A SUSTAINABLE VISION FOR URBAN INDIA

A SUSTAINABLE VISION FOR URBAN INDIA

A.K. JAIN

PUBLICATIONS

KALPAZ PUBLICATIONS

DELHI-110052

A Sustainable Vision for Urban India

Rs. 1260

ISBN: 81-7835-683-X

Published in 2008 in India by
Kalpaz Publications
C-30, Satyawati Nagar,
Delhi-110052
E-mail: kalpaz@hotmail.com
Phone : 9212729499

Laser Typesetting by: Quick Media, Delhi
Printed at : G. Print Process, Delhi

Contents

Contents

Preface

After 6 decades of the Independence, India still has about one-fifth of its population, a mammoth 250 million, below the sustenance level or poverty line. It raises the question of the relevance of the planning process. It is necessary to have a hard look at the ongoing perceptions, processes, plans and programmes.

The urban and environmental challenges prompt a reconsideration of the values, goals and means of achieving them. There is a need of abandoning the prevalent reactive tendencies of urban form, which follows fiction, finance, fear and fragmentation. There is an urgent need to evolve the concepts and innovations in shaping the urban environment by shifting the paradigm toward urban integration, and evolve a new model for the contemporary city, which is designed with nature and relates to local culture alongwith global openness.

In place of fast-paced economy oriented development, it is necessary to adopt the beauty of simplicity, spirituality, sincerity, and sustainability. Learning from the inherent wisdom of nature and cities of the past, a city should be infused with contemporary sensibilities. India, while moving towards urbanization is passing through a rare historic moment in aligning urban growth and development with political, economic, and social trends. What is required is to actively engage and draw inspiration from actual social and physical conditions with ethics of care, respect, and honesty. A city is like an organism always growing and evolving and self-adjusting according to new needs that arise. Such a city should menifest the networks, human relationships and connections.

A sustainable city should promote community empowerment together with decentralisation, devolution and deregulation of planning process. It should support and encourage a pro-poor, people-centered approach towards self-rule, self-reliance and self-build with the local and simple solutions based on a comprehensive understanding of the issues and processes. As a tribute to India's poor, deprived and hard working people, this book is dedicated towards the goal of sustainable urban India. It attempts to build a dream, a new vision, which can be translated into livelihoods; a comprehensive approach which is simple and beautiful. Writing is a solitary pursuit. I am grateful to many people and organisations in this endeavour. First mentions should be made I my family for all the help and encouragements. The Delhi Development Authority has provided me a unique opportunity in gaining a rich experience on the subject. School of Planning and Architecture New Delhi provided me the opportunity to teach and interact with the young minds. I am grateful to Kalpaz Publications for taking up publication of this book in a dedicated and most congenial manner.

A.K. Jain

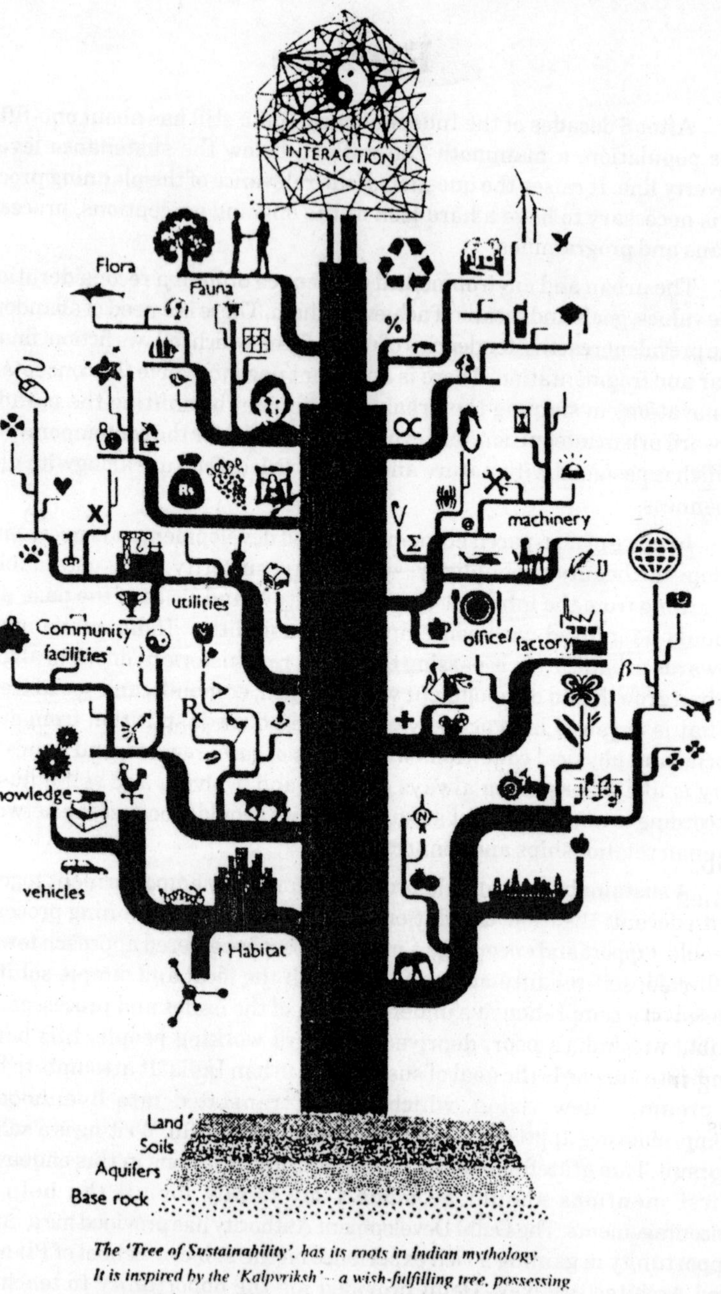

The 'Tree of Sustainability', has its roots in Indian mythology. It is inspired by the 'Kalpvriksh' — a wish-fulfilling tree, possessing a perennial source of bounty. It symbolises long life, health, wealth, shelter and prosperity that last for a 'kalp'. Kalp is the longest time period known on Earth and equals 4,320,000,000 years.

Adopted from ABN-AMRO 06-07 Sustainability Report, India

1

INTRODUCTION—AN URBAN VISION

"Vision-it reaches beyond the thing that is, into the conception of what can be imagination gives you the picture. Vision gives you the impulse to make the picture your own" —Robert Collier

Urban India has increased more than ten times in size during last 100 years – from 26 million in 1901 to 285 million in 2001, which is 28 per cent of the total population. By 2020, urban population will be 40 per cent of the total population and by 2050 the figure will be 50 per cent. The share of urban population has risen from 17.2% in 1951 to 27.8% in 2001.

The number of cities with a population of more than one million has gone up from 5 in 1951 to 35 in 2001. Of these, 8 cities have population between 3 million and 5 million and 6 cities: Delhi, Mumbai, Kolkata, Chennai, Bangalore & Hyderabad, have a population of more than 5 million. These megacities are the nodes of economic growth of India.

By and large, the nature and extent of growth of Indian Cities is unplanned and unanticipated, the provision of services is not proactive, but reactive. The demand for services such as transport, water, and sewerage continually outstrips supply resulting in a situation of perpetual scarcity and shortages.

Pressure is evident on the basic services. About 54 per cent of urban households do not have access to toilets and 64 per cent are not connected to the public sewerage system. Almost 50 per cent of solid waste remains uncollected. Although 89 per cent of urban population is covered by treated water supply, water is supplied only for a few hours per day. City roads are clogged. Though vehicle population in India increased 80-fold in the last 40 years, road area increased by only 5 per cent. Little attention has been paid to development of mass rapid transport systems in most major cities. Only 17 of the largest cities have organized bus services, and only three cities – Mumbai, Kolkata and Chennai – have a suburban rail system. A good network of roads coupled with efficiency mass urban transport system makes a substantial contribution to the efficiency of the cities and enables them to become a catalyst of the economic and social development.

A World Bank study estimated that poor quality if life results in about 30,000 premature infant deaths, 17 million respiratory disease-related hospital admissions and 1.2 billion restricted activity days. The Central Public Health Engineering estimates 100 per cent coverage of safe water supply and sanitation services would cost Rs. 1,79 billion by 2021. The estimates by the Rail India Technical and Economic Services put the cost of providing transport infrastructure in cities with 1 lakh plus population over the next 20 years at Rs. 2,070 billion. The 1996 India Infrastructure Report had assessed an annual investment of Rs. 280 billion till 2005 at 1996 price level for urban water supply, sanitation and roads. This makes the issue of augmentation the basic infrastructure services and making the Indian Cities sustainable and livable a daunting and a major challenge.

Urban Poverty and Employment

The livelihood-poverty-development linkage is critical to the long-term sustainability of cities. The increasing levels of urban income and education provide an important springboard to develop a range of livelihoods that are linked to new economy areas. Biotechnology, Information and Communication Technology (ICT), advanced materials, human and financial employment generation, there is a need for a strong emphasis on community-based activities in the areas of water supply, sustainable and renewable energy, education and health. To maintain a sustainable metabolism for the cities, a key challenge will be coping with the rural migration to urban areas in an inclusive manner, without disrupting the local, social and cultural fabric and without compromising the equity, efficiency and sustainability. The Government of India has formulated a National Policy on Street Vendors, and the city plans have to make mandatory provisions for this sector.

In order to address to the needs of the majority of the people, that is poor, a major focus area has to be Local Economic

Promotion and Poverty Reduction. Among young people there is a widespread perception that the future holds nothing for them. As a result a large number of the unemployed are forced to take on informal, illegal or uncertain jobs. While entrepreneurial potential and development opportunities lie untapped, the cities and municipalities lose out on tax revenue. This sort of situation is not attractive for investors, and the economic development stagnates, while the vicious circle of poverty perpetuates, as such, there is an urgent need to focus on the promotion of small and medium-sized enterprises (SME) and the local and regional economy of the city. The growth opportunities of existing enterprises, value added chains that are labour intensive, facilitating business start-ups and attracting new business will enhance the competitiveness of the city.

Infrastructure

At today's costs, the total infrastructure investment to make India a world-class economy within ten years has been estimated at Rs.500 lakh crore. These pertain to urban development (Rs.175 lakh crore), roads (Rs.40 lakh crore), water supply (Rs. 15 lakh crore), power (Rs.67.5 lakh crore), river grid (Rs.67.5 lakh crore) and industrial upgrade (Rs. 125 lakh crore). Due to this massive investment in infrastructure, the present volume of construction business valued at Rs. 25 lakh crore / year would zoom up three times to that of Rs. 75 lakh crore / year. This will help in achieving 8.5 per cent GDP growth on a sustained basis. Whether we plan it or not, this will witness runaway growth of our cities. This is in fact already happening in most of the Indian cities. This calls for an urgent need to regulate, direct and divert the investments in a planned way and provide matching infrastructure, land and services. There is an urgent need to strengthen the revenue base and capacity building of the local authorities. The municipalities shall have to change the ways of taxes and start charging economic costs for services together with the outsourcing non-core activities. Options like tapping the bond markets require an administrative reform that is competitive, participatory and accountable. For mobilizing private sector resources, Special Purpose Vehicle has been developed by the Government of India so as to make infrastructure projects financially viable. Already there are several success stories of management contracts for Municipal

Services. While opening up the financial options, regulatory mechanism should be in place. The role of the intermediaries and expert/professional organizations to mobilize the support of institutional and domestic banks and financial institutions is crucial.

Often the resettlement option and the process of relocation takes the slum-dwellers far away from their work sites without appropriate transport connectivity. Public funds are often invested to provide housing to the slum dwellers. In-situ rehabilitation and upgradation should be considered as the priority options so as to rejuvenate the existing community with minimum disruption and loss of physical and social assets. It can be financed by using part land as a resource and by offering optional loans for home improvements. This requires working out a sound micro-credit policy and infrastructure support. NGOs, self help groups and financial institutions can play a major role in evolving effective systems for channelizing the credit. Experience has shown that macro-investment in basic infrastructure can transform and leverage the micro-investment in low cost shelter and slum upgradation. This is reflected in the New National Urban Housing and Habitat Policy framed in 2007 by the Ministry of Urban Housing and Poverty Alleviation. In Mumbai private sector has been mobilized in the task of slum rehabilitation by using land as a resource. In Delhi, the Delhi Development Authority has embarked a pilot project for mass housing of rehabilitation tenements with the private participation.

Ecology and Environment

For worsening urban crisis, there is an urgent need to focus upon the improvement in energy services. Despite a containment of user demand using 'Factor 4' technologies and decentralized generation, alternative and renewable energy sources, such as a solar energy, offshore wind turbines, biomass-based energy generation, gas and clean coal for thermal power, the grid and hydrogen as the major energy carriers, need to be explored. The concept of energy efficiency begins with Zero-fossil Energy Development (ZED), which should be incorporated in city planning.

Water

In the Indian cities water is emerging as the most critical sustainability constraint. A range of technical and institutional options ranging from centralized surface storage to decentralized rainwater harvesting and re-cycling, together with design and water management options are to be explored. As a mandate, and urban planning exercise should address to management of watersheds on community basis; surface and sub-surface storage; rationalization of land and water use, re-cycling, re-use and local biological treatment of urban and industrial process water. A vision plan for water supply focusing upon local, unexploited opportunities is a major stepping stone in dealing with urban water supply in the effective manner.

Transportation

A least-cost life cycle analysis of transportation systems across a range of carriage ways and modes (pedestrians, road, light rail, rail, water, sea and air) should be able to establish an optimum long-term mix. A mix of bicycles, people movers, hyper-trams, hyper-buses and ferries generally provides a safer, faster and cheaper services that the inefficient personal car. Data shows that the number of vehicles in urban India has increased 80 times, but road area has gone up by only five per cent. This calls for proportionate development of road and parking areas, grade separated corridors, multi level parking and options to explore subterranean space for circulation and planning. The Government of India (Ministry of Urban Development) has framed a National Urban Transport Policy (2006) which deals with all these issues in a comprehensive manner. Transport policy intimately linked to pollution control including noise, which should be part of City Transport Plans. Providing a barrier free environment is another mandatory requirement for planning and design of outdoor and indoor environment.

Participatory Planning

Effective participatory planning among all the stakeholders, mediation between competing or conflicting interests would help in bringing about change and lasting improvements to the living environment. To translate the sustainability principles by city design, the following six critical areas can be identified:

Jobs : Job sites located within communities reduce time spent travelling to work.

Corridors : High density commercial and residential corridors focus growth along transit routes.

Walkability : Interconnected street systems link residents with the services they need.

Green Space : Green Spaces provide recreation opportunities and connect people with natural systems.

Infrastructure : Integrating natural systems based on the principles of conservation of natural resources and recycling that reduce infrastructure costs and environment impact.

Housing : A range of housing types allows residents of differing economic situations to live in the same neighbourhoods and have access to the same services.

Management and maintenance aspects need to be given serious attention at the design stage. Not only the buildings, but the cities need to be intelligent and green, and should be visualized to cater to the needs of the future. For environmental and micro-climate focus, the concepts of site planning, building design technology and materials have to be re-examined. It is at the design stage, that the environmental efficiency and compatibility of a building are largely determined, which is popularly called 'Green Architecture'. The building should incorporate flexible systems which respond to the changing micro-climate needs and carrying conditions of natural ventilation and light. The design should obviate outdoor and indoor pollution. It should provide for rain water harvesting, recycling and exploitation of non-conventional sources of energy (such as photo-voltaic system). The design of openings and glazing should allow flexibility. In large public buildings, the use of intelligent systems can be employed.

Urban Reforms

Today, the most important challenges for urban India are the urban reforms and the transformation of current institutions and systems of governance that are necessary to a sustainability transition. Efficiency, ethics and equity are the key goals. This would require 'space' for urban governance, participation and new forms of partnerships. These transformations should start with local and community-based governance and an open government. The 73rd and 74th Constitutional Amendment Acts and Good Governance Campaign of the Ministry of Urban Development, Government of India provide the institutional basis for a process of devolution based on subsidiary, built around local communities. The new institutions of self rule and governance can help creating a vibrant urban culture and a sense of ownership among its citizens within a dispersed city. Decoupling environmental pressure of economic growth, while continuing to satisfy human needs requires an integral effort. The solution lies with the people and the governance.

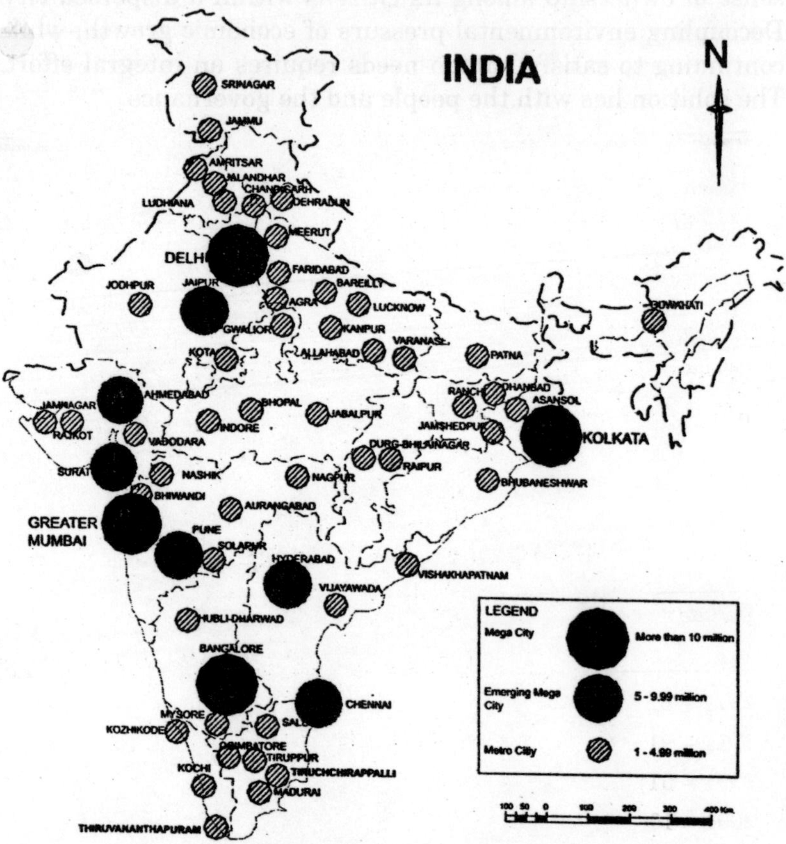

Emerging Mega and Metro Cities of India - 2001

2

THE CHALLENGES OF URBAN DEVELOPMENT

When the world was created, God made everything a little bit incomplete. Rather than making bread grow out of the earth, God made wheat grow so that we might bake it into bread. Rather than making the earth of bricks, God made it of clay so that we might bake the clay into bricks. Why? So that we may become partners in completing the work of creation.

—The Midrash

In India urbanisation is widely deemed as the "engine of economic growth". Urban population of India increased ten fold from 27 million in 1901 to 285 million in 2001. Increase in the number of urban settlements in the country, standing at 5161 in 2001, up from 3768 a decade earlier.

Urbanisation In India

Decade	*No. of Cities/ Towns*	*Urban Population*	*Annual Growth Rate (%)*	*Urbanisation (%)*
1971 – 81	2590	109.1	3.79	23.53
1981 – 91	3378	159.1	3.09	25.7
1991 – 01	3768	217.6	2.73	27.79
2001 – 10*	5161	285.9	2.3	30.3
2010 – 20*	—	—	2.5	34.7

* Projected

Source: Census of India, 2001.

The present rural dependence on 68 per cent employment through agriculture is unsustainable in the long term as it could lead to social unrest spurred by the economic disparities between urban and rural populace. Economic development in agriculture, industry and services necessitates accelerated focus on investment and development of physical infrastructure in order to achieve cost effectiveness of the logistics chain from supply to manufacture and from product to delivery end.

India's economic turnaround has largely been witnessed after the policy of economic liberalisation and democratic decentralization, along with other policy changes, and the urbanization has been a natural corollary of development.

CHANGES IN POLICY CONTEXT

Command economies	⇨ Market Economies privatisation
Low environmental awareness	⇨ High environmental awareness
Centralised System	⇨ Decentralised System (73 & 74th CAA)
High deficit spending	⇨ Structural adjustment
Govt. Domain over Infrastructure & Housing Dev.	⇨ Incentives for Infrastructure Investments & Private Sector in Housing
High subsidy Regime	⇨ Users pay principle, low subsidy

However, there is a serious disconnect between the policy context and the spatial contact. The following gaps are conspicuous between the policies and plans:

Spatial Planning

(*i*) Spatial Planning Gap : The policies, ideas and vision often do not get translated on ground in absence of realistic spatial plans.

(*ii*) Implementation Gap : The plans do not get translated into action.

(*iii*) Missing links in livelihood, poverty, and development chain.

(*iv*) Need for devolution of governance and localisation.

Planning as an attempt to synthesise the diverse activities, perspectives, aspirations and resources into a composite whole is a complex and dynamic process. The process of planning depends upon the local political, socio-economic, physical, infrastructural and administrative realities. During last decades the peoples' aspirations and focus of planning have become enlarged - from the local spatial, infrastructure, housing, architectonic and functional aspects, to global, environmental, organizational, governance, conservation of heritage, urban, aesthetics, employment and poverty alleviation, human dignity, empowerment and participation.

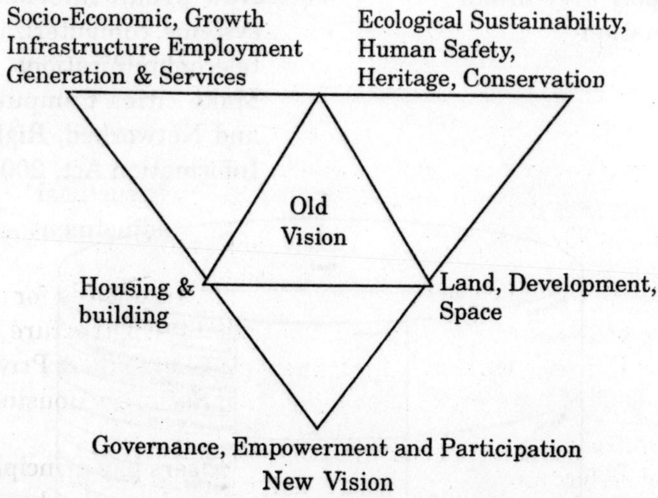

The present approach to planning needs to be reviewed keeping in view in following ongoing paradigm shifts:

PARADIGM SHIFTS IN PLANNING PROCESS

Focus on statutory planning	⇨ Performance orientated planning; focus on implementation
Government does all	⇨ Public-Community-Private Partner-ship, Corporati-sation of Urban Local bodies, contracting out.

Comprehensive planning ⇨ Strategic and action planning.

Focus on spatial and physical aspects ⇨ Approaches incorporating institutional and financial aspects, planning for economic development.

Meeting basic functional needs, planning as a social function ⇨ Emphasis on quality and innovative demand driven planning.

Rigid legislation ⇨ Legal reforms facilitating participatory planning & flexibility.

Monopoly over urban information ⇨ New urban information systems, computerization, telecommunications, GIS, Make cities Computable and Networked, Right to Information Act, 2005.

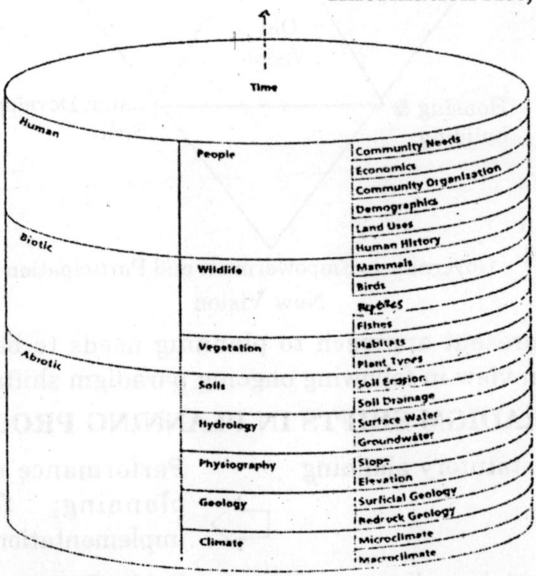

The Layer- Cake Model (Wallace, McHarg, Roberts and Todd 1971-74) illuminates the relationship among the Human, Biotic and Abiotic systems across space and time. This signifies a delicate relationship between Human Development and Environment, which needs to be understood and respected for a sustainable world

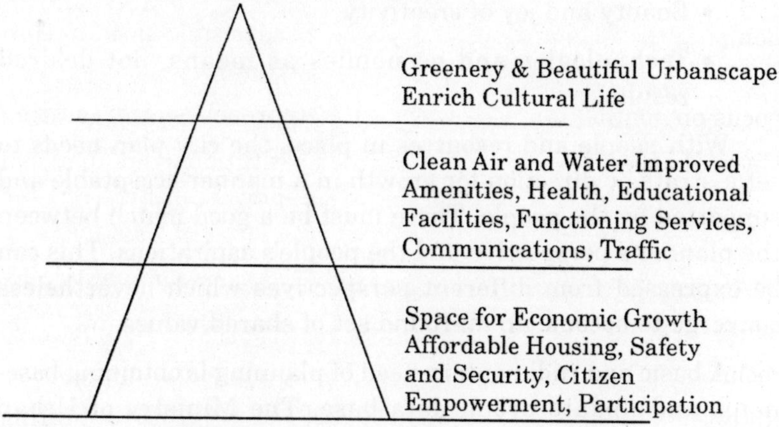

The Aspiration Pyramid

In view of the new aspirations of the people and emerging economy, City Plan should address the following critical issues:—

- Clear long term vision, SMART (Specific, Measureable, Actionable, Realistic and Timely) Goals and Commitments
- Future land use challenges
- The potential carrying capacity, water conservation/ supply and ecological footprint of urban system.
- Economic development and poverty related challenges
- Energy, transportation and water resources constraints and opportunities
- Environment, pollution control and climate change related challenges
- Heritage and conservation potential
- Governance and institutional capacity

The planning and development are linked together with the following ecological and human factors :-

- People centered, place specific planning
- Balance between economic development and environmental concerns
- Conservation of irreplaceable treasures: heritage, nature and cultural resources

- Beauty and joy of creativity
- Technologies and economies as means, not desired results.

With people and resources in place, the city plan needs to set a strategic direction for growth in a manner acceptable and supported by the people. There must be a good match between the planner's perspective and the people's aspirations. This can be expressed from different perspectives which nevertheless converge to become an all-round set of shared values.

A basic and rudimentary need of planning is obtaining base-maps and update urban data base. The Ministry of Urban Development has undertaken National Urban Information System (NUIS) Project, which will assist the States and Cities in this task. The NIUS project, which aims to help the mapping of more than 5000 urban settlements by emerging techniques of GIS and satellite based a remote sensing and aerial photographs, in conjunction with conventional techniques for effective planning. The National Urban Information System (NUIS) would develop a holistic Urban Information System which combined with the National Natural Resources Management Systems (NNRMS) on a National Mission Mode. The National Urban Information System Scheme (NUIS) covers various components of Urban information system, as given below:

- Land and Natural Resources
- Settlement Pattern
- Study of Slum Bastis and unplanned areas
- Improvement of Urban Environment
- Re-densification of Towns/Cities
- Plan Implementation, MIS and Digital Cadastral database
- Land Monitoring
- Monitoring of Land Regulation and Urban Fringe
- Transport Planning and Environmental Assessment and Safety.

Shelter and Housing Policy

About 40 per cent of the total slum population of India resides in the 35 one-million-plus cities. India needs to build 33 million houses in the next five years, of which 16.75 million are for urban areas. As part of the growth process, the poor will continue to move to the economic growth centres in urban areas and stay in slums. Urban areas also create a demand for services that permit many to earn a living, while waiting for better opportunities. Urban dwellers demand low-cost services and personal help that the slum dwellers make available. Particularly the concerns of the elderly, disabled and children need to be attended in a dedicated manner.

The National Urban Housing and Habitat Policy, 2007, has been formulated to address the issues of sustainable development of infrastructure and public-private partnership for housing and slum rehabilitation. 20 member task force set by the Ministry of Urban Employment and Poverty Alleviation reviewed the 1998 National Housing and Habitat Policy and has proposed a new framework in the context of housing finance, infrastructure, development, land assembly and social housing.

The policy aims to bridge the gap between demand and supply of housing and infrastructure, and to build synergy, convergence and integration of housing and related infrastructure interventions. Besides, the Public Sector acting as 'enabler', the policy postulates increased role of Private and Corporate Sector in Land Acquisition and Assembly, Partnerships (JVs & SPVs) and Resource Mobilisation. The policy lays emphasis on safety net for EWS/LIG and proposes 20-25% reservation for EWS/LIG and other weaker sections of society in land & housing (SC/ST/OBCs, women, Street vendors and physically handicapped). The policy advocates using land as a resource for slum improvement and integration of VAMBAY & NSDP. The mobilization of global resources, as well as capturing the private sector, local, micro- savings by innovative fiscal concessions, have been emphasised.

Slum Rehabilitation—Mumbai Model

The main plank in favour of in-situ rehabilitation is that the squatters continue to stay at the same place hence their livelihood is not disturbed. There are fewer chances of their selling the allotted tenements and shifting elsewhere. However, compared to relocation into plots, it is a capital intensive propositions. It works by using the land as a resource with accompanied relaxation in Development Controls and bank loan arrangements.

- 1990s – In the new D.C. Regulations special provisions were made for Slum Redevelopment, but slum dwellers were reluctant to pay the contribution for the scheme.
- 1995 – A committee was formed to devise a scheme for rehabilitation of slums existing as on January 01, 1995.

Slum Rehabilitation in Mumbai is envisaged under three categories:

- DCR-30(10) Schemes : In-situ rehabilitation/redevelopment
- 3.11 Schemes : Relocation of squatters from Road/Railway/Airports/ROW areas
- 33.14 Schemes : Transitory shifting/accommodation of JJ units on rental basis

The basic tenets of In-situ Rehabilitation scheme in Mumbai are:

- JJ clusters existing up to January 01, 1995 taken up for rehabilitation. If at least 70% residents agree, the project can be taken up by a co-operative housing society of the slum dwellers/NGOs or by the developer/land owner etc.
- Land as a resource is utilized.
- Each dweller is given a Dwelling Unit (DU) of carpet area measuring 20.9 sq. m. and a covered area of about 25 sq. m. to 30 sq m. having a multi-purpose room, an alcove for kitchen and a toilet, free of cost. Wherever possible, effort is made to provide a 2 room unit.
- Both Residential and Commercial units are rehabilitated.
- Units of commercial activity are given equivalent area of existing unit, limiting to 20.9 sq. m.
- Passage upto 2 m. wide, one Society office, one balwadi and one welfare center, each of 20.9 sq. m. carpet area, for every 100 JJ units and part thereof is not counted in FAR/FSI.

- Rehabilitation Component : Built up area + common passage + society office + balwadi + welfare center.

Development Control Norms

- Over and above the FSI required for rehabilitation, equivalent FSI is permitted on the plot for free sale component.
- The maximum FSI permissible is 2.50. If the required FSI, for the rehab and free sale components, exceeds 2.50, the Transfer of Development Rights (TDR) are issued for the balance FSI (free sale component) to be utilized elsewhere.
- The density of Slum Rehabilitation units (25 sqm plinth area) permissible is minimum 360 DUs per hectare, and a max. of 1080 DU per Ha.
- The developer has to deposit Rs. 20000/- per dwelling unit for subsidizing the house tax for a fixed period and maintenance of the complex. The interest on this amount helps to accomplish the same.
- Rehab tenement allotted to a slum dwellers cannot be sold for a period of 10 years. However it can be transferred to legal heir.
- The scheme can be taken up on a minimum plot size of 500 sq. m. and the ground coverage is 25%. The change of landuse is not required; the construction of JJ units is done in addition to the permissible FSI as per land-use provisions.
- If the number of units required to be rehabilitated from the site is less than 500 DUs, the number of surplus DUs constructed at the prescribed density are handed over to the Government for resettlement from other sites.

In-Situ Slum and JJ Rehabilitation (Tehkhand Pilot Project, Delhi,

According to Master Plan for Delhi – 2021, and Report of Madhukar Gupta Committee to Make Delhi Slum Free (2005), the prevailing 'site and services' (Relocation of Slum & JJ) approach needs to be progressively abandoned and substituted by an alternate approach, with the following approach:

- Resettlement, should be based mainly on built up accommodation of around 25 sq. m with common areas and facilities, rather than on the model of horizontal plotted development.
- The concept of land as a resource should be adopted to develop such accommodation with private sector participation and investment
- Incentives by way of higher FAR, part commercial use of the land and, if necessary and feasible, transfer of Development Rights, should be provided.
- A cooperative resettlement model should be adopted with tenure rights.
- The provision of accommodation should be based on cost, with suitable arrangements for funding/financing, keeping in view the aspect of affordability and capacity to pay.
- The sites should be integrated with the overall planned development of the area, particularly keeping in view the availability of employment avenues.
- Arrangement for temporary transit accommodation is to be made.
- Community Based Organisations (CBOs) and Non-Governmental Organisations (NGOs) should be closely involved in the process.
- A dedicated Slum Clearance and Urban Renewal Authority, or a Corporate Body, should be created.

Tehkhand Pilot Project, New Delhi covers an area of 14.3 Ha. located Okhla Ind. Area(Zone-F). Proposed construction will provide of 3500 houses for resettlement of slum dwellers and 750 high category houses (free sale houses), Development controls/Planning Guidelines.

- Maximum density: 600 dwelling units per hect, ± 10% variation.

  Max. FAR of 250.
- Commercial component upto 10%.(mainly for self employment opportunities of Slum & JJ dwellers and making the scheme financially viable).

- Minimum component of the land area for rehabilitation of squatters has to be 60%.

  Maximum area for remunerative use 40%.
- Area of Dwelling Unit for rehabilitation 25 sq m
- Common parking is to be provided.
- No restriction on ground coverage (except set backs)

Planning Norms For Facilities

1. Primary school - 800 sq m per 5000 population
2. Senior Secondary School - 2000 sq m per 10,000 population

The following multi-facilities can be clubbed in a composite facility centre – (500 – 1000 sq m)

(*i*) Multi-purpose community hall - 100 sq m.

(*ii*) Basti Vikas Kendra - 100 sq m.

(*iii*) Religious site - 100 sq m.

(*iv*) Police Post - 100 sq m.

(*v*) Health Centre - 100 sq m.

(*vi*) Park/Shishu Vatika - 200 sq m.

(*vii*) Area for essential retail outlets, e.g. Dairy, Fair Price Shop, Kerosene shop, etc.

(*viii*) Provisions for informal trade units and weekly market.

Parking – 0.5 ECS per 100 sqm of total floor area.

For General Housing @ 2.0 ECS/100 sq m of total floor area.

The sites for facilities such as senior secondary school, religious, community hall, shopping centre etc. and primary school shall revert back to the DDA.

Water System

Water stress is a growing problem in most parts of India, and Delhi in particular due to excessive water consumption and population growth. There is a need to give a close look to the issue of water supply and explore the unexploited opportunities for saving water and augmenting its supply.

All measures should be taken to reduce unaccounted flow of water (UFW), production losses at existing plants. The existing drainage basins shall be made self-sustainable in water management by integrating water-sewerage-drainage systems. It is imperative to not only to initiate new projects and upgrade present infrastructure, but also to promote water conservation through an integrated and a community driven model, comprising of complimentary short term and long term measures.

To improve the water supply in accordance with the projected requirement, all measures are to be taken to reduce unaccounted flow of water (UFW), production losses at existing plants. The existing drainage basins shall be made self-sustainable in water management by integrating water-sewerage-drainage systems. It is imperative to not only initiate new projects and upgrade present infrastructure, but also to promote water conservation through an integrated and a community driven model, comprising of complimentary short term and long term measures as given below:

(*i*) Recycling of treated wastewater with separate lines for potable water and recycled water. For this, dual pipe supply system has to be introduced in a phased manner in all the areas.

(*ii*) Ground water recharging through rain water harvesting, conserving water bodies and controlling groundwater extraction. Groundwater extraction is to be controlled through registering boreholes and recharging according to test yields. Ground water management is to be enforced by concerned agency.

(*iii*) Focused planning and action is required to prepare and implement rain water as roof water harvesting schemes both with the aim of optimizing water use and ground water recharge. For this suitable mandatory provision to be made for planning and construction of various schemes.

(*iv*) The planning should dovetail watershed management, and arrest the run-off. It should ensure the conservation of natural valleys, water bodies and aquifers. The concepts of 'zero run-off drainage', with retention ponds, sediments traps and balancing lakes should be adopted, with a segregated wastewater disposal system. A green network overlapping the blue network would protect the ecology of aquifers, and also provide a pleasant environment. Simple methods of site planning, which incorporate porous/semi permeable paving, drop inlet/down pipe, sediment trap, retention ponds, etc. will contribute in maintaining ground water table.

(*v*) Rivers, major drains and canals, with indiscriminate dumping of wastes, have become polluted and foul. These need strict pollution control measures and eco-sensitive land use controls. Water flow needs to be controlled and stabilized and marked at each kilometer station. The valleys should be zoned as water portals, so that these are flanked with greenery, farmlands and forests.

(*vi*) One of the prime objectives of development should be to improve the quality of river-water, to secure its continuous flow and to encourage the return of aquatic life. This needs improvement of drainage, waste water treatment and pollution abatement by sewerage improvement. The surplus water during the monsoons should be retained in balancing ponds along the riverbed rather than allowing it to the downstream areas.

(*vii*) The drains and waterfront can be landscaped in the form of interconnected parkways. There is no need for elaborate gardening of the greenways, but wild, simple and natural stretch by itself would be ecologically important. Such trails could be one of the cheapest forms of drainage and recreation.

(*viii*) Water supply in new areas should incorporate separate lines – one for washing, water coolers and garden taps, the second for supplying potable water. All non-residential buildings having a discharge of over 10,000 litres a day should incorporate a wastewater recycling.

(*ix*) The wasteful practice of 'drill, pump, and spill' has to be replaced by efficient methods of water conservation, use, and recycling as standard and mandatory procedures. There is a need to incorporate the mandatory stipulation of water saving/waterless flushing system in the Building Bye-laws.

(*x*) Where the hazard of pollution exists, the minimum charge for operating permits should cover the expenses of adequate policing and controls. Mandatory performance bonds and liability insurance should pay for all damages plus any corrective measures, which might be needed. As a governing rule, no new development, manufacturing, process or operation of any polluting activity should be permitted, which may result in the significant degradation of any water resource.

(*xi*) About half of the water that is treated and distributed at public expense is non-revenue water. This is due to unrecorded usage or illegal taps and water connections. Reducing water losses is cheaper than augmenting water capacity for such losses.

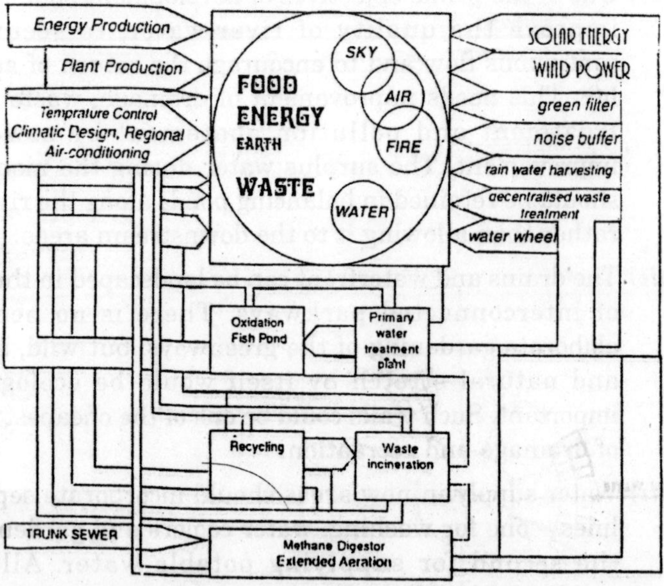

The waste management process should embody the principle of circular metabolism, which means recycling wastes to produce energy, adoption of eco-technology for zero polluting energy (wind, solar and water wheel), development of green filters, noise buffers and rainater harvesting

Sewerage and Sanitation

A basic mandate of sustainable development is that all the urban areas should be served by regular sewerage system. The areas where immediate regular sewerage system is not available, low cost/mini-sanitation system could be adopted. For this, the surface drainage and sewerage systems should be developed in an integrated and decentralised manner. The following are the key action areas in this regard:

Waste Product Gas Plant - an Integral System

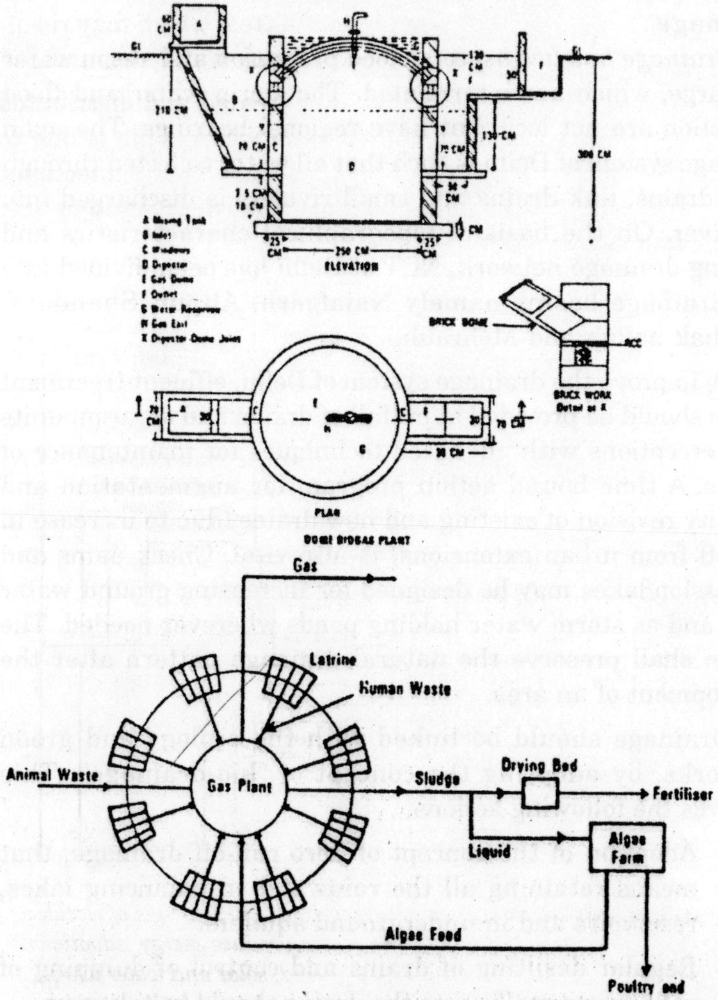

Decentralised STP's with capacity of 40-60 MGD at the Subcity Level (10-15 lakh population) and at Community Level.

Environmental Impact Assessment (Mandatory for new development).

- Common Effluent Treatment Plants in Industrial Estates.
- Eco-Parks Mandatory for all STP's and CETP's.
- Rehabilitation of Existing/Old Sewage Lines correlated with Redevelopment.
- Recovering Energy/Gas as fuel from Sewerage.

Drainage

Drainage has two aspects: flood protection and storm water discharge, which are interrelated. The storm water and flood protection are not local but have regional bearings. The main drainage system of Delhi is such that all water collected through main drains, link drains and small rivulets is discharged into the river. On the basis of topographical characteristics and existing drainage network, NCT of Delhi has been divided into five drainage basins namely Najafgarh, Alipur, Shahdara, Khushak nallah and Mehrauli.

To improve the drainage system of Delhi, effluent treatment plants should be provided at outfall of drains and aeration units at interceptions with advanced techniques for maintenance of drains. A time bound action program for augmentation and capacity revision of existing and new drains (due to increase in run off from urban extensions) is also vital. Check dams and depression/lakes may be designed for increasing ground water table and as storm water holding ponds wherever needed. The design shall preserve the natural drainage pattern after the development of an area.

Drainage should be linked with the ecology and green networks, by adopting the concept of "bio-drainage". This Involves the following actions:

- Adoption of the concept of Zero run-off drainage, that means retaining all the rainwater in balancing lakes, reservoirs and in underground aquifers.
- Regular desilting of drains and control of dumping of solid waste/malba into the drains should be taken up.
- Drainage to be integral part of Road Development Plans/ flyovers/Grade Separators.
- GIS based drainage mapping and planning.

- Sub-wells need to be developed under flyovers for trapping rainwater. Pump houses in low-lying areas should be operational with back-up power.
- Remodelling of selected drains may also be required considering the upstream flow in the region.

Solid Waste Management

The problem of solid waste management is assuming serious proportions due to increasing population, urbanisation, changing lifestyles and consumption patterns. The garbage from unauthorised developments, slums, JJ settlements, etc. is not collected which further adds to the environmental degradation. The projected average garbage generation in Delhi for horizon year 2021 is @ 0.68 kg per capita per day and total quantum of solid waste would be 15750 tons/day.

Management of solid waste involves waste generation, segregation and storage; waste collection; waste transfer/ transportation; treatment, recycle, reuse, recovery; and disposal. For effective waste management, its segregation at the community and neighbourhood level is imperative. The waste shall be segregated and collected, in separate chambers at dalaos. For this, involvement of rag pickers with RWAs, CBOs and NGOs ia to be recognised and encouraged.

For biodegradable and recyclable waste, which is segregated at the source, decentralised treatment at neighbourhood level may be adopted, while for silt, centralised treatment may be followed. The other type of specialised waste includes biomedical waste; hazardous waste from industries; construction debris and fly ash; meat processing centre etc. Disposal of bio-medical waste is to be as per Bio-medical Waste Rules and hazardous waste requires special handling. Proper dumping, recycling and reuse of construction debris and fly ash have to be linked. Meat processing centre waste is to be recycled for chicken feed etc.

Considering the nature of solid waste and the economic aspects of its disposal, major part of solid waste especially silt has to be disposed of in sanitary landfills. But wherever recycling is possible, it should be preferred than disposing of the waste in sanitary landfill sites. More viable alternatives to landfills are vermiculture, fossilisation, composting etc. Waste Minimisation Circles (WMCs) should be constituted and made effective.

Implementation and monitoring & Bio-Medical Wastes (Handling & Management) Rules, 1998, for hospitals, nursing homes, and clinics should be taken up.

Keeping in view the fact that finding new sanitary landfill sites in Delhi Is becoming extremely difficult, there is no option, but to resort to alternative and decentralised methods of waste treatment, reduction, recycle and reuse, which include vermiculture, fossilisatlon and composting.

Public Transport

Public Transportation, and not the car, should be the basis of design of the future urban space. Networked just-in-time public transportation systems using light rail hypertrams in dense neighbourhoods and guided hyper-buses in lightly loaded areas, could be the least cost solutions, with lowest ecological footprint. This can be serviced by a rapid hydrogen-powered river hyperferry network. High speed intercity rail line, air transport and the containerization with radio tagging of goods enable automated rapid goods movement across different levels of aggregation. Piggybacking on the passenger network should be integral component of regional network planning. Transport policy intimately linked to pollution control including noise, which should be part of City Transport Plans. Providing a barrier free environment is another mandatory requirement for planning and design of outdoor and indoor environment.

National Urban Transport Policy 2006

National Urban Transport Policy 2006 prepared by Ministry of Urban Development, Government of India, has been framed with the objective to ensure safe, affordable, quick, comfortable, reliable and sustainable access and transport within the cities. This is sought to be achieved by:

- Integration of Urban transportation at the urban planning stage, for integrated land use and transport planning.
- Equitable allocation of road space between people and vehicles.
- Transport systems that encourage greater use of public transport and non-motorised modes.
- Establishing regulatory mechanisms that allow a level playing field for all operators.
- Introducing Intelligent Transport Management Systems.
- Addressing concerns on road safety
- Reducing pollution levels through planning enforcement, norms and cleaner technology.
- Capacity Building.
- Raising finances, through innovative mechanisms and mobilizing private sector in public transport.
- Public participation and cooperation in adopting 'Green Transport'.

Noise Reduction and Traffic Calming

Noise is emerging as a major pollutant and irritant and is a constant source of pain and disturbance and cause of health hazard. Against a permissible level of 50-60 dB (A), the sound levels in cities often exceed 80 dB(A). Faulty and leaking silencers, over-use of horns and vehicles plying on rough roads accentuate noise level from the traffic. Besides this, the noise from commercial and industrial activities, unabated use of sound amplifiers, generator sets and fire-crackers often disturb the peace.

By proper planning, such as location of public, semi-public and commercial activities along major transport arteries, a buffer can be created for residential zone. The green buffer with thin leave trees, land formations, mounds, embankments, etc. along major road would provide effective barrier to transmission of noise. It is also necessary to effectively enforce Noise Pollution (Control) Rules, 2000 and, to notify certain areas as 'No Horn Zone' (e.g. residential areas, University Campus, institutional areas, road intersections & flyovers). The design and surface material of roads and pavements should also ensure reduction of noise. The concerned authorities should prepare areawise traffic calming schemes and a Noise Monitoring and Control Plan (NMCP).

Barrier Free Environment

A major consideration in the planning and design of outdoor and indoor movement should be that people with disability, older persons and people in wheel chairs could move around without the help from others. This requires that:

- Vertical and horizontal circulation, rooms and toilets in a building should be barrier free and disabled compatible;
- Paths and pavement shall be flat, uniform and slip-free;
- Orientation points and guide routes must be provided for usually disabled people;
- Paths and pavement shall be free from unnecessary obstacles;
- Information and warning signs must be understandable, clear and well lit;

Areas where passengers can alight from vehicles should be closed to entrance, preferably within 10m. The line of vision between alighting area and entrance shall be free so that waiting can see each other. The network of pathways should be continuous and easy for older/disabled to follow and perceive. Paths shall be clearly distinguished from the roads for motor vehicles.

Large open areas should be provided with guide routes and guide rails with orientation aids. Guide routes should be without obstacles and hazards, where a disabled person can walk. Guide rails are used by people who have difficulty in walking, to provide supports and assistance, and by visually disabled people as orientation aid. Guide rail should continue past resting sections and at least 300mm past the beginning and end of the flight of steps or the ramp.

Signs, symbols and texts should be easy to detect and to read. Placing and design are dependent on the information content, but disabled person and the mentally retarted people should also be taken into account. Advertisement signs, benches and other objects should not be allowed to be placed temporary in a pedestrian area since they constitute a danger to disabled persons and cause inconvenience to them. Warning makings should be placed on the surface of the pavement to indicate unexpected permanent obstacles in a pedestrian area.

If there are steps leading up to a main footpath, and alternative route should be provided with a ramp. Long flights of steps should be divided with resting landing after every 10 to 12 steps, and such landings should be well illuminated. The height and depth of the steps should be the same along the entire flight. The step height should be preferably be 120mm and may not exceed 150 mm. The pedestrian crossings should be placed along the shortest route with proper markings. They should be provided with a ramp for wheel chair.

Traffic lights should have both light and sound signals. The outdoor environment should ensure continued accessibility and serviceableness. Footpaths, pavements and pedestrian crossings should kept free from dampness and spilling of water to prevent slipping. Plants should be cut back so they do not encroach on footpath. Public transport should provide easy access and mobility with comfortable boarding and embarking for the older people and handicapped. Bus stops, vehicle design and facilities like public toilets, telephones etc. should be sensitively design so as to meet the needs of the aged/ handicapped.

Movement of pedestrians in the city is an important aspect, especially after the introduction of MRTS. Safe passages for pedestrian movement is to be identified by the concerned agencies. This will become possible with restructuring of the landuses along the MRTS corridors. While restructuring land uses along the MRTS corridor, the following facilities will be provided:

- Parking lot for passengers embarking and disembarking.
- Pedestrian passages to nearby transport node and workplaces.

- Facilities like public conveniences, toilets, taxi stands, parking for wheel chairs etc.
- Signages
- Security and first aid arrangements, resting places, benches etc.
- Landscape, shaded public areas, street furniture

Planning for the Elderly, Disabled and Children

As for census of India the proportion of elderly population is expected to show an increasing trend, while the proportion of children population will decrease. Accordingly, the standards and provision for housing for elderly, geriatic healthcare, schools, playgrounds, maternity/child care centres etc. need to be incorporated.

The National Policy on Older Persons, 1999, recognises shelter for the elderly as a basic human need and commits that the stock of housing for different incomes segments will be increase. It stipulates that housing schemes for urban and rural lower income segments to earmark 10 per cent of the houses/ house sites for allotment to older persons. As such it is proposed that the development of a network of dedicated housing/hostels and old age homes should be made in his whiles together with the following provisions:

- Provide helpline and home-help assistance to older people in managing, maintaining and improving their existing homes.
- Provide community centres offering day care service, library, hobby-rooms, games, catering service, etc.
- Make neighbourhoods more attractive for older people and ensure improved physical and social planning.
- Consult older people to identify their specific needs in housing design, services and domestic equipment.
- Ensure personal security and safety, provide emergency signalling system.
- Design of the dwellings to ensure greater flexibility of use by all ages and handicapped persons.
- Make existing neighbourhood and dwellings more easily accessible.

- Encourage a social network within the local community.
- Make available opportunities to utilise the potential and capacities of older people.
- Link housing with income generation by the older persons.
- Introduce reverse mortgaging arrangement to release some of the equity tied-up in a house.
- Nursing and medical care visits to be provided for bed-ridden elderly people on regular basis.
- Silver Human Resource Centre/Training Institutions should be integrated with housing.
- Institutions for protecting the rights of mentally disabled and the elderly suffering from senile dementia, medical care information centres, Rehabilitation hospitals, health centres and Geriatric Hospitals for elderly population should be planned.

Livelihood, Poverty and Development Linkage

Of the 285 million urban Indians, 70 million are poor. National Sample Survey Organisation data shows the incidence of urban unemployment is much higher than that of rural

Low Cost Conventional Pit Latrine

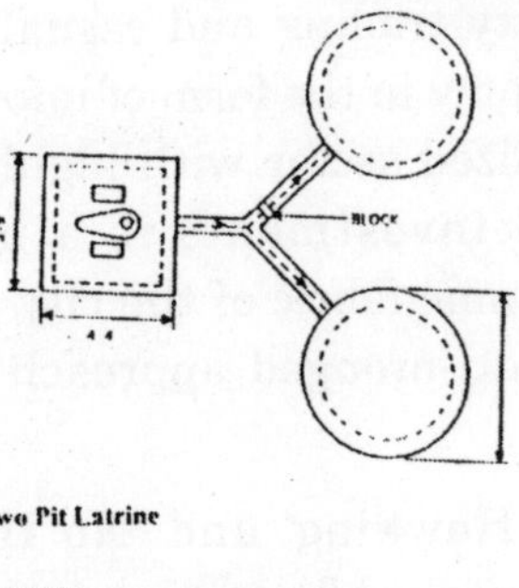

Two Pit Latrine

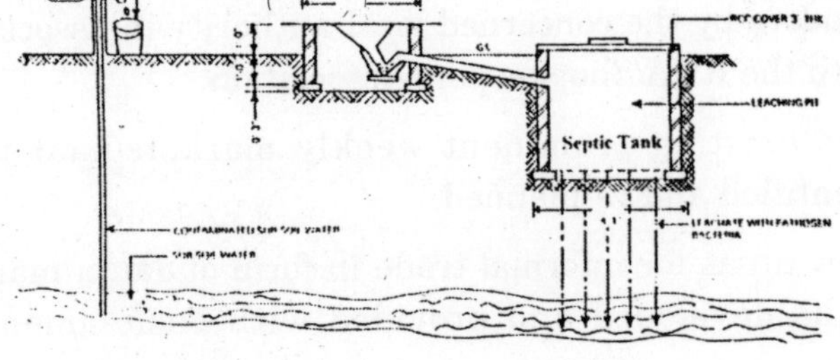

unemployment. There were 14 urban persons unemployed per 1000 in the year 2003, compared to five for rural India. Also the NSSO data shows that most urban employment (33 per cent) is in production related work, which means the service sector boom is not helping. The livelihood-poverty-development linkage is critical to the long-term sustainability of the cities. The increasing levels of urban income and education provide an important springboard to develop a range of livelihoods that are linked to new economy.

Informal Sector—Implementing National Policy on Street Vendors

A survey conducted by the Directorate of Economics and Statistics in Delhi (1997) on unorganized trading activity in Delhi estimated the total number of unorganized trading enterprises as 2 lakh and the number of persons employed around 3.18 lakhs. The contribution of this sector in terms of Gross value added to the economy of Delhi was estimated at Rs. 1.01 lakh per enterprise per annum.

Large sections of unemployed and underemployed population in Delhi and outside, look forward for self-employment in the informal sector. They bring forth multitutde of small enterprises, petty trading and casual labour. As such Delhi has a parallel economy in the form of informal sector. This vernacular and disorganized sector with highly reduced needs of space, services and investments is a major source of employment in the economic fabric of the city. Master Plan for Delhi-2021 adopts a multi-pronged approach to cater to this sector, as given below :

- Earmarking of 'Hawking' and 'No Hawking' Zones. Specific areas be marked for stationary and mobile street vendors by the concerned local authority in association with the RWA/Shopkeepers Association.
- The existing prominent weekly markets/haat to be identified and re-planned.
- New areas for informal trade in form of Janta markets to be developed and provided with basic amenities

in housing, commercial, institutional and industrial areas.

- Provision of common basic services, like solid waste disposal, urinals/toilets, water point and lighting.
- Institutionalising this sector by adopting mandatory norms of space for hawkers / vendors.
- To evolve innovative designs of stalls, push-carts and mobile vans of various sizes and with cleaning facilities.

The following norms are prescribed for the provision of informal sector units:

- Planned Commercial Centres - 3 to 4 units per 10 formal shops
- Govt. and Commercial Offices - 5-6 units per 1000 employees
- Wholesale Trade & Freight Complexes-3-4 units per 10 formal shops
- Hospitals - 3-4 units per 100 beds
- Bus Terminal - 1 unit per 2 bus-bays
- Primary School - 3-4 units
- Sr. Secondary Schools - 5-6 units
- Regional / District Parks - 8-10 units at each major entry
- Neighbourhood parks - 2-3 units
- Residential Area - 1 unit / 1000 population
- Industrial Area - 5-6 units per 1000 employees

Devolution, Governance and Localisation

The 73rd and 74th Constitutional amendments and Good Governance Campaign of the Ministry of Urban Development, Government of India provide the institutional basis for a process of devolution based on subsidiarity, built around local communities. Kerala State's People's Planning Programme (Janakeeyasoothranam) and Bangalore's Janagraha (Citizens

Movement) are good examples of participatory governance. The new institutions of self rule and governance can help creating a vibrant urban culture and a sense of ownership among its citizens within a dispersed city. Decoupling environmental pressures of economic growth, while continuing to satisfy human needs requires an integral effort. The solution lies with the people and the system of governance. Simulation models should be developed to explore the blue-skies area of future livelihoods, lifestyles and time-use. The break-through concept of Lifetimes – a human time-use based resource accounting system, enables lifecycle time-use accounting and imputed economic value simulation. This would cross-link environmental accounting systems with human capital planning approaches and should determine the broad directions and investments for the sustainability transition scenario.

74th Constitutional Amendment Act of India

As per the 12th Schedule of the 74th Constitutional Amendment Act of India, 18 new tasks have been defined as in the functional domain of the ULBs, the most important of which are:

1. Urban Planning including town planning.
2. Regulation of land-use and construction of buildings.
3. Planning for economic and social development.
4. Roads and bridges.
5. Water supply for domestic, industrial and commercial purposes.
6. Public Health, sanitation, conservancy and solid waste management.
7. Fire services.
8. Urban forestry, protection of the environment and promotion of ecological aspects.
9. Safeguarding the interests of weaker sections of society, including the handicapped etc.
10. Slum improvement and upgradation.

11. Urban poverty alleviation.
12. Provision of urban amenities and facilities such as parks, gardens, playgrounds.
13. Promotion of cultural, educational and aesthetic aspects.
14. Burials and burial grounds; cremations, cremation grounds and electric crematoriums.
15. Cattle pounds: prevention of cruelty to animals.
16. Vital statistics including registration of births and deaths.
17. Public amenities including street lighting, parking lots, bus stops and public conveniences.
18. Regulation of slaughter houses and tanneries.

Good Urban Governance Campaign

The Ministry of Urban Development, Government of India with the United Nations Centre for Human Settlements in September 2001, launched Good Urban Governance Campaign. As a follow up it has been launched at the States and at local levels, for interactive and participatory roles of civil society, service providers and other stakeholders. The campaign proposes that good urban governance is characterized by the following interdependent and mutually reinforcing norms:

- Sustainability in all dimensions of urban development.
- Subsidiarity of authority and resources at the closet appropriate level.
- Equity of access to decision-making processes and the basic necessities of urban life.
- Efficiency in the delivery of public services and in promoting local economic development.
- Transparency and accountability of decision-makers and all stakeholders.
- Civic engagement and citizenship
- Security of individuals and their living environment.

Good Urban Governance Campaign engages the cities, partners and the community in a vigorous debate on the issues of concern. These norms are supported by a wide range of operational principles, which are based on lessons of experience and reflect regional conditions. Their implementation must be grounded in the local reality of urban planning and management.

Peoples' Planning Programme (Janakeeya Soothranam) Kerala

India with a strong commitment towards democracy, enacted constitutional 73rd and 74th Amendment Acts in 1992. Subsequently, state legislature promulgated provisions for three tiers of Panchayat viz. Grama/block and zila pachayats along with urban local governments viz. Nagar Panchayat/Municipal council/Corporation.

The State of Kerala has been a pioneer in decentralized planning. In 1996 a new planning process was introduced in Kerala through the launching of people's campaign for decentralized planning popularly known as janakeeyasoothranam. The people's planning campaign empowers local people to prepare plans for local development. 35-40 per cent of the State's plan funds are devolved to the local government; who formulate projects for their needs and implement projects through actively involving people at various stages of formulation and implementation. So far about 1200 plans (DR) and more than 100,000 projects have been prepared. Technical Advisory committee of experts in various fields, such as, town planning, agriculture, irrigation, watershed development, transportation, housing, health, finance and power provides research inputs in the planning process, enabling application of latest research in local planning. Training workshops, awareness campaigns, handouts, handbooks, manuals, capacity building and interactive web sites are integral part of the local planning process. The Kerala experience provides an innovative example of bridging the divide between research and local action. It brings together the people and the government, long range planning and short range prgrammes and synchronises the planning with the implementation. The State Government has devolved about 35 to 40 per cent of Plan funds to the local government. There has been meaningful participation of the local population.

Bangalore – Janaagraha : Citizens' Movement

Janaagraha: Citizen-in-government participatory democracy movement covers Bangalore's 100 wards. It works out how the money earmarked for works could be best utilized as per the needs and local demands of the residents and aims at moving from representative democracy to participative democracy.

AREA	366 sq. km
POPULATION	5.6 million
ROAD LENGTH	4,000 km
ANNUAL BUDGET OF CORP.	Rs.1,025 crore
ANNUAL BUDGET OF DEV. AUTH.	Rs.1,100 crore

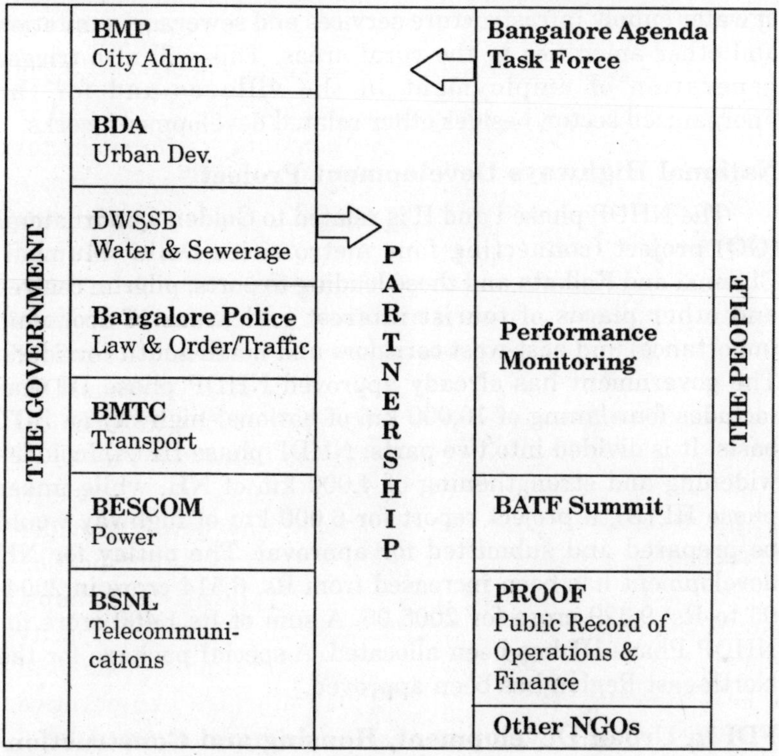

BMP: Bangalore Mahanagera Palike, **BDA:** Bangalore Development Authority, **BWSSB:** Bangalore Water Supply & Sewerage Board,

BMTC: Bangalore Metropolitan Transport Corporation, **BESCOM:** Bangalore Electricity Supply Company, **PROOF:** A campaign built around citizens right to information, **BATF Summit:** Six monthly review of the seven departments listed in the chart.

Bharat Nirman and Provision of Urban Amenities in Rural Areas (Pura)

The Government of India announced this programme with a target to bring 10 million hectares of land under assured irrigation, road connectivity to all villages with a population of 1000 and construction of addition 60 lakh houses for the poor in rural areas. The government has also decided to provide a corpus of Rs. 8,000 crore to the Rural Infrastructure Development Fund. The World Bank agreed to provide a $ 3 billion loan for its Rs. 1,74,000 crore Bharat Nirman programme to develop rural infrastructure. The scheme is accompanied by a programme of provision of urban amenities in rural areas (PURA). It has been launched with the objective of the provision of water supply infrastructure services and sewerage, sanitation and other amenities in the rural areas. This will also trigger generation of employment in the villages and for the unorganized sector, besides other related development works.

National Highways Development Project

The NHDP phase I and II is related to Golden Quadrilateral (GQ) project (connecting four metro cities-Delhi, Mumbai, Chennai and Kolkata and those leading to ports, pilgrim centres and other places of tourist interest and areas of economic importance) and east-west corridors and north-south corridors. The government has already approved NHDP phase III that includes four-laning of 10,000 km of national highway on BOT basis. It is divided into two parts: NHDP phase III (A) includes widening and strengthening of 4,000 km of NH, while under phase III (B), a project report for 6,000 km of highway would be prepared and submitted for approval. The outlay for NH development has been increased from Rs. 6,514 crore in 2004-05 to Rs. 9,329 crore for 2005-06. A sum of Rs.1,400 crore for NHDP Phase III has been allocated. A special package for the North-east Region has been approved.

FDI in Urban Development, Housing and Construction

The Ministry of Commerce has issued the guidelines for FDI up to 100 per cent under the automatic route in townships, housing, built-up infrastructures and construction development projects. It will include housing, commercial premises, hotels, resorts, hospitals, educational institutions, recreational facilities and city/regional infrastructure, subject to the following guidelines. Minimum areas to be developed under each project would be as under:

- Serviced housing plot : 10 hectare (Minimum)
- Construction development Project : 50,000 sq.mt. (minimum built up area)

In case of combination project, any one of the above two conditions would suffice.

The investment would further be subject to the following conditions :

- Minimum capitalization of US$ 10m for wholly owned subsidiaries and US$ 5m for joint ventures with Indian partners. The funds would have to be brought in within six months of commencement of business of the company.
- Original investment cannot be repatriated before a period of three years from the completion of minimum capitalization. However, the investor may be permitted to exit earlier with prior approval of the government through the FIPB.
- At least 50 per cent of the project must be developed within a period of five years from the date of obtaining all statutory clearances.

As per scope of FDI in construction, the overseas construction companies can build townships, large buildings, commercial complexes and supermarkets in India. FDI in construction envisages to promote housing in a big way.

Key Resources

Apart from the human capital, the following are the key resources of city development:

- Land and Natural Resources
- Water, energy and other infrastructure services
- Finance
- Heritage and Cultural Resources
- Administrative systems, political apparatus, implementing agencies, institutional capacity and legal framework

These resources need to be constantly preserved, developed and reviewed to meet the needs of people in the context of time and space. Cities account for over 55 per cent of the country's GDP and more than 90 per cent of total government revenues. Delhi, Mumbai and Kolkata contribute around 60 per cent of the total value added in manufacturing. But only a fraction of all this is ploughed back to cities. A critical analysis of municipal finances by the National Institute of Urban Affairs reveals that the municipal spending levels in India, are abysmally low. At an annual per capita of Rs.574, this level of expenditure is 130 per cent lower than the 1963 norms.

Some of the State Finance Commissions have suggested a formula for sharing resources between the state government and the local bodies and the measures to be taken to improve the financial position of the local bodies, which need to be implemented without delay.

Urban infrastructure Financing

The central and state governments promote private initiatives and public private partnership in urban infrastructure sectors such as water supply, sanitation, public transport, land development, etc. The government has a commitment to provide support in the form of equity contribution, package of concessions, dedicated levies to repay loans and transparent regulatory framework. Private sectors are encouraged to negotiate concessions required to make their investments safe and paying. The city of Visakhapatnam is a good example of how cross subsidization between consumer groups can make water supply system run on commercial principles. The Ahmedabad Municipal Corporation has launched the country's first municipal bonds.

Special Purpose Vehicle (SPV) mechanism has been proposed for infrastructure projects that are financially viable but facing difficulties in raising resources in current situation. Such projects can be funded through financial SPV having Rs. 10,000 crore for core projects to extend loans for projects in roads, ports, airports, tourism, etc. The current budget (2005-06) has also provided Rs. 1,500 crore assistance for making projects financially viable to attract greater private participation.

Examples of Management Contracts for Municipal Services

Services / Tasks	*City*
Sanitation and Public Health • Conservancy/drain cleaning • Sanitation/maintenance for STP • Construction and maintenance of toilets	Guwahati, Bangalore, Jodhpur, Ludhiana, New Mumbai, Faridabad, Delhi, Dharwad, Aurangabad, Kalyan, Jaipur, Kochi.
Solid Waste Management • Garbage collection/disposal street cleaning • Compost plant, solid waste	Chennai, Guwahati, Ahmedabad, Rajkot, Baroda, Bangalore, Kochi, Mumbai, Pune, jalandhar, Amritsar, Ludhiana, Jaipur, Baroda, Kalyan.
Roads and Bridges	Delhi-Noida, Indore (Rau)
• Link bridge • Road Construction, bypass	Panvel Ahmedabad, Kochi, Bangalore
• Road maintenance • Street lighting	Jaipur, Ranchi, Rajkot, Faridabad, Jodhpur
• Light rail transit system	New Mumbai, Hyderabad
Water Supply • Maintenance of water supply system	New Mumbai, Tirupur, Vishakha-pattnam
Tax Collection • Collection of entry tax	Guwahati, New Mumbai
• Other local taxes/charges Parking lots/collection of charges	Guwahati, Pune
Parks and Gardens • Development and maintenance of gardens and parks/play grounds/ sports complex/swimming pool/ planetarium, traffic islands.	Rajkot, Baroda, Mumbai, Faridabad, Hubli-Dharwad, Bangalore, Kochi, Ranchi, Aurangabad, New Bombay, Kalyan, Pune, Amritsar,
• Social forestry, tree planting along streets	Ludhiana, Jalandhar, Jaipur Baroda, Jaipur
Others	
• Waste water recycling	Chennai
• Bus terminus/shelters	Ranchi, Kochi
• Ward security	Ahmedabad, Rajkot
• Market development	Ahmedabad, Kalyan
• Maintenance of vehicles	Rajkot
• Land development	Faridabad
• Maintenance of libraries	Faridabad
• Milk market	Hubli-Dharwad
• Octroi post	Nashik

Urban Renewal and Reforms

The Jawaharlal Nehru National Urban Renewal Mission (JNNURM) has been initiated by the Government of India, which aims at providing incentives to cities to undertake institutional, structural and fiscal reforms, necessary to improve service delivery systems that are sustainable, enhance local economic performance, and bring about transparency and accountability in the functioning of municipal governments. Preparation of a City Development Plan (CDP) is a pre-requisite for accessing the funds under the JNNURM. For mega cities and cities with million plus population, the JNNURM is a two-tiered programme for urban infrastructure development and poverty alleviation-employment generation.

The scheme being implemented in a 'Mission mode' to cover 63 cities, each comprising a population exceeding one million, State capitals and 23 other cities of religious and tourist importance. An estimated provision of Rs. 50,000 crore for a period of seven years is to be given as Grant-in-Aid for leveraging additional resources. Access to resources will be contingent on some mandatory reforms like effective implementation of the 74th Amendment of the Constitution, rationalization of stamp duty to 5 per cent over a seven-year period, repeal of the land Ceiling Act or reforming the Rent Control Act coupled with Municipal Reforms on accounting procedure, improving the tax efficiency and application of user charge apart from some optional measures. It will be monitored through a National Committee under the Minister of Urban Development and State level Steering Committees under the Chief Minister.

The Mission consists of two sub-missions: one on urban infrastructure and governance and the other on basic services to the urban poor. The Government has also launched two parallel schemes : an urban infrastructure development scheme (for small and medium towns) and a housing and slum development programme. The objectives or these reforms are to improve the financial condition of local bodies, their credit-worthiness, ability to access market capital for taking up new projects, secure public participation and commercial sustainability in the provision of services. The Urban Renewal Mission will entail investment partnerships among the Centre, State governments and urban local bodies.

Apart from about Rs. 50,000 crore in building urban infrastructure across the country under the Jawahar Lal Nehru National Urban Renewal Mission (JNNURM) during the next 7 years, there is going to be unprecedented massive investments in the urban and rural development through the schemes of Urban Infrastructure Development, Bharat Nirman (Rs.1,74,000 crore) National Highways Development Project, Gramin Sadak Yojana, Private Sector and Foreign Direct Investments, Public-Private Partnership, etc. This is a unique opportunity for urban managers and the planners to redirect the course of urban growth towards new generation infrastructure and well planned and sustainable development. The task is enormous and demands proactive, accelerated, orchestrated and coordinated actions for integrated planning. This is a "never again" opportunity for urban turnaround of Indian cities towards the global standards.

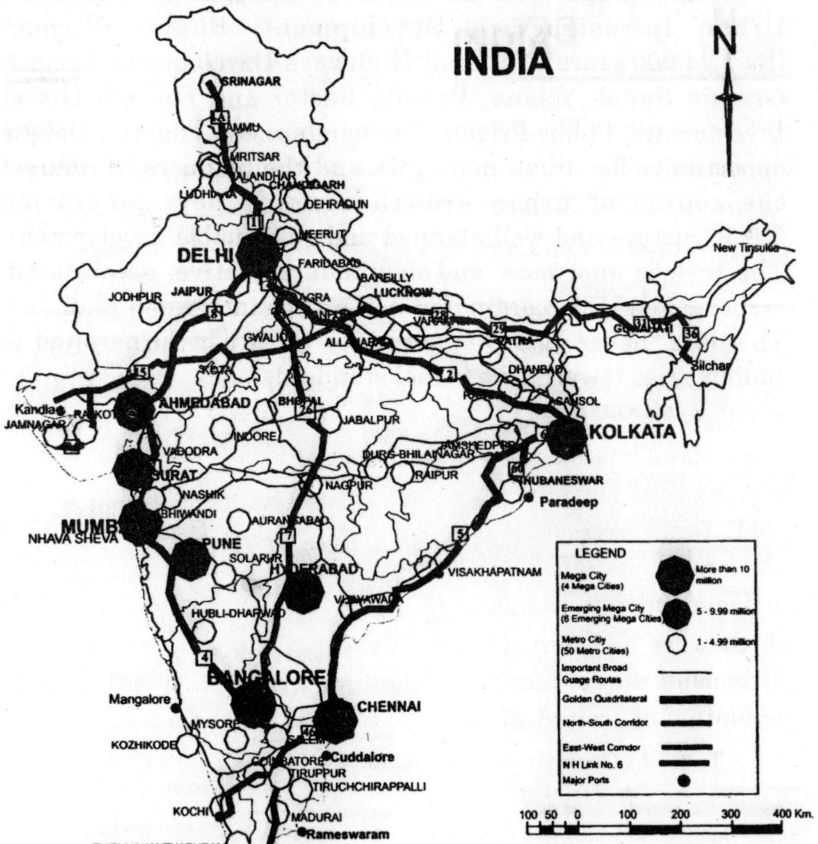
INDIA
N
SRINAGAR
DELHI
New Tinsukia
JODHPUR
JAIPUR
FARIDABAD
BAREILLY
LUCKNOW
AGRA
MEERUT
DEHRADUN
LUDHIANA
GWALIOR
ALLAHABAD
PATNA
DHANBAD
ASANSOL
Silchar
Kandla
JAMNAGAR
AHMEDABAD
BHOPAL
JABALPUR
INDORE
KOLKATA
VADODRA
SURAT
NASHIK
BHIWANDI
MUMBAI
NHAVA SHEVA
PUNE
AURANGABAD
NAGPUR
RAIPUR
DURG-BHILAINAGAR
JAMSHEDPUR
BHUBANESWAR
Paradeep
VISAKHAPATNAM
HYDERABAD
VIJAYAWADA
HUBLI-DHARWAD
BANGALORE
CHENNAI
Mangalore
MYSORE
KOZHIKODE
SALEM
COIMBATORE
Cuddalore
TIRUPPUR
TIRUCHCHIRAPPALLI
KOCHI
MADURAI
Rameswaram
THIRUVANANTHAPURAM
Tuticorin
LEGEND
Mega City (4 Mega Cities)
More than 10 million
Emerging Mega City (6 Emerging Mega Cities)
5 - 9.99 million
Metro City (50 Metro Cities)
1 - 4.99 million
Important Broad Guage Routes
Golden Quadrilateral
North-South Corridor
East-West Corridor
N H Link No. 6
Major Ports
100 50 0 100 200 300 400 Km.

3

URBAN SPACE FOR NEW ECONOMIC BOOM

We live in Flow City. Systems are the roots of design, nourishing the spaces we try to make beautiful ... Projects in urban design, architecture, and landspace architecture that aren't made with an understanding of flows and connectivity are destined to fail.

—Kristina Hill

India, the seventh largest country in the world in terms of area (330 million sq. km.), has a population of 1,027 million (2001), which is the second only to China. During last 150 years, there had been a 32 fold increase in population in urban India against less than five fold increase in the rural India. In 2001, there were 5161 towns and approximately 5,80,000 villages. Accordingly to the Census of India, the towns and urban agglomerations (UA) were grouped into six population sizes, which were 3,969 in number. By 2051, the number of these settlements would increase to around 6,500, which will have a population of around 47.50 per cent (Table-1).

Table 1 : Growth in Number of Settlements : 1901-2051

Census Year	Urban Population (in millions)	Percentage of Urban to total Population Population	No. of urban Settlements/ Agglomerations	Rural Population (in millions)	Percentage of Rural to total Population	No. of in habitated Rural Settlements (in millions)
1901	26	11.00	1,827	210.00	89.00	0.59
1951	62	17.29	2,845	289.00	82.81	0.58
2001	285	27.78	3,969	742.00	72.22	0.58
2051	820	47.50	6,500	912.00	52.50	0.57

Spirce : Census of India + projections for 2051

According to the Census, urban areas have been classified into six size-class categories based on population, as given below:

Class I	-	100,000 and above
Class II	-	50,000 to 99.999
Class III	-	20,000 to 49,999
Class IV	-	10,000 to 19,999
Class V	-	5,000 to 9.999
Class VI	-	Less than 5,000

As given below (Table 2), in 2001, 27.78 per cent of the urban population of India resided in around 4,492 towns/ UA:

Table-2 : Number of Towns and urban Population by Size Class, 1991-2001

Size	*No. of Towns/ UAs*	*Population in Millions*	*No. of Towns/ UAs*	*Population in Millions*	*Percentage increases between 1991-2001*	
	1991		*2001*		*Towns/UAs*	*Population*
Class I	296	138.80	407	188.11	37.5	35.50
Class II	341	23.31	407	27.04	19.4	16.00
Class III	927	28.08	1,111	33.34	19.8	18.70
Class IV	1,135	16.50	1,355	19.11	17.6	15.60
Class V	725	5.53	999	7.21	37.8	30.30
Class VI	185	0.61	213	0.76	15.1	23.80
Total	3,609	212.83	4,492	275.57	24.5	29.50

Source : Census of India

The Census of India is considering the reclassification of settlements from Class I to Class VI towns to megacities, metrocities, medium and small cities and large, medium and small towns (Table-3). This hierarchical reclassification corresponds to central place villages and other villages grouped as panchayats (Table-4).

Table-3 : Emerging Re-classification and Growth of Urban Areas

Sl. No.	Reclassification Areas	2001 (actual)			2051 (projected)		
		No. of settle-ments	Popula-tion (in millions)	Percentage of urban Population	No. of Settle-ments	Popula-tion (in millions)	Percentage of Urban Population
1.	Megacities (>10m + as UA's with MC's + other LSG's)	3	42.38	14.74	15	180	22.10
2.	Metrocities (1 to 10m as UA's with M.C. + other LSG's)	32	65.48	22.96	85	218	26.60
3.	Medium Cities (0.3 to 1m as UA's with M.C. + Other LSG's)	88	38.64	13.54	300	150	18.25
4.	Small Cities (0.1 to 0.3m as UA's with M.C/ M.CL + other LSG's)	308	48.20	16.89	600	120	14.60
5.	Large Towns (20,000 to 0.1m as UA's with M.CI. + other LSG's)	1515	63.17	22.24	2000	100	12.15
6.	Small Towns (<20,000 as NP's)	2,023	27.48	9.63	3,500	52	6.30
	Total	3,969	285.35	100.00	6,500	820	100.00

Source : Census of India + projections for 2051

Note : M.CI. – Municipal Council, NP – Nagar or Town Panchayat, LSG – Local Self Government including rural panchayats

Table-4 : Emerging Scenario of Rural Settlements – 2051 (Estimates)

Sl. No.	*Classification of Village*	*Estimated Number of villages*	*Number of rural Panchayats (Estimated)*	*Average population per Panchayat*	*Total estimated Population (in millions)*	*Percentage of total country population (Estimated)*
1.	Central Place Villages as rural growth centres, each with separate panchayats	35,000	35,000	10,000	350	20.00
2.	Other villages, grouped as panchayats	5,35,000	1,07,000 (approx.)	5,250	562	32.5
	Total	5,70,000	1,42,000	—	912	52.50

During 1990-91, the urban sector contribution in per capita GDP was 3.62 times more than the rural sector (Table-5). The planning and development of human settlements and provision of infrastructure are much better in urban areas. Rural population migrate to urban areas due to more employment opportunities, better facilities and limited capacity of rural economy to accommodate the increasing population.

Table-5 : Urban and Rural Shares of GDP

Sl. No.	*Year*	*GDP at factor costs at Current Prices (Rs. Billion)*			*Per capita GDP in Rs.*		*Ratio of urban and Rural per capita GDP*
		Urban	*Rural*	*Total*	*Urban*	*Rural*	
1.	1950-51	27	67	94	422	225	1.97
2.	1980-81	673	759	1433	4222	1449	2.91
3.	1990-91	2355	1570	3925	10844	2297	3.62

Source : Planning Commission, Task Force reports on Urban Development, 1983 Mulkh Raj, Urbanization, Infrastructure and Besieged Growth Potential (Mimeo), 1993.

The 2001 census indicates India's urban population as 28% as compared to 17% in 1951, which is projected to increase to almost 40% in the next 30 years. Most of this growth will be in the smaller cities of the Class I category or towns with over one lakh population, the share of which is 65% in 2001, as compared to 25% in 1901. The Trends indicate the highest growth of smaller cities in the vicinity of the metros, which are becoming extremely unaffordable and unlivable. As such, some of the smaller, high-growth settlements, are in the periphery of the bigger ones. Delhi urban agglomerate's average annual growth rate between 2000 and 2005 was 4%, (compared to Mumbai's 2.6% and Bangalore's 3.2%), partly due to higher growth of its feeder towns, such as, Noida and Ghaziabad, which had the highest growth rates in the country at 6.96% and 6.38% respectively. The challenge of urbanization may therefore lie in both the small towns and the urbanized corridors that build up between cities, like the Mumbai-Pune stretch, or the corridors from Delhi to Jaipur, Chandigarh, Mathura, etc. As such the solution does not lie just in the development of towns, but planning in a broader perspective of the region and urban corridors. This needs starting with identifying key development drivers – such as a new expressway, an airport, a new railway line or an SEZ. Within a regional framework, the planning and development of towns and cities, integrated with the socio-economic and environmental objectives should be taken up.

It is estimated that one per cent growth in infrastructure yields a cascading effect of 2.5 per cent growth of GDP. To improve the infrastructure development of cities and to exclude them to act as the new growth centres, there is a need to focus upon sector specific infrastructure (railways, power, civil aviation, water, communication, transport, sanitation and waste management etc.), social infrastructure and evolve fiscal and monetary policy initiatives. It also needs a wide public and private sector participation, alongwith capturing the Foreign Direct Investments. Agriculture still provides livelihood for 68 per cent of our population while contributing 24 per cent to our GDP. Sustained growth of manufacturing, coupled with the services sector in non-metropolitan towns and growth centre can significantly alter the trends on urbanization. Every Indian city is a hive of so called informal economy, i.e. without formal approval of the government. The poor have houses but no titles; crops but no deeds; business without licences. The informal economy is people's spontaneous response to the state's failure and its law, rules and regulations. This parallel economy is in many ways more authentic, hardworking, and creative than legal economy, which needs to be encouraged by the planned development.

With the ongoing globalization, corresponding to the policies of democratic decentralization and economic liberalisation, the course of urban growth is moving at a fast pace towards new generation infrastructure. This makes the need for evolving a new forms of planning, development and governance which are pro-poor, participatory and flexible. The plans should address the immediate concerns of the citizens, without loosing the sight of long term vision. There is a need to give disaggregated attention to every aspect and each sector, while weaving them into a comprehensive whole. The whole process has to adopt a new paradigm which is participatory, democratic and decentralized.

Planning in a democratic context is an exercise of balancing between the competing and conflicting demands, long term vision and immediate concerns. It is a conflict resolution between political exigencies and professionalism, between future permissiveness and post-facto regularisation. On one hand the democratic and constitutional right of the population, including the inmigrants to live and work is to be protected, on the other the land, water, and ecology need to be preserved. Planning is an art to co-exist the opposites - livelihood and lifestyle, Economic Right and Social Left. It is essential to look back to look forward – so that the city conserves its heritage, as well as is futuristic too. At the same time planning has to be essentially pro-poor and inclusive, encompassing the vulnerable people, children, elderly and working women. The planning process should encourage the self build, self-help potentials of the people. This means a complete rethinking and moving from government driven, subsidy oriented provision of shelter and services to self-generating housing, services and opportunities for self-employment. This would mean opening up access to land, finance, services and other resources for community driven development and reversing the present concept of single use zoning to multiple use zoning, together with redefining the urban legal framework.

Governance and Planning Reforms

An emerging challenge pertains to the urban reforms and sustainable transformation of current institutions and systems of governance. Efficiency, ethics and equity, using a minimal throughput of energy, with the least impact on nature are the key goals. This would require 'space' for urban governance, participation and new forms of partnerships. These transformations should start with of local and community-based governance and an open government. The 73rd and 74th Constitutional amendments provide the institutional basis for a process of devolution based on subsidiarity, built around local communities. The new institutions of self-rule and governance can help creating a vibrant urban culture within a dense yet dispersed city. Decoupling environmental pressures of economic growth, while continuing to satisfy human needs requires an integral effort. The solution lies in a participatory system of governance and planning framework, with the following key reforms:

- Localisation and decentralisation of planning
- Community partnership and planning, interfacing administrative and political constituencies
- Corporatisation of planning organisations

- Government as facilitator for people-centred planning.
- Adoption of principles of Devolution, Debureaucratisation, Deregulation & Decontrol
- Efficiency, equity and employment generation and economic potential as the basic criteria.
- Release access to land, housing, services, finance and information by public-private partnerships.
- Promote micro-enterprises and micro-banking.
- New methods of land assembly and development.
- Regularisation of land tenure; simplify and expedite land registration.
- Review and simplify property taxation.
- Emphasise cost recovery and adopt "user pays" principle.
- Eliminate monopoly practices, including government monopolies.
- Make urban development self-financing and self-sustaining by developing the concepts of Excess condemnation, TDR, Accommodation Reservation, land pooling and readjustment, development and conversion charges, betterment levy, additional FAR charges, BOT, franchising, contracting out, etc.
- Simplification and devolution of planning procedures and controls.
- Replace lowest tendering system by alternative/project management contract systems.
- Replace building byelaws by development control rules/planning permissions, remove unnecessary controls.
- Review all urban legislations and scrap outdated ones.
- Establish regulatory authority for urban development and privatization.

- Minimize legal complexity, maximize enforcement and empower the community.

The new economic boom and private sector investments in real estate have unleashed the growth of small and medium towns. However in spite of huge investments, the reality is rather dismal. Most of the smaller cities lack the basic amenities and services, like public transport, communications, drinking water supply, power, sanitation, health facilities and employment. The planning of these towns, integrated with governance, financial and legal reforms, can act as a major resource, which should be based on a broader regional framework.

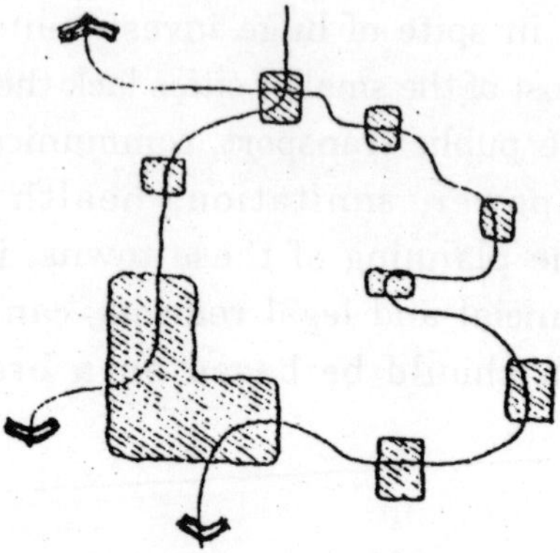

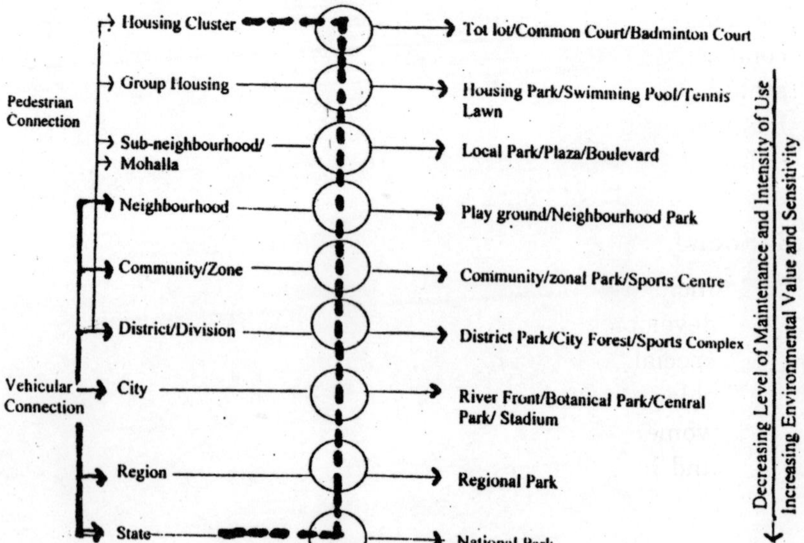

Hierarchy of Open Space System Based on Environment and Activity Classification

4

BETWEEN LIVELIHOODS AND LIFESTYLES

Only connect!... Only connect the prose and the passion, and both will be exalted, and human love will be seen at its height. Live in fragments no longer. Only connect, and the beast and the monk, robbed of the isolation that is life to either, will die. —W.M. Forster

The *raison-de-etre'* of habitat planning is wide ranging and complex. A habitat system caters to a wide range of interest and stakeholders – poor and rich, children, women and elderly, business, public and political. The broad objectives as given below, have been organized around social, economic and environmental perspectives:

I. Social Objectives

1. Inclusive community development, with special attention to older people, poor, women, children and handicapped	• Access to land, services and social facilities • Promote health through social infrastructure, greenery & Sports • Strengthen social and cultural life • Shelter for All
2. Equity	• Diversify housing opportunities and affordability • Promote accessible local facilities
3. Mobility and communications	• Enhance mobility including walking, cycling and public transport

	• Enhance communication networks & facilities
4. Healthy living	• Improve local environment (air, land, water) / pollution control
	• Encourage an active life-style
	• Facilitate access to health facilities
5. Safety and Security	• Reduce the chance of accidents, disasters, dangers, violence, fires etc.
	• Provide security / police / fire safety infrastructure
	• Encourage a sense of ownership and belonging
6. Freedom of choice	• Diversify local facilities, work and social contact
	• Open up life-style and movement options
7. Local decision-making	• Building local social capital through the participatory process
	• Create local partnerships and trusts
	• Increase user control of local systems
II. Economic Objectives	
8. To promote wealth creation, poverty reduction and employment generation	• Diversify entrepreneurial opportunities, learning, specialization, etc.
	• Recycle financial resources
	• Promote urban regeneration, mixed use, commercial and work centres
	• Shelter intertwined with jobs and poverty reduction
	• Plans for local employment, informal sector, street vendors

	• Enhance education and training opportunities • Encourage public transport, walking and cycling
III. Environmental Objectives	
9. To enhance environmental quality	• Create an attractive public realm • Promote local distinctiveness and value local heritage • Reduce noise and vandalism • Create robust, adaptable and high-quality buildings
10. Greenery, landscape, flora and fauna	• Enhance bio-diversity, green networks, parks, playgrounds, and sports complexes • Realize urban 'brownfield' potential thus reducing urban sprawl • Recovery of water bodies, rivers, lakes & rain water harvesting
11. To safeguard natural resources	• Manage water resources and sustainability • Reduce demand for non-renewable resources, encourage energy efficiency, Encourage Factor 4 Technology • Close local resource loops(re-use and recycling)
12. To cut greenhouse gas and carbon emissions	• Increase energy-efficiency of buildings. • Promote renewables and combined heat and power • Reduce car reliance and the need to travel

Looking back most of the city plans have largely benefited the middle class and organized sectors, whereas the poor have remained marginalized. For a change, it is essential to start the process from the other end, with the following approach:

- Target the 'other half'.
- Mandatory provision of a component of shelter for EWS/ LIG in all Government/Private/Cooperative Housing.
- Shelter as a participatory and evolutionary process.
- Access of poor to land and tenure.
- Urban services and public transport integral to housing development.
- Development controls to encourage development of EWS/ LIG Housing
- Incentives and mandatory norms to mobilise private sector and community for Slum rehousing.
- Shelter interwined with jobs and poverty alleviation
- Mixed use zoning in place of single use zoning
- Mandatory norms for informal sector and street vendors

The Indian cities manifest three types of urbanism – planned, unplanned and regualrised. The perceptions of the planners often lead to the policies and plans which are oriented towards the organized and middle classes, while the poor are left to fend for themselves. These are largely the results of impressionistic ideas and myths of land use zoning and planning. There is a need to evolve the ideas based on a clear understanding of the purpose of planning and to quarantine the perpetual myths of planning, urbanism, zoning, densities, low-rise and mixed land use. Considering the above objectives and approach, the Master Plan for Delhi-2021 (MPD-2021) is an attempt to evolve a 'Livelihoods Strategy' in preference to 'Lifestyles':

A Pro-poor Strategy

The poor in the cities is an underclass composed of bottom 15 to 20 per cent, who are often caught in a cycle of perpetual poverty due to non-access to government programmes, land, finance, employment and services. They often have a poor image of themselves and almost no hope from the government and have no idea of the 'development'. Due to systemic disfunction of income distribution and housing markets, the poorest families find themselves excluded from the ownership of any form of assets. In this situation 'Housing for All' needs to be added with 'Guaranteed Livelihood for All'. This should comprise of a basket of minimum essential needs of the poorest ranging from survival to development of skills, health, education, shelter and employment.

The people time and again, and in spite of several barriers, have demonstrated their capacity in contributing in housing sector. It is necessary that their resources, energy and skills are channelised and captured by an enabling approach. The housing and development authorities should reverse their roles and participate in the housing development programmes of the people. This means redefining the concepts of land use and land tenure together with legal framework (e.g. development control norms, building bye-laws and regularisation of unauthorized colonies). Local governments should earmark lands for informal sector including squatting and holding zones as an integral part of planned development, together with housing areas for the cooperative societies and otherwise organized communities.

A major priority area of intervention in promoting a synchronized development of shelter and poverty reduction is to evolve a new legislative and planning framework, including innovative development controls and removing barriers in the development of low income housing linked with micro-enterprise. There is a need for the state/local bodies to formulate decentralized programmes, which allow various options (including design and layout) to the community and provide necessary technical and administrative and financial supports.

In order to establish links between shelter and poverty reduction, it is necessary to revise the concepts of planning, land use, tenure and building regulations. There is a need to adopt innovative systems of land pooling and to harness private sector resources in services, housing and development. The integrated programmes should be worked out on the following premises:

- A decentralised programme which optimizes the resources of public-private sectors and the community.

- Providing a new legal and administrative framework together with incentives to support the initiatives of the community and private sector.
- Access to finance, mobilizing small savings through cooperatives and micro-credit institutions/NGOs.
- A programme in which urban authorities concentrate on developing land, trunk and basic services, including transport, health and safety.
- A new planning framework removing barriers and controls in the development of self generating and sustainable settlements.

The availability of serviced urban land is a critical issue. There is a need to optimize the availability of urban land to the urban poor for planned growth of housing and home-based enterprise. A new framework has to be èvolved for the dilapidated old areas, so as to trigger a process of self-generating renewal. The concepts of mixed land use, redensification, and instruments of 'Accommodation Reservation' and 'Transfer of Development Rights' can be useful tools in this task.

The category of the urban poor, mainly comprise the inhabitants of squatter settlements and informal service providers. Such services include domestic help, hawkers and vendors, and low paid workers. These include both existing population and future migrants. In terms of housing requirements of the city, this continues to be the single biggest challenge and would require a mix approaches and innovative solutions. New housing in the form of one or two room units, can be developed through public and private agencies and through Cooperative societies. As this category constitutes bulk of the housing stock that has to be catered at an affordable price to the lowest income bracket as housing for Economically Weaker Sections (EWS), this is often done by cross-subsidization. It may be suggested that in every housing scheme, at least 15 per cent of the saleable net residential land should be reserved for EWS housing and pooled on a zonal basis to have its even spread in different parts of the city and not concentrate at one place. In old built up areas, this may be mandatory part of the redevelopment scheme, whereas in urban extensions, the acquisition and development cost of this land should be borne by rest of the project. Such reserved lands should be handed over to a designated agency for promoting housing for low income and weaker sections.

Private sector participation in land assembly, development and housing should emphasize the housing for urban poor through the following strategies:

(*a*) In-situ slum rehabilitation, using land as a resource;

(*b*) Housing for urban poor should be about fifty per cent of total number of dwelling units to come up in future;

(*c*) Re-categorization of housing types, development control norms and differential densities to make EWS/LIG housing viable and economical;

(*d*) Compulsory construction of at least 35% of dwelling units or 15% of permissible FAR, whichever is higher in the form of EWS & LIG units by all developers of group housing.

In view of growing demand for housing and shortage of urban land, there is need for optimal utilization of land in following ways;

(*i*) Shift from plotted housing to group housing;

(*ii*) Optimum utilization of land and enhanced density pattern.

(*iii*) Relaxation of ground coverage, FAR and height.

Redevelopment, both in planned and unplanned areas can be incentivised through various measures, such as permission to reconstitute and amalgamate plots, higher FAR etc., covering built up areas, such as:

(*a*) Planned areas along major transport corridors; underutilized/low density areas; and resettlement colonies.

(*b*) Unplanned areas: villages; unauthorized colonies and Jhuggi-Jhompri (JJ) Clusters.

Besides linking shelter and employment, the network of facilities should be integrated with housing development, which include night shelters, community hall Anganwari, adult education centre, School for mentally/physically challenged, Social Welfare Centre, Dharamshala, Reformatory and Orphanage, Old Age Home, Care Centres for physically and mentally challenged, women's hostels, etc.

Small Home Based Enterprise

Indian cities are characterized by multiple use of space and large number of households, especially poor use their home for livelihood. In Delhi too, inspite of a statutory Master Plan, small enterprises continue to flourish in the homes. A large proportion of about 2.3 lakh retail enterprises with an employment of 5.4 lakh engaged in trade, commerce and allied services operate from the residential areas. The Master Plan for Delhi – 2021 (MPD-2021) has recognized the phenomenon of Mixed Use and has adopted a multi-pronged strategy to promote home based enterprises with the following measures:

(*i*) Regularisation of non-polluting industrial clusters in residential areas and also allowing 121 types of household industries in residential premises.

(*ii*) Continuance of Commercial Use in inner city residential areas/Special Areas.

(*iii*) Small shops of maximum 20 sqm area, trading in or dealing with the 24 items, of daily needs allowed on ground floor in all residential premises, irrespective their being under Mixed Use Streets/Commercial Streets.

(*iv*) Proposed network of service markets, informal sector of trade, weekly markets etc.

(*v*) Commercial activity / retail shops, etc. permitted on notified mixed use street, local commercial streets and Pedestrian Shopping Streets.. 2183 such streets have already been notified by the MCD / GNCTD, of which 809 are Mixed Use Streets, 777 Commercial Streets and 597 Pedestrian Shopping Streets.

This will not only save the home-based enterprises from punitive action, but also provide self-employment opportunities to a large number of the poor and the middle income groups. This also makes the residential areas more lively, secure, and comfortable, provided environmental and other safeguards are adopted together with augmentation of infrastructure services and parking.

World over the concept of "smart growth" is gaining acceptability which is based on the premise of mixed land use. When homes are located within the walking distance to grocery stores or employment centres, alternative to driving such as walking becomes viable. The mixed land use also provides a more diverse and sizeable population and wider commercial base to support the public transit. The acceptability of smart growth among town planners has resulted in transformation of many cities on the concept of mixed use as a means to conserve energy and also to reduce the number of private vehicles on roads. While the separation of land uses was intended to protect the communities from polluting industries and businesses, it has led to a pattern of development in which stores, housing and schools are often placed so apart that they can only be reached by motorized transport. Improved environmental regulations and private sector innovation mean that many businesses are now cleaner than they were many decades ago when zoning was first introduced to separate place of work from houses, thereby eliminating much of the need for their strict separation from homes and commercial establishments. By liberalized Mixed Use policy, private car use can be reduced and the provision of efficient public transport becomes more viable.

Planning is an exercise in conflict resolution – between political exigencies and professionalism, between future permissiveness and post-facto regularisation. On one hand the democratic and constitutional right of the population, including the in-migrants to work and get accommodated in the cities is to be protected, on the other, its air, water, greenery and ecology are to be preserved. Caught between 'livelihood' versus 'lifestyle', between 'economic right' versus 'social left', the planning is an attempt to balance the opposites.

Social Infrastructure

A large segment of the urban population inhabitates in the sub-standard areas, such as, unauthorized colonies, urbanized villages, old dilapidated housing areas, resettlement colonies etc. The conservation and revitalization of such areas is necessary while for traditional areas environment upgradation and improvement is needed. It would be desirable to take up all existing developed residential areas one by one for environmental improvement through (*i*) plantation and landscaping, (*ii*) provision of infrastructure-physical and social and proper access, where lacking, (*iii*) possibility of infrastructure management of the last tier through the local residents. Non-government Organizations, which come forward for establishment of adult literacy centers, crèches, balwaris and likewise institutions should be encourage to supplement the social actions of the concerned government departments and the housing agencies. The capabilities of the families for increasing income need should be explored; suitable provisions for income earning opportunities be made within or near these settlements and monitored. The present method of regularization of unauthorized colonies may not be helpful in improving the low level of physical environment existing in these colonies. For improvement of physical and social infrastructure, the house owners in these unauthorised colonies should be asked to form into societies and these societies should come forward with plans for improvement and upgradation.

The villages should get the modern services and amenities and should also be catered for their traditional cultural styles. Around these settlements educational, health and recreational facilities and work areas should be developed for the benefit of the village population.

The rapid urbanization has led to scarcity of urban land and subsequent overall shortage of Public and Semi Public facilities, like religions, hospitals, dispensaries, schools, colleges, training institutions, police lines, compost plants, police stations, electric sub stations, tourist complexes, clubs, amusement parks etc. They need to be strengthened and provided both by public and private sectors.

There is a need to evolve standards and a system for provision of micro level utilities / facilities and garden/street furniture, such as public toilet/urinals, bus shelters, telephone/ PCO booths, police control room, security / guard rooms, pump rooms, dhobi ghats, machine wash centers, etc.

Social Security

The cities represent the paradigm of social organization. The human destiny is intimately tied up with their amorphous urban structure. The physical manifestation of a city may eliminate certain problem or at the same time may create new hazards and special tensions. Entailed by technological conveniences, the order and immutable regularity of a city could provide an mnemonic metaphor.

There is a greater need to integrate land use activities, different communities, vocations, professions and income groups in a composite manner. The urban structure has to be evolved keeping in view its geographical features and potential to provide a safe and manageable city. The security has to be built-in, rather than being dependent upon the police force and legal / administrative controls. In the urban context, "decentralization" and "homogeneity within heterogeneity' are the watch-words. Planning as a sociological function should address itself to the demand of safe and manageable cities. This requires evolution of various planning options based upon the premises of safety and security.

According to the Indian Seismic Zone map, several cities like Delhi are placed in Seismic Zone IV, which means high damage risk zone. In the past, several earthquakes of Richter magnitude 5.5 to 6.7 have occurred in Delhi and other cities. Such natural and man -made disaster neither can be prevented nor predicted. However, with the technological advancement to some extent mechanism can be developed to mitigate the after effects of the disaster. Areas of vulnerability can be identified and necessary measures can be proposed by the concerned agencies. The concerned local bodies should keep updating the building byelaws to safeguard against disasters and ensure effective and impartial enforcement. Micro-zonation surveys should be referred for land use planning and be considered while preparing the city plans. It is proposed to introduce the concept of Disaster Management Centres to handle the security aspects. Besides this, the existing network of police station, police post, and fire stations is to be strengthened.

It is essential to have a clear picture of the evolving shape of the city and to understand the dynamics of urban form. Every city should have a spatial framework which establishes the long-term pattern of land use, density and movement. The framework and accompanying policies can provide a key focus for cross-sectoral stakeholder debate and the enrichment of the knowledge and cultural framework.

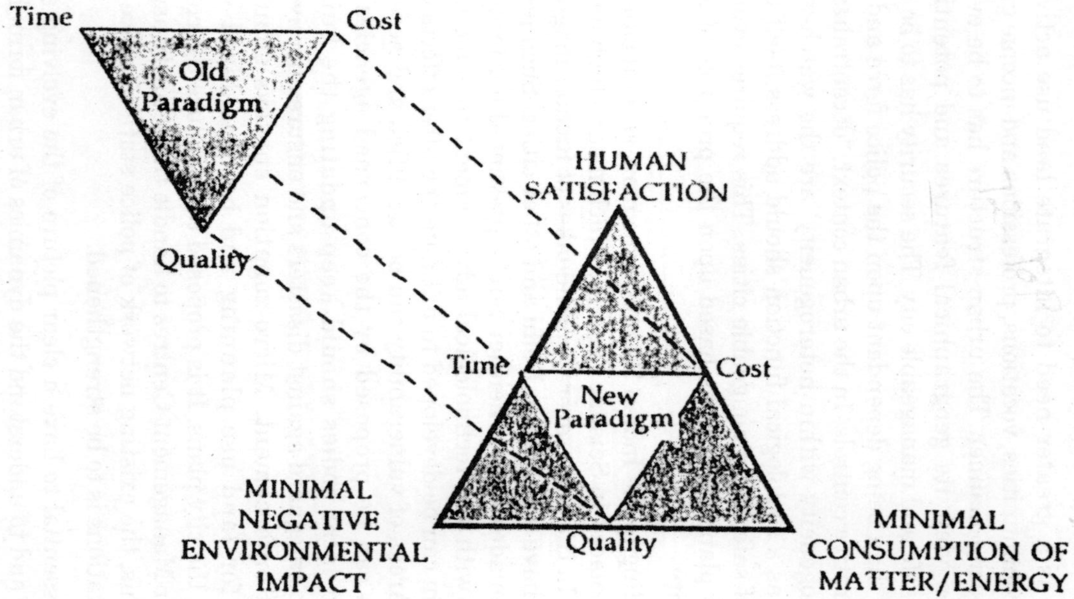

Old and New Paradigm

5

URBAN POLICY AND PLANNING REFORMS

A touch of irrationality is a saving grace for us, a stroke of luck which gives us some breathing space, a loose fit in the machine which makes us alive. Life, intelligence, goodness probably came out of this free play and this lack of restraint. Leave some ears of wheat in the field for the gleaners, he said. Perhaps we shall learn one day that the most reliable machines leave room for the unexpected.

—Michel Serres

Ongoing policy reforms in the urban sector including economic liberalisation and democratic decentralisation demand the compatibility of the contemporary planning process in India which may involve certain radical changes. Planning is the foundation of the development superstructure comprising of land, housing, infrastructure and construction. It can either act as a barrier to the policy reforms or can become a catalyst of new generation changes.

As per 2001 Census, there are 5161 cities and towns in India inhabiting a population of 285 million. Of these about 1500 master plans have been prepared, many of which are statutory. The Delhi Plan with the approval of Parliament in 1962 was the first comprehensive exercise and has been a model of modern town planning in India. Apropos of the economic and urban reforms and with new forms of governance, a debate is in the offing on the fundamental premises of planning and its necessity.

Policy Reforms

During last decades the government of India initiated radical policy reforms in the form of 74th Constitutional Amendment Act (74th CAA) and economic liberalisation. The Union Ministry of Urban Development during recent years took up the Habitat themes of "Inclusive Cities", "Cities without Slums" and "City to

City Co-operation". The Govt. of India and the United Nations Centre for Human Settlements (UNCHS) had also launched "Good Urban Governance Campaign". It is seen as an integral process of urban improvement and better sense delivery. The hypothesis is that better infrastructure service, security of tenure, political empowerment and participation in civic decisions will lead the urban poor to higher levels of economic and social life. The UNCHS campaign for Good Urban Governance gave emphasis on inclusive cities, participatory, transparent and accountable management, community empowerment, poverty reduction, capacity building and security of tenure. There is a clear paradigm shift in the approach, which envisages public-private partnership, a facilitating approach, institutional capacity building and legislative and procedural reforms.

In the context of new National Urban Housing and Habitat Policy (2007), the Corporate, Private and Cooperative Sectors are to take the lead role in terms of land assembly, construction of houses and development of amenities within the projects. Emphasis is on creation of housing stock on ownership and rental basis. Corporate sector is to be encouraged to provide for hosing for staff and to facilitate their employees in acquiring their own houses. Cooperative Sector is to be given preference in allotment of land and house sites to encourage housing development. State Governments have taken up schemes in collaboration with the private sector for slum redevelopment on cross-subsidization basis.

The policy reforms also encourage the preparation of district and metropolitan development plans, which integrate investments and their spatial implicaitons, and need a suitable plan making mechanism and techniques. This requires serious consideration so that the planning framework responds to the climate of new economic policies and democratic decentralisation. In order to enable the implementation of the new strategy, it would be necessary to restructure town planning departments, development authorities and the local bodies and to equip them to the new policy changes. The challenge is to evolve a decentralised, localised planning structure with public-private partnership approaches.

In spite of basic policy reforms, the planning generally continues to be performed in the conventional manner – top down approach, centralised, comprehensive and controlling in nature. Except few states, the planning functions are yet to devolved to the local bodies, as enshrined in the 74th CAA. The state town planning departments sitting in the headquarters, continue with the old practice of preparing the master plans of various cities and towns. These plans generally depend upon the conventional theme of "government does all". They are based on policies like large scale acquisition, mass public sector housing and infrastructure development to be provided by the government sector. They tend to control the development, rather than promoting it. The private sector often complains that planning controls prevent and inhibit enterprise. The negative answers to most of the applications and inordinate delays occurring through planning process have become a normal phenomenon. Planning process is performed by the government authorities under all kinds of bureaucratic restrictions. This results in long delays, arbitrary decisions and discretionary interpretation of the plans and regulatory framework. Government controlled planning often leads to dull uniformity squeezing out the variations which fail to respond to different income groups, perception, tastes and life styles.

The bureaucrats and planners sitting in judgement do not necessarily have the superior knowledge required. The ability to visualise future growth or to have superior knowledge or judgement is not a prerogative of a group of official planners than another group which may be lacking the official position. Development activities are usually suspended or frozen due to non-finalisation of the plans. Regulatory and organisational problems are attributed generally to the insufficiency of staff in the planning department. Due to limited, expensive and time-consuming process of development, the whole development becomes more expensive. Planning may create a false market and in huge alterations in property values by determination of locational suitability of road network, infrastructure and land use. As such, there is widespread politics of influence and it is a fact that fortunes can be made or lost due to official decisions. As a result, besides illicit payments, the pressure groups, local leaders and politicians temper the planning decisions.

A major pitfall of planning had been the adoption of the borrowed concept of single use zoning against the popular mixed use syndrome. The restrictions on land use, zoning regulations and compartmentalisation of activities hinders the opportunities of self-employment. Small enterprises, which are traditionally operated from the living places, are required to be shifted to discriminated commercial/industrial areas, which become beyond the affordability of general masses. Shifting of offices, industries and other commercial activities due to prevention by land use zoning results in great loss of jobs and discourages growth. Bulk of the working force in Indian cities constitutes the 'informal sector' or the 'unorganised sector' of employment. A consequence of strict zoning had been alarming loss of intensively lively urban urban atmosphere and variety which prevailed in the traditional cities. The proposals attempting to 'rationalise' and 'compartmentalise' land uses are contradictory to develop residence work-place relationship. Invariably the master plans taking cognisance of the census data on population growth and urban concentration recommend that the migration to the city should be curbed. This stems from thinking that rural migrants by swarming to the city ruin the city life and create housing and services problems by utilising the infrastructure without paying the taxes. This is a perverse and colonial view of urbanisation, which looks upon cities as the exclusive preserve of the rulers and the rich with the paraphernalia of the service sector.

Large scale land acquisition for urban growth had been a favourite pipe dream of the planners in India. Modelled on Delhi's strategy, predominantly the state and urban bodies take upon themselves the role of the developers, city builders and housing suppliers. The exclusion of the private, informal and unorganised sector from the development and housing process, in spite of severe restrictions, could not be sustained. At present about half of the housing stock in Delhi is comprised of informal, organic or unauthorised units and the fact remains that the government bodies, local authorities or organised sector all over have proved to be inadequate to meet the demands. The land policies, plans, byelaws, zoning regulations fail to accommodate most of the sub-standard, self-help and community housing development (hence unauthorised), comprising nearly half of the total dwelling units built every year. Often the city development plans prove to be the impediments to organic, indigenous and community approach to employment and housing largely catering to the poor section of the society.

The avowed objectives of planning often stand defeated in the face of changing hazards to the community, viz, critical shortages of basic services, particularly water and power, traffic congestion, massive encroachments, noise pollution, haphazard signboards and hoarding, and other forms of nuisance. It is a sheer wastage of manpower and resources of the local bodies largely preoccupied with checking of deviation in individual buildings upto nearest centimeters, when there is no machinery and resources available to check the major sources of nuisance and pollution causing critical threat to social health, convenience and safety.

The studies indicate that to obtain planning permission for a group housing project, it would take 4 to 8 weeks in Singapore whereas in India, it may take few years and would involve dealing with at least 20 to 30 organisations/government bodies. The effect of delays and time loss is spectacular. This not only hinders city and economic development but inverts the creation of jobs. The propensity of planning officials to reject a development plan on technicality, instead of passing it subject to appropriate changes, results in loss of time and energy. The growth of local wealth and tax base is suspended and the jobs are lost (except the job of the officials). There is a built-in bias against growth, expansion and extension and most of the official planners are afraid to take a positive view, largely because they want to avoid allegations of corruption and favourism. The 'status quo' attitude imposes inflexibility which does not respond to the changing needs of a developing and dynamic society. The provision of administrative discretion has bequeathed a system in which the planning officers can intervene with all kinds of prejudices, which are not compulsory and mandatory.

Often there is a built-in bias against growth, expansion and extension and most of the official planners are afraid to take a positive view, largely because they want to avoid allegations of corruption and favouratism. The 'status quo' attitude imposes inflexibility which does not respond to the changing needs of a developing and dynamic society. The provision of administrative discretion has bequeathed a system in which the planning officers can intervene with all kinds of prejudices, which are not compulsory and mandatory. The complex, many a times contradictory and overdetailed rules, regulations and byelaws fail to protect the endowed objectives of public health, safety and convenience, but are used as the tools for denial of the proposals and schemes, sometimes to expropriate illegal favours and thus breed corruption. The existing institutions are incapable of controlling the process of urbanization, providing basic needs for the majority of the people or halting environmental deterioration. The masses are disadvantaged by complexity of laws, impenetrate bureaucracies, onerous system of taxes, fees and licences, regulations, which are a barrier to self-help and their access to resources. Making human settlement institutions more effective and more responsive to people's needs and aspirations should be a major goal.

Changes in Planning Process

In view of above challenges, there is a need for a paradigm shift in the planning approach and process.

In order to translate new policies and paradigm into practice, the planners have to prepare themselves for a new role and much wider responsibilities. As a bridge between the civil society and the politico-economic structure, the planners have to perform the role of the catalysts of change.

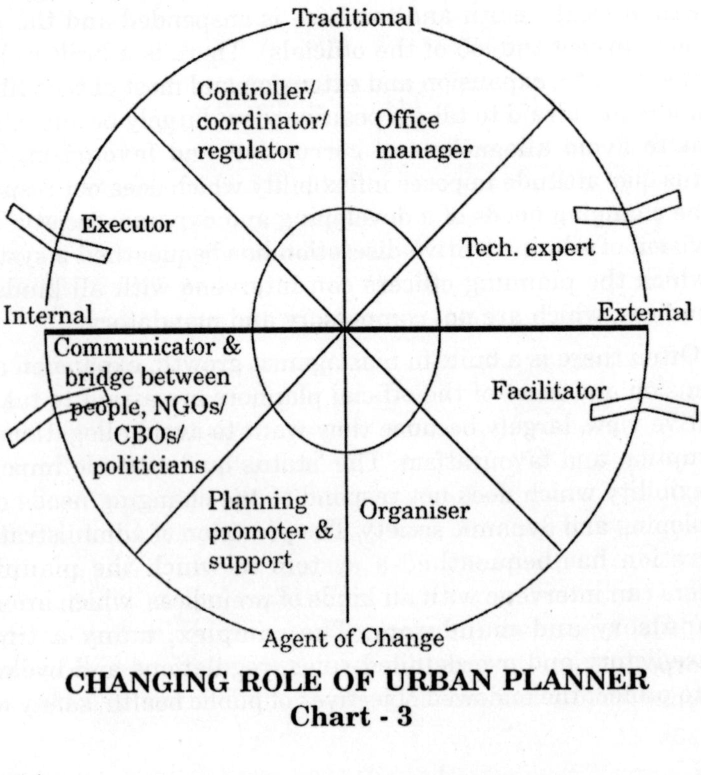

CHANGING ROLE OF URBAN PLANNER
Chart - 3

At the organisational level, the local bodies and town planning departments have to gear up for a major shift in their roles. Traditional town planning has to be replaced by strategic and Action planning and Building Bye-laws and Development Controls to be replaced by a comprehensive regulatory framework with an orientation to support and promote the planned development by the community/private initiatives.

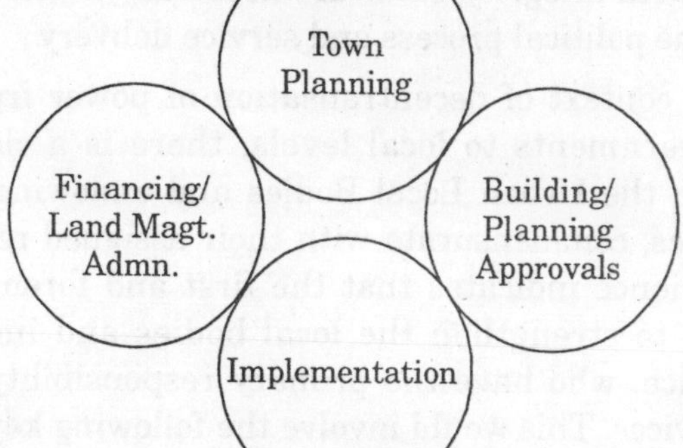

PLANNING AND URBAN DEVELOPMENT: THE TRADITIONAL ROLES

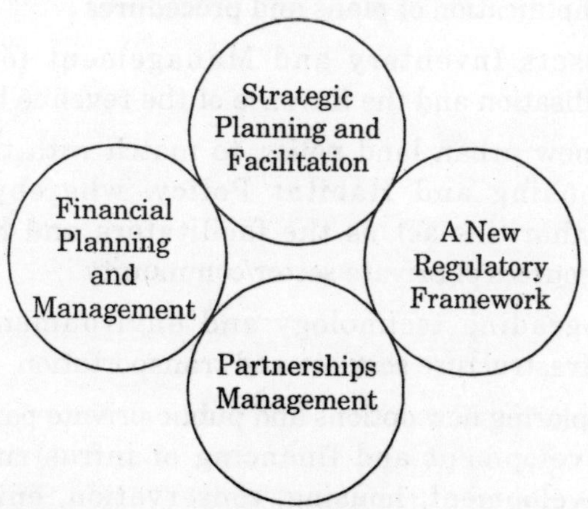

CHANGE IN ROLES FOR POLICY REFORMS

This requires a rigorous capacity building - at individual, corporate and organisational levels. They have to reaffirm their commitment towards the profession, society and city. As the agents of change there is a need to integrate a broader cross-section of professionals and develop an aptitude of flexibility.

With the ongoing globalisation, economic liberalisation and devolution of power to local bodies, gone are the days of armchair professionals. Their insulation from the general masses and the political system may be catastrophic in the changing environment, where participatory decision making is becoming institutionalised. Among the professionals, who require expertise exercised with integrity, skills are necessary to strike a balance between the political process and service delivery.

In the context of decentralisation of power from Central/ State Governments to local levels, there is a clear need to strengthen the Urban Local Bodies and endowing them with the finances, commensurate with their assigned responsibility. The experience indicates that the first and foremost priority should be to strengthen the local bodies and improve their performance, who have the primary responsibility to provide urban services. This would involve the following key initiatives:

- the introduction of short and medium-term, Integrated Action Planning, to complement comprehensive long term objectives
- simplification of plans and procedures
- Assets Inventory and Management for optimum utilisation and the increase of the revenue base
- a new urban land policy, to match with the National Housing and Habitat Policy, whereby the local authorities act as the facilitators and harness the resources of private sector/community
- upgrading technology and environment focus for Infrastructure services and transportation
- exploring new options and public-private partnership for development and financing of infrastructure, land development, housing, conservation, environmental improvement and slum/JJ rehabilitation.
- adoption of Multi-year Investment Planning to match priorities of state budgets/5 Year Plans with urban projects

- a new approach towards Development Controls, to mobilise private sector in provision of services and community facilities, and adoption of concepts like white zoning, Accommodation Reservation, Transfer of Development Rights (TDR), Excess condemnation, etc.
- networking with international and national urban prgrammes, e.g. Citynet, Healthy Cities, UMP, etc.
- mandatory performance management system and MIS
- networking with NGOs, CBOs and private sector for planning, management and maintenance.

A leveraging strategy should be adopted so as to encourage private sector to participate in infrastructure/city development for which there is an urgent need of intersectoral cooperation. It is necessary to explore the areas where the government can cooperate in partnership. With the private sector participation, encouraging cooperation, partnership and competition is a critical area of concern.

There are numerous success stories of innovative partnerships in various areas of development, as given below:

- Reforms in Municipal Administration – Andhra Pradesh,
- District Planning Committees – Kerala
- Efficiency Enhancement – Ludhiana
- Devolution of Powers – Allahabad
- Fiscal empowerment – Bangalore, Chennai, Guwahati, Indore, Jaipur, Mumbai, Ludhiana, Mysore, Patna, Vijayawada
- Accrual Based Municipal Accounting system – Tamilnadu
- Partnership in Urban Services – Nasik, Panvel, Pune, Jaisingpur, Baroda, Chennai, Tiripur, Hyderabad, Visakhapatnam, Indore, Delhi-NOIDA, etc.
- Geographic information system – Mirzapur
- Asset Management – Mirzapur
- Property tax – Mirzapur, Nagpur, Patna
- Poverty alleviation, slum rehabilitation and micro-credit–Ahmedabad, Mysore, Pune

- Municipal Bonds – Ahmedabad, Bangalore, etc.
- Innovative building bye-laws – Greater NOIDA.

A major effort should be made to reverse system of top-down planning and management. Planning should relate to local social, cultural and environmental conditions and facilitating popular participation in habitat development. It should encourage new forms of popular participation through stimulation of direct action groups, public-private joint ventures, and non-governmental organisations dedicated to community action. This requires an increased flow of information to the people and to nongovernmental organisations, and improves the feedback of information from the people to institutions. Capacity building of institutions and training of community leaders would improve and assure grass-roots participation in government support programmes. New ways will be needed to share and co-ordinate responsibilities among local, regional and state authorities and also between planning, housing, transport, energy supply, etc. Authority for decision making should be decentralized to increase community control over actions affecting them.

Planning Controls versus Promotion Supports

During recent years significant changes have taken place in land use zoning, planning norms and parameters, sub-division regulations etc. These include Master Plan of Delhi 2021, Simplified Development Promotion Regulations of Urban Affairs and Employment (1996), General Development Control Regulations for Navi Mumbai, CIDCO (1994), and also the regulations of Singapore Redevelopment Authority, Chennai Metropolitan Development Authority and Greater NOIDA. The innovative concepts of zoning such as given below should be included in the Planning and Development Controls:

- Planning Unit Development Zoning (PUD)
- Transferable Development Rights (TDR)
- Performance Zoning
- Evolutionary Zoning
- Floating Zoning
- Conditional Zoning

- Incentive Zoning
- Accommodation Reservation
- White Zoning
- Excess Condemnation
- Squatter holding zoning

Also various kinds of planning permissions charges/taxes required to be paid thereof may form part the subordinate legislation. These may include –vacant land tax, Development Charges, impact fees, betterment levy, conversion charges, Purchasable Development Rights, misuse charges, parking levy/ charges, additional FAR charges, etc.

In the context of changing scenario and increasing role of private sector there is a need to evolve a new set of regulatory framework, which are simple, transparent, responsive, flexible and clear.

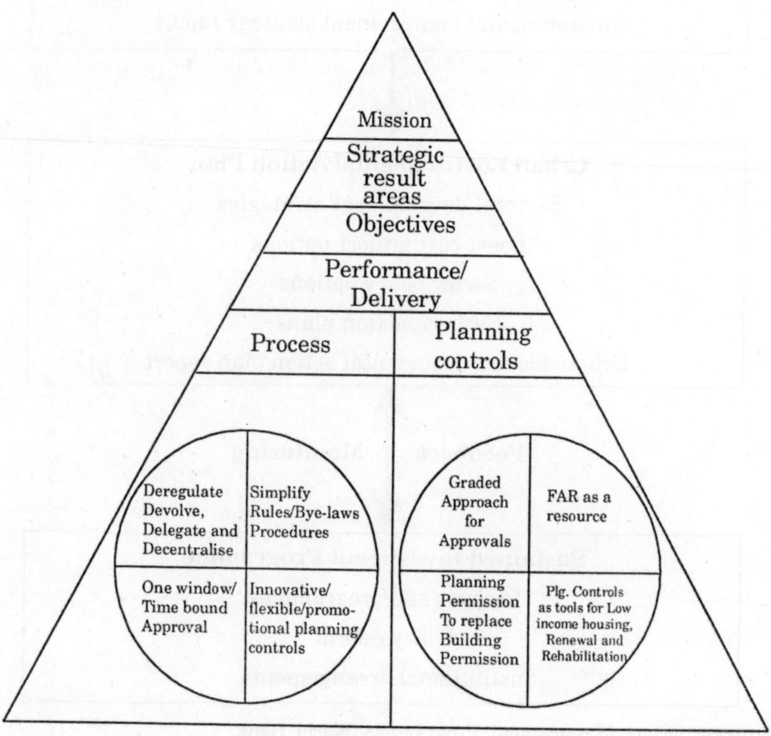

The Urban Environment Planning Process

Rapid Urban Environmental Assessment and Consultation

Decision to begin process

Basic environmental indicators

Urban environmental profile

Public consultation and forum

political commitment

↓

Urban Environmental Management Strategy

Long-term environmental goals

Phased strategy to reach goals

'Priority geographic areas

Needed policy reform and institutional actions

Environmental management strategy report

↓

Urban Environmental Action Plan

Sectoral development strategies

Least-cost project options

Sector policy options

Sectoral action plans

Urban-wide environmental action plan report

Feedback ↕ **Monitoring**

Sustained Investment Programme

Projects and programmes

Policy reform

Institutional arrangements.

Source: Urban Management Programme, World Bank

Keeping in view the availability of large number of qualified professionals in the private sector, prevalent corruption and harassment, it is time to review the need of Building Bye-laws which can be replaced by zoning/planning controls so that the infrastructure services, environment, aesthetics, parking and other public concerns like safety and health are safeguarded rather than internal features of buildings. This will facilitate development which is environmentally appropriate and would meet the social needs of the public at large. In order to avoid sustained litigation between the developers and local bodies, these should have a strong legal backing.

In place of emphasis on individual buildings, the focus should be on environment, infrastructure services, and area based schemes. The zoning and urban controls have to address to emerging issues of environment, services, urban design, renewal and conservation. These should ensure welfare of the handicapped/disabled and weaker sections of the society. As a basic principle, the regulation of building activity should make it redundant for an official to enter a private building. This means that the controls and bye-laws should do away with the regulations for internal features, like room size, ventilation, sanitary fittings, etc. Building bye-laws should be extremely simple and limited to the external elements of buildings, such as bulk, envelope, height, set-backs, parking etc. Registered Architects may be given powers to sanction the building plans, subject to conformity with the zoning/development controls. This would reduce the burden of the local bodies and eliminate corruption to a great extent.

This would comprise of no approval stage, prototype sanction, sanction by registered architects, instant sanction, Block Sanction, Planning Permission and Urban Design Approval. For example, no sanction may be required for plots upto 50 sqm. and for plots upto 500 sqm. sanction by registered architects should be sufficient. For multistoreyed buildings, group housing, layouts, redevelopment schemes, etc., sanction of local authority in respect of Zoning Regulations, planning permission, urban design approval and approval of Fire Department should be necessary. The requirement of obtaining various permission and building sanction may be reduced to grant of planning permission which may be necessary for any scheme above 4 ha., where the role of qualified town planner and Landscape Architect becomes mandatory.

Floor Area Ratio (FAR)

The FAR is the most crucial aspect of Planning Regulations and has a direct bearing with the property value. There are large variations in FAR in the country, which are usually arbitrary and fail to capture the value addition due FAR for city development and municipal services. In the urban context, planning regulations can use FAR as a major resource for the local bodies, who have a responsibility to provide infrastructure services and confer development rights. It would be pertinent to provide a basic FAR of 100 (FSI of 1.0) in the regulations together with an upper ceiling for which the planning/local body may be empowered to charge Purchasable Development Right Levy for FAR in excess of a basic FAR (say 1.0). Thus, Planning Regulations can act as a gold mine for the local bodies, who are always short of the funds for development of infrastructure. This will also help in the localisation of the planning and regulatory functions conferred under the 74th Constitutional Amendment Act, 1992.

Low Income Housing

The present development control framework is not conducive to promote low-income housing through cooperative/private sector. The difficulty arises in balancing FAR and density and there is generally gross under-utilisation of FAR for EWS/LIG housing. As such, it is recommended to regulate development controls only through FAR so that use of limited urban land can be maximized. It is also proposed to review the standards like minimum width of roads, parks, standards of community facilities and open space etc. which are realistic and affordable. In this regard, IS-8888 should be reviewed and incorporated in the Local Codes/Planning Regulations.

Most of the co-operative societies cater to middle and high income groups, and there is hardly any provision for community services, personnel and informal sector working as domestic servants of the residents. It is proposed that a bonus FAR of 10 to 15 per cent may be allowed which will be utilized for construction of tenements upto maximum 25 to 40 sqm. plinth area. These tenements should revert to development authority or the local body for community services personnel/EWS. This will generate a large housing stock without any investment of the local/government bodies.

Rehabilitation of Squatters/Slum Dwellers

By using FAR as a resource and by promoting formation of cooperative societies of slum and squatter clusters, the private sector and slum residents can be activated in resettlement and self-help upgradation programmes. For this, an incentive FAR (upto 50 percent) may be allowed and 10 percent of FAR may be permitted for commercial activity, by sale of which in the market, the whole scheme can become self-financing. Also, relaxation in set-backs and density should be available for such schemes. In this way, planning regulations can act as a tool of providing access to housing and services to economically weaker sections and slum dwellers.

Renewal and Reconstruction

The inner city areas, urban villages, and regularized unauthorised colonies need renewal, upgradation and reconstruction. The concept of incentive zoning will promote redevelopment of such areas if they are offered incentives of FAR, ground coverage and mixed land use and will discourage unauthorized construction. The regulations should be framed keeping in view the requirements of circulation, parking, services and community facilities. For freehold properties upto 2000 sq.m. there may be no need to surrender land for community facilities and road widening and for larger areas benefit of FAR should be available for land required for facilities and road widening.

After 30-40 years, most of the public housing usually becomes ripe for renewal. To facilitate urban renewal of housing complexes more than 20 years old, the submission of original building plans may not be insisted upon and power of attorney transfers may be acceptable. Such system will facilitate better use of dilapidated derelict old buildings and housing, which have become redundant with fast changing life-style and economic prosperity. The concept of **white zoning** adopted in Singapore has proved to be effective tool of urban turnaround of dilapidated, old areas. Under this, the developers/owners join together and work out a viable renewal or redevelopment scheme. This is examined by Singapore Redevelopment Authority and sanction is given for mixed use or proposed activities as may be justified from services, transport and economic viability points of view. The Redevelopment Authority provides budgetary and infrastructure support to the developer, who transforms the area into something beautiful and functional. The narrow streets have been widened, where the owners do not loose FAR due to its widening, and modern infrastructure services could be extended in erstwhile sub-standard areas.

Legal and Regulatory Framework

The maze of archaic legislation, which governs habitat sector and municipal resources, hardly inspires the people and the investor confidence. Rather than encouraging fiscal discipline and prudent management of debt, it places severe limits on municipal resource raising, a thorough revision of the regulatory framework is thus a need of the hour. An important issue that needs to be considered is the setting up of a regulatory authority for decisions related to fixing tariffs, quality of service etc. This was felt needed in the U.K. after privatisation of power, water and urban services so that other monopolistic trends of private sector operators and fall in quality of service does not take place. The Australian initiative of the utilities commission to take care of such issues of public interest in the delivery of urban services such as power, telecommunication, roads, etc. is worth mentioning. In India this could be done through State Level Regulatory Bodies or at the level of important cities, which are financially strong and could decide upon the nature of tariff and other service related matters.

Another important legislative instrument is the regulation of Public Private Partnership in city infrastructure provision through BOO, BOOT, etc. financing and managing mechanism on the lines of the federal law brought out by the Philippine government. The sustainability of infrastructure project depends on the success of policy planners in implementing a strong techno-Financial and techno-Legal regime based on viably rates of return for private sector participation. The techno-financial and techno-legal regime should support each other so that a conducive and sustainable environment is maintained for constant investments in the sector.

An Agenda for Planning Reforms

In the above context and to compliment with the ongoing policies of economic reforms and democratic decentralisation, there is a need to embark upon several basic changes in the planning approach. The focus is to remove the barriers created by planning, with service delivery on ground with speed and efficiency. The key areas where such changes are necessary are given below:

Decentralised Governance

(73rd and 74th CAA)

- From Statutory/comprehensive planning to Integrated Action Planning, with focus on implementation and flexibility
- Localisation and Decentralisation of Planning
- Community Partnership and constituency planning interfacing administrative and political constituencies.
- Corporatisation of planning organisations.
- Strategic Planning with a view to mobilise private sector.
- Integrating physical planning with Institutional, Financial and Infrastructure Plans.
- Government as Facilitator and Catalyst in planning for self-rule, self-build and self-reliance.
- Political apparatus for people centred planning.

Market Economies and Privatisation

- Efficiency, equity and employment/economic potentials as the criteria of planning.

- Emphasis on quality and innovative demand driven planning.
- Incentives for infrastructure and housing investments.
- Release access to land, housing, services, finance and information by public-private partnership.
- Focus at the grass roots and a pro-poor perspective.
- Planning to promote micro-enterprise and micro-banking.
- Mixed landuse as a tool of planning for poverty reduction strategy.
- New methods of land assembly and development.
- Regularise land tenure
- Simplify and expedite land registgration
- Review and simplify property taxation
- Emphasise cost recovery and 'user pays'
- Develop enabling strategies.
- Upgradation of infrastructure in slums and lower income population areas.
- Identify and incentivise private and community sector institutions.
- Target subsidies to the poor.
- Empowering the community.
- Encourage self-build housing and small businesses.
- Eliminate monopoly practices including government monopoly.
- Make urban development self-financing and self-sustaining by developing the concepts of Excess Condemnation, TDR, Accommodation Reservation, land pooling and readjustment, development and conversion charges, betterment levy, additional FAR charges, BOT, franchising, contracting out, etc.

Environmental Concerns

- Developing local environment Standards.
- Environment Impact Analysis
- Circular Metabolism for infrastructure systems
- Blue network planning.
- Waste Management and Recycling
- Services upgradation
- Cyclic Renewal
- Urban form and housing appropriate for environment and ecological compatibility.
- Energy saving, adoption of non-conventional sources of energy.
- Rainwater harvesting
- Industrial zoning, typology and locational decision.
- Public transport policy, plans and technology as major ingredients of environmental protection.
- Health concerns of planning, housing, services and slum/ inner city renewal.
- Micro-climate, pollution, dust and noise minimisation.
- Conservation of heritage.

Planning Promotion Supports in place of Controls

- Reduce the number of approvals required for private sector participation.
- Time limit for approvals
- Devolve and delegate powers to approve.
- One window system
- Replace lowest tendering system by alternative/Project Management Contract Systems

- Replace building approval under Building bye-laws by Planning Permissions.
- Resort to Free Development Zoning and White Zoning in City Plans.
- Invoke concepts of Transferable Development Rights (TDR) and Accommodation Reservation (AR).

Information Technology:

- Develop GIS and computer aided design for planning.
- Human Resource Management and Capacity Building.
- Assets Management.
- Need for Systems Approach.
- Computerise land/property records and digitise plans, layouts.
- Community/CBO/NGO Networking.
- Online planning and property information.
- Flexible zoning and dynamic networking
- Computerised system of approvals/planning permission.
- Intelligent services, buildings and transport.
- Development of I.T. infrastructure and Parks.
- Environment monitoring
- MIS

Legal and Management Reforms:

- Review all planning/building legislations and scrap outdated ones.
- Remove unnecessary controls
- Simplify procedures.
- Reduce regulatory complexity and dergulate wherever possible.
- Establish Regulatory Authority for urban development and privatisation.

- Minimize legal complexity, maximize enforcement and empower the community.
- Effective horizontalisation among actors, resources and people.

The policy and planning reforms will go a long way in the urban transformation and planning in concert with new economic policies and democratic decentralisation. It is imperative that the planners and urban managers reconsider their approaches, ways and procedures and their impact on the economy, infrastructure and housing. The planners will have to redefine their roles so that they provide necessary supports to the growing importance of market philosophy, while safeguarding the social interests of the poor sections of the society.

Dimensions of Environment Quality

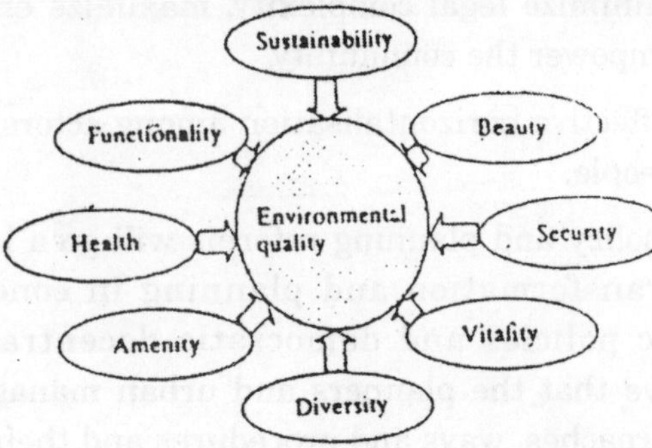

Environmental Planning and Management (EPM) Process

Source UNEP

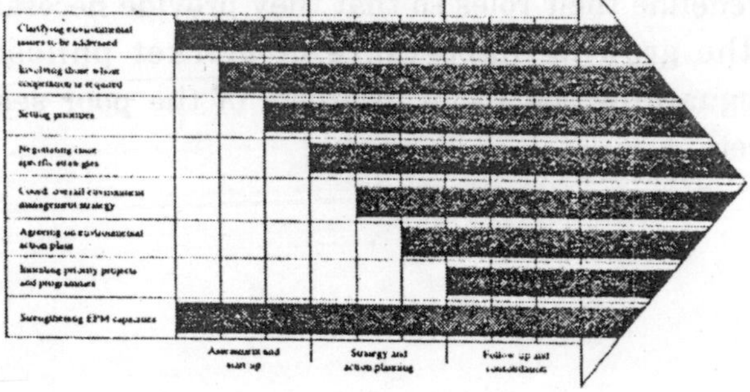

Source: Adapted from Jochen Eigen, 1992

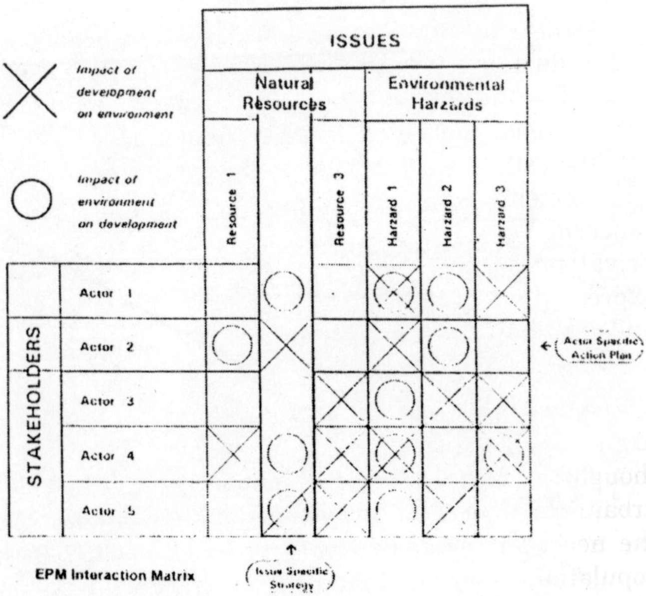

EPM Interaction Matrix

6

NEW PARTNERSHIPS FOR INDIAN CITIES

The great challenge of the 21st century is to strengthen the forces of integration and weaken the forces of disintegration and destruction.

—Former President Bill Clinton

The Indian cities are the nodes of economic growth, mobilisation and consumption. However, the sustainability of the Indian cities is hampered by several factors, such as, inadequacy of the capital stock (land, water supply, mass transport and housing), poverty and environment degeneration. The cities in India face the problems of overcrowding, sanitation and pollution and acute shortages of water, power, housing, transport, open space and public facilities.

According to the Planning Commission, Government of India, during 1993-94 about 36 percent of India's population was below the poverty line, (37 percent rural and 32 percent in urban areas). During 1999-2000 the methodology was changed and the estimates of urban poverty ratio came between 21.6 to 23.6 percent. However, urban poverty continues to be a major concern. With the recent policies of economic liberalisation, privatisation and globalisation, the apprehensions are often expressed with regard to the survival and welfare of the poor and need for adopting pro-poor development strategies for their economic emancipation.

In the past, the solution to urban ills was often seen to lie in preventing further urban expansion. Now, the answer is thought to be greater investment in cities. The problem is not urbanisation itself but more the inability of some cities to afford the necessary infrastructure to keep pace with the rate of population change and increase in construction as income rise.

Many now argue that with adequate public and private investment and improved urban management, most cities should be able to improve their local environment and reduce their contribution to global environment degradation.

In order to translate new policies and paradigm into practice, a framework of the objectives is to be prepared. It should clearly spell out economic, environmental, financial, social, constitutional and political objectives. With the ongoing globalisation, economic liberalisation and devolution of power to local bodies, gone are the days of armchair professionals. Their insulation from the general masses and the political system may be catastrophic in the changing environment, where participatory decision making is becoming institutionalised. Among the professionals, who require expertise exercised with integrity, skills are necessary to strike a balance between the political process and service delivery. With the private sector encouraging cooperation and competition in the critical areas of concern such as given below:

- Land assembly and development.
- Transport services, clean technology and laws for environmental safeguards.
- Water, sanitation, drainage and waste management.
- Housing alongwith community utilities services, open space and facilities.
- Slum upgradation, rehabilitation and their city renewal.

New Partnerships

Public Private Partnership in land, housing and infrastructure development has been in practice in certain States in India with a varying degree of success. Some of the examples are *Haryana joint development mode* based on the Haryana Development and Regulation of Urban Areas Act. Other interesting example is that of the *Lucknow Development Authority* model. In Chennai Metropolitan Develoment Authority in a guided urban development model under the *Tamil Nadu Urban Development Project* forms a joint venture with private land-owner and developers. Guided Urban Development was formulated with a view to ensure fare return on investment to the private land owner/developers and availability of relatively large proportion of service site for allotment of lower income families at affordable prices.

The Bengal Ambuja Projects of Udayan has shown the way for new partnership in housing development. The success of partnership between *West Bengal Housing Board and the Gujarat Ambuja Cement Group* has lead to the setting up of other Joint Ventures by the Bengal Government i.e. Bengal Pearless Housing Development Company, Bengal DCL Housing Development Company, Bengal IFB Housing Development Company and Bengal Shrachit Housing Development Company.

Private Sector in Slum Rehabilitation is a viable option in the redevelopment of the slum/squatter settlement area. Part area retained for the rehabilitation of the slum dwellers, while the remaining part of the land is developed for concomitant commercial or middle income/high income group housing with the primary objective of subsidising the rehabilitation of the existing slums. Such an approach is being tried out in Mumbai. The private builders/developers are also encouraged to undertake such developments in which the interests of the slum dwellers are not undermined in any way. The initiative of the Government of Maharashtra through the Shivshahi Punarvasan Prakalp (SPP) with participation of MHADA and MMRDA with additional funding coming from HFIs is another institutional mechanism to address the shelter requirements of the economically weaker sections and low income populations to a substantial extent.

NGO/CBO Initiatives in Housing: The Non-governmental and community sectors are forms of the private sector which are however not profit making and derive their existence from the voluntary service to deprived communities. This sector has at most times provided many innovative housing solutions where other formal sector agencies have failed.

An innovative scheme for down marketing housing credit for the urban poor as cash loan to the individual beneficiary for construction of houses with beneficiary family participation has been initiated as a special programme by the Government of Kerala during the 50th anniversary of India's Independence. This novel scheme is a self help programme by the beneficiary households organised as *Community Development Societies (CDS)* in all the 58 municipalities and corporations of Kerala with a special arrangement for savings of the order of 15% of house cost in HUDCO's Public Deposit Scheme, which has a growth in addition to acting as a cash security.

Other than this, self-help initiatives of SEWA, Ahmedabad, for shelter upgradation of poor self-employed women living in slums, with a clientale of 3600 poor women in urban slums is an important effort. Also SPARC, Mumbai alongwith Mahila Milan have floated two schemes at Hyderabad and Pune, benefiting 115 households, women have been engaged in the manufacture of building components and supervision of construction.

The process of partnerships integrates various stages of strategic planning, partnership development, capacity building and implementation. Accordingly, an action agenda can be developed to promote PPP arrangements for institutional, legal and financial aspects at the Central, State and local government levels.

THE PROCESS OF PARTNERSHIPS

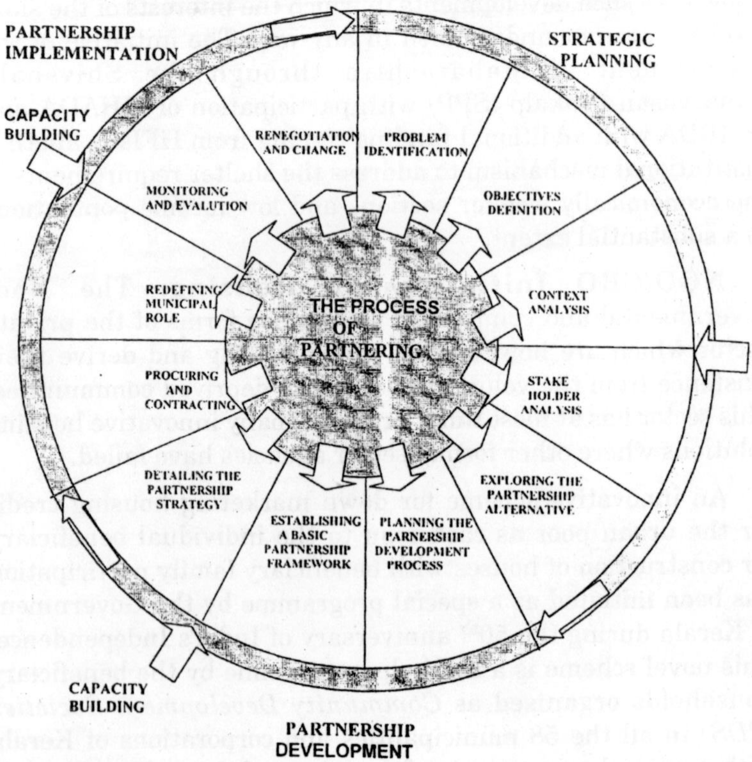

Source: DFID

Inter-Governmental Action Agenda for Promotion of PPP Arrangements

Action areas	*Central*	*State*	*Local*
Institutional	Establishment of PPP Promotion Agency Development of Privatisation Policy Evaluation and Impact Assessment Studies	State Level PPP Promotion Agency Follow up of Privatisation Policy Evaluation and Impact Assessment Studies, Inter-municipal Co-operation	Capacity Building to identify services movable for PPP and modes and modalities to operationalise PPP through traning and initial use of consultants Local level evaluation and Impact assessment
Legal	Preparation of guidelines and model Acts to facilitate PPP at various levels of services	Modification of Acts, by laws and codes as per requirements	Modification of bye-laws and codes to encourage PPP Formulation of regulations to ensure efficiency and equity by PPP
Financial	Promotion of institutioanl Finance Bilateral/ Multilateral Aid Development of appropriate instruments Provision of Tax incentives Extension of institutional finance to PPP on the same terms as per public agencies	Promotion of Sate level Financing Institutions Rationalisation of State Municipal Fiscal Transfers Development of a Service specific mechanism to provide subsidies	Determination of appropriate cost recovery and pricing policies Application of equity and affordability considerations.

Source: Adapted from Meera Mehta and other sources.

Financing and Resource Mobilisation

Urban infrastructure development is usually funded through budgetary support from central/State Governments and Local bodies through its 5-Year Plans and Annual Plans. The resources have been supplemented with funds from LIC, World Bank, other multi-national and bi-lateral programmes (ADB, OECF, KFW, ODA, DFID, DANIDA, CIDA, SIDA, EU, USAID, etc.) routed through Central/State Governments to supplement the plan allocations partly as grants and partly as loans according to a pre-determined formula.

As these funds were passed on to the States and ultimately to the local projects as part of the budgetary system, the concept of commercialisation could not be introduced in infrastructure sector. Not only the funds were made available partly as grants and partly as softer loans, the recovery of costs from the beneficiaries could not be effectively introduced. However, with resource constraints, the availability of funds for these sectors could not keep pace with the growing demand. On the other hand, the investment made every year generated the recurring demand for operation and maintenance in the subsequent years. Gradually, needs for operation and maintenance took priority and availability of funds for expansion and new projects diminished further.

Most infrastructure services are technologically complex, requiring large capital investments, large quantities of energy and requiring constant maintenance. To the extent that the pricing of such services remains constant or relatively inelastic, or worse still, the services are not priced at all, the costs of services are an increasing burden on relatively static municipal resources and state budgets. This has let to a steady deterioration in the maintenance of city level infrastructure services, throughout India.

It is increasingly clear, that cities and citizens get infrastructure that they deserve and desire. There is a price that people have to pay for the improvement in quality and levels of efficiency of the city services. If the citizens are not ready to pay a realistic price for those services the cities and citizens pay a larger price later, not only leading to adverse physical environment and quality of life but also leading to gross inefficiencies and economic decay.

The operations of housing finance institution have been on an upward spiral and in the past few years presumably on account of the facilitatory environment created by the consecutive budgets. The establishment of the Mortgage Credit Guarantee Scheme under the aegis of NHB would help the Housing Finance Institutions in widening their coverage while offering protection from major defaults.

In view of the fact that high stamp duties and archaic rent laws have been a hindrance to the sustainable development in housing and real estate. The proposal for an Urban Reforms Incentive Fund with Rs. 500 crore contribution would cover issues relating to revision of Rent Control Acts, Urban Land Ceiling and Regulation Act, rationalization of stamp duties and evolving appropriate building byelaws. It would help in adoption of appropriate user pay instruments in enhancing sustainability of projects and urban local bodies besides promoting Public Private Partnerships in civic infrastructure.

The strengthening of urban local bodies is important as they form the managerial hubs of the cities contributing to the development of housing and infrastructure. In this context a proposal for a City Challenge Fund for enhancing the credit worthiness of the urban local bodies has been mooted. In addition, the proposal for a Pooled Finance Mechanism and the enhancement of the limit of municipal tax-free bonds from Rs. 200 crores to Rs. 500 crores would facilitate additional resource mobilisation by the Urban Local Bodies. The proposed Infrastructure Equity Fund of Rs. 1000 crores, with contributions from insurance companies, financial institutions and banks would also provide support to innovative infrastructure projects.

In order to ensure safe and sustainable housing, healthy and efficient development of the real estate sector is an imperative. The boom in the real estate market in the early nineties had led to mushrooming fly-by-night developers, driven by the motives of profit-maximisation, with little commitment to the profession. The large-scale destruction to housing in urban areas and the damage to engineered buildings during the Gujarat earthquake have evinced the need for greater accountability with focus on design and quality control in construction.

Capacity Building

Capacity building, aims at the development of human resources, the establishment of well functioning organisations within a suitable work environment and a supportive socio-political environment, for improving the performance of institutions and personnel. However, considering that the scarcity of adequately qualified and trained personnel is one of the biggest obstacles to improving the performance of urban bodies in India, it is training as an integral part of capacity building, that is essential to enhance the performance of institutions and of people.

If figures are anything to go by, then the scale of training required in India is indeed large and extensive. According to 1993 estimates, the total urban sector training need is somewhere between 3,25,424 and 3,28,944. These figures, however, are only indicative of the magnitude of training required in the urban sector in India; actual numbers could be much more.

In the context of decentralisation and improved policies for urban development, training as a subset of capacity building has been successful in addressing the needs of organisational development of municipal bodies and the need for technically competent staff with a professional body of local government financial managers. But even though efforts towards training for better urban management have been undertaken at the national as well as the regional level in India, training opportunities in general, for municipal employees have been few. Even where they have been undertaken, training programmes for urban management have failed to have the desired effects. In this light, it is necessary to realise that while there is a definite and obvious need to increase the number of trained personnel to take up the responsibilities of urban management, it is just as important that training programmes and curricula becomes realistic and need (demand) oriented rather than subject (supply) oriented.

The developing and nurturing of partnerships has been identified as the new tool for the achieving progress without hampering resources for future generations. Education and capacity building has to play an important input in this agenda if it has to be successfully implemented. At this moment there is a woeful lack of manpower and management resources as no one could be termed as an "urban manager" who could comprehensively foresee and manage the overall development of the urban area. The planners of today are specialists in particular fields like transportation planners, architect planners, engineer planners, social planners, etc. There is a need for professional managers who could comprehend the problems conceptualize options and conceive solutions to urban development through a comprehensive vision of the present and the future. Capacity Building efforts along with policies have to be developed to allow for greater awareness and attitude towards formation of Public Private Peoples Partnerships (PPPP). Future education/capacity building efforts have to be aimed at the development of the pre-requisites for sustainability reflected in the four interrelated principles of transparency, efficiency, mutual understanding and partnership. This education has to be directed towards the building up of a responsible civic society that can direct future development efforts. In fact, if the future society has to be sustainable, all have to be educated to work in synergy with each other. This means a change in role of the urban professional – from controller to catalyst of charge, from office manager to organizer and from technical expert to facilitator. The actioning of capacity building plan involves redefining the policies, goals, roles and procedures with the participation of the civic society. The stages from cooperation to coordination to integration are to be developed synthesising financing/economic, spatial, technical and institutional aspects.

Le Corbusier classified the human environment in seven categories: The right angle, the hand, the character, the fusion, the human body, the spirit and the environment. The composition progresses hierarchically (from bottom to top), from the intuitive nature of man to the comprehensive and global mode of human world

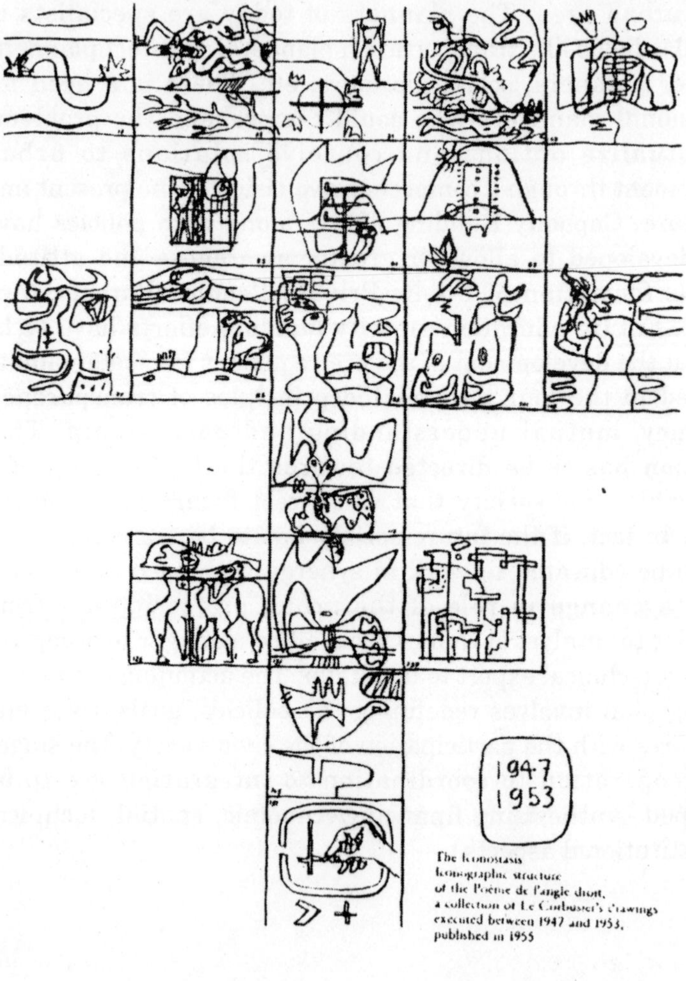

The Iconostasis
Iconographic structure
of the Poème de l'angle droit,
a collection of Le Corbusier's drawings
executed between 1947 and 1953,
published in 1955

7

LAND POLICY AND MANAGEMENT

But for the boundary, the mind is still trapped within a frame. The mind exerts its highest creativity —Akira Yamamoto

Land management involves a wide range of direct and indirect actions to affect the use of land. Direct actions include land use planning, regulatory measures such as zoning and fiscal policies, and land development projects such as land readjustment; indirect measures include provision of land related information, more efficient transaction in land, improved credit for land and housing purchase and improved institutional coordination.

There are different cultural/ideological approaches to land ownership. In China, land is viewed as a public resource, with use rights subject to Government approval. Thailand and Philippines, land is subject to private ownership and transactions. The approach in Indonesia is an intermediate stage between two extremes. These approaches have significant impacts on the government's land policies, which are integral to urban system and its cross-sectoral linkages. How efficiently the land market works can be seen from the perspective of the city administration, real estate developers, business and households, in particular the urban poor. From the viewpoint of the city government, a good example is the system under implementation in the Tokyo region, i.e. using preferred and deferred areas to implement a coordinated land development strategy. From the viewpoint of real estate developers, one of the best examples is that of Bangkok, where there are minimal planning and building regulations. From the urban poor viewpoint, good examples are land sharing and its variations, and cross-subsidy system in Manila where lower interests are charged for smaller loans.

The efficient operation of the land market requires good information on land availability, price affordability, together with the government interventions, for example, credit policies and regulatory systems.

Planning and regulatory systems have important roles in land management by guiding and controlling the spatial impacts or externalities of the multitude of short term decisions by the private sector. These are linked to issues of governance, sectoral investments, fiscal policies and other aspect of urban management. There are several examples of efficient integrated planning and regulatory systems. In Seoul, fiscal policies are being used to encourage the faster use of vacant land and to discourage speculation. In Jakarta, Manila and Dhaka, more effective strategic planning / structural planning technical approaches are being used rather than static, costly and unrealistic master plans. In Manila, more effective forms of public participation in the development process are being introduced.

There is a need to re-examine planning parameters especially in the light of new concerns for environmental sustainability. Housing and infrastructure standards should be reassessed in terms of affordability and techniques for incremental upgrading of standards. New techniques such as environmental impact assessment and fiscal regulations may be more effective than traditional zoning procedures. Community participation is important in creating a sense of "ownership" of land development plans and policies among the community affected. There is need to establish mechanisms for more effective methods of involving the community in the planning and development process.

The urban poor have typically no access to affordable land and / or housing in the right location, i.e. in areas with easy access to employment. Poor households, are often faced with the choice of either staying in illegal and usually unsafe settlements without basic services and security of tenure, or to live on the city fringes with long and expensive journeys to work.

There are a variety of techniques to improve the urban poor's access land involving direct subsidies through public housing, sites and services projects, housing credit schemes and slum upgrading programs. A number of innovative on-site policies have been tried such as land sharing in Bangkok and its variations in Mumbai, Kuala Lumpur. A good example is Myanmar's hut-to-apartment scheme, where government sells land to private developers provided that they give a percentage of the houses constructed to its low income households on the site. The Community Mortgage Programs in Bangkok and Manila are helping the urban poor.

Indirect mechanisms such as provision of credit for low-income housing are important to complement direct mechanisms such as slum upgrading. Planning standards for land development and house construction for the poor should allow and encourage incremental construction. To minimize displacement of the poor in land development projects, in situ slum redevelopment, regularisation and tenure rights should be adopted.

To encourage the production of housing, especially for the urban poor, there is need to prescribe mandatory norms for EWS/LIG housing in all general housing schemes. There is also a need to provide financial and other incentives for rental housing, especially those which are specifically targeted for the poor.

Currently, land management is often divided among many agencies at the local, regional and international levels with inadequate vertical and horizontal coordination. Frequent problems include:

- The need to examine the relevance of land development agencies. In many countries the original function of such agencies, i.e. to govern the use of public land and / or built-up land banks, is absolute. Most public land is already used and the higher price of land makes it very difficult to devote resources to purchase significant areas of land.

- Often the development authorities are both developers and regulators, where the conflicts of interests may arise, alongwith inadequate links with the local government.

- At the city level, there are inadequate mechanisms for linking spatial planning to financial, economic and sectoral planning. In addition, there are inadequate mechanisms for cross-boundary coordination in the context of the metropolitan region.

Coordinated spatial / financial / institutional planning was the objective of the Capital Investment Folio (CIF) developed for the Metro Manila Commission in the early 1980s. The CIF approach remains very relevant for megacities and can help in coordinating the phasing of spatial plans with infrastructure investment strategies and allocating responsibilities for action. A similar process was developed for the Jabotabek Metropolitan Development Plan. The Kuala Lumpur Structure Plan is an example of effective delineation of functions for urban development at various national, metropolitan and local levels, including coordination of planning and financing systems.

- The respective roles of the different levels of government involved in planning, financing, provision of services and other urban activities should be clearly defined. This presupposes that appropriate roles at each level have been defined.

- It is critical for there to be effective mechanisms for the coordination of physical and financial strategies. In addition, given the importance of megacities to national economies, coordination mechanisms should be developed between megacity management and national economic and financial planning organisations.

- New methods for the involvement of private formal and community organisations in the process of land management should be developed, since the private sector as a whole will remain responsible for the vast majority of megacity urban development.

Typically bulk of shelter is provided by the private sector and the majority of this by individual. There is an urgent need for governments to focus more on 'enabling' policies to support households in their search for land and shelter. Examples of such assistance include reducing the cost of land transfers, providing some forms of legal tenure to informal sector households and other policies already discussed, such as deregulation.

Several cities have taken the initiatives to streamline land transaction procedures and integrate information management, including Bangladesh, Philippines and Australia. Improvements are being made in the areas of cadastral mapping, land registration and titling, institutional streamlining, reductions in the number of approvals for land development, etc. which can benefit individuals and corporate land developers.

Land Information System

Megacity organisations in both public and private sectors need to have good information on land in their region, including ownership, price, conditions on use, affordability in relation to shelter, land value increases in relation to overall inflation rates etc. In general, megacities in the region have poor land information systems with consequent financial and other costs to both the public and urban managers. Among other problems, land data may not be available for public access, the information base may not cover the metropolitan region and there may be unwillingness to share information on the part of government officials. Improved land information systems can also help governments to introduce urban indicators designed to measure the impacts of land development policies and programs over times.

Singapore has a comprehensive land information system which meets the needs of all government departments with particular interests in land as well as providing a 'one stop shop' for the public. Malaysia has developed a computer-assisted mapping system originally intended for managing land registration information, which has become a multi-purpose GIS.

- A good land information system base is essential to land management in obtaining a range of benefits including clear property title, efficient and transparent land transactions, better evaluation of government land policies and more efficient locational decision-making by the private sector. Public access to such information is vital.
- With the advent of computer systems, the overall costs of introducing GIS and similar data bases for the metropolitan region should be for outweighed by the benefits. While many national, regional and local organisations have strong interests in improved land information systems, the urban development authorities should take the lead in establishing such systems, with linkages with local urban research institutes.

As megacities expand there are important choices in the form of urban growth which may be summarized as "city-out" versus new towns. The various sub-issues include:

- The need to analyse land supply within a regional context, taking account of policies for economic decentralisation.

- The need to consider sustainability factors, e.g. forms of urban expansion which minimize energy use, minimize development on high value agricultural land, avoid vulnerable groundwater resources, optimize use of land (e.g. mixed areas, multiple use of buildings, etc.)
- The need to provide for accountable local planning and decentralised decision-making on land issues within a metropolitan strategic framework.
- The role of infrastructure, particularly transportation, in guiding megacity expansion.

In the Tokyo region, effective coordination of urban expansion is provided by the designation of 'development promotion' and 'deferred development' areas, each accompanied by various financial and other regulatory mechanisms, including wide availability of land information. In the National Capital Region (Philippines) urban expansion is being coordinated with policies for government support to a number of economic growth centres (e.g. Subic, Clark, Mailaque), i.e. in support to a decentralised megacity structure.

- As megacities expand there is an increasing need for close liaison between economic planning organisations, metropolitan and local governments to coordinate land policies and programs. This becomes especially urgent as megacities become more involved in the global economy.
- There will be a need for a strategic plan which addresses the 'new' issues of sustainable urban expansion and which and which reflects the high priority need for land use / transportation planning.

Cross-cutting Issues

Related to two generic aspects, the quality of life and the impact of the global economy, there are important cross-cutting issues concerning Land Management:

- Land and Transportation Planning Integration – transport planning is one of the most effective ways of guiding megacity expansion.
- Sustainability Issues – land development involves the critical issues of environmental, financial and institutional sustainability.
- Informal Sector – The informal sector requires equal attention in urban management.
- Regional Context – various aspects of land development should be viewed from the regional context such as water and drainage, transportation and environmental-development interactions (natural and man-made).
- Institutional Coordination – land management by its very nature involves the concerns of many public and private institutions and requires horizontal and vertical coordination.

There is a need to clearly define the roles and functions of organisations involved in land management at the national, regional and local levels. This becomes specially urgent with the emergence of Metropolitan Regions covering many local governments. Land development at the macro level should reflect national and regional economic development objectives, taking into account the land-related impacts of the global economy. There should be careful evaluation of urban expansion choices, in most cases it will be realistic to support market-driven city-out urban expansion, using transport, telecommunications and administrative decentralisation and guiding mechanisms. Enhanced public participation in land policy development and implementation is vital to generate 'ownership' of plans and programs.

Land development policies should be analysed in terms of their impact on income groups, particularly the urban poor. Innovative techniques for assisting the urban poor in access to land and shelter should be developed, including on-site solutions for squatting, new policies to support private rental housing and access to credit facilities. Enabling policies and techniques to help individual households obtain land and shelter should be developed, including streamlined land transaction procedures, provision of tenure to informal sector households, deregulation and other indirect actions. Planning and regulatory systems should be re-evaluated, focusing on the use of more effective plans, the potential for deregulation and the needs of sustainable urban development. Spatial planning activities should be merged within the wide urban management process so as to allow effective integration of spatial, financial, economic and institutional strategies.

Developing a comprehensive land information system can benefit both a wide range of government organisations and the public.

Spatial scale of urban environmental problems

SPATIAL SCALE	HOUSEHOLD/ WORKPLACE	COMMUNITY	METROPOLITAN AREA	REGION	CONTINENT/ PLANET
Key infrastructure and services	shelter water storage onsite sanitation garbage storage stove ventilation	piped water sewerage garbage collection drainage streets/lanes	industrial parks roads interceptors treatment plants outfalls landfills	highways water sources power plants	
Characteristic problems	substandard housing lack of water no sanitation disease vectors indoor air pollution	excreta laden waters/soils trash dumping flooding noise/stress natural disasters	traffic congestion accidents ambient air pollution toxic dumps	water pollution ecological areas lost	acid rain global warming ozone layer

Source Bartone (1990) in UMP. Towards Environmental Strategies for Cities. World Bank, 1994

8

ECOLOGY OF SUSTAINABLE DEVELOPMENT

Mercury, with his winged feet, light and airborne, astute, agile, adaptable, free and easy, established the relationships of the gods among themselves and those between the gods and men, between universal laws and individual destinies, between the forces of nature and the forms of culture, between the objects of the world and all thinking subjects.

—Italo Calvino

Cities today are in the centre-stage of environmental pollution, land degradation and loss of bio-diversity. Concentration of intense economic process and high levels of consumption in cities increase their resource demands, beyond their boundaries, cities affect traditional rural economies and their culture.

The urban professionals are increasingly aware that efforts to improve environment must focus on major urban centres. Cities today dominate global resource consumption. They take up only 2% of the world's land surface while they use over 75% of the world's resources. Sustainable urban development is, therefore, the most pressing challenge before the humanity in the 21st century. Could the vast appetites for resources and their hugo waste discharges be curtailed? Can they become a resource and energy efficient home for the humanity? Could efforts to improve the environment performance of our cities also create new opportunities for urban employment ?

The main problem with cities today is that they have become centres of mobilisation rather than civilisation. They are nodes of an increasingly economic activity, with the volume of travel saving reacahed unprecedented levels in recent years. The urban economic culture has a deep impact on the human mind, which has become too preoccupied with the pursuit of personal gain. The city of the future, to be sustainable, will have to re-establish the concept of civilisation, with greater dependence on local production for local consumption, with greater concern on the livability of local environment, and with a greater emphasis on creating public spaces for people to enjoy.

New Directions

Based on the past trends and technological advancement, the following predictions can be made for the future urban perspective:

- New balance will be struck between scientific-technological advancement and human development; emergence of bio-architecture and eco-technologies.
- Future demand of infrastructure will overtake the level of building and housing construction.
- Environment, employment and equity will be the major concerns of city development. This includes poverty reduction and an equitable access to land, finances, services and environment.
- The structure of a city will be determined not by its geometry but by the human activities within it.
- Possibly many cities will be replaced by conurbation.
- Water will be a critical issue and major problem in urban areas.
- Higher level of mixed land use, replacing single use zoning.
- System which are adaptable according to customer demands and development of energy and environment.
- Information Technology as a major tool and determinant of city development, economy and industry.
- Solar energy will hold the key of power supply during the next century. Renewable and nonpolluting energy sources will overtake present power sources.
- Much higher use of subterranean space and Earth Tunnels for climatic control, utilities, transport and other infrastructure will be witnessed.

- Commercial use of solar energy.
- Biotechnology will play a major role in waste treatment, recycling and conservation of biodiversity.
- Evolution of 'Intelligent Infrastructure' and new automation systems, including Telecommunity, Transmission superhighways, etc.
- Quest for quality and survival of the excellence.

In this context, new attitudes and directions will replace the present ones with the following key themes:

- Holistic in place of reductionist
- Diversity in place of uniformity
- Decentralised in place of centralised
- Small scale in place of large scale
- Collaboration and partnership in place of autonomous
- Facilitator in place of manager
- Participatory in place of pre-planned
- Organisational in place of functional
- Urbanistic in place of architectonic
- Sustainability in place of development
- Mass customisation in place of mass production.

One of the central focus of urban development during 21st century would be human development with focus on alleviation of urban poverty. The cities manifest vast gulf of incomes and living standards. The living conditions in pavements, poorly serviced slums and squatter settlements are bordering the inhuman levels. One out of every three persons lives below the poverty line, and about 90% of our urban poor live in unplanned settlements and self-built housing, lacking rudimentary services. The planning framework has not been able to serve these vast population. It is necessary to evolve a new framework to channelise the urban resources in a manner, which serves the poor, and is affordable by them.

Improved services, environment and housing enablo the poor to integrate themselves with the network of transactions in the urban system has a whole. This propensity, which is highly desirable from the point of view of socio-economic development, underscores the need for launching programmes of in-situ upgradation and old city improvements as growth points of the urban process. The strategy may comprise of formulating around the sub-standard areas several programmes of physical, social and economic upgradation, which could promote backward and forward linkages between housing and other programmes, such a nutrition, health, environmental improvement, education and employment. However, the strategy of development should contain a strong commitment to the widest possible public participation.

The economic reforms call for a significantly increased role by the private sector in development. Local bodies have to gear up to encourage non-governmental organisations and private sector to provide services and supports for urban development. Their capabilities need to be strengthened to harness the potential of community, cooperative and private sector resources in the development of the city. They have to reorient their role as a facilitator for which new instruments and institutions need to be created in order to achieve higher levels of mobilisation of resources, for equitable participatory service delivery.

In order to enable the implementation of a new strategy, it would be necessary to restructure the local bodies and service departments and to equip them to the changing political set up. The process of urban development is not just an aspect of physical and economic growth, but it is profoundly linked with the political system and community participation. The challenge is to find ecologically sustainable, socially just, economically viable and culturally transferable technological and managerial innovations which are appropriate to meet the needs of the 21st century.

City Metabolism

The critical question today is as humanity moves towards urbanisation, whether living standards in our cities can be maintained by curbing their environmental impacts. To answer this question, we have to draw up balance sheets quantifying and comparing urban resource flows. Use of energy and other resources largely depends on the way cities function, as well as their living standards. The metabolism of most cities is essentially linear, with resources flowing through the urban system without much concern about their origin and destination of wastes. In other words, linear metabolic process implies that inputs and outputs ate largely unrelated. Whether it is the use of timber, pulp, paper, consumer goods or fossil fuels, their consumption results into generation of wastes, fumes and pollution. Often urban sewage system are linear, collecting human wastes and discharging it downstream or in the open lands, which get contaminated by sewage, toxic contents and hazardous chemicals.

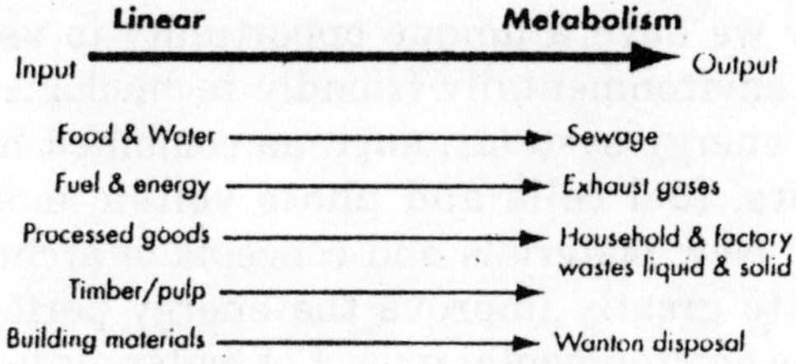

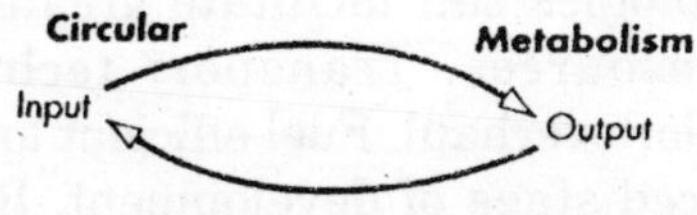

Circular Metabolism

The linear metabolic system of cities is different from nature's circular metabolism, where every output by the organism is also an input which renews and sustains the living environment. Cities should develop a self-regulating, sustainable circular metabolic system, so as to make them viable with the environment on which they depend. Outputs have to integrate with the production systems, incorporating the principles of Recycle, Reuse, Reduce and Recover. The purpose of recycling of paper, metals, plastic and glass and conversion of organic materials into compost is to return waste products which is harmless to the land and environment. By design, city form, size, locational decisions, administrative restructing and efficient mass transit system, many of the environmental problems of cities can be contained.

Looking at the damage which our urban development has inflicted upon the environment, one of the prime agenda, is to explore the possibility of creating a living environment which is self-sufficient, ecologically balanced and culturally stimulating. We need to look at the fundamentals of human settlements, and evolve a system whereby we can establish harmony with nature by ensuring minimum waste. This can only be done by creating a unit of living in which each resource is put to maximum productive use and 'cycled' for reuse. A viable necessity for Indian cities is effective utilization of urban waste energy from incineration plants and sewage treatment for generation of energy which can be employed for lighting, heating and air-conditioning.

Eco-Technology

Today we have a unique opportunity to use a whole new range of environmentally friendly technologies in our cities. Efficient energy systems, such as combined heat and power generators, fuel cells and photo voltaic modules are now available. New materials and concepts of architectural design allow us to greatly improve the energy performance and to reduce the environmental impact of materials used in buildings. Recycling technologies can facilitate greater efficiency in the urban use of resources. Transport technologies are also undergoing a major overhaul. Fuel efficient low emission vehicles are at an advanced stage of development. Rapid urban transit systems are starting to reappear, which would reduce the dependence on private transport.

Today the adoption of eco-technology for infrastructure and building is essential for environmental sustainability. Whether we are concerned with transport, water supply, sewage, or the provision of adequate housing, the conventional approach has to change. The engineers, architects and planners have a great responsibility to help create receptiveness for the emergence of a new kind of urban form and architecture 'that combines climatic responsiveness with functional efficiency and a pleasing environment. This is an ethical responsibility that transcends the traditional brief of the profession. With cities as our main home today, we have to redefine their cultural and environmental function.

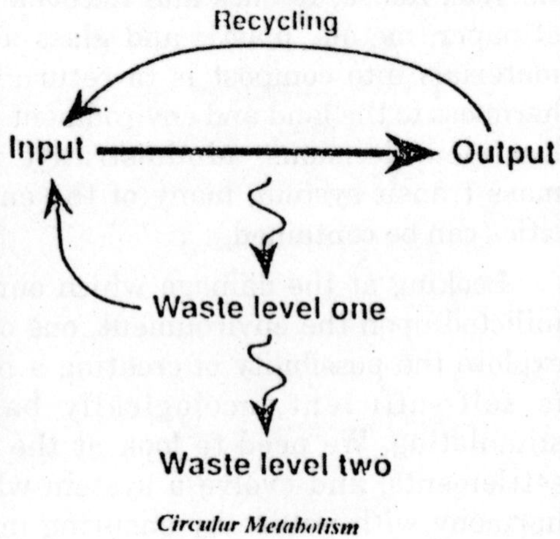

Circular Metabolism

The cities worthy of the new millennium will be energy and resource efficient, as well as culturally rich and socially responsible. In our major cities inward investment in resource efficiency will contribute significantly to achieve higher levels of employment. The investment in infrastructure will make a vast difference to health and living conditions in the cities.

Energy Efficiency

Wind, earth and water are the primary energy sources of the world. It is the solar energy, conserved through billions of years, that we are now enjoying as fossil fuels. The energy crisis of the 1970s jolted the world into greater awareness for alternative energy developments. We have to realise that it is solar energy that is the only source of our past and future energy, it is the sun that converts water into water vapours and makes it fall back on the land surface. It is this fallback on the photosynthetic conversion of the solar energy that enables the vegetation to grow and survive on the earth surface. It is again the sun that helps to generate oxygen and helps the survival of the entire life on this world.

Passive design of buildings for climatic comfort is not only essential for a conducive environment, but also important to save demands of energy, particularly electrical power. This is an expensive and recurring overhead which can be minimised by proper design and strategies. Lighting often accounts for nearly half of the electrical consumption. By proper approach and a comprehensive strategy energy efficiency and economy can be achieved. These can be summed up as under:

- Architectural design
- Integration of architectural design with lighting (both day-lighting and artificial lighting)
- Lighting Technology

Energy efficiency of lighting installations *interalia* depends on :

- Efficiency of various components of the systems (lamps, ballast and luminaries)
- The way in which they are used (they are strongly influenced by the control systems and day light availability)
- Maintenance.

It is important to pay attention to the strategies which can be used to reduce the power consumption. The most important factors for reduction of energy used for lighting are the incorporation of daylight design in all the buildings on a mandatory basis, and Adoption of energy efficient practices by :

- Regulation and standards of lighting
- Regulation and standards of lighting products
- Energy labeling of lighting products
- Imposition of limits on building connected lighting load (fixing lighting power density limit expressed in watts per square meter of floor area)
- Imposition of minimum efficiency of lighting installations (by specifying average installed circuit efficiency in Lumens per Watt for lighting equipments).

For energy efficiency, load management techniques and energy accounting should be adopted. Schemes to minimise power thefts/losses by improved metering arrangements should be enforced. Low energy consuming gadgets and Non-conventional energy sources like recovering energy from sewerage, solar energy should be used for street lighting, lighting at public spaces, open areas, traffic signals, hoardings etc. For energy efficiency, the following critical areas need to be attended:

(*i*) The concept of energy efficiency should begin with the idea of Zero-fossil Energy Development (ZED) which envisages an urban form and design of passive building envelope that reduce the demand for power to the point where it becomes economically viable to use energy from renewable resources. This involves a holistic approach combining the issues and actions at various levels of planning, design, construction and maintenance leading to a sustainable and energy efficient regime. The city geometry, restructuring and zoning with self-contained neighbourhoods could minimise the need to travel and substantial saving of recurring energy/fuel consumption. Integrated mass transport system, traffic and transit operation and management, better tele-communications, promoting bicycles and NMV transport, is another major area of energy efficient habitat. The introduction of energy audit and design of energy efficient buildings by site planning, heights, form, construction and materials and reducing energy demand by passive micro-climatic design approach, intelligent energy controls, heat recovery, landscape, opening design, furnishings, etc., are the critical considerations. The key to future is a cybernetic form of sustainable energy, which integrates symbiosis, recycling and energy chains.

(*ii*) Load management techniques and energy accounting should be adopted. Schemes to minimise power thefts/ losses by improved metering arrangements should be enforced. Non-conventional energy sources like recovering energy from sewerage, solar energy should be used for street lighting, lighting at public spaces, open areas, traffic signals, hoardings, etc.

(*iii*) To meet the part of the estimated requirement by non-conventional sources/solar energy and other actions, the following stipulations are proposed:

- For all establishments with floor area of more than 300 sqm, solar energy should be mandatory.
- Compulsory Solar Panels for public advertising, lighting in open areas, public utilities, streets, etc.
- As alternate mandatory arrangement during power cuts to replace generators/inverters etc.
- Adoption of Load Management Techniques.
- Tariff restructuring and improved metering arrangement to minimize power thefts/losses.
- Interim single point connection in unauthorized colonies and jhuggies.
- Private Sector Participation in different stages of Power generation, transmission and distribution.
- Incentivising energy savings and use of energy efficient gadgets.
- Public awareness, capacity building and training.

(*iv*) As per Asian Development Bank's report (1997), potential in saving energy due to better overall efficiency in domestic sector is about 20%.

There is strong case for replacing low efficiency incandescent lamp with high efficiency fluorescent tubes or CFL's without compromising with the lumens output. Similarly for the refrigerators which account for 30% of total electricity consumed, measures like increased thickness of foam insulation, use of high coefficient compressors increased evaporator surfaces, use of tighter door seals and through technical improvements can reduce consumption from 540 KWH/year to 300 KWH/year (for a 165 litre refrigerator).

Incandescent bulbs, neon tubes and fluorescent lamps are giving way to light-emitting microchips that work longer, use less power and allow the use of light in new ways. The chips, which are known as light emitting diodes, or LED's have huge performance advantages in many mundane tasks (such as traffic lights). They consume 80 per cent less electricity than the bulbs, and last up to 10 times as long. Moreover, they have the safety advantage of gradually fading instead of burning out. The eventual result will be huge savings in energy and maintenance costs.

It is necessary to have regulatory standards which encourage the users to reduce electricity consumption. This may include the adoption of following measures :

- Utilisation of heat reflective insulation on the roofs.
- Use of non-conventional and renewable sources of energy
- Adopting energy efficient building design
- Use of technology which would consume minimum energy to maintain desired human comfort conditions. For example, replacement of bulbs by fluorescent lamps/ CFLs may bring in substantial savings in electrical consumption.

Solar Energy

India is endowed with abundance of sun. However, its potential in producing energy is still to be explored. In a cloudless region, a roof area of 100 sq.mtr. receives about 500

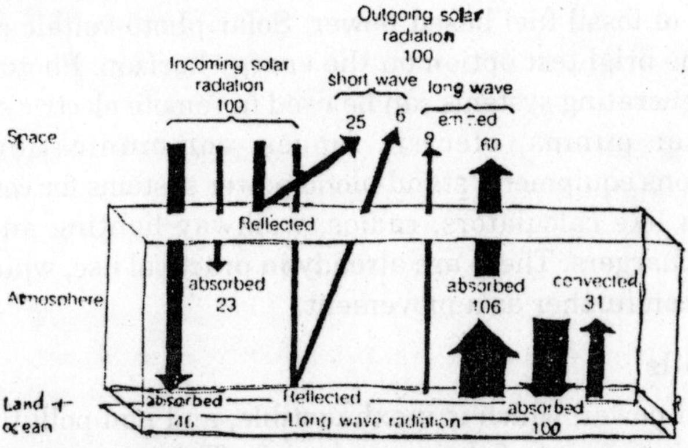

The Earth's energy budget scaled to 100 outgoing arbitrary units of solar radiation

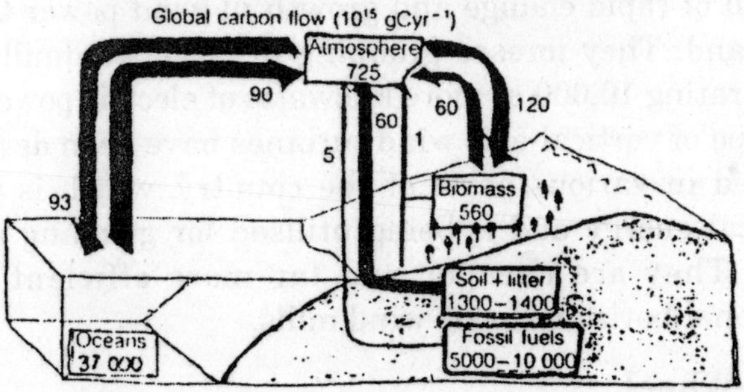

Global Carbon Flow

KW per day from eight hours of sunshine. In the hot-arid regions (the greatest solar radiation intensity occurs between latitude 15 and 35 north or south) more than 3,000 hours of solar radiation could be obtained and even in the warm-humid rigion there are about 2300 hours. Where there is lack of conventional materials such as coal, oil, or gas, it is that use is made of the solar energy which is generally abundant in the tropics. Solar water heating for domestic hot water or as part of a home heating scheme has become more widely used in some countries as a response to the energy and environment crisis. As solar energy is initially captured in the form of heat, it is therefore best use of a variety of heating purposes. Solar water heaters (e.g. for canteens, schools, homes and hotels), solar steam cookers and water distillation units provide examples of practical applications of solar energy.

Solar Photo-Voltaic Cells

The dream of clean, abundant, low-cost solar power for the future has been around for a long time where there is no fuel to burn, of fossil fuel based power. Solar photo-voltaic cell was one of the brightest option on the energy horizon. Photo voltaic power generating systems can be used in remote electric supplies for water pumps, electric fences, communications and navigations equipment; stand-alone power systems for consumer products like calculators, radios, walkway lighting and auto-battery chargers. These are already in practical use, which need to be taken further as a movement.

Windmills

Wind power, which is inexhaustible, and non-polluting, is a promising way out of the energy crisis. The scientists feel that a period of rapid change and growth in wind power technology is at hand. They foresee grouping of large windmills, capable of generating 10,000 or more kilowatts of electric power. Already new type of vertical-axis wind turbines have been designed and installed in various parts of the country, which is producing electrical energy and is being utilised for grinding and pump water. They are cheaper and far more efficient than the traditional horizontal-axis wind mills.

Water-Wheel

Flowing water can be used to turn a water wheel, which can be used as source of energy. If the site has a running stream a mini-dam can be built at the higher plateau. The water flows downhill and can run a mini power house to generate electricity by turning a turbine. The energy can alternatively be used for sawmill flour grinding and to pump water.

Rainwater Harvesting

India having a total geographical area of 329 million hectares, has an extraordinary diversity of ecosystems. Most parts of the country are endowed with the monsoon season of rainfall, celebrated by the poets throughout. Rain water had always been an asset which was treated with respect and preserved with care. This is evident in numerous lakes, ponds, baolis, wells, tanks, channels, and canals found all over the country in almost every city and village. However, during the recent times the concept of water conservation has remained neglected. This has resulted into severe shortage of water and ecological imbalance.

With the heavy and indiscriminate deforestation, construction of buildings, roads, etc., this natural percolation of water has been upset. This has resulted in the lowering of local water tables and disappearance of perennial springs that once kept our rivers flowing. The uncontrolled flow of water is also resulting in severe floods. So the immediate means necessary to avoid these tragedies are to make efforts to maximize the localised water conservation.

The drainage along the natural contours should be the starting point of layout planning and land development. The concept of zero-run off with a series of retention ponds, sediment traps and balancing reservoirs provides an economical and pragmatic solution to drainage and water harvesting. Green ways and parkways along the natural drainage channels should be planned and developed for their protection. The natural drainage channels should be segregated from waste water and sewerage network.

Various methods can be adopted for rainwater harvesting at the project level, depending upon the ground contours, rainfall and requirements vis-a-vis economic considerations. These include the following :

- Underground rainwater storage
- Contour trenching
- Pits, deep holes and wells
- Stepwells, tanks and Baolis
- Ponds, balancing lakes etc.
- On channel storage and ground water recharge
- Channel and canals.

For a building project, underground rainwater storage is a pragmatic initiative, the rooftop water tank can be filed by a bamboo pump or electrical motor for raising the water. By solar energy the condensed water is passed through a filter or coal, sand and marble chips to provide clean potable water.

Although the best way to save water is to use it sparingly, another option is to treat waste water and reuse it for various purpose. Recycled water can be used to irrigate the grass in parks and along embankments. Increasingly, areas with chronic water shortage are installing recycling systems.

Water Recycling

Conserving the scarce water and recycling used water is a major challenge in the urban areas of India. For this a new technology, known as root zone cleaning system seems promising. It consists of a receiving tank into which the toilet, kitchen and bath water flows by gravity; a mud area where suitable reeds, rushes and other plants are grown; and an outlet tank in which the water cleaned by tho natural process is accumulated. The processed water is clean and without any smell. Fish and amphibians living and growing within it show that the'water is clean and system is successful. Chlorination, which removes germs and bacteria, leaves chemical residues, which are unfavourable for human consumption. This is not so with waterborne plants, which oxygenate the water and help organic activity. As the water moves through the roots of the plants, the acids released interact with the bacteria and similar strong chemicals can also be broken down and rendered harmless by this simple natural process. The basis is the hydraulic principle whereby water is pushed up through a tube narrower than the water contained. In this case the ground water rises up the stems of certain aquatic plants and biochemical conditions are established which initiate the cleaning process. Thus, it is a combination of aerobic (using oxygen) as we as anaerobic systems, offering the advantages of the both. In the past few years, various versions of this acquatic plant based technology for purifying water have come in practice in India (notably in Kolkata). A variation of this process is fish culture. Within days golden tilapla fish degrades the effluent and dark colour and odours are removed from waste, making it suitable for reuse.

Recovery of Rivers, Lakes and Water Bodies

A priority of urban development is to improve the water bodies and the quality of water. This involves rationalisation of land use, controlling encroachments, installation of water purification facilities, improvement of drainage, waste water treatment, sewerage treatment and furtherance of advanced treatment. This would lead to preparation and implementation of attractive and pleasant river-front development schemes.

Bio-Architecture

The materials used in buildings, their compatibility with climatic conditions, energy contents and environmental performance of buildings are interlinked. It is necessary to rationalise the use of building materials for conservation of energy and environmental efficiency of built environment.

The development of simple, small eco-technologies integrated with bio-architecture, which use replenishable fuels and adopt recycling, provide environmentally sustainable and economical alternatives to the present energy crisis and pollution caused by it. Reducing energy demand by low energy design strategies is crucial for the sustainability of the Indian cities.

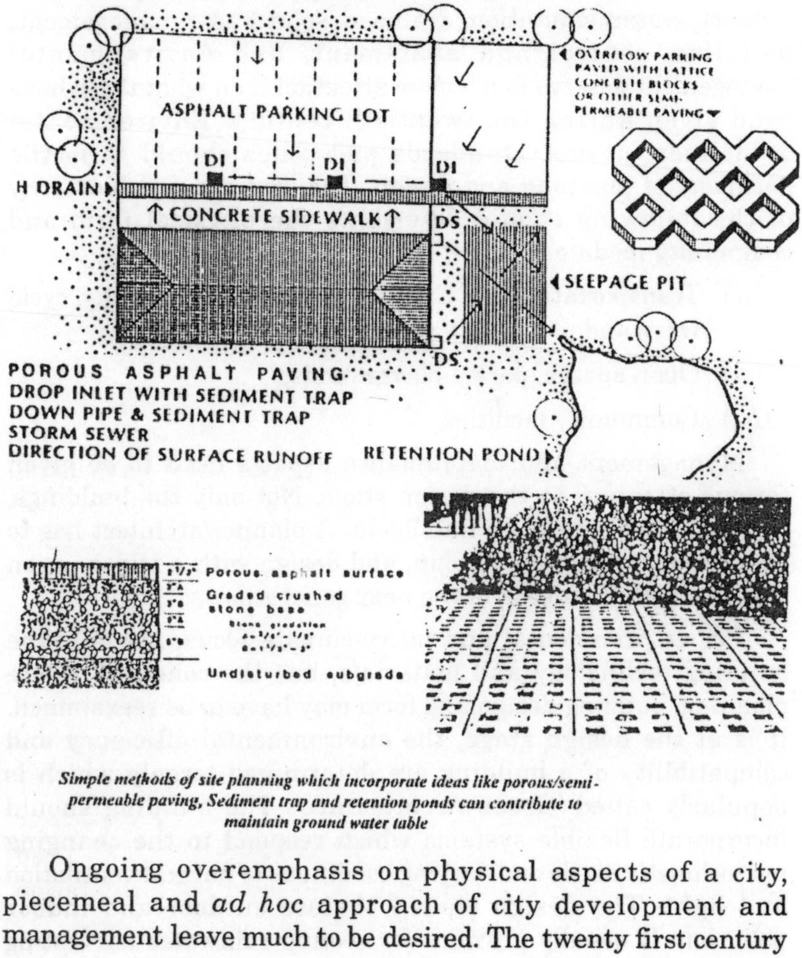

Simple methods of site planning which incorporate ideas like porous/semi-permeable paving, Sediment trap and retention ponds can contribute to maintain ground water table

Ongoing overemphasis on physical aspects of a city, piecemeal and *ad hoc* approach of city development and management leave much to be desired. The twenty first century city in India should discern a much more professional approach, which should match and accelerate India's potential. It is rather sad that we have the potential but outdated institutional structure does not facilitate its harnessing. It is essential to develop the institutional structures and capacity building for best of planning capabilities.

The starting point of planning and should be ecology and environment, for which comprehensive environmental policies, plan, parameters and programmes need to be evolved and adopted. The urban pattern, linkages, density pattern, size of settlements, etc. should be based on environmental considerations. The aspects of energy, topography, climatic comfort, water, sanitation, drainage, solid waste management, pollution control and abatement, and environmental management deserve much more attention than what these have been given during the twentieth century. Environmental guidelines, norms, standards and codes should form the backbone of planning and design. The systems and hierarchy of the following should determine the physical form and community module :

(*i*) Transportation and Circulation (including parking, cycle ways and pedestrian precincts)

(*ii*) Open spaces, parks, playgrounds,

(*iii*) Community facilities

Management and maintenance aspects need to be given serious attention at the design stage. Not only the buildings, but the cities need to be intelligent. A planner/architect has to be a visionary. He has to plan, and design with a wider vision and visualise the needs of the next generation.

For environmental and micro-climate focus, not only the building technology and materials, but the concepts of site planning, building design and form may have to be reexamined. It is at the design stage, the environmental efficiency and compatibility of a building are determined largely which is popularly called 'Green Architecture'. The building should incorporate flexible systems which respond to the changing microclimatic needs and varying conditions of natural ventilation and light. The design should obviate outdoor and indoor pollution. It usually provides for rooftop rainwater harvesting and recycling of wastewater and exploitation of non-conventional sources of energy (such as photo-voltaic system). The design of openings and glazing should allow flexibility. In large public buildings, the use of intelligent systems can be employed with gain. These concepts are already in vogue and buildings such as Living Kapsulo, Palau (Pacific) Amro bank, New Amsterdam, Islamic Centre, Paris are examples of bio-architecture approach.

The following should be attended for design with nature:

- Natural Eco-system
- Water supply and quality
- Air quality
- Noise reduction
- Erosion Control
- Flooding Prevention
- Landscape features
- Flora and fauna
- Open space integrity

A basic consideration of human intervention in natural system should be "carrying capacity" of an area. The carrying capacity of an area is the population or level of activity that can be sustained for a given length of time without depletion of the resources or breakdown of the biological (natural) systems.

The urbanisation during the 21st century will demand urban services, transport, communication, buildings, housing, employment and work centres during the first 20 years, what had been achieved in the entire 20th century. There will be new set of priorities, viz., environment, equity, employment, economy and efficiency. Information technology will play a major role in the process of urbanisation, development and management. The architects, planners and engineers have a vital role in this task, as they are concerned with sustainable development and environment.

Dust potential and SPM are intercepted by trees, reducing it upto 10 to 25%

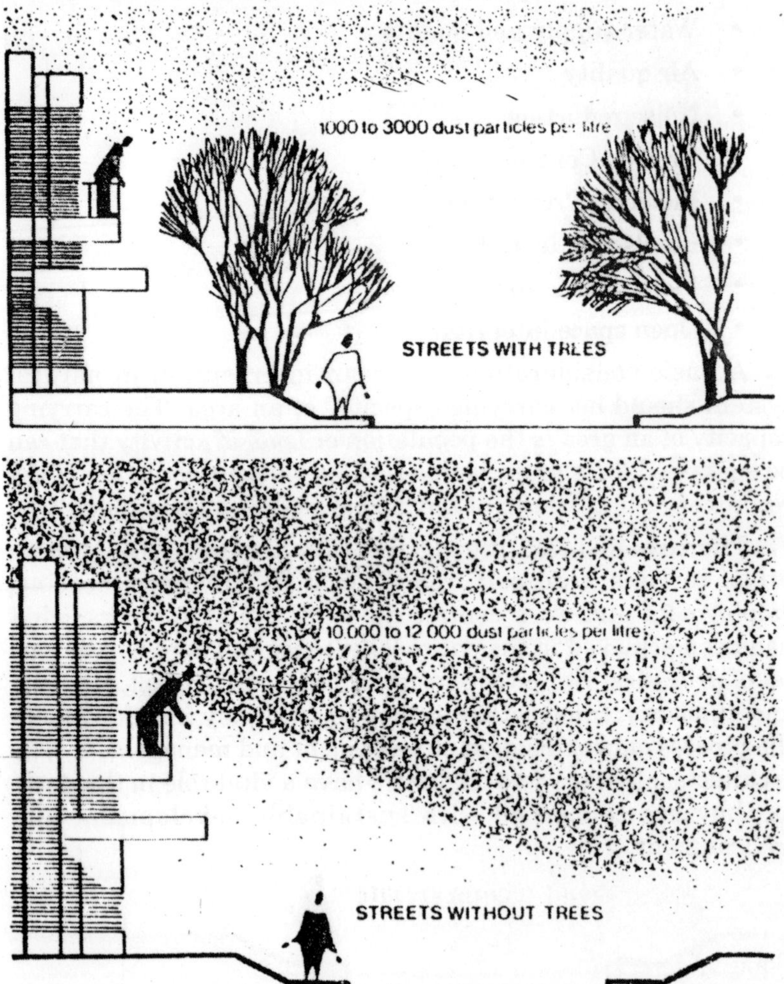

9

URBAN GOVERNANCE AND INFORMATION TECHNOLOGY

Connections Lost, Found, Severed, Invented, Disconnected, and Secured—
Nan Ellin

India's is a continuing story of the persistence of patterns of the past amidst epochal changes. During last 2000 years the sub-continent which had about 20 million people; has grown fifty times. It is the future of this mass that comprises a seventh of all humanity that is cause for both celebration and concern. If India has held together as an entity across the latter half of the 20th century, the vibrancy and flexibility of its democracy has played no small part.

The success of India rests on its collective ability as a society and as a legacy of a civilisation, though the ideal of equality is so often a mirage in the land of multi-layered hierarchy. The great upsurge of those at the margins of society; of adivasis, Dalits and women is still in its early phase. Much will depend on how far their concerns are addressed and their right to dignity given the recognition it deserves and demands. The polity's successes and failures will be the touchstone for not just our rulers but all those who make up and believe in India not merely as an idea but as an ideal.

India is heir to the travails and legacies of a long past. The flexible and open-ended idea of India that the republic was founded on, had a second, oft neglected dimension — the dream of levelling the layers of privilege and status that had burdened our society. The urge for harmony and the striving for equity went together. Neither has remained unaffected by the tumult of the last six decades.

This social inequality between the "privileged" and the "under-privileged" has grown further over the centuries. In feudal times, the rulers, the Maharajas, the large land owners and the British were the privileged classes. This distortion was sought to be remedied 58 years ago through the creation of a republic based on the principle of equal rights for all our citizens. Sadly, however, this has not been remedied. On the contrary, the disparity has increased. The many years of "socialist" economic policy seem to have resulted in the emergence of a new "privileged" class of politicians, government officials, large land owners and businessmen, who derive enormous power though patronage and even corrupt practices, which influence economic and fiscal policies often to the detriment of national interest. The spirit of contribution to national development and the creation of national wealth is increasingly being subordinated to abject self-interest. The national fabric of values is being eroded rapidly, making increasingly difficult for individuals to succeed on their merit alone.

The Planning Commission occasionally rings alarm bells at the rising cost of "delivery" of government services — at present more than 65%. Public servants' rising demands for a good life are eating into funds. While the Central deficit soars, the economies of the States are collapsing. Which means lesser availability of funds for poverty alleviation. Rajiv Gandhi once remarked that "only 15 paise out every rupee really reaches the poor."

Sri Aurobindo remarked that India's real role was to be the guru among the nations of the world. While we see Indians doing well outside India, inside India they are still floundering. Why is it that the Indian cities, as the crucibles of culture are not able to nourish or promote the remarkable capacities of its own people? A prime role of the cities in the twenty first century would be to restore the cultural heritage and combine science, development and traditions in a global perspective. For example, if a unitary consciousness is indeed the basis of the universe, it would combine the advances of biochemistry along with an understanding of the life-force and the soul which mirror the human being that is cosmic in nature.

The new culture would interface material potentials with the glory of the spirit, values and welfare of all beings. As classical

India combined a vast flowering of art, architecture, music and dance, alongwith numerous philosophies, our cities should menifest human values and cultural enrichment. They should respect the vast variations in cultures, faith, languages and customs, rather than merely accepting material affluence as enough. It would raise the poor and the down trodden and help all people become happy and free.

The world is now entering into a global age in which pluralism must be foundation of world culture. It is a new age of dialogue and respect in which we must learn to honour and cherish all the cultures of the world, with a firm belief in tolerance and synthesis. Our settlements must embrace all human beings and their cultures as part of one great family.

This is crucial since the cities today are trapped between a destructive consumerism and a rigid religious exclusivism on the other leading to a growing psychological and social unrest.

In a pluralistic society such as ours the State must be equidistant from all religions and at the same time be equally supportive of all of them. In a democracy, differing outlooks and lifestyles need to be respected. Elected politicians and public servants must be committed not to religion but to ethics. At the level of ethics there is a vast and wide degree of consensus among all religions. The human rights and ethical principles for public life can be codified and applied to State policy. Ethical principles are universal and they uphold the inviolability of the dignity of the human being. Amidst our national problems we must consciously protect our ancient culture from the degrading invasions.

If we are able to draw upon our spiritual heritage, learn to love each other, and while nurturing a grand vision of our future, there will be nothing to stop us from going forward to a future worthy of our past and of the promises of the present.

For this a new vitality and creativity is necessary that honours the country's venerable traditions, but does not restrict itself to past forms and conventions. It requires a new generation of thinkers who are global in outlook but grounded in the practical spirituality. Indian professionals must return to their cultural wellsprings and create a new vision for humanity. We can see how traditional Indian disciplines as Yoga, Ayurveda and Vedanta are gaining respect worldwide for their integral and holistic approach. The new world order of computers and the information revolution offers the country a situation quite favourable to its unique spiritual and intellectual talents. But for this to occur India must stand up to blaze a new trail to the universe that dwells both inside and outside of ourselves.

If Indian cities are to matter globally in this unfolding scenario, it will need to unleash the full potential of its greatest asset, namely its human capital. The world over, Indian nationals have achieved international recognition and acclaim in the fields of science and technology, medicine, economics, culture and the arts. In addition, they have demonstrated outstanding ability as entrepreneurs and innovators. Many of these achievers have shone outside India - the result of access to good education and an environment which recognises and rewards achievement. The ability to shine, unfortunately, is often thwarted on Indian soil where access to good education is subjectively restricted and where creativity and true enterprise are often discouraged. We are not a country of equal opportunity for all. Perhaps the reason for this partly lies in our polity, governance, culture, and traditions.

Information Technology

A new phenomenon is taking shape in India: the emergence of the information industry. Increasingly, the traditional factors of production - land, labour and capital - have become less important when compared with information and technology; economists have termed this as the 'expansion of the production frontier'.

Tomorrow' s cities will be dominated by knowledge industry. The emphasis will not be on physical or tangible assets, but on intangible assets, on knowledge. The intellectual capital of a city will determine its rank and competitiveness. Intangible assets include research and development, patents, propriety technologies, database and human relationships. There will be a major shift in the definition of work. Information and knowledge will be both the raw material as well as the product.

The world's major growth industries - microelectronics, pharma, biotechnology and telecommunication - are already brainpower industries. These industries, in turn, stimulate other industries to become knowledge based.

In the next 20 years, Information Techology will play a major role in converting illiterates into literates; in converting normal governments to smart governments and provide direct employment to more than 10 million people through IT Enabled Services and E-business. According to Nasscom's vision 2020, it will contribute towards 28 per cent of India's GDP. Thus, if any industry will contribute the maximum to India's economy in next decade, it will undoubtedly be the internet led I.T. industry and E-business or E-Biz will lead the way. Internet has bought India on the threshold of its second tryst with destiny.

Governance and IT

Government functioning tends to be complex, slow, and shrouded in a cloak of mystery and secrecy, with bureaucrats unwilling to share information with the public. With emerging technologies aiding transparency, governments cannot remain insulated for long from the public. Decision-making has to become more transparent and accountable.

Unfortunately, the use of information technology in government has meant a mere shift from a manual system to a computerised one. Without existing procedures being overhauled so that they can deliver superior service to citizens, such a change is pointless.

Andhra Pradesh is an excellent example of how states can incorporate information technology in the day-to-day functioning of the government, and re-engineer the manner in which services are provided to common citizens. Under its 'one-stop non-stop' approach, a pilot project called TWINS (Cities Integrated Network Services) integrated 18 services of six departments over one counter. It provides fast and easy access to government services, makes the government appear much simpler, and also cuts down on corruption.

In this new scenario, participation in the democratic process would be meaningful only if everyone has access to knowledge and information. It also has the danger of creating a new class divide; of information haves and have-nots. According to Peter Drucker, humanity will increasingly polarise into two employment categories: the intellectual, cultural and business elite (the mobile and independent, knowledge workers), and the rest (the immobile and dependent, service workers). Unless some equality is ensured in terms of access to information, there can be no true democracy and participation.

In Andhra Pradesh, the government is able to keep database of citizens, which helps in better targeting of welfare programmes and minimise misuse of funds; Virtual town hall meetings allow citizens to watch the proceedings of municipal meetings, and also enable them to participate in decision-making, which otherwise is not subject to public debate. This participation in the form of interactive sessions, panels and discussion groups, planning consultations, chat lines, and electronic online voting is becoming commonplace in Andhra Pradesh. Expanding cable television networks have made it possible to deliver the electronic information into the homes of the people.

In future, the prosperity of cities will most likely be measured in terms of PCs per household and bandwidth per capita. India needs to develop its telecommunications infrastructure rapidly, so that it can provide connectivity at affordable rates to large sections of its people. Fortunately, it is easier, and cheaper, to extend telecommunication networks to rural areas than it is to build road communications.

It is evident that the urban problems are going to be the major issues of the coming century due to the massive growth of cities. The country's future power structure, as well as social and economic structure would depend upon how its urban areas are managed and developed, for which the use information technology is inevitable. This helps in capacity building of service provides and empowers the citizens immensely.

Urban Vision

"Few dream and transform the dreams into thoughts and thoughts into actions. I would like to tell the young that the vision is bigger than us. The developed India needs a revolution in the minds of the young. Enter into it. Ignited minds are indeed the powerful resource to transform this nation from the developing nation of 50 years into a developed nation in less than two decades of time. Technology is the prime mover for the vision for the nation"

— Dr. APJ Abdul Kalam

The basic question is whether there is dream of the future of our human settlements? On the face of alround crisis, infrastructure services, environmental degradation, failure of local bodies, growing squatter settlements and unauthorised colonies, it is doubtful whether there is any vision or a perspective and whether present system allows it.

India's bright future seems darkened by the rapid growth and concentration of population in large urban centres. It has already exerted pressure on natural resources, which has seriously impaired the environment and capacity of cities to cope with the compulsions of growth. Everybody needs an intact environment. The protection of the climate, the forests, the rivers, the air and the soil will have to be a common endeavour. The great challenge for the future is how can be harmonize what is needed for economic competitiveness and guarantee environmental sustainability?

Humanity's future will only be secured when we are more careful with nature and our interaction with it in a sustainable way. This will require not only increasing the efficiency of resource management, but it also implies sustainable lifestyles which will entail giving up consumerism. The President of India in his address to the nation on the eve of Republic day 2000, succinctly summed up: "One half of our society guzzles aerated beverages while the other has to make do with palmfuls of muddied water. Our three-way fast lane of liberalisation, privatisation and globalisation must provide safe pedestrian crossings for the unempowered India". Mobility has its price: use of resources, harmful chemicals, and noise damage both people and the environment. Transport for the future will have to be different. In spite of various problems the 21st century promises to be a dynamic, though a turbulent, one. some of the dynamic changes that are in the offing today have all the potential of leading humanity to the solution of some of the global problems. As the rate of social, scientific and technological progress continues to mount, the broad contours of the future come into increasingly sharper focus. Information technology yields considerable optimism for the future towards a major leap.

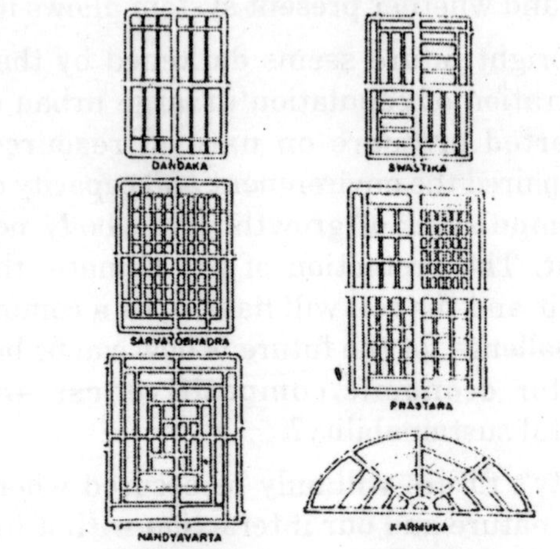

Vastupurush mandal : Ancient Cosmic diagram as a basis of spatial composition and organisation. The celestial zoning of deities and men in a hierarchical system of inter-squared modular grid. The innermost zone belongs to Brahma, the god, which is, surrounded by the king and the Brahamins. The next zone is for the warriors and then businessmen. The peripheral area is for the menial workers.

10

REDISCOVERING THE TRADITIONAL WISDOM

Designing is like improvisation, finding a sound for each place.

—Walter Hood

After the independence of India in 1947, a new era of urban development started. It reflected the political commitment to build a new India. With socialist visions of mass production, centralized governance and comprehensive planning, it laid foundations of rural and regional development and slum clearance. New industrial towns were developed and plans for capital cities were prepared. Forerunners among them were Delhi Master Plan, prepared with the help of the Ford Foundation and Chandigarh by Le Corbusier. The ideals of town planning visualized city as a great industrial and economic generator alongwith the ideals of socialism achieved by slum clearance and mass housing. The colonial perceptions of old city as "Slum" perpetuated, and a new zeal of building "modern and model" city prevailed. With an overemphasis on demographic criterion, functionalism, economic and physical development, the historical, social, aesthetic cultural and environmental characteristics were often marginalized.

Today, coupled with shortages of basic services, degrading environment, squatting, population pressures, and unregulated growth, the resultant built form of Indian cities is complex, amorphous and chaotic. It no more reflects a coherent response and ambience to its heritage and environmental. The situation is reaching a break down level and today there is a common falling in deprivation and the loss of totality and harmony. There is fragmentation and alienation of man at all levels: individual, societal, physical and psychical.

The questions that we must explore and address are – is it possible to develop an indigenous approach to arrest the ongoing feeling of dislocation, deprivation and degradation? Can we develop a sustainable approach for the conservation and preservation of our urban heritage and environment?

Evolution of Built Form

Starting from the caves and nest-building of higher apes, the built form has evolved with the human beings. Through the stages of semantics, organic and vernacular settlements, it reached to a sedentary stage of evolution. The modern built form developed from a host of complex factors, most of which are empirical and homogenous continuum of scientific knowledge of economics and mathematics.

The complementary space was seen as a symbolic manifestation of cosmic system, attempting to unite the opposed substantial domains and contrasting phenomenon. The conceptual orientation of space had been a basic part of a cognitive system or ontology.

In India most well known icongraphic system had been the 'Mandala'. It is the cosmography of universal order and a source of self identification within the order of the universe. The form of a city was derived on the principles of Vastupurush Mandal. It established an interrelationship of physical form of a settlement with the spiritual, cosmic and behavioral system. It determined the basic form, its location, zoning and orientation of various functions in a settlement. It was interrelated with the Mandala, the context of surroundings, like the planets in the astrological chart. A system of astha(8), Navgarh (9 planets), 24 matrika pithas, etc. was devised as a numerical symbolism and for orientation and linkages of the settlement system.

The Vastrupurush Mandala had been so universal that it could be applied to an altar, a temple, a house, a city or the entire cosmos. The symbol relates physical form with the outer form and the inner vision. The Mandala had been not only a spatial axiom but a temporal process as well. It is a module encompassing the principles of organ a city : interrelationship of parts, interdependence of systems, resonance and synchronically.

The latest, and perhaps the most well known metaphysical interpretation of Mansara Cosmology has been the city of Jaipur. Built in early eighteenth century by Jai Singh II, a ruler with deep interest in astronomy and astrology, it is a geometric allegory of cosmic predestination, negotiated with the morphological situation of the site.

The underlying principle of Mandala is the theme of macrocosm and microcosm. It binds human beings with their physical world and immediate environment-the-city, the village or a house. Within the overall organisation and structure of the cosmos, everything is interlinked and integrated. Like a Jiva (human body), the settlement performs different functions, that of body, head, atman and nerves, i.e. channels of communications. This not only includes built form, but also the water bodies and open space and their association with the divine.

Vastu Shastra had been seen as the art of integration of Vastu (Space), Purush (the human beings) and Mandala, that incorporates Prakriti – i.e. five basic elements of nature (Panch – bhutas), and Kal (Time). The Indian Vedic knowledge offers an integral vision of Vastu, Purush and Prakriti. The elements of nature are set into an order that causes a process of cultivation and purification. There is a five fold order comprising of origination, building, interlocking, overlapping and transcending.

Vedic insight provides a beautiful hypothesis of relationships of Kal (absolute time) and space. This leads to the basic principle of creation. Space is the ultimate substance filled with minute particles called 'Parmanu' (nucleus). Every Parmanu is a minute space possessing energy. It is absolute abstraction of the universe of the ultimate form. The space is luminous as the particles are always emitting light. This material is called Vastu which is external and metamorphosises itself into the manifest world. It is super-potential and hypersensitive. It vibrates in dimension of time (Kala). The space is sensitive enough to order these vibrations into rhythms. The fusion of space and time, when interlocked with Prakriti and Purush takes the form of Vastu. The architect or artist assumes the role of Jivaatman, the microcosm. The macrocosm is the Parmataman. They are all linked by common vibrating measures and resonate by virtue of Kala measure. This is a spiritual experience, leading one to the world of peace and bliss. The architect, therefore, has to understand the underlying principles of Prakriti, Purush, Pran and Kala (time), in order to evolve an integral vision and process of planning, design and building.

COMPONENTS OF VASTU-PURUSH-MANDALA

VASTU (Space/Settlement)

- Interlocking & harmonious inter-relationship among Purush, Prakriti & Kala which bestows auspiciousness, exuberance and beauty.

PURUSH (Mankind)	*PRAN (Life)*	*OBJECT*
Peace	Creation	Fertility & Compassion
Harmony	Movement	Clarity, Purity & Integrity
Happiness	Actions	Bliss, Joy of creativity
Tranquility	Destruction	Cyclic Rejuvenation
Spiritual Attainment	Stillness	Enlightenment

PRAKRITI (Nature)

Element Vision	*Symbolic Colour*	*Symbolic Process*		*Sense*
Earth (Brahma)	Yellow	Differentiation/ origination	Nivritti (Freedom)	Smell
Water (Vishnu)	White	Transformation/ binding	Pratishtha (Dignity)	Taste
Fire (Rudra)	Red	Propagation/ Interlocking	Vidya (Knowledge)	Form
Air (Uswara)	Dark	Conditoning/ overlapping	Shanti (Peace)	Touch
Ether (Sadasiva)	White	Continuity (Transcending)	Santya (Spiritual Tranquillity)	Sound

The traditional vision seeks consciousness to order these components into an organic and interactive relationship through understanding, feeling, thought and action. Consciousness is expressed in the objects and events, and the expression continues on through perception, interpretation, judgement and comprehension. The ordering of subsistence ensures harmony, peace and purity in life. The ordering of distinction on the basis of time, place, ethnic groups and aesthetic considerations allows the formation of distinctive lifestyles. It facilitates achieving an equilibrium between the natural elements and the human being and between internal and external energies.

Today this cycle has been disrupted leading to breakdown of human, social and physical / environmental inter-relationship. There is a need to re-establish a balance and organic relationship between the nature, human consumption (space, air, water, food, energy) and the economy. The challenge is to re-establish the uterine relationship between nature and man. The ecological cycle, which has been disrupted by indiscriminate economic and physical demands of development needs to be revived. Looking at the damage which our cities and development have inflicted upon the physical, social and cultural heritage, one of the prime agenda is to explore the possibility of creating a living environment which is self-sufficient, ecologically balanced and culturally stimulating. We need to relook at the fundamentals of human settlements and rediscover the sustainable habitat so that harmony and inter-relationship between nature and life can be re-established.

A habitat is not just its physical attributes, but also its cultural, mythical and metaphysical contents, which include the following:

- Sense of pride, faith and image, dreams and aspirations
- Cultural, educational and intellectual development
- Multi-culturalism
- Sense of belonging, social interaction
- Spatial experience

- Environmental compatibility
- Equity, participation and affordability
- Physical infrastructure, networks and communications.
- Incrementality
- Personal, social and economic opportunities, employment generation
- Pluralism, change and renewal
- Safety and security
- Meeting functional needs
- Health, physical comfort, and privacy

Sustainable development is basically a concern of 'design with nature'. It means development and human interventions in natural system to the extent of carrying capacity of an area. The carrying capacity of an area is the population or level of activity that can be sustained for a given length of time without depletion of the resources or breakdown of the biological (natural) systems. In order to address to the needs of the majority of the people, that is poor, a major focus area has to be local economic promotion and poverty reduction. Among the young generation there is a widespread perception that the future holds nothing for them, as a result, a large number of the unemployed are forced to take on informal, illegal or uncertain jobs. While entrepreneurial potential and development opportunities lie untapped, the cities and municipalities lose out on tax revenue. This sort of situation is not attractive for investors, and the economic development stagnates, while the vicious circle of poverty perpetuates. As such, there is an urgent need to focus on the promotion of small and medium-sized enterprises (SME) and the local and regional economy of the city. The growth opportunities of existing enterprises, value added chains that are labour intensive, facilitating business start-ups and attracting new businesses will enhance the competitiveness of the city.

The natural ground forms are best accepted as given. They are the resolutions of myriad forces at work over a long span of time. To adapt to them is to harmonise with the forces and conditions by which they have evolved. By means of site reconnaissance and soil surveys the most productive land can be designated for lawns, gardens or crop production or can be preserved in its natural state. The basic idea should be to achieve a harmonions inter-relationship between the people, nature and time. This can be achieved by an interactive ordering of the elements of nature, viz, land, water, energy, air and space.

The backbone of new urbanism is the synergy at the policy, planning and design levels. Planning and urban development should integrate employment, housing, slum rehabilitation, industry, transport, energy, water, waste management, sanitation, and drainage into a composite whole. It should not only look back to cultivate indigenous knowledge and resources but also relate to the future growth potential and environmental constraints. It is necessary to remember what Mark Twain said "...... do not part with your dreams, you may exist but cease to live!"

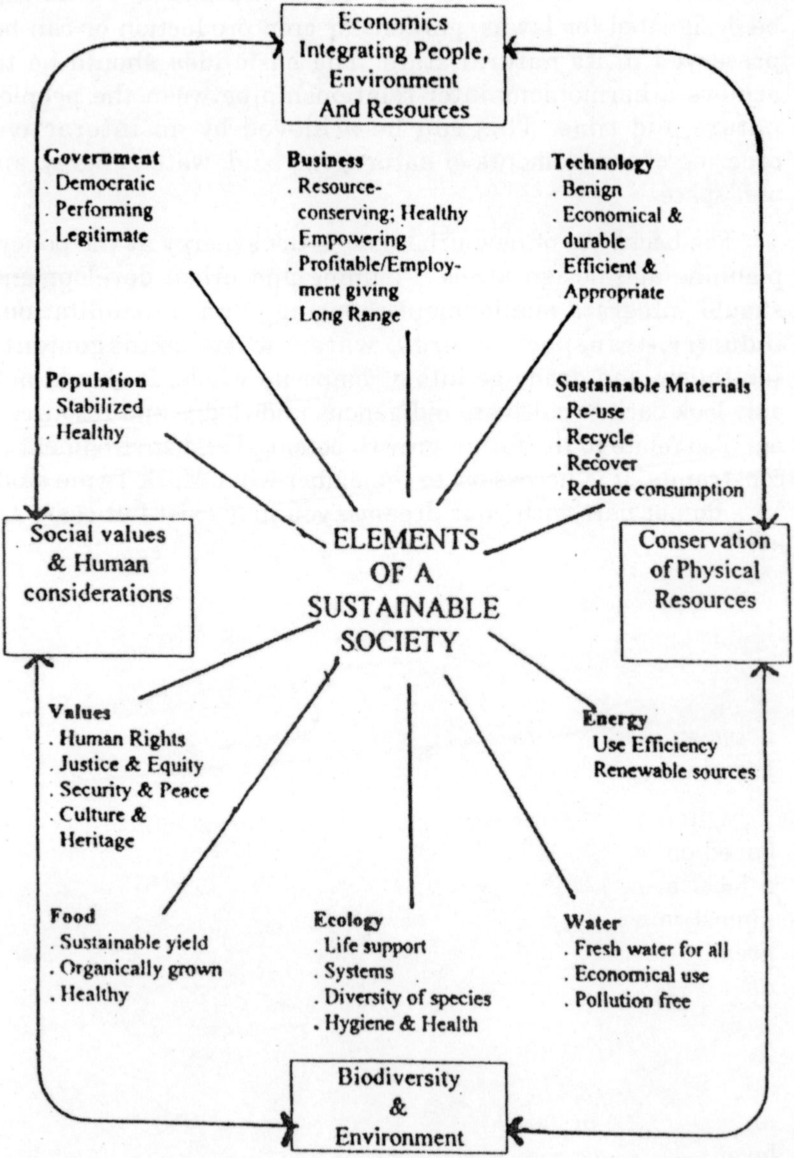

Elements of A Sustainable Society

11

DECENTRALISED AND PARTICIPATORY LOCAL PLANNING PROCESS

"Go in search of your people, love them, learn from them, plan with them, serve them, begin with what they have, but of the best of leaders when their task is accomplished, their work is done, the people all remark, we have done it ourselves."

—Lao Tsu (500 BC)

The conventional Development Plans are prepared by the Town and Country Planning Departments, often without people's participation. By and large it is purely a professional exercise, obviously disowned by people and decision-makers. A major drawback of the conventional development plans is that these are seldom integrated with the Five Year Plans and budgets of the State or country, thus there has been gap between planning and implementation, and mismatch between the plans, projects / programmes and financing.

Often no attempt is made for either identifying a key sector based on character of the area or coordinating allied sectors of a local area. Local experience and indigenous knowledge are almost missing from the conventional planning process. In the preparation of the local plans, scientific study and analysis are usually lacking and there are gaps between research and local actions. Over-emphasis on the physical / spatial aspects frequently results into overloading organization, socio-economic and legal aspects. The close door approach often leads to predominance of individually benefited projects rather than city level and long range perspective. Often the official plans are criticized for their slow progress and rigidity. The ownership of the plan is very important in a democratic process, alongwith a scientific approach and use of modern technology, which should be blended with the peoples's participation.

Concept of Decentralised Planning Process

The concept of decentralized planning process is based on a combination of top-down and grass-root-up approach. The State of Kerala, has been a pioneer in decentralized planning. The State covers an area of 38,863 sq.km. and has a population of 32 million (2001) in its 14 districts. The State is known for its highest literacy rate in India (91%) and for its educational, healthcare and labour welfare facilities. In 1996, a new planning process was introduced in Kerala through the launching of people's campaign for decentralized planning, popularly known in Malayalam as 'Jankeeyasoothranam'. This was undertaken during the preparation of the Ninth Five Year Plan of the State.

The people's planning campaign empowers local people to prepare plans for local development for which the State's Plan funds are devolved to the local government; who formulate and implement the projects by actively involving people at various stages. So far about 1200 plans (DR) and more than 100,000 projects have been prepared. Technical Advisory Committee of experts in various fields provides research inputs in the planning process, enabling application of latest research in local planning.

Considering the spirit of 73rd and 74th Constitutional Amendments, draft Local Development Plan at Gram Panchayat/ Municipality level is prepared first. Then regional plan, i.e., Integrated District Development Plan (IDDP) is prepared on the basis of Local Development Plans of the constituents of the District, and forwarded for the sanction of the government. Afterwards the draft LDP is modified and forwarded for sanction based on the sanctioned IDDP.

Organisational Set-up for LDP and IDDP

Fig.1 shows the organizational set-up of District Planning Committee created for the preparation of LDP and IDDP. As shown, the District Planning Committee (DPC) constituted under 74th Constitutional Amendment is the apex body with the Department of Town and Country Planning acting as the nodal agency for the preparation of the plans. A coordination committee is formed at district level consisting of mainly elected political heads of Local Self-Government Institutions (LSGI). The objective of the committee is initiating the process of the preparation of the LDP by respective LSGI.

Fig. 1. Organisational Set-up for the preparation ofIntegrated District Development Plan and Local Development Plans

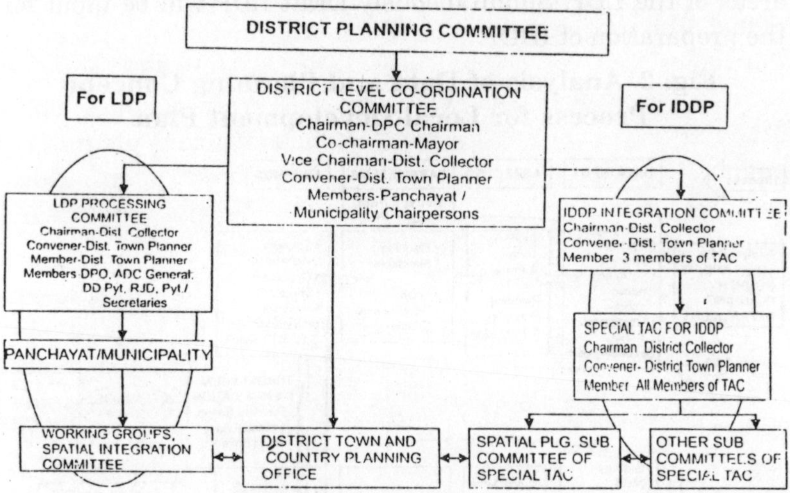

Abbreviations

IDDP – Integrated District Development Plan

LDP – Local Development Plan

TAC – Technical Advisory Committee

Source: Adapted on the basis of Easow and Thomas (2005)

For the preparation of the LDP, Panchayat Municipality is the apex body. Under each LSGI, eleven Working Groups, namely agriculture, industries, poverty reduction and social security, schedule caste and tribe, health, education, infrastructure, environment, financial resources and watershed development, are constituted for data collection and for a brief analysis of each LDP. Each Working Group consists of elected representatives, government officials, NGOs etc. A core committee of these Working Groups is formed as Spatial Integration Committee (SIC). SIC of LSGIs has a key role in the preparation of their LDP and has the overall responsibility right from data collection to report writing. Figure 2 indicates the process of the data analysis and planning concepts for the preparation for Local Development Plan. An integrated finding of the analysis will result in identification of thrust areas, followed by planning concept, policies and strategies and finally Draft LDP. These are formulated jointly by Town and Country Planning Department and Spatial Integration Committee. The findings from the IDDP analysis also form an input for the identification of the thrust areas of the LDP. Simultaneously Draft LDP will be input for the preparation of IDDP.

Fig. 2. Analysis of Data and Planning Concept Process for Local Development Plan

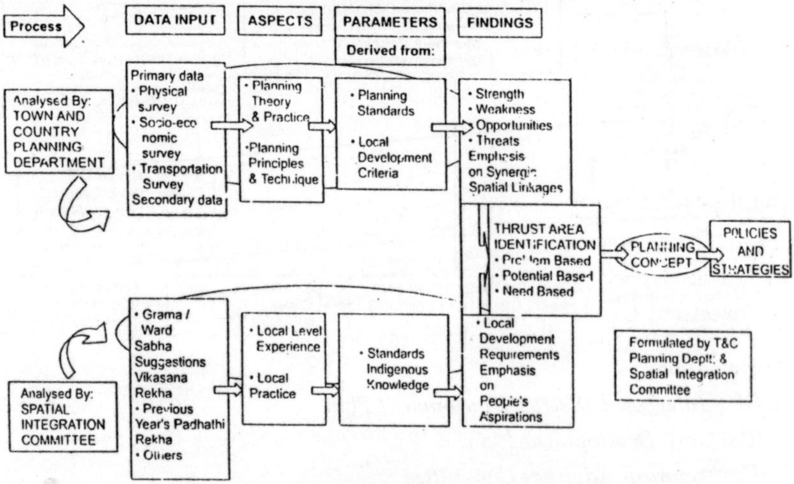

Source: Adapted from Easow and Thomas (2005)

For the preparation of the IDDP, a Technical Advisory Committee (TAC) is constituted and its members are elected representatives like DPC members (who act as chairmen of the various sub-committees), district heads of government departments (normally convener of the subcommittee), NGOs, representatives of research wings and educational institutions, etc. This special TAC has 19 members of sub-committees on : 1. Agriculture 2. Irrigation 3. Water shed Development and Land Utilisation 4. Forest and Environment 5. Animal Husbandary and Dairy Development 6. Fisheries 7. Industries and Co-operation 8. Transportation and Housing 9. Health 10. Drinking Water and Sanitation 11. Education 12. Finance 13. Social Welfare 14. Poverty Alleviation and Rural Development 15.

Power and Communications 16. Scheduled Castes and Scheduled Tribes (SC & ST) Development 17. Tourism, Culture and Sports 18. Human Resource, and 19. Spatial Planning. Spatial Planning Sub Committee of the Special TAC is the key committee of the whole project for plan preparation and also acts as the implementation committee of the project. A core committee is also constituted from Special TAC for validation of suggestions of the special TAC. Figure 3 indicates the process of preparation and synchronization of Local Development Plans and Integrated District Development Plan.

Preparation Process of LDP

At the State level, a steering committee functions within the Town and Country Planning Department, for both the LDP and IDDP, which is headed by the Chief Town Planner. As given below, there are four main stages involved in the preparation of an Integrated District Development Plan.

Fig. 3. LDP & IDDP: The Planning and Synchronization Process

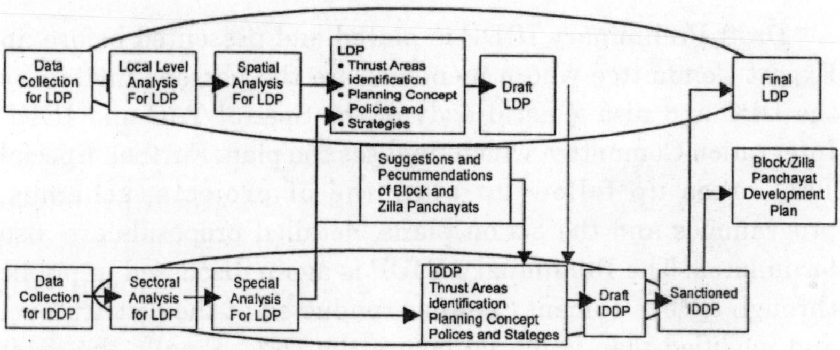

1. Preparatory Works

- Preparation of the base map of the district;
- Preparation of checklist for secondary data collection and collections of other relevant materials, etc.

2. Data Collection and Compilation

- District level secondary data collection through Special TAC and various departments;

- Feeding the data into the computer and linking with the GIS.

3. Analysis

In preparation of IDDP analysis are undertaken twice – one by various Sub-Committees of Special TAC, named as sectoral analysis and other done by the Department of Town and Country Planning, named as Spatial Analysis. Analysing the past trends of development of the sector, study of present scenario, identification and prioritization of problems and potentials, identification of solutions and enhancement of potentials, evaluation of ongoing / committed projects and programmes, formulation of sectoral policies and suggestions, etc. are some of the assignments in the sectoral analysis.

4. Plan Formulation

After the analysis, and thrust area identification the planning concept is developed alongwith formulation of the strategies and policies. Based on all these the final product, named as Draft Integrated District Development Plan is evolved.

Draft Preliminary IDDP is placed and presented before an Expert Committee whose members are the persons invited by the DPC and also general body of the Special TAC and IDDP Integration Committee which finalises the plan. Further, Special TAC takes up follow up planning of projects, schemes, programmes and the action plans, detailed proposals are also formulated. The Preliminary IDDP is again discussed in public through a Development Seminar conducted at the district level and modified plan is placed before the DPC. Finally the draft IDDP is forwarded to the government for sanction.

Processes involved for the final LDP are given below:

- Modification of draft LDP based on sanctioned IDDP by the SIC.
- Modification of the Draft LDP based on the Development Seminar.
- Sanctioning of LDP by the DPC

Components of LDP

The Local Development Plan consists of two basic components:

(*i*) Perspective Plan for 15-20 years, which contains:

- A policy Plan
- Spatial Strategies for optimum utilization of resources
- Infrastructure plan

(*ii*) An Execution Plan for 5 years which contains:

- Strategy for development incorporating physical, social and economic dimensions
- General land use plan
- Infrastructure plan
- Transportation plan
- Sectoral strategies for integrated development
- Development Code / Controls

Components of IDDP

The IDDP consists of two basic components:

(*i*) A Perspective Plan for 15-20 years:

- Settlements pattern giving hierarchy and functions of settlements
- Development policies for integrated development,
- Regional Infrastructure Plan

(*ii*) An Execution Plan for 5 years:

- Strategy for integrated development
- Transportation networks
- Location criteria for services and facilities
- Rationalisation of fund allocation
- Specific projects to be implemented.

A salient feature of the decentralized planning is the funding for the preparation of the LDP and IDDP. The plan preparation project of LDP and IDDP originated from Kollam District and had been formulated as a joint project of all the LSGIs of the district. The entire LSGIs of Kollam district were allocated funds from their Tenth Five Year Plan, as given in Table-1:

Table 1. Allocated Funds Distribution from the Tenth Five-Year Plan in Kollam District (Kerala)

Sl. No.	*LSGI*	*2003-04*	*2004-05*	*2005-06*	*Total*
1.	Jilla Panchayat	Rs. 40,000	Rs. 5,75,00	Rs. 25,000	Rs. 6.40,000
2.	Block Panchayat	Rs. 90,000	Rs. 50,000	Rs. 25,000	Rs. 1,65,000
3.	Grama Panchayat	Rs. 98,000	Rs. 40,000	Rs. 25,000	Rs. 1,63,000
4.	Municipal Council	Rs. 1,81,500	Rs. 50,000	Rs. 25,000	Rs. 2,56,500
5.	Municipal Corporation	Rs. 2,82,000	Rs. 60,000	Rs. 25,000	Rs. 3,67,000

The Lessons Learnt

The Kerala experience provides an innovative example of bridging the divide between planning and Local Action. It brings together the people and the government, long range planning and short range prgrammes and synchronises the planning with the implementation. The preparation of about 1,200 plans (DR) and more than 100,000 Projects during last 7 years indicates the success of the campaign. The State Government has devolved about 35 to 40 per cent of Plan funds to the local government. There has been encouraging active participation of the local population in the planning process and workshops, through the awareness campaigns, handouts, handbooks, manuals, capacity building and interactive web sites.

The Kerala experience provides useful lesson for decentralised and participatory planning framework which needs the following key reforms:

- Localisation and decentralisation of planning.
- Community empowerment, partnership and constituency planning.

- Government as facilitator for people-centred planning.
- Adoption of principles of Devolution, Debueaucratisation, Deregulation & Decontrol.
- Efficiency, equity and employment generation and economic potential as the basic criteria.
- Release access to land, housing, services, finance and information by public-private partnerships.
- Planning to promote micro-enterprises and micro-banking.
- New methods of land assembly and development.
- Regularisation of land tenure; simplify and expedite land registration.
- Review and simplify property taxation.
- Emphasise cost recovery and "user pays"
- Eliminate monopoly practices, including government monopolies
- Make urban development self-financing and self-sustaining by developing the concepts of Excess Condemnation, TDR, Accommodation Reservation, land pooling and readjustment, development and conversion charges, betterment levy, additional FAR charges, BOT, franchising, contracting out, etc..
- Simplification and devolution of planning and building controls and approval.
- Replace building byelaws by development control rules/ planning permissions.
- Review all urban legislations and scrap outdated ones.
- Simplify procedures
- Establish regulatory authority for privatization and PPP.
- Minimize legal complexity, maximize enforcement and empower community.

Legal & Para- legal Reforms

The prevailing understanding of legislation is a hierarchy of laws – (*i*) the Constitution, (*ii*) The Acts (Central and State), (*iii*) Regulations, byelaws, rules and Mandatory administrative/ government orders, (*iv*) Statutory Plans, zoning, development controls and architectural controls. In a democratic context where people are involved, the 'legislation' is to be seen in a broader context, beyond its punitive aspect. There are various examples of 'para-legal' measures, which have been successfully adopted for urban planning and development by way of a participatory process. These are often in the form of:

- Policy Planning Guidelines
- Charter
- Code of Conduct and Ethics (social, community, professional and religious)
- Incentives (such as land use flexibility, Transferable Development Rights Waive of Building Byelaws
- Standards, norms and specifications
- Empowerment Zone Partnership and Community Enterprise Promotion.

A major para legal provision can be Empowerment Zone Partnerships and Community Enterprise Promotion for urban regeneration. The key lies in community empowerment which requires decentralisation, deregulation, devolution and decontrol, together with better coordination and allocations at all levels – the government, local authority and the community:

Community Level	*Local Authority Level*	*Community Level*
Remove regulatory barriers	Invest state resources or funds	Involve the entire community
Simplify programme & rules	Decentralize	Plan comprehensively
Co-ordinate programmes	Develop and Decontrol Co-ordinate programme	Leverage private resources
Invest broad resources	Simplify procedures and approvals	Streamline planning process, monitoring implementation and accountability

The Kerala case study demonstrates that an emerging challenge in the urban and legal reforms pertains to the transformation of current institutions and systems of planning. These transformations should start with of local and community-based governance. The 73rd and 74th Constitutional amendments provide the basis for a process of devolution based on subsidiarity built around local communities.

The planning legislation is to be viewed in a broader context, which should include para-legal measures, comprising of a set of policy planning guidelines, charter / code of conduct, community empowerment and partnerships. These require concerted actions at the government, local and community levels, where planners can play the role of a catalyst.

The earlier studies believed that an area of trees 30-40 square meters supplied the oxygen requirement for one man. However, this is to be seen with respect to type of plants, pollution level, micro-climate and other factors

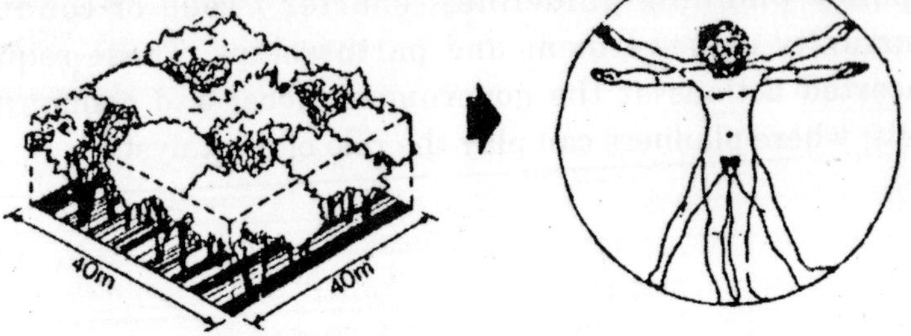

Plants reduce Particulate Air Pollution

Source: Spirn

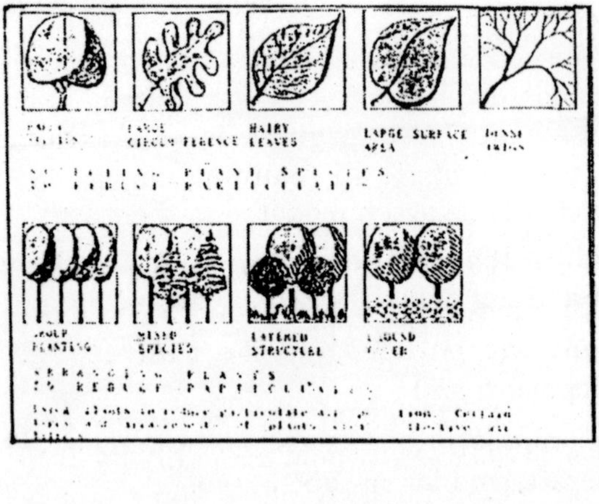

12

CONCEPT AND CONTENTS OF LOCAL AREA PLAN

Our concern is for the joy of the community for the sense of belonging.

—Alison and Peter Smithson

The Master Plan for Delhi-2021 has introduced the concept of Local Area Plan which means the plan of a ward/sub-zone to be prepared and approved by concerned local body. Based on the Master Plan and Zonal Plans framework, the planning at Local level should set up a broad framework for participatory planning. It aims to ensure that the plans for development are realistic and respond to the local needs.

Within the overall framework of Structure Plan/Master Plan or zonal development plan, the Local Area Plan sets out detailed policies and specific proposals for the development and use of land, and should guide most day-to-day planning decisions. The preparation of local plans gives local communities the opportunity to participate in planning choices about where development should be accommodated in their area.

In providing the detailed framework for the control of development and use of land, local plans need to:

- Set out the policies for the control/regulation of development; and
- Make proposals for the development and use of land and to allocate land for specific purposes.

These proposals are to be shown on Survey base maps. A local plan may designate any part of the city/municipal area as an action area for development, redevelopment or improvement. The Local Area Plan should include the policies and proposals for the development and use of land and, in particular, those which will form the basis for deciding planning applications and determining the conditions attached to planning permissions with sufficient precision to enable them readily to be implemented and performance measured.

The plan proposals should illustrate each of the detailed policies and proposals in the written statement, defining sites for particular developments or land uses and the areas to which specified development control policies will be applied. Boundaries of locally or nationally designated areas, such as, heritage sites/ zones, conservation areas, redevelopment areas, etc.

Local Area Plans should necessarily have the following:

(*i*) Title, its legality, plan approving authority,

(*ii*) Purpose and context

The plan should make clear in the introduction what its role and purpose is and briefly explain the planning framework within which it is prepared i.e. national and regional policies and, where appropriate, structure plans. A brief explanation should be included of the plan's relationship with the authority's other policies, programmes and management strategies, and with the planning policies of neighbouring authorities.

(*iii*) Vision, strategy, aims, objectives and target

Each plan should also include in the introduction a clear and concise statement of its main aims, objectives and targets, and the strategy for achieving them, having regard to the likely level of resources available, both public and private sector. Taken together, the strategy, aims, objectives and targets should provide a clear vision of what will be achieved by the implementation of the plan, and make clear the authority's priorities at the outset. When consulting at pre-planning stage it may sometimes be useful to include for discussion, alternative policies and proposals together with an assessment of their relative merits.

The establishment of aims, objectives and targets in the plan and a clear indication of how the policies and proposals will be implemented, by which agency and over what period, will assist monitoring of both implementation and the effectiveness of policies.

The Local Area Plan should be clear, succinct and easily understood by all those who need to know about the planning policies and proposals which apply in the area. The needs of different groups should be carefully considered in determining the approach and style of the plan. The use of a plan summary and a full index will help to make the plan more accessible. Jargon should be avoided as far as possible. Where it is necessary to use technical terms, these should be explained in a glossary.

The written statement should be clear and concise and should be limited to those policies and proposals which genuinely provide a strategic framework for local plans and development control. Policies and proposals should be clearly and unambiguously expressed, with sufficient precision to enable them readily to be implemented and their performance measured. In the event of a contradiction between the written statement and the diagrams, the written statement prevails.

Preparing a Local Area Plan

A Local Area Plan should generally include the following:

- Vision statement
- Site and its context
- Policy review and objectives
- Programme of requirements
- Planning principles and parameters
- Concepts and proposals
- Proposed development process
- Feasibility appraisal
- Implementation aspects
- Costs, phasing and timing of development.

The following are the major components, which provide a framework of the Local Area Plan:

- Land uses
- Organisation of space for various activities:
  - Housing, slums and inner city areas, villages, etc.
  - Unauthorised colonies
  - Work centres, commercial use
  - Mixed use streets/areas
  - Transportation, parking, cycle track, walkways, pedestrianisation, etc.
  - Parks, playgrounds and sports

- Community facility
- Utilities and services

- Archaeology, ancient monuments, listed buildings, and conservation areas
- Sites of special scenic interest
- Local nature reserves, protected flora and fauna, nature conservation, and green strategies.

The following critical areas should be systematically documented, analysed and addressed in the process of Local Area Planning.

1. Ecology

- Landscape setting and type
- Land form, contours, drainage, geology, soils, etc.
- Hydrology (including rivers, streams, lakes, ponds, and swampy or floodable ground, sub-soil water, etc.)
- Flora, fauna, trees and hedgerows
- Climate, wind direction, microclimate, orientation, etc.

2. Human Impact

- Census data related to settlements/area, component of migrants, children, women and older persons, occupations, incomes, poverty assessment, informal sector, homeless, health conditions.
- Boundaries of the site and area
- Contamination, pollution, noise, sub-soil water, sewerage, solid waste disposal etc.
- Aesthetics quality
- Heritage resource and historical development, settlement pattern, archaeology, cultural characteristics, local history, events / festivals, place names,

3. Public Realm

- Planting
- Street furniture
- Structures

- Safety and security
- Maintenance

4. Ease of movement

- Public transport roads, railways, cycle tracks, etc.
- Access to site including bicycles, service vehicles and pedestrians (including those with restricted mobility
- Parking
- Pedestrian routes and flows
- Cycling corridors
- Transport proposals, assessment and green travel plans
- Air quality

5. Legibility (ease of understanding)

- Identity, image and perception
- Local views
- Strategic views '
- Vistas
- Landmarks
- Skyline
- Roofscape
- Gateways
- Thresholds
- Boundaries and barriers
- Nodes

Planning Checklist

It is useful to work out a list of site data that will be required in order to guide the evolution of the parameters, options and proposals for Local Area Planning. An illustrative checklist alongwith typical impact questions is given below:

General Site Context:

– Geographic location, adjacent land use patterns, access system, nearby destinations and facilities, stability or change in development pattern.

- Ecological and hydrographic system of the region.
- Nature of the area economy, other proposals or projects nearby and their effects on the site.

Typical Impact Questions:

- Will important locations or resources become inaccessible to the general public?
- Will the project put an undue traffic load on its surroundings?

PHYSICAL DATA, SITE AND ADJACENT LAND

(1) Geology and Soil:

- Underlying geology, rock character and depth, fault lines.
- Soil types and depth, value as an engineering materials and as a plant medium, presence of hazardous chemicals or contaminants.
- Areas of fill or ledge, liability to slides or subsidence, water mining - potential.

Typical Impact Question:

- Will the soil be contaminated?
- Can the soil absorb likely wastes without damage?

(2) Water:

- Existing water bodies - variation and purity.
- Natural and man-made drainage channels - flow, capacity, purity.
- Surface drainage pattern - amount, directions, blockages, flood zones, undrained depressions, areas of continuing erosion.
- Water table - elevation and fluctuations, springs, flow directions, presence of deep aquifers.
- Water supply - location, quantity and quality.

Typical Impact Questions:

- Can the drainage system accept the additional runoff?
- Will lands be flooded, erosion be induced, or water bodies caused to fluctuate?

- Will the water table rise or fall, affecting vegetation, basements or foundations?
- Will ground water be contaminated, or the recharge or draw-down of aquifers be affected?

(3) Topography:

- Contours
- Pattern of landforms - typology, slopes, circulation possibilities, access points, barriers, visibility.
- Unique features

Typical lmpact Question:

- Will unique or valued landforms be damaged?

(4) Climate:

- Regional pattern of temperature, humidity, precipitation, sun angles, cloudiness, direction and speeds.
- Local microclimate : warm and cool, slope wind deflection and local breeze, air, drainage, shade, heat reflection and storage, plant indicators.
- Ambient air quality, dust, smells, sound levels.

Typical Impact Questions:

- Will local micro-climates be affected adversely - by the deflection or funneling of wind, the shading or reflection of sunlight, the drying or humidifying of the air; the intensification of dismal temperature ranges'?
- Will air pollution increase or dust or obnoxious odors be generated?
- Will the project increase or decrease disturbing noise levels?

(5) Ecology:

- Dominant plant and animal communities - their location and relative stability, self-regulation, and vulnerability.
- General pattern of plant cover, quality of wooded areas, wind firmness, regeneration potential.
- Specimen trees - their location, spread, species, elevation at base, whether unique or endangered, support system needed.

Typical Impact Question:

- Will important plants be disrupted ? Will it be difficult for them to relocate or to regenerate themselves?
- Will rare or endangered species be destroyed or pest species increase?
- Will the project cause eutrophication of water bodies or algal blooms?

(6) Man-made Structures and Networks:

- Existing buildings : location, outline, floor elevations, type, condition, current use.
- Networks : roads, paths, rails, transit corridors, sewers, water lines, gas, electricity, telephone, etc. their location, elevations, capacity, condition.
- Fences, walls, decks, other human modifications to the landscape.

Typical Impact Questions:

- Will present and planned roads and utilities serve the site without adverse impact on adjacent areas?
- Will the project require a substantial investment in surrounding roads and utilities?
- Can these new facilities be adequately maintained and operated?
- Will new structures conflict with or damage existing ones?

(7) Sensory Qualities:

- Character and relationship of visual spaces and sequences.
- Viewpoints, vistas, focal points.

Typical Impact Questions:

- Is the new landscape in character with the existing one?
- Are existing views and focal points conserved and enhanced?
- Are the new buildings compatible in character with the existing structures to be retained?

SITE AND ADJACENT LAND

(1) Site values, rights, constraints:

- Ownerships, easements and other rights.
- Zoning and other regulations that influence site use and character.
- Economic value and how it varies across the site.
- Accepted "territories".

Typical Impact Questions:

- Will the economic values of the site or its surroundings be depreciated or enhanced?
- Will ownerships or customary "territories" be significantly disrupted?

(2) Past and future:

- History of the site and heritage value.
- Public and private intentions for future use of site.

Typical Impact Questions:

- Are historic structures conserved?
- Are archaeological sites, listed buildings and heritage zones conserved?
- Does the plan disrupt or facilitate change?
- Does it conflict with any existing plans for the future?

Coorelation of Data:

- Subdivisions of the site : areas of consistent structures, character, problems.
- Identification of key points, axis, area best left undeveloped, areas where intensive development is possible.
- Ongoing changes, and those likely to happen.
- Ties to context - current and possible linkages, areas where consistent use is desirable, patterns of movement to be preserved.

13

SHELTER FOR THE URBAN POOR

"Long did I cherish a desire, neither for wealth or fortune, but my house tucked away in a corner of the earth, where I could be with my thoughts." —*Rabindra Nath Tagore*

According to the Ministry of Urban Housing and Poverty Alleviation (2007), the total housing shortage in India (as per 2001 Census) was about 24.71 million Dwelling Units (DUs), out of which 21.78 million DUs relate to the Economically Weaker Sections (EWS), while 2.89 million DUs are required for Low Income Group (LIG). The housing shortage during the 11th Plan period (2007-12) is expected to be 26.53 million DUs, out of which just 0.004 million DUs will be in High Income Group (HIG) and Middle Income Group (MIG).

About one-half of the population of India's major metropolitan centres, like Delhi, Kolkata, Mumbai and Chennai are living in various types of illegal, squatter and slum settlements. The proportion is even higher in other cities. It is a paradox that the number of homeless, squatters and slum dwellers in the Indian Cities is increasing in proportion to public housing programmes. In spite of ever increasing investments in housing, the problem remains stupendous. This informal solution to the deficiencies of housing and urban development programmes in open defiance of planning legislation illustrates the extent to which popular measures regulate the process of change and provide shelter to the poor.

The prevailing approach towards the problem of housing is dominated by demographic, economic and technological attitudes. The problem of slums, squatters and homeless is seen as a by-product of population growth and migration to urban centres. Normally, the programmes and policies are based on the following premises:

(*i*) Housing is a centralised and organised activity;

(*ii*) Housing is a package of final product.

(*iii*) The standards have to be in consonance with the affordability and investments.

(*iv*) Stratification of Society according to economic levels

(*v*) To cover a vast proportion of population with limited investment, the size of dwelling units, their specifications/infrastructure norms are continually lowered.

(*vi*) Standardisation of space, development and construction.

Housing Typologies

Urban housing is characterised by a very segmented market with a complex network of access, as summarised below:

- Informal Settlements
- Traditional Villages
- Unauthorised Colonies (Regularised)
- Public Housing Plots
- Government Employee Housing
- Public Housing Flats
- Housing Cooperatives
- Planned Colonies
- Old City Housing

Shelter of the Lowest Income Group

The poor live in various types of housing, which includes pavement dwellers (or doorstep dwellers), in dilapidated old buildings, hutments, spontaneous, irregular colonies, etc., as given below:

Shelter Typology Problems and Solutions

Type	*Solutions*
1. Rundown walk-ups in core areas (generally third generation households) as renters protected by rent control.	Cooperatising; buying off land lord (at 100 times assessed rent in Mumbai) – Reconstructing at site with municipal support with transit accommodation provided during construction with ownership of constructed units through soft loans/subsidised rentals.
2. Pavement/doorstep dwellers in core areas (generally new entrants to the city as individuals).	Sanitation through night shelters, pay and use toilets, health facilities; when households formed, a few could be rehabilitated in Site & Services Schemes; otherwise they move in spontaneous colonies.
3. Spontaneous colonies in core and intermediate areas-in marginal lands (generally second generation households near place of work space) – single/double storeyed construction of non-permanent material.	Granting tenural rights and sanitisation of environments (paving, street lighting, drainage, individual ablution facilities, potable water) or gradual reconstruction/upgrading. They qualify for relocation if colony in full or part is required for a public purpose (e.g., road widening).
4. Spontaneous colonies in peri-urban areas (generally new migrants). Single storeyed improvised shelter.	Sanitisation of environment and granting tenural rights over a period of time.
5. Site and service schemes serviced plots with or without built ablution facilities and sometimes a roof-single or double storeyed in peri-urban areas.	Reduced planning and space standards – heavy initial public investments.
6. Built units in 4 storeyed walk-ups in peri-urban areas or 8-16 storeyed slab blocks in central areas on subsidised rentals.	Regular public housing which not be lowest income group housing

Source : Adapted from UN-Habitat, 1998, AMDA and other sources

The settlements of the poor are usually categorized, as slums and squatters (jhuggi-jhompri), etc.. It is necessary to understand where and how they live in the city, a broadbrush picture of which is given below:

How the Pook Live and Sustain

Type	*Sub-Type*	*Main Economic Activity*	*Main Locations*	*Interventions*	*Storeys*
Squatters On-street	– Linear and sporadic by individuals	Daily wage employment	Inner city pavements	Transient Services	Gr.
	– Linear and sporadic	Information trade + Supplementary employment	Marginal Strips in intermediate or periphery Zones	Transient Services	Gr.
Squatters Off-street	– Amorphous areas occupied by households	Informal trade + Supplementary employment	Areas in intermediate or Periphery zones	In-situ upgrading through infused services	Gr.
	– Defined area reorganised	Regular employment or Organised trade + supplementary employment	Sites in intermediate or Periphery zones	In-situ reorganisation of services and designed built space.	Gr.+1
Inner City Slums	– Defined area incrementally transfromed	Organised trade + supplementary employment	Areas in inner city	In-situ transformation through infused services and flexible bye-laws	G G+1 G+2
	– Define sites of walk-ups reconstructed	Regular Employment	Sites in inner city	In-situ designed re-construction	G+3 G+4
Organised	– Serviced plots	Informal trade + supplementary employment	Planned locations in intermediate or Periphery zones	Planned and designed relocation	G/G+4
	– Serviced plots and built wet areas	Regular/ Organised employment	-do-	-do-	-do-
	– Serviced plots and designed built units	-do-	-do-	-do-	-do-

Source : Adopted from E.F.N. Ribeiro/ AMDA (May, 2000)

Starting with the Slum Area (Improvement and Clearance) Act, 1956, and the objective of the public agencies had been to make the city slum free and provide housing to the slum dwellers. In this process, a variety of approaches, such as provision of built / low cost housing, site and services schemes, Low-cost built up housing, cluster housing etc. have been tried. In general, a three pronged strategy had been adopted for improvement of the shelter for those residing in the slums and Jhuggi-Jompri (JJ) Clusters. These are:

(*i*) Relocation / resettlement,

(*ii*) On site upgradation,

(*iii*) Environmental Improvement in JJ Clusters/Slum areas.

What Went Wrong?

In spite of various efforts 'nothing ever gets built on schedule or within budget' has almost because a dictum. The problem of shelter, especially for the poor, looms large all over. It would not be justifiable to blame the professionals/ building industry or the government. In fact no single reason would be enough to explain the reasons for this situation.

CHEOP'S LAW
Nothing ever gets built on schedule or within budget.

Several gaps, missing connections and barriers can be identified for the persisting shortage of shelter, such as given below:

- Gap Between planning, design and engineering practice

GAP BETWEEN PLANNING / DESIGN AND SYSTEMS BUILDING

- Missing Connections between:
  - Planning and systems Building
  - Design and Modular Coordination
  - Technology and Artisanal building practices
  - Management and Public Participation
  - State / formal sector and Informal Sector

No breakthrough can be achieved unless the following barriers are broken:

- Planning and design (which synthesise policies, strategies and practices)
- Legal framework and procedures (you get third rate quality for third rate payment)
- Financial resources
- Technological and operational

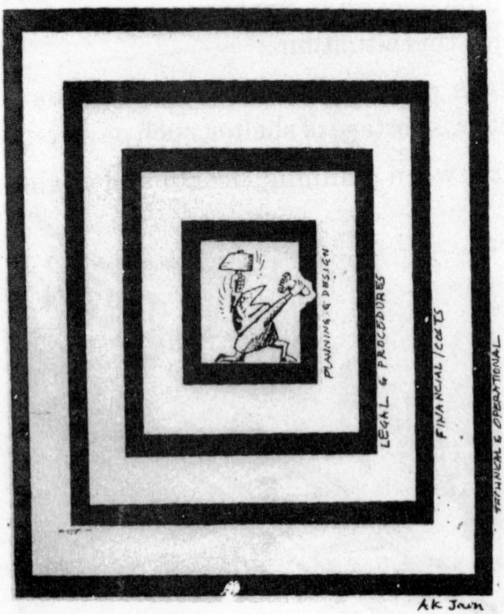

Shelter for the masses is not a simple technological issue or a mere problem of the finances. It is a complex amalgam of a host of factors, which need to be tackled at all levels and in a holistic manner:

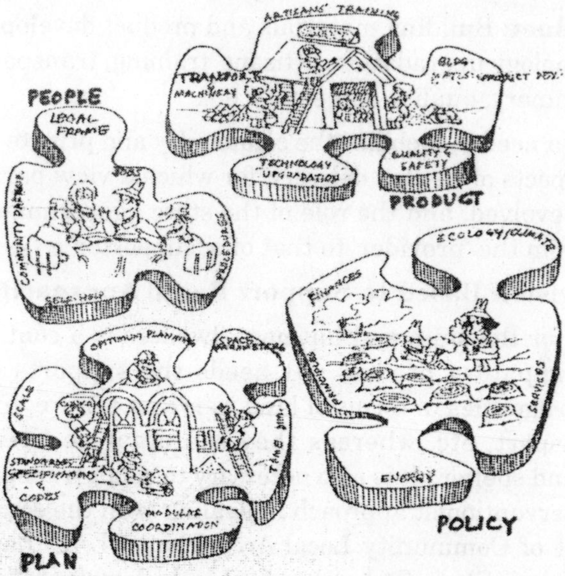

- **Policy :** Urbanisation, housing, land, finance, ecology, infrastructure services, public-private partnership, building industry, labour, etc.
- **Planning:** City and housing development, space standards, specifications and codes, scale of cooperation, optimum land use planning and development, controls,

time dimension, modular coordination and design synthesis, etc..

- **People** : Socio-economic characteristics, community participation, procedures, self-help, legal framework, etc.
- **Product**: Building materials and product development, technology upgradation, artisans' training, transport and machinery, quality and safety, etc.

There is a need to mobilize the community and private sector in all the aspects of shelter delivery, for which a view paradigm needs to be evolved, and the role of the state / government has to change from the 'provider' to that of a 'supporter'.

From Provision Based to Support Based Approach

Shelter for the slum and hutment dwellers is a continuous and a participatory process. It needs the supports of the government agencies in terms of land, services, tenure, finance, public transport, etc. whereas they can organise their own structures and shelter. It is also necessary to adopt transparency and non-interventionist approach in dealing with the squatters. The concept of Community Local Area Plan (CLAP) has been used in Nagpur Slum Redevelopment, which provides useful clues to mobilise the local resources and potential of the Slum/ JJ dwellers in improving their living conditions. Shelter within the support-based approach, should be planned and implemented as a participatory process. People's participation in housing programmes has been widely accepted and adopted. Agenda 21 expressed this global commitment to the concept stating that "international co-operation, local partnerships and citizen participation are central to improving the urban environment" (UNCED 1992).

In a people-centred process, the adequacy of housing, utilisation of resources, productivity and economic efficiency can be redefined according to their satisfaction of people's need, not according to an imposed idealistic material standard. The reference in the support-based approach is the standard of living and the satisfaction of human needs and not the amount of consumption. The consideration of people's needs requires that they should be in control of the pace of the process and the decisions taken throughout.

Comparison between Provision-Based and Support-Based Approaches

Characteristics	*Provision-based Approach*	*Support-based approach*
Aim	- Reduce housing shortage. - Provide sufficient formal housing and eliminate substandard housing. - Aim is measured by productivity.	- Improve living conditions. - Increase affordable and appropriate housing options. - Aim is measured by resourcefulness.
Basic Conceptions	- Housing is a product; its value is for what it is - Housing is commodity political instrument; product, industry and technical field. - Experts and politicians know better about housing. They have to control provision to ensure efficiency. - When people build houses for themselves, they are substandard. - Housing operation can be centrally managed.	- Housing is a process; its value is for what it does. - Housing is people-centred process based on participation enablement and partnership. - People know better their housing needs and fulfil them if supported. They have to control provision to ensure fit. - When governments build houses for users, they do not fit their needs. - Housing process has to be locally based.
Strategies	- Provide houses on behalf of people. - Centralise resources and housing construction. - Building public housing by government sector. - Housing projects are standardised, large-scale and built fast and instantly to control cost and efficiency. - Mass housing and slum removal.	- Support people in housing themselves. - Decentralise resources and decision-making. - Build people's capacity to manage the process. - Housing programmes are localised, small-scale, diversified and built incrementally to engage people. - Sites-and-services and upgrading.

Characteristics	*Provision-based Approach*	*Support-based approach*
Actors and Roles	- Central Government is provider and local government is the implementer. - People are unknown during provision and recipients of allocated end-products. - Professionals are planners, large-scale contracting companies are builders.	- Central government is enabler to local government that are enablers to local actors. - People as individuals and communities are genuine participants and controllers. - Small-scale contractors are builders, professionals are supporters, NGOs and CBOs are mediators.

Source : Based on UN Habitat and other sources

Redefining the Goals

The experience of last 6 decades of planning and housing development in India distills the following basic objectives and principles for shelter:

- The planning and housing should focus upon the deprived 'Other Half'.

An inclusive –Citywide strategy for EWS / LIG housing : provision of a component of shelter for EWS / LIG compulsory for all government / private / cooperative housing

- The provision of a component of Shelter for EWS / LIG should be compulsory for all Government / Private / Cooperative Housing in a city wide strategy. The private sector should participate in this social responsibility.
- Shelter is a participatory and evolutionary process
- Access of poor to finances, serviced land and tenure are essential
- Slum rehabilitation and social housing should not be only the responsibility of the public sector, but incentives and mandatory norms should be able to mobilize private sector and community. In this endeavour land and community are the major resources.
- Shelter is intertwined with the jobs and poverty alleviation
- Mixed use zoning should replace single use zoning
- Mandatory provision for informal sector/street vendors should be integral part of planned development

The challenge is to translate the above concepts into workable action plans, regulatory policies and programmes.

Housing Strategy

The housing strategy should incorporate the development of new housing areas, upgradation, re-densification and redevelopment of existing housing areas, including unauthorized colonies, villages and the inner city. The future requirement of shelter provision will be dominated by small dwelling units. In view of the limited availability of land and increased requirement of housing, plotted residential development should be discouraged. There is a need to re-examine the myth of low rise housing for the poor and to encourage multi-storied housing options, as being done in Mumbai, Pune and other cities.

It is necessary to adopt a multi-pronged strategy for provision of housing and for delivery of serviced land by involving the private sector to a significant extent, public agencies and co-operative societies, etc. The overall responsibility for provision of land and facilitation of adequate housing to meet the projected demand lies with the government which should devise ways of collaboration with the private agencies. Planning norms, land use zoning, density, FAR, and building controls are to be reviewed so that new areas can be opened up for low income housing as well as the redevelopment of existing areas can be triggered. It is essential to optimise utilization of land with a view to increasing net residential density. A fixed density could lead to under-utilisation of FAR or imposition of artificial limits to optimal use of land, which is a scarce commodity.

To make the construction activity more environment friendly, the choice of alternative building materials and techniques have to be promoted. New building technologies including pre-fabrication are to be explored for housing. Standard specifications may also be reviewed incorporating innovative building systems and materials.

The three basic traditional concerns of housing and building pyramid have been – 'Cost, Quality and Time'. In the present scenario, the pyramid has to have a wider context, which should include Human safety and satisfaction, Ecological Sustainability and Aesthetics and Creative Environment. A new paradigm is emerging for housing, construction and building sector, and correspondingly the plans, designs, engineering and management should be framed in this wider context. The heterogeneous character of the country, its people and their socio-economic-physical characteristics demand evolving a variety of plans and designs incorporating flexibility together with differentiated approaches according to contextual peculiarities.

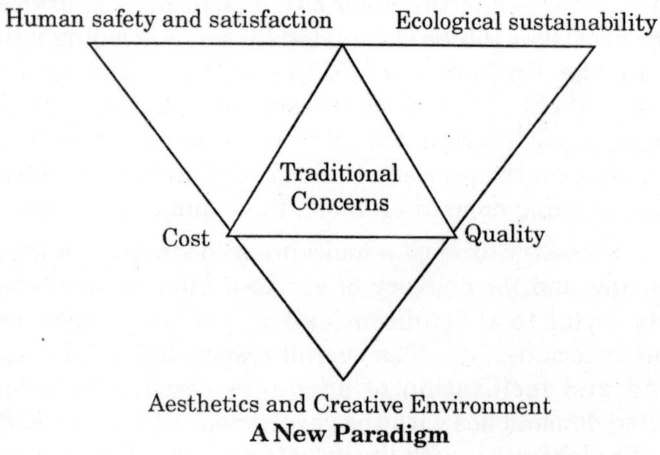

A New Paradigm

Rehabilitation/Relocation of Slum & JJ Clusters

A major emphasis should be to adopt a variety of approaches for shelter with the participation of the communities. The driving force for the Collective Slum Rehabilitation can be by the formation for the cooperative societies, as well as taking up slum rehousing through the developers and government agencies by way of the incentive of Floor Space Index or Floor Area Ratio (FAR). Land is scarce and a most valuable commodity which is to be used optimally with adequate provision of smaller units at an affordable price for the lowest income brackets.

Besides reserving adequate land for low income housing, every group housing should ensure that minimum 15% of FAR or 35% of the dwelling units, whichever is more, is dedicated for the EWS and lower income category. A liberalized FAR of 400 has been proposed for slum rehabilitation in Delhi Master Plan – 2021, against the FAR of 250 in Mumbai. This implies that the pattern of EWS housing shall be multi-storied.

Development Options

Instead of promoting a single development model for obtaining secure land tenure and improving housing and living conditions, a range of options can be tried and tested by the communities. As the work spreads out and scales up, these strategies can be expanded, refined and adapted to suit the particular needs, aspirations and conditions of the community. The five broad strategies listed below provide the options for slum and Jhuggi Jhompri communities:

1. **Upgrading**: Slum upgrading is a way of improving the physical environment and basic services in existing communities, while preserving their location, character and social structures. Besides improving the physical conditions and quality of life in these poor communities, the physical improvements made under an upgrading process can act as a springboard for other kinds of development like income generation, welfare, etc.
2. **Relocation:** The greatest advantage of the relocation strategy is that it usually comes with housing security, through land use rights, outright ownership of some kind

of long-term land lease. But relocation sites are often far from existing communities, job opportunities, support structures and schools. Community members who want to keep their old jobs or attend the same schools must bear the burden of additional traveling time and expense and must adapt themselves to a new environment. In cases of relocation, communities face the cost of reconstructing their houses at the new site and in some cases the additional burden of land purchase payments. But tenure security tends to be a big incentive to invest in housing and environmental development at the new community.

3. **Land sharing:** Land sharing is a Slum/JJ settlement improvement strategy which allows both the land-owner and the community people living on that land to benefit by dividing the land and allowing the community to buy or rent a portion of the land to the landowner to develop commercially. In land sharing, the community gets secure tenure via land ownership of long term leasehold, and the people can then work together to design and construct their own new housing on their portion of the site.
4. **Reconstruction:** In this strategy, existing Slum/JJ communities are totally rebuilt on the same land, or on land that is nearby, within the same general area, either under long term lease or outright purchase. The security of land tenure at the new site provides the community with a strong incentive to invest in their housing, through rebuilding or new construction. Although the reconstruction option involves making considerable physical changes within the community and requires some adaptations to a new environment, the strategy allows people to continue living in the same area and to remain close to their places of work and this is a crucial compensation for the expense and difficulty reconstruction involves.
5. **Reblocking:** Reblocking is a more systematic way of improving the infrastructure and physical conditions in

existing communities by making adjustments to the layout to install sewers, drains, walkways and roads in such a way that ensures the continuity of the community. Communities can then develop their housing gradually, at their own pace. When communities opt for reblocking, some houses may have to be moved and partially or entirely reconstructed to improve access or some lanes may have to be realigned to enable drainage lines, water supply systems or sewers to be constructed. Reblocking is often undertaken in cases where communities have negotiated to buy or obtain long-term leases for the land they already occupy. In both cases, the process of reblocking is an important step in the progress towards land tenure security and improved housing.

Alternative Shelter Delivery Approaches

1. **Public Housing:** In this socialist style housing system, resettlement plots or ready-built housing units are developed by the State and supplied to people, usually on a subsidised basis, making the government a supplier of shelter.
2. **Market Sector Housing:** In this system, private entrepreneurs design and develop shelter projects (in various forms, ranging from individual houses to condos to blocks of flats) and sell or rent those units at rates which allow them to meet their development costs and turn a profit. This system looks at shelter not as an essential human need but as a commodity where the prevailing pre business systems of finance and governance offer many incentives to develop these kinds of profit making projects. But despite publicity to the contrary, this sector has been unable to reach the poorest.
3. **People Sector Housing:** in this housing delivery system, individual families construct their own housing, on land which they have bought themselves or been granted, instead of buying it ready-made from the developers.

4. **Cooperative Sector:** Shelter which is planned, financed and developed by groups of people includes options like the coopeartive housing projects. This housing delivery system works best in situations where there are financial engagements to finance them, legal instruments to give legal status to the groups which develop them, and tradition of community organization to support the process.
5. **Collective Community Rehabilitation:** In this new shelter delivery system, the communities within a given constituency link together, survey their housing problems as a group, and then enter into a collaborative process with their municipal governments and with other concerned organizations in the city to jointly developing programmes which resolves those problems and which allows all those communities to be developed, with government finance and support. The form that development takes in each individual community is flexible, and could involve in-situ upgrading, relocation, land sharing or reblocking. More important than the form is the fact that the housing plan covers all the settlements and carries out.of a process in which all the local stakeholders look at the situation and plan together. The cornerstones of this process essentially are the following:

    - Collective land management.
    - Collective financial management
    - Collective social management
    - A decentralised community based management system.

The Collective Community Rehabilitation process will include: integration with city development plan, social development, community organization development, savings activities development, income generation and welfare. A working Committee which networks with local communities must include the representatives of the local community, Local Authority, Service Agencies and the NGOs.

The Collective Process

To improve the living conditions and tenure security of lakhs of poor, Jhuggi-Jhompr/Slum households is a staggering task. The big challenge is how to ensure that communities lead the process, that local cooperation between stakeholders becomes the key strategy for implementing the upgrading, and that housing for the poor becomes an issue which belongs to the city as a whole. To promote a comprehensive community development, which brings about improvements to all aspects of people's lives, it is necessary to take the following upgrading plans:

- **Infrastructure development plans:** paved lanes and roads, water supply and electricity systems, storm and sewage drains, solid waste disposal, at household and community levels.
- **Environmental development plans** may include tree planting and greenery, community gardening, waste-water and trash recycling, alternative energy systems, playgrounds, recreational areas, etc.
- **Social development plans** may include vocational training, employment and welfare center, youth and day-care center, clinics, hostels for poor or elderly members, community centers, cooperative offices, multi-facilitiy centres, communication system, fire-fighting facilities, etc..
- **Economic development plans** for the community may include developing markets or community stores, establishing conservation or tourism areas, enhancing people's earning through community enterprises, loans for small businesses, support for household workshops, or vocational training.

Financial Models and Options

The finance is a critical factor in any Slum Rehabilitation Strategy. There are pros and cons of various financial models, and no single model can be advocated in toto. Keeping in view, the radical option to transfer the subsidy directly to the community, a combination of various models as given below would lead to a hybrid, vector financial model of Collective Community Rehabilitation:

1. Cost-recovery Model
2. Subsidy model
3. Municipal upgrading Model
4. Basic Services Model
5. Environment Improvement of Urban Slums Model
6. Community savings Model
7. Cooperatisation Model
8. Land sharing/In-situ Reconstruction
9. Collective Community Rehabilitation Model (a combination of the above models)

The Government of India has launched Jawahar Lal Nehru Urban Renewal Mission, comprising of 'Basic Services to the Urban Poor' (BSUP) and Integrated Housing and Slum Development (IHSDP). The scheme also provides funds for slum and squatter rehabilitation projects.

Land and Services

The availability of serviced urban land is a crucial issue for Slum Rehabilitation in Delhi. There is a need to optimize the availability of urban land to the urban poor for their housing. The new framework for the Slum & JJ Clusters would trigger a process of self-generating settlement and resettlement. The concepts of mixed land use, redensification and instruments of 'Accommodation Reservation' are the effective tools in the task. A leveraging strategy by taking up the pilot projects should encourage the community and private sector to participate in Slum and JJ Rehabilitation.

While developing the city level shelter, land and infrastructure plans, there is a need to relate those with the urban poor and to redirect the resources for the economic emancipation and self-reliance of the poor. These must involve transformation and innovation in the relationship among people, governments, financial institutions etc., the success of this collective enterprise depends upon the involvement of people at the grass-root level for which civic engagement, sustainability and equity are the guiding principles.

The empirical evidence suggests that provision of housing to the urban poor really helps them in climbing up the poverty line and accelerate in the social and economic ladder. This requires evolving a multipronged strategy based on community empowerment together with decentralization, devolution and deregulation strategies for a pro-poor, people-centered approach. The policies should be so devised as to empower the community towards self-rule, self-reliance and self-build. The success of the participatory approach would depend on local, low cost and simple solutions based on a comprehensive understanding of the issues and processes.

14

TOWARDS HOUSING FOR ALL

In the planning and designing of new communities, housing projects, and urban renewal, the planners both private and public, need to give explicit consideration to the kind of world that is being created for the children who will be growing up in these settings.

— Urie Bronferbrenner, Two Worlds of Childhood (1917)

Looking back most of the city plans have largely benefited the middle class and organized sectors, whereas the poor have remained marginalized. For a change there is a need to invert the planning process, starting from the other end, as given below :

- Target the 'other half'.
- Mandatory provision of a component of shelter for EWS/ LIG in all Government/Private/Cooperative Housing.
- Shelter as a participatory and evolutionary process.
- Access of poor to land and tenure.
- Urban services and public transport integral to housing development.
- Development controls to encourage development of EWS/ LIG Housing
- Incentives and mandatory norms to mobilise private sector and community for Slum rehousing.
- Shelter interwined with jobs and poverty alleviation
- Mixed use zoning in place of single use zoning
- Mandatory norms for informal sector and street vendors

Delhi with a population of around 160 lakh (2007) covering an area of 1483 sq.kms. poses a huge challenge of housing and related issues.

DELHI – Population Growth

Year	*Population (in Lakhs)*	*Decadal growth rate (%)*
1961	26.6	52.5
1971	40.7	52.9
1981	62.2	53.0
1991	94.2	51.5
2001	137.8	46.3
2021(projected)	230.0	26.4

As per 2001 Census Delhi had 33.8 lakh census houses and 25.5 lakh households. Number of total houses exceeded the number of households by 8.3 lakh units. Occupied houses were about 31 lakh, number of vacant houses being almost 3 lakh. 82% of houses were used for residential purposes. Houses used for residence and residence-cum-other uses totaled 24.5 lakhs. This compared quite well with 25.5 lakh households. As compared to 1961, there had been a progressive increase in the percentage of population living in slum and JJ clusters and unauthorised colonies.

Delhi presents a variety of housing typologies, with complex processes in their growth, operation, morphological and spatial configurations, which are distributed in two major types of housing developments: one, in the organised public, regular and cooperative housing (15.1 lakh families i.e. 47% families) and the remaining 15.9 lakh families living in traditional/slum areas, illegal and squatter settlements. Almost 1 lakh persons are estimated as homeless. The proportion of organised public sector housing stock is continuously reducing, while the production of unorganized, decentralised and illegal housing (slum areas, squatter settlements and unauthorised colonies) is twice the output of organised/formal sector. The estimates project a need to build around 24 lakh dwelling units, for the year 2021 when the population of Delhi is projected to be around 23 million.

The Issues

The studies bring out the following facts:

(*a*) About 50% of the housing stock (15.9 lakh) in Delhi is comprised of indigeneous and non-formal settlements.

(*b*) About half of the families in Delhi fall under the category of Economically Weaker Sections and Low Income Groups

(*c*) About two thirds of EWS/LIG families live in the slum and squatter settlements.

(*d*) Squatter clusters, characterised by fragmentation, small scale of operation, decentralisation and self-generation are serving the housing needs of the poorest, whereas unauthorised colonies which are medium scale and comparatively more organised are catering predominantly to the MIG.

HOUSING SITUATION (1961-2001)

		1961	*1991*	*2001*
1.	Slum & JJ Clusters	—	1,38,996 (7.8%)	3,29,217 (10.51%)
2.	Individual Housing on Regular Plots	32591 (6.9%)	2,35,224 (13.2%)	5,10,597 (16.30%)
3.	Employer Housing	31562 (6.7%)	99,792 (5.6%)	1,24,823 (03.98%)
4.	Unauthorised colonies	36300 (7.7%)	4,40,154 (24.7%)	7,59,203 (24.24%)
5A.	Site and Services	—	2,97,594 (16.7%)	4,40,793 (14.7%)
5B.	Built Housing	4700 (1.9%)	3,02,940 (17%)	4,99,946 (15.96%)
6.	Traditional Urban Villages	3,23,686 (68%)	2,67.300 (15%)	4,67,916 (14.94%)
	Total	4,71,881	17,82,000	31,32,495

Sources : Census of India, Slum & JJ Wing, MCD, DDA, GNCTD, etc.

GROWTH OF SQUATTERS

Year	*No. of clusters*	*Households/jhuggis*
1981	409	
1990	929	2,59,334
1994	1080	4,00,000
1998	1100	4,78,175

Source : Food & Civil Supplies Deptt. & GNCTD & Slum & JJ Wing, MCD (*e*) Cooperative housing in Delhi is not catering to the needs of housing for low income and Economically Weaker Sections.

(*f*) Organised public sector of housing production, though substantial, has been marginally effective in serving the shelter needs of the poor.

(*g*) Data confirms that housing is generator of employment, economic growth and productivity.

(*h*) A substantial proportion of employment the City is in the informal sector, small and micro-enterprises. Data on informal sector and unemployment indicates a shift towards higher productivity, and growth in the size of the informal sector. The share of male work force employed in the informal sector ranged between 22 per cent to 68 per cent in 1993 and 25 per cent to 71 per cent in 1998.

(*i*) The female work force plays a major role in setting up of small and micro enterprises (between 60 per cent to 87 per cent). Employment opportunities for the males in the informal sector have also increased.

Master Plan for Delhi-2021 (MPD-2021)

MPD-2021 projects that by the year 2021 the population of Delhi would be around 220 –230 lakhs for which about 22000 hectares of land will be required for urban extension. This will accommodate around 14 lakh dwelling units, of which 50-55% of units should be for the urban poor. The urban extensions are proposed to be developed with the following land use distribution:

Land Use Distribution

Land use	*% of Land*
Residential	45-55
Commercial	4-5
Industrial	4-5
Green/Recreational*	15-20
Public & Semi-Public Facilities	8-10
Circulation/Transport	10-12

*This does not include green areas under various specific gross land use categories.

Together with development of new areas, a major thrust area is the recycling and redevelopment of old dilapidated areas, such as :

- Areas along MRTS/Major Transport Corridors
- Underutilised/Low-Density, Old/Housing Areas.
- Special Area, Villages, Resettlement Colonies, and Unauthorised Colonies

It is proposed that unauthorised colonies (about 1600) are to be regularised and are proposed to be effectively incorporated in the mainstream of urban development, with infrastructure development, services and facilities.

Land is to be used as a resource to trigger the process of private sector participation with mandatory provisions for EWS housing/slum rehousing. Existing urban areas are proposed to be redensified so as to meet about 40% of additional housing requirements (about 10 lakh Dwelling units).

Urban Extensions

As per the Master Plan norms about 50 percent of the area proposed for development in the urban extension would be required for city level infrastructure, transportation, public and semi-public facilities, industrial and commercial complexes, and EWS/Resettlement housing, which by and large are to be developed by the DDA/Government agencies. Out of 22000 Ha. proposed for Urban Extension-2021, about 2200 Ha. is required for essential facilities like colleges, schools, hospitals, fire stations, Police Station etc., another 3300 Ha. to 4400 Ha. for city level parks, and about 2500 Ha. for city level roads / transport corridors. Major city level activities are proposed to be provided in the facility corridors to developed along major Roads (30 meters and above), which would be flanked by Residential Communities and neighbourhood in the following hierarchy:

	Population	*Area*
1. Housing Area	5,000	8 - 10 Ha.
2. Neighbourhood	10,000	18 - 20 Ha.
3. Community	1,00,000	200 - 225 Ha.
4. District	5,00,000	1500 Ha.
5. Zone / Sub-City	10,00,000	4000 Ha

Housing and Land Requirements for Delhi-2021

Sl. No.	Housing Type	Development Agencies	%age	EWS/ LIG Component	No. of DUs (Lakhs)	Redev. (Lakhs)	New (Lakhs)	Net Land for New Housing
1.	Slum & JJ 1. In-situ Rehabilitation 2. Relocation/ Reconstruction 3. Up-gradation	Public Agency Private Agency Co-op Society	25	25	6.0	2.40	3.60	900 Ha.
2.	Houses on Independent Plots & Redevelopment	Public Agency Private Agency	8	4	1.92	1.22	0.70	200 Ha.
3.	Group Housing (Min. 35% of total DUs mandatory 2 room and less)	Public Agency Private Agency Co-op Society	42	14	10.08	2.0	8.08	4000 Ha.
4.	Employer Housing	Central/State Govt.	4	2	0.96	0.34	0.62	400 Ha.
5.	Unauthorised Regularised colonies infill	Co-op Society/ Residents' Association/ Private agency	15	6	3.60	2.60	1.0	
6.	Other Housing areas, Upgradation of Old areas/ Traditional areas/ Villages	Public Agency Private Agency Co-op Society	6	3	1.44	1.44	—	
	Total		100	54%	24.0	10.0	14.0	5500 Ha.

In order to develop about 14 lakh dwelling units in new areas, about 5500 Ha. of net housing area would be required. It is necessary to utilize optimally the urban lands and take up redevelopment/redensification of the existing urban areas. For this the resources of both – the government and private sector need to be mopped up and interfaced with the overall city development.

It is envisaged to develop about 75,000 new housing units per year in the Urban Extensions, 42% of which are to be provided by group housing by the public / private & cooperative sectors. This implies development of about 31500 DUs per year (or 120-150 Ha. net housing area), for which it is necessary to create a land bank. The lands falling along the major transport corridors are proposed to be developed or redeveloped in an integrated manner with the participation of land owners.

It is observed that the practice of prescribing FAR and density norms without distinguishing between housing categories often results in making smaller size of housing unaffordable (as land cost per dwelling unit will be higher than larger size units), besides under-utilisation of the utility networks and scarce urban land. The norms should provide options to achieve the density and FAR-both in walk-up structures, without lifts or in high-rise construction. A uniform density often leads to under-utilisation of FAR. Therefore, the following density norms, with corresponding category of dwelling unit (DU) are proposed:

Slum Rehabilitation / EWS housing (upto 30 sq.m)-600 DUs/Ha

Category I (above30-upto40sq.m.)–500 DUs/ Ha

Category II (above40-upto80sq.m.)–250 DUs/ Ha

Category III (above80sqm) – 175 DUs/Ha

Private sector participation in shelter for the poor has been envisaged through the following strategies:

(*a*) In-situ slum rehabilitation by using land as a resource;

(*b*) Compulsory construction of at least 35% of dwelling units or 15 % of permissible FAR, whichever is higher in the form of EWS units by all developers of group housing.

(*c*) Incentivising Redevelopment of existing housing areas by enhanced FAR.

In order to optimize housing stock within the existing urban areas, the MPD-2021 has relaxed the development control norms for Residential Plots. Max. height of 15 Mtr. has been allowed and Floor Area Ratio and ground coverage have been substantially enhanced. This will also enable regularisation of existing housing stock to a large extent. With a view to provide more space for lower income strata of society, FAR has been enhanced from 225 to 350 for plots upto 100 sq.mts.

The massive housing needs necessitate working out an integrated and multi-pronged strategy based on the following premises:

- A decentralised programme which optimizes the resources of public-private sectors and the community.
- Providing a new legal & administrative framework together with incentives to support the initiatives of the community and private sector.
- Access to finance, mobilizing small savings through cooperatives and micro-credit institutions/NGOs.
- A programme in which urban authorities concentrate on developing land, trunk and basic services, including transport, health and safety.
- A new planning framework removing barriers and controls in the development of self generating and sustainable settlements.

The availability of serviced urban land is a critical issue. There is a need to optimize the availability of urban land to the urban poor for planned growth of housing and home-based enterprise. A new framework has been evolved for the dilapidated old areas, so as to trigger a process of self-generating renewal. The concepts of mixed land use, redensification, and instruments of 'Accommodation Reservation' and 'Transfer of Development Rights' have been identified as the tools in the task.

Small Home Based Enterprise

Indian Cities are characterized by multiple use of space and large number of households, especially poor use their home for livelihood. In Delhi too, inspite of a statutory Master Plan, small enterprises continue to flourish in the homes. A large proportion of about 2.3 lakh retail enterprises with an employment of 5.4 lakh engaged in trade, commerce and allied services operate from the residential areas. MPD-2021 has recognized the phenomenon of Mixed Use and has adopted a multi-pronged strategy to promote home based enterprises with the following measures:

(*i*) Regularisation of non-polluting industrial clusters in residential areas and also allowing 121 types of household industries in residential premises.

(*ii*) Continuance of Commercial Use in pre-1962/MPD-1962 residential areas/rehabilitation colonies and in inner city.

(*iii*) Regularisation of retail shops, etc. under Mixed Use Regulations by notifying mixed use streets and local commercial streets/areas. About 2300 such streets have already been notified by the MCD/GNCTD.

(*iv*) Small shops of maximum 20 sqm area, trading in 24 items of daily needs on ground floor in all residential premises.

This will encourage home-based enterprises and provide self-employment opportunities to a large number of people. This will also make the residential areas more lively and secure, provided environmental and other safeguards are simultaneously adopted, together with augmentation of infrastructure services.

Redevelopment of Existing Urban Areas

The modality for redevelopment is based on the incentive of enhanced FAR and application of concept of mix-use zoning. The basic objective of redevelopment is to upgrade the old, dilapidated areas by implementing schemes on the basis of physical and socio-economic conditions in the following way:

(*i*) Influence Zone along MRTS Corridor for redevelopment and renewal should be identified on the basis of physical features such as metro, roads, drains, high tension lines and control zones of Monuments / Heritage areas, etc.

(*ii*) The residents / cooperative societies/ private developers should get the layout and services plan prepared in consultation with the concerned authority for approval.

(*iii*) Within the overall Redevelopment / Regularisation plans, building plan approval shall be at following two stages:

(*a*) Planning Permission for an area of around 4 Ha. This permission may not be required in case an approved layout / Redevelopment / Regularisation plan exists.

(*b*) 1. Cluster Block for a minimum area of 3000 sq.m. The owners should pool together and reorganise their individual properties so as to provide minimum 30% of area as common green / soft parking besides circulation areas and common facilities.

2. Individual buildings shall be given sanction by the concerned authority within the framework of cluster block approval.

(*c*) The norms of Group Housing with respect to ground coverage, basement, parking, set backs etc. (except FAR) shall be applicable.

(*iv*) Amalgamation and reconstitution of the plots for planning purpose will be permitted.

(*v*) To incentivise the redevelopment a maximum overall FAR of 50% over and above the existing permissible FAR on individual plots subject to a maximum of 400 shall be permissible. Higher FAR shall however not be permissible in redevelopment of Lutyens Bungalow Zone, Civil Lines Bungalows Area and Monument regulated Zone.

(*vi*) In case of plots with service lanes, the lane area may be included in the scheme. However, no FAR / coverage will be granted and the area shall be used as public area.

(*vii*) The standards of housing density, minimum width of roads and community facilities can be relaxed, wherever justified, by planning considerations (e.g., pedestrianization of the area).

(*viii*) The Public and Semi-public uses and services like hospitals, dispensaries, colleges, schools, police stations, fire stations, post offices, local government offices, parking etc. shall be retained in their present locations as far as possible and if not, relocated as part of the redevelopment scheme. Alternative sites shall be indicated in the Redevelopment Schemes / Zonal Development Plans. Any change or addition thereof shall be in accordance with the overall policy frame prescribed in the plan.

(*ix*) Reduced space standards may be adopted for community facilities / social infrastructure for the areas have been proposed. The land required for any public purpose may be acquired with the consent of the owner through issue of Development Rights Certificate in lieu of payment towards cost of land as per the prescribed regulations. The concept of Accommodation Reservation i.e. allowing construction of community facilities without counting in FAR may also be utilized.

(*x*) Subject to preparation and approval of integrated / comprehensive Redevelopment schemes and provision of parking and services, up to 10% of the FAR may be allowed for commercial use and 10% of the FAR for community facilities with a view to trigger a process of self-generating redevelopment.

(*xi*) The circulation pattern should include segregation of pedestrian and vehicular traffic, entry control, access of emergency vehicles to every block, provision of adequate parking etc.

(*xii*) Appropriate levies for increased FAR, and landuse conversion shall be charged from the beneficiaries by the competent authority as per prevailing rules / orders.

(*xiii*) Urban Design and Heritage to be ensured as per the guidelines.

(*xiv*) The land use shall be governed as per the Master Plan/ Zonal Development Plan. The non-residential use will be permitted as per the provisions of the Mixed Use Regulations and Special Area Regulations.

Group Housing Norms

Minimum size of plot	-	3000 sq.m.
Maximum Ground Coverage	-	33.3%
Maximum FAR	-	200

Height : No Restriction, subject to clearance from AAI/Fire Department and other statutory bodies.

Parking @ 2.0 ECS/100 sqm built up area

(*i*) The density may vary (10% variation permissible in all categories) for specific categories as given below:

(*a*) Category I (upto 40 sq.m) - 500 DUs/Ha.

(*b*) Category II (above 40-upto 80 sqm) 250 DUs/Ha.

(*c*) Category III - 175 Dus/Ha. (above 80sqm)

(*ii*) Plots for group housing should be located on roads facing a minimum width of 18 mt. ROW (13.5 m ROW for redevelopment areas and 9m ROW for Slum Rehabilitation / Special Area and Villages).

(*iii*) Additional floor area up to a maximum of 400 sq.m shall be allowed to cater to community needs such as community / recreational hall, crèche, library, reading room and society office. In addition to above, 100 sq.m. area shall be permissible for Senior Citizen Recreation Room.

(*iv*) The Central Government in consultation with the DDA may relax density and other norms for public housing and projects of national importance.

(*v*) The developer shall ensure that minimum 15% of FAR or 35% of the dwelling units, whichever is more, are constructed for Community-Service Personnel / EWS and lower category. Such flats should have a carpet area between 25 - 40 sqm.

(*vi*) Ground coverage up to 40% may be allowed to achieve low-rise high-density housing without lifts.

(*vii*) Levy on additional FAR shall be at rates notified with the approval of Government from time to time.

(*viii*) Stilts: If the building is constructed with stilt area of non-habitable height and is proposed to be used for parking, landscaping etc. the stilt floor need not be included in FAR.

(*ix*) Basement, if constructed, and used only for parking, utilities and services shall not be counted towards FAR.

Slum Free City

For making Delhi a city without slums, an eight point programme has been proposed:

(*i*) Resettlement, whether in the form of in-situ up-gradation or relocation, should be based mainly on built up accommodation of around 25 sq. m with common areas and facilities, rather than on the model of horizontal plotted development.

(*ii*) The concept of land as a resource should be adopted to develop such accommodation with private sector participation and investment, to the extent possible.

(*iii*) Incentives by way of higher FAR, part commercial use of the land and, if necessary and feasible, Transfer of Development Rights should be provided.

(*iv*) A cooperative resettlement model with adequate safeguards should be adopted with tenure rights being provided through the institution of Co-operative Societies.

(*v*) The provision of accommodation should be based on cost, with suitable arrangements for funding / financing keeping in view the aspect of affordability and capacity to pay.

(*vi*) In cases of relocation, the sites should be identified with a view to develop relatively small clusters in a manner that they can be integrated with the overall planned development of the area, particularly keeping in view the availability of employment avenues in the vicinity. Very large resettlement sites could lead to a phenomenon of planned slums.

(*vii*) Suitable arrangement for temporary transit accommodation for families to be rehabilitated should be made. This may preferably be near or at the same site and the utilization of these may be synchronised with the phases of implementation of the scheme of in-situ up-gradation.

(*viii*) Community Based Organisations (CBOs) and Non-Governmental Organisations (NGOs) should be closely involved in the resettlement process.

According to MPD-2021, the schemes for Collective Community Rehabilitation/ Relocation should be explored with the possibility of involving private sector/slum cooperatives. In existing resettlement colonies, redevelopment, regular servicing and maintenance, which are overdue, are to be based on the guidelines and incentives as applicable for the Squatter Rehabilitation Scheme with the following broad guidelines:

(*i*) Minimum plot size 2000 sq.m. (facing a min. road of 9m).

(*ii*) Maximum density - 600 units per ha. ± 10% variation.

(*iii*) The scheme should be designed in a composite manner with an overall maximum FAR of 400 on the residential component of the land and FAR on the remunerative component of the land shall be as applicable for the relevant land use.

(*iv*) Mixed land use / commercial component up to 10% of permissible FAR.

(*v*) Specific situations may require clubbing of scattered squatters with JJ sites in the neighbourhood to work out an overall comprehensive scheme.

(*vi*) The minimum component of the land area for rehabilitation of squatters has to be 60% and maximum area for remunerative use has to be 40%.

(*vii*) Area of dwelling unit for rehabilitation shall be around 25 to 30 sq.m.

(*viii*) Common parking is to be provided which can be relaxed wherever required, except for the parking for remunerative purposes.

(*ix*) No restriction on ground coverage (except set backs)

(*x*) Schemes shall be approved by concerned local body.

(*xi*) Schemes / designs should be compatible for disabled.

Land Management Policy

The Report of the National Commission on Urbanisation (1988) states that the objectives of urban land policy as outlined by the Urban Land Policy Committee appointed by the Government of India (Ministry of Health) in 1965 still broadly hold good. These are:

1. To achieve an optimum social use of urban land.
2. To make land available in adequate quantity at the right time and for reasonable prices to both public authorities and individuals.
3. To encourage cooperative and community effort and bonafide individual builders in the field of land development, housing and construction.
4. To prevent concentration of land owner-ship in a few private hands and specially to safeguard the interest of the poor and underprivileged section of the society.
5. To use land as a resource for financing urban development by recouping the unearned income which otherwise accrues to private landowners.

To this list, the Planning Commission Task Force on Planning of Urban Development added the following objectives:

6. To encourage the socially and economically efficient allocation of urban land so that land development is done in a resource-conserving manner and that the magnitude of land used is optimal.
7. To promote flexibility in land-use in response to changes resulting from a growing city.

Delhi since 1961 has been pursuing the policy of Large Scale Acquisition, Development and Disposal. With the policies of economic liberalisation (1991) and Democratic Decentralisation (1993), together with ever-increasing shortage of serviced urban land, housing and other resources, it is necessary to evolve the alternative approaches. From the experience of other cities in India, one notices replicable ingredients for alternative strategies for access to land, as given below:

(*a*) Guided land development for large areas/urbanizable blocks;

(*b*) Land pooling for compact areas (institutionalized as Town Planning Schemes in Gujarat and several other States);

(*c*) Land reconstitution/redevelopment (for in-situ upgrading in small parcels in core areas);

(*d*) Acquisition for a public purpose under the Land Acquisition Act, 1891.

(*e*) Joint sector model of land assembly and development (Greater Noida, CIDCO, New Mumbai).

(*f*) Transferable Development Rights (in Hyderabad, it works for built up areas).

(*g*) Saleable FAR and mixed use concept (for regeneration urban potential from land intercity urban assets).

(*h*) Land Pooling and Redistribution Scheme (Town Planning Scheme, Maharashtra.)

(*i*) The concept of 'Excess Condemnation' (can be used for major roads/transport and facility corridors).

The land policy reforms should open up new ways of land banking/land assembly and housing development.

A New Management Structure

No breakthrough can be achieved without overhauling the existing institutional framework and developing a new management structure to achieve effective coordination, cost controls, and efficient delivery. The salient areas pertaining to inter-disciplinary management of housing development are the following:

(*a*) Professional land management and new system of land assembly based on public-private partnerships.

(*b*) Better financial management and exploring innovative areas of resource optimization, reducing administrative overheads; affordability as a major concern.

(*c*) Flexibility in planning, design and management to facilitate improved solutions for affordability and evolutionary upgradation of services/facilities, renewal etc.

(*d*) Better control over time, Management Information System, monitoring, bridging gap between demand and supply, overcoming delays and cost over-runs.

(*e*) Decentralisation, Community participation, Horizontalisation, Constitution of Project Management Groups and new ways of contracting and monitoring.

(*f*) Technological interface, with reference to the specifications, physical/social infrastructure, construction, maintenance and energy and environment concerns.

(*g*) Capacity building, competitiveness, training, exchange, and learning from other good practices.

(*h*) Transparency in process of housing management and disposal.

(*i*) Legal reforms, including Acts, Bye-laws, regulations and procedures.

(*j*) GIS data base for land management, services and housing.

(*k*) Issue of identity cards to all slum and squatter families and computerized records.

(*l*) Rationalising subsidies

(*m*) To deal collectively with the Slum/JJ communities, rather than individual families.

(*n*) A two-tiered tenure system – land to be leased collectively to the community, shelter to the individuals (preferably jointly in the name of husband and wife).

In spite of the fact that high level industrial development and sophisticated technological innovations have permeated in almost every field and serving the society, in case of housing, these are functioning in a primitive way involving wastages and delays. Low productivity, high costs, long building cycles, non-standardization and poor quality are the main challenges of building and housing. At present a large proportion of housing activity is carried out by the individuals in a sporadic, semi-industrial manner, outside the monetary sector. Socio-economic changes all over the world make it necessary to change these conventional methods by others more in accordance with the present technological era. This is underlined by the key position of housing and building within the national economy. It is necessary to evolve an integrated "systems" approach in planning, design and development of housing. Close coordination and consistency between planning, design, production and management of housing are indispensable pre-requisities of systems approach, alongwith modular coordination and standardization.

Urban Density and Fuel Consumption relationship for 32 cities (1980)

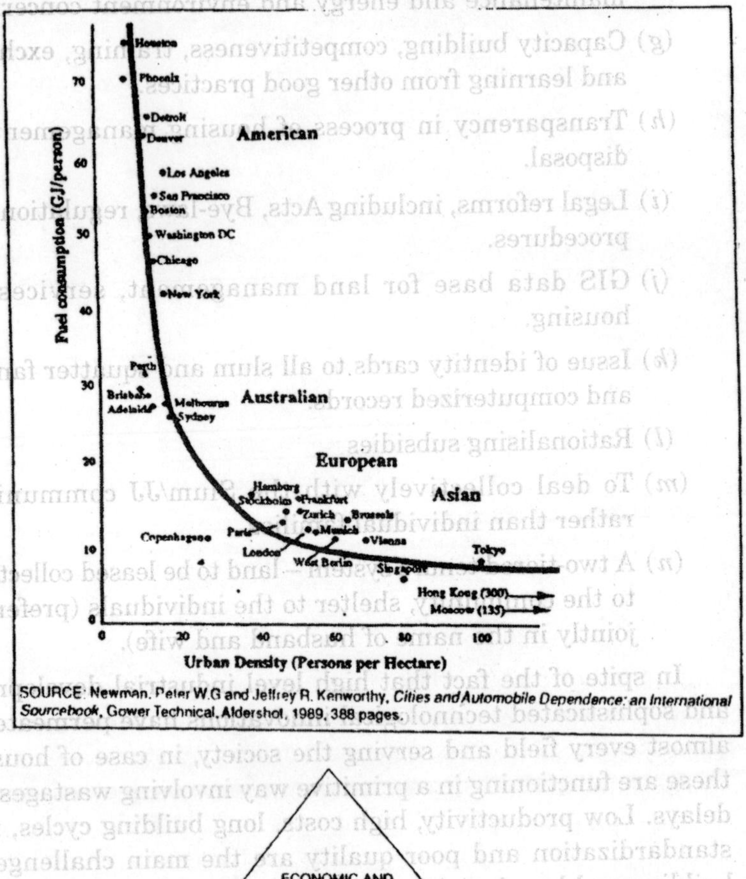

SOURCE: Newman, Peter W.G and Jeffrey R. Kenworthy, *Cities and Automobile Dependence: an International Sourcebook*, Gower Technical, Aldershot, 1989, 388 pages.

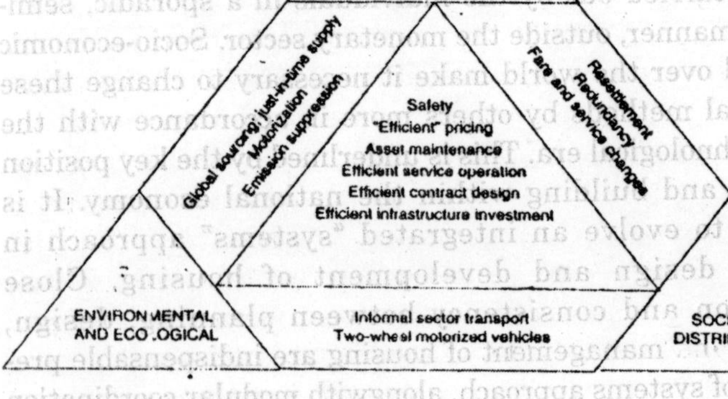

15

SUSTAINABLE TRANSPORT

We are building too many walls and not enough bridges.

— Scott Carson

The total population of million plus cities in India increased to 145 million in 2001 A.D, and there were about 60 million two-wheelers and 8 million cars in metropolitan cities. Increased use of personalised motor vehicles is choking the already congested roads. An inefficient urban transport system impedes the growth of urban economy and leads to several problems like air pollution, high incidence of traffic accidents, etc. The link between transportation and environmental quality has been long recognised, although the perception of the relationship has changed over time. Concerns at local level like noise, air pollution, loss of green space, traffic delays and accidents have transcended to the fundamental issues of survival of the ecological system.

The effects on the environment due to various modes of transportation can be broadly summarised as follows:

Modes of travel	*Effects on the Environment*
Rail	• Noise and Vibration
	• Accident Risks, and hazards
	• Damage to Wildlife and farmlands
	• Land requirement for right of way
	• Depletion of fossil fuels
Road	• Air Pollution at a local and global level
	• Noise and vibration
	• Accident risks

	• Damage to wildlife and farmlands
	• Land requirement for right of way, parking, terminals, workshops, fuel filling stations, etc.
	• Pollution for surface water
	• Depletion of fossil fuels
Air	• Noise
	• Accident risks
	• Congestion of access roads to airports
	• Land needs for infrastructure
	• Air Pollution
Water/Marine	• Alterations in natural water system due to construction of ports, canals
	• Land needs for infrastructure
	• Accident risks
	• Water pollution, vibrations, noise and oil spill effecting marine life
	• Depletion of fossil fuels

The cumulative effect poses a considerable burden on the society in the form of deaths and fatal causalities in road accidents, pollution, noise, stress etc. Emissions of Carbon dioxide and nitrous oxides continue to endanger the human health. Diesel emissions increase health hazards, including cancer and asthma. Traditional solutions to cope up with the demand of increasing traffic have resulted into widening of roads up to the brim thus eating away the area meant for the pedestrians and cyclists. Every year there are new roads, fly-over and bridges to facilitate higher speeds and to accommodate increasing volume of traffic. Underground and surface parking lots are developed at enormous costs, which often deprive the people of invaluable green lung-space. Their needs are outgunned by a well-armed car lobby. The building of new roads and widening of existing roads are, however, reaching the stage of saturation. It is becoming well nigh impossible to obtain land and remove encroachments for widening of the road network. The solutions like underground metro network are often projected as the panacea for traffic and environmental problems of the cities. These are often long range and too expensive. Alternatives, such as surface railway for intra-city transport could be less costly and short range. About 55% of the railway passengers are comprised of its suburban services. 11.5 percent of the total earnings of the railways are from the suburban traffic. In spite of this the Ministry of Railways has taken a stand not to make any further contribution in intra-urban transport. It is necessary that the stalemate is resolved so that the railways could contribute in solving the problem of public transport. Various studies are available which indicate the relationship among the capacity, costs and emissions of various transport modes. The following table gives a simplified and comprehensive picture:

Capacity, Cost and Emissions of Various Transport Modes

Mode of Transport	*Person per Hour per lane*	*Total Cost per Passenger Kilo-metres (US$)*	*Total emissions per Passenger KMS*
Walking	1,800	Negligible	0
Bicycle	1,500	×	0
Motorcycle	1,100	×	27.497
Car	500-800	0.12 – 0.24	18.965
Bus			
Mixed traffic	10,000 – 15,000	0.02 – 0.05	1.02
Bus-only lane	15,000 – 20,000	0.02 – 0.05	0.89
Separate Busways	30,000	0.05 – 0.08	×
Light rail transit surface exclusive	20,000 – 36,000	0.10 – 0.15	
Coal			4.3520
Gas			0.1876
Fuel Oil			0.6261
Rapid Rail Transit			
Surface (coal)	50,000	0.10 – 0.15	4.9651
Elevated (gas)	70,000	0.12 – 0.20	0.2307
Underground (fuel oil)	70,000	0.15 – 0.25	0.7102

Sources: United Nations Center for Human Settlements (Un-Habitat). Transportation Strategies for Human Settlements in Developing Countries (Habitat, Nairobi, Kenya, 1984). p. 25.

The World Bank, Urban Transport (The World Bank, Washington, D.C., 1986). p. 53.

Asif Faiz et al., Automotive Air Pollution: Issues and Options for Developing Countries, Working Paper No. 492 (The World Bank, Washington, D.C., August 1990). Table 20, p. 43.

The National Urban Transport Policy (2006) recommends short-term and long-term planning for transportation for all cities, working out Transport System Management (TSM), technology up-gradation, private sector partnership, energy efficiency, transportation linked with sustainable development, regulating car industry and dovetailing inter-city movement system with intra-city transport. The policy also suggests integration of road and rail transport and establishment of Unified Metropolitan Transport Authority (UMTA) for metropolitan cities.

Transport Infrastructure and the Ideal City

Although the roads are the lifeline of socio-economic development, the available road capacities are grossly inadequate in most of Indian cities. In addition to the proposed mass transport system, road network capacity will have to be substantially augmented in order to cater to transport demand. It is estimated that additional 70,000 lane Km of major road network in metropolitan cities will have to be added through new roads and widening over the next 20 years.

Rapidly increasing demand for transport and the resulting traffic congestion have led to pressures to build new transport infrastructure. Although, as a long-term measure many of these capital-intensive transport systems are justified, the fact remains that most of the cities can ill-afford the expenses of these solutions. Thus, there is an inescapable need to consider the other alternatives, keeping in view the following are the basic premises for a sustainable and ideal city:

- maximum 8 to 10 minutes walking distance from the Residence / work place to public transport node
- no automobiles except taxis at peak hours, as all citizens move by public transport and bicycles.
- Homes with nearby stores, restaurants, movies and cultural activities.
- Abundant parks, pedestrian streets, greenways, wide sidewalks, bicycle, paths.
- High and low income citizens meeting as equals in public spaces.

- Autonomy and freedom of movement for children and the elderly.
- Very low levels of noise and air pollution.

Land Use and Urban Structure

The basic objective of transport planning should be transport conservation, which includes review of land use concepts and systems of transportation. This requires radical changes in the concepts of land use by integration and higher level of mix of communications, housing, jobs, recreation and transportation. The basic purpose of transportation should be efficiency, equity, ecology and land economy. The geometry of town planning plays an important role in this and the pattern of urban development requires restructuring for transportation efficiency. The concept of decentralisation by regional planning has not been very successful so far. There are various hurdles and conflicts between various States which come in the way. The concept of urban constellation may be more pragmatic and responsive to market forces and potential of development of settlements around the metro-cities.

Various studies are available which draw the following general findings:

(*i*) The ownership of the private vehicles in urban areas is growing three to four times the population growth rate.

(*ii*) Higher the density, lesser is the gasoline consumption per capita.

(*iii*) Higher the prosperity, higher is the car ownership.

(*iv*) Mixed land use (generally found in unplanned city, inner city) reduces the demand of transport.

(*v*) The construction of flyovers, underpasses is a temporary solution to congestion on the roads. Likewise metro/underground railway may not necessarily reduce the volume of personal vehicles on the roads.

(*vi*) Promotion of cycles, NMVs and IPT modes of transport is vital for Indian cities, which need dedicated and safe right of way and certain radical incentives.

(*vii*) Linear urban morphology is more conducive for mass/public transport system (as compared to polynodal, polycentric geometry).

(*viii*) In Indian cities transport infrastructure usually guides the mode of development and land use. Planned residential areas along major arteries get converted to commercial and other uses, which could be so preplanned.

(*ix*) Parking is emerging as a major urban problem and requires preventive, as well as curative, enforcement measures.

(*x*) More and bigger roads create more traffic jams. They stimulate real estate development around them and thus generate more traffic. Bigger roads stimulate longer trips.

(*xi*) Public funds are always scarce. Resources devoted to road construction and maintenance leave other critical sectors such as education, health and recreation of the poor people unattended.

(*xii*) Low density city cannot be served by efficient low-cost, high frequency public transport.

Integrated planning of intra-urban and inter-urban transport can bring about a new pattern of urban population distribution, settlement structure, industrial growth and lead to environmental conservation. This will require re-examining the concept of single land use zoning and city structure which should be based on conservation of transport. Further the following areas need priority for sustainable transport:

- Reorganisation of land-use of central area including the circulation in view of emerging traffic pattern
- Rationalisation of land-use and density with due consideration of parking requirements, pedestrianisation, efficient use of road right of way.
- Integration of buses, trams route with MRTS, Metro rail, circular rail corridors, LRT and waterways.
- Integration of Bus and Rail stations, terminals, with surface dispersal facilities and services such as parking, taxi stands and potential urban renewal developments including the land-use restructuring.
- Introduction of integrated traffic and transit operation, control and management, setting up of Unified

Metropolitan Regional Transport Authority for planning and implementation.

- Exploring the potential of using subterranean space for transport and parking.

Planning should ensure that the transport infrastructure corresponds to social demand. The choice of heavy and costly public transportation systems in several large towns (such as Delhi, Bangalore, Ahmedabad) raises doubts about the viability of these infrastructures, which must be supported by user charges. Urban planners can not neglect the economic dimension of these problems. A coherent spatial policy may in the first place encourage the revitalization of existing inner areas. High priority needs to be given to the improvement of their functioning and upgradation of their infrastructure.

Smart growth practice advocates mixed use practice and higher densities and much has been written all over about the myths of conventional planning. It has been accepted world over that higher density does not overburden services, and it does not require more infrastructure support. It has also been established that higher density does not create congestion. It has also been established that higher density is better environmentally. It is globally accepted that mixed use (MLU) helps in revitalising community life and attracts pedestrians back on the street. It is also established that in today's service economy communities find that by MLUs they are able to balance the quality for life criteria to determine where people will settle.

World over the concept of smart growth is gaining acceptably which is based on the premise of mixed land use. When homes are located within the walking distance to grocery stores or employment centres, alternative to driving such as walking becomes viable. The mixed land use also provides a more diverse and sizeable population and wider commercial base to support the public transit. The acceptability of smart growth among town planners has resulted in transformation of many cities on the concept of mixed use as a means to conserve energy and also to reduce the number of private vehicles on roads. While the separation of land uses was intended to protect the communities from polluting industries and businesses, it has led to a pattern of development in which stores, housing and schools are often placed so apart that they can only be reached by motorized transport. Improved environmental regulations and private sector innovation mean that many businesses are now cleaner than they were many decades ago when zoning was first introduced to separate land from houses, thereby eliminating much of the need for their strict separation from homes and commercial establishments. Smart growth supports the integration of mixed land uses into communities as a critical component of achieving better places to live.

Transportation needs can not be considered an independent variable. The needs are greatly influenced by urban form and access policies. Mobility patterns in 8 high income cities show the tremendous variation in car use, distances travelled, public transport use at similar levels of income. It has been shown that people may use different modes and technologies, public or personal transport, but the daily average motorised travel time varies relatively little. The travel time for all modes, including journeys by foot and by bicycle, differ little as everyone has the same time constraints with 9-10 hours work day. In low-density cities which are car dominated and have high road space, car owners travel long distances relatively fast, but have high travel times. It is difficult to establish efficient public transport systems in such cities. On the other hand, those cities that have a dense settlement pattern, tend to be more public transport friendly and more citizens use non-motorised forms of transport, (such as Tokyo, Singapore and Hong Kong).

Contrary to prevailing beliefs, car use is much higher in cities that have strict zoning and very little mixing of business areas with residential areas. Houston in USA with wide roads, low density (9 persons per ha.) and separation of residential areas, has very high use of cars (25,400 km per person per year) and long average travel time (90 minutes) compared to Hong Kong which has a high density low car use (1,300 km per person per year) and low travel time (40 minutes).

Mobility Patterns in High Income Cities

Motorised mobility (Private) km / year / person	*Cities*	*Motorised mobility (all modes) km / year / person*	*Daily motorised travel time, minutes*	*Share of the journeys by foot, bicycle and public transport, per cent*	*Density person/ha.*
25,400	Houston	25,600	90	5	9
12,100	Melbourne	13,100	70	26	14
5,600	London	7,700	60	51	59
5,500	Paris	7,300	50	56	48
6,300	Munich	8,900	60	60	56
4,300	Tokyo	9,900	70	68	88
4,700	Singapore	7,900	60	48	94
1,300	Hong Kong	5,000	50	82	320

Source: Jean Vivier, 2001

From the above, it can be concluded that:

- Private car use can bc reduced with mixed land use policies
- Provision of efficient public transport and taxi/free-wheeler services can reduce private vehicle use.
- Public transportation is not very successful if we do not have mixed land use policies in a city along with high density living.

Preventing Transport

Transportation policy and planning have dominantly been concerned with moving people by mass transport, modernisation and introduction of new systems of transport. Construction of bridges, flyovers, widening of roads, metro etc. have been pursuing during the last two decades. The net result is to sustain and subsidise inefficient and loosing public transport undertakings which consequently encourages personal transportation. As such, the paradox of transport policy has been that very ills it must resolve are the consequences of such a policy. This has also relegated para-transport and traditional modes into background. Classical case is of the bicycles in Delhi which declined from 30% in 1970 to 5% in 2001. The surveys indicate drastic reduction in the volume of the cycle traffic in the cities whereas there has been phenomenal growth of light-fast vehicles.

Communications provide a viable substitute for transportation. As such, transportation policy is to be linked with telecommunications, electronic mail, video-conferencing, radio-paging, mobile-phones, computer networking, E-mail etc. as the alternatives to physical movement. Likewise there is a need to redesign the system of goods movement. Containers and computers can very effectively avoid unnecessary goods movement.

Non-motorised Transport and Bicycles

Transportation is an element of total civic life and must match the cultural and social factors. Transportation decisions are also subject to political compulsions. According to Michael Replogle, 25% to 80% of urban transport in Asia is by non-motorised vehicles (NMVs). In view of this, it is necessary to encourage pedestrian and cycle movement, together with para-transport modes. The volume of traffic catered by such modes can never be replaced by capital intensive mass transport systems.

According to the studies, there are 45 million cycles in India against 1.5 million cars. Although there is a ratio of 1:30, but in term of its transport contribution, it is meagre as compared to other countries like China, where 80% of trips are by bicycles and 20 to 40% in Netherlands, Sweden, Japan and Germany. Bicycle has an efficiency of 30% and provides 40w of tractive power at 20 km per hour. It has carrying capacity of 100 to 180 kg load. It is most economical and as such an ideal social means of transport. Bicycles are most energy efficient using 55 calories per passenger. It is non-polluting and environment-friendly. Cycles are space-saving, occupying one sixteenth of car space. Whereas cars can cater to 120-220 persons per meter width of roads, cycles can carry 1500 persons. It is also time saving and affords flexibility and personal freedom due to its size and flexibility. It is accessible in narrow streets, undulating terrain and difficult areas.

However, there have been various hurdles in the development of bicycle transportation. The main problem arises from the low priority in planning and mixing up of bicycles traffic with fast vehicular traffic. In Delhi where cycles are only 10% of vehicular modes, 30% of fatal accidents involve cyclists. It is necessary to overcome the problem of cycle and NMV transport, for which the following proposals need consideration:

- Planning and development of dedicated bikeways, NMV streets and lanes, which should be adequate, direct, shortest, safe and attractive. These should be user friendly and as far as possible dedicated.
- Cycle need to be given proper priority, or at least equal treatment with motorised vehicles. For safety of cycle traffic, it is necessary to develop under-passes on major roads and signal control lock system as prevalent in the countries of the West.
- Development of network of cycle rental and parking centres.
- Taking up of bicycle friendly town/zone pilot projects.
- Comprehensive network planning of cycle tracks.
- Cycle design improvement.
- Provision of bicycle tracks through major parks and city forests so as to encourage use of cycles.
- Provision of finances for bicycles and NMVs.

Keeping in view the importance of cycle as sustainable and healthy transport, it is necessary to initiate several actions to promote the use of cycles. The design of cycle has to appeal to the younger generation who looks for speed, comfort and glamour. There is need to develop new models of cycles, which are hi-tech and hi-speed. The use of computer chips, multi-gears, batteries, hydrogen and photovoltaic cells for energy and music system can be thought over. It was not very long when transistor radio became a fad and cyclists were often seen carrying one. The designers have to get out of a variety mould and reinvent the cycle. New designs should address to the disadvantages of the bike as urban transport-fatal accidents, toil, weather, low speed, lack of wider variety etc. There is a need of innovation, new technology and research, which could restore the place of bicycle in urban transport. Bicycle being the biologically driven vehicle, proper attention should be given for easy and comfortable riding, together with the geometrics of the cycle tracks and landscaping along cycle tracks. It is also necessary to evolve cycle as a family transport and also design special cycles for the handicapped, aged and women.

Rickshaw as Intermediate Public Transport

The cycle rickshaw, a popular mode of passenger transport in Indian cities, should be redesigned for efficiency, safety and speed. According to one estimate, in Delhi 250,000 cycle-rickshaws are operating. Likewise in many Indian cities large number of cycle-rickshaws act as a major mode of public transport. However, in many cities, the civic authorities are banning the movement of cycle-rickshaws in certain localities and rickshaw pullers are often the subject of harassment by the local officials. In spite of these hardships, the rickshaw is continues to remain the most popular, easily available and cheap mode of transport for intra-city travel or within a crowded locality. In a crowded place like Delhi's Chandni Chowk, if all the cars and trucks are banned, rickshaws can create a far better transportation system, both in terms of passenger transport and cargo transport, than any other mode of transport. The amount of space they occupy versus the amount of luggage they carry is a lot more. By proper design, rickshaw can also emerge as a family vehicle, replacing the expensive, polluting and dangerous motorised vehicles. Motorised versions or rickshaws can replace the school buses, which are often unable to serve the congested localities and sometimes lead to fatal accidents. The planning of neighbourhood and location of schools, colleges and such activities should be conducive for use of bicycles. Cycle and cycle-rickshaw tracks must be planned separate from the fast vehicular traffic and development of cycle parking should be integrated with the markets, transport modes, schools, colleges, parks etc. An integrated network of cycle trails, subways, overpasses would go a long way in making cycling pleasant and safe.

Sustainable Transport Policy Planning

Transport, land use, economic development and environment are often inter-dependent. Transport policy, as such, needs to be evolved on the basis of environment, economic and social considerations. The major components of sustainable transport policy are pollution control, efficient service, accessibility, safety, efficient pricing, asset management and efficient investment. The policy instruments should essentially cover greening of urban transport, noise control, emission standards, TSM, optimising capacity potential, promoting use of NMV and cycles, flexible laning, parking policy, minimising traffic congestion, road and cordon pricing, carrying capacity, telematics and financing.

Greening of Urban Transport

The challenge of urban transport can be substantially met by recapturing the streets for pedestrians, cyclists and fuel efficient, low speed two wheelers. After decades of efforts to travel faster and farther, the objective now must be to provide access to people and places by 'green' modes of urban transport, which include communications, walking, bicycling, intermediate public transport modes and trains. Inherent with it is the aim to curtail the need for commuting and shorten the distances by various strategies, such as telecommunications, electronic mail, mixed land use zoning etc. Polluting and life-endangering transport modes have to be discouraged and relegated in the margin, while environment friendly modes of transport need to be given the centre-stage. It is necessary to develop an ecologically sound, extensive and well-equipped public transport system that is not a source of physical injury, or air and noise pollution. The provision of 'green lungs', 'pedestrian precincts' and 'exclusive bicycle tracks' and facilities are integral to the development of transport system. As such the 'greening of urban transport' has to become a basic objective of city development and transportation planning.

City must be lined with cycle tracks, pedestrian streets, greenways and parks. It must be served by low-cost, high-quality predominantly surface transit/bus systems. Such a city can be more socially just more environmentally sustainable, more competitive and happier.

The experience of fuels in transportation has been extremely poor. It is well known that two-thirds of the SPM causing air pollution in metro cities is usually contributed by vehicular traffic. The pollution continues to impair the human health, therefore, it is necessary to develop alternative fuels, which include electricity/battery, CNG propane and solar energy.

Transport Systems Management: Transportation Systems Management (TSM) techniques offer low cost solutions to urban transport problems. Some of the measures that can be adopted in our cities are as follows:

Road widening/traffic free zones and TDR: In the inner city area, where the traffic volume has grown many times, it is generally suggested either to ban certain narrow roads to traffic altogether, and where feasible, take up road-widening by acquiring the land. However, as the cost of acquisition of land in the cities is very prohibitive, the local bodies find it difficult to bear the same. A novel solution to this problem, which has been adopted in the Municipal Corporation of Greater Mumbai, is the scheme of "Transferable Development Rights (or TDR) wherein the owners of properties on either side of the streets to be widened have to compulsorily relinquish the required extent of land needed to widen the street free of charge in lieu of increased FARs. The TDR can also be sold (like shares) in the market.

Flexible laning : In the case of most of the cities in India, there are inward tidal flow of vehicles towards the City Centre in the mornings and vice-versa in the evening, Wherever the arterial roads catering to such traffic have a width of six lanes or more the "flexible laning" concept can be adopted. However, such a system would require the road-dividers to be movable and enforcing strict lane discipline.

Traffic Signals Management: Computer Controlled Traffic Signals Management System provides flexible-time traffic signaling, depending upon the volume of traffic and area-wide traffic signal co-ordination. Priority can be accorded to public transport vehicles at the traffic crossings. The technology for this purpose is readily available in India.

Parking Policy: About one-fourth of valuable road space in our cities is being taken away by parked vehicles. There is a need to adopt norms for parking, regulate parking spaces, develop multi-storied parking with the help of private sector-use sub-terranean space for parking, stipulate higher parking charges for commercial vehicles and workshops in residential areas. Strict enforcement of parking discipline is inescapable in this context, so that the moving traffic can at least make use of whatever road spaces are available.

Parking is one of the critical problems faced by the city, which is becoming serious due to distortions in land use, unauthorized encroachments, longer trip lengths accompanied by higher private vehicle ownership due to poor public transport and easy financing of private vehicles.

As such the parking policy should be a critical consideration, which should be evolved keeping in view the following:

(*i*) Reviewing parking norms for various land uses

(*ii*) Optimizing parking space

(*iii*) Multi-level parking provisions at the venues of public concentration/ in commercial areas/Metro Stations etc.

(*iv*) Identify & Remove Bottlenecks

(*v*) Minimizing the need for use of Private Transport

(*vi*) Land use – Public Transport Synergy

(*vii*) Conservation of Transport

(*viii*) Development Controls incentives and disincentives

(*ix*) Review of mixed land use policy

(*x*) Constitution of a Unified Transport and Parking Authority

Park-n-ride facilities: Provision of park-and-ride facility particularly at suburban railway stations in and around the metro-cities can greatly help in reducing the number of private vehicles on the urban roads. Creation of such facility can be easily privatised.

Peak hour congestion: The use of private cars and trucks should be banned on all major public roads in all major cities during peak hours. Where individuals still wish to ply their vehicles during peak houses, they should be required to obtain a permit on payment of a fee.

Minimum occupancy vehicles: The system of "minimum occupancy vehicles" can be introduced during rush hours in all million plus cities along specified roads and bridges as in vogue in the developed countries so as to reduce peak hour congestion.

Cordon pricing: With a view to reduce traffic congestion in the Central Business Districts (CBD), a "Cordon Pricing System" for cars, heavy trucks and other such vehicles should be introduced. This would imply charging of an "entry fee" for the cars, trucks and other vehicles into notified CBD during specified hours.

Carrying capacity: The concept of "carrying capacity" of roads needs to be recognised. As in Singapore, State Transport Authority can fix annual ceilings on the number of new registration certificates to be issued for cars/two wheelers in million plus cities and any vehicles other than those so registered for use in a particular "city" should be required to pay an extra toll of fee upon entering the municipal limits.

Financing

Involvement of the private sector in urban transport in bringing in additional resources is also suggested. It must, however, be recognised that the high costs, low profits and long gestation periods of Urban Transportation Projects do not always make them financially viable. To attract the private sector to participate in mass transport projects, the government will have to participate in the equity of such projects and provide certain concessions/benefits such as provision of interest free/low interest subordinate debt, incentives for property development, etc. Other methods worth consideration for financing urban transport can be following:

- Levy on petrol/fuel for mass transport projects.
- Using land and FAR as resources.
- Using air-rights over railway/road/terminals.
- Wiping off indirect subsidy given in allotment of land to petrol pumps.
- Levying parking charges.
- Generating international funding
- Leasing and issue of bonds to mass transport projects.
- Excess condemnation in construction of highways/MRTS and simultaneous development of land/terminals.

- Rationalisation of passenger/vehicle taxes.
- Surcharge on property tax.
- Misuse and parking charges.

To sum up, traditional solutions to cope up with the demand of increasing traffic have resulted into widening of roads up to the brim thus eating away the area meant for the pedestrians and cyclists. Every year there are new roads, fly-over and bridges to facilitate higher speeds and to accommodate increasing volume of traffic. Parking lots are developed at enormous costs, which often deprive the people of invaluable green lung-space. Their needs are outgunned by a well-armed car lobby.

The basic objective of transport planning should be transport conservation, which includes review of land use concepts and systems of transportation. This requires radical changes in the concepts of land use by integration and higher level of mix of communications, housing, jobs, recreation and transportation. The basic purpose of transportation should be efficiency, equity, ecology and land economy. The geometry of town planning plays an important role in this and the pattern of urban development requires restructuring for transportation efficiency.

The objective must be to provide access to people and places by 'green' modes of urban transport, which include communications, walking, bicycling, intermediate public transport modes and trains. Inherent with it is the aim to curtail the need for commuting and shorten the distances by various strategies, such as telecommunications, electronic mail, mixed land use zoning etc. It is necessary to develop an ecologically sound, extensive and well-equipped public transport system that is not a source of physical injury, or air and noise pollution. The provision of 'green lungs', 'pedestrian precincts' and 'exclusive bicycle tracks' and facilities are integral to the development of transport system.

The major components of sustainable transport policy should be pollution and noise control, efficient service, accessibility, safety, efficient pricing, asset management and efficient investment. The policy instruments should cover TSM, optimising capacity potential, promoting use of NMV and cycles, flexible laning, parking policy, minimising traffic congestion, road and cordon pricing, telematics and financing.

16

DELHI'S TRAFFIC AND TRANSPORTATION

You can never plan for the future by the past. — Edmund Burke

In Delhi during the period 1981 - 2001, cars increased by 10 times - from 20 per 1000 households to 200 cars in 2001. Two wheelers increased by 7 times - from 60 per 1000 households in 1981 to 410 in the year 2001 . In 2005, total number of vehicles in NCTD were 40 lakh, which are more than the combined number of vehicles in other 3 major metros in the country. Total road length in NCTD increased from 15000 Km in 1981 to 23000 Km in 1993 and 26000 Km in 2000, whereas the number of vehicles per km. increased from 37 in 1981 to 134 in 2000 (four fold increase). RITES survey indicates rise in the vehicular trips by personalized fast modes from 16.6% in 1981 to 27.4% in 2001. Vehicular trips by bus marginally increased from 59.7% in 1981 to 60.5% in 2001. Around 83% are intra-city trips. Multi-nodal land use pattern of Delhi generates large number of intra-city trips due to increased use of personal modes of transport. With the phenomenol increase in number of vehicles, one of the major problem being faced is congestion, overcrowding and acute shortage of parking space. There is absence of adequate organized parking space because of which valuable road space is being used for parking.

It clearly necessitates the need to evolve certain innovative solutions to the problem and better integration of city transportation network and land uses. The basic idea is to shift personal vehicular trips to public transport (Metro, ring railways, buses etc.) and make roads comparatively less congested.

Synergy between Transport and Land Use

There is a need to achieve synergy between land use and transport, so that there is lesser need of commuting and consequential conservation of energy, time and resources. There is a need for better public transport and the redevelopment of influence zone along metro and major Transport Corridors. It is necessary to address to the critical problems and future transportation needs way of an integrated Multi-nodal Transportation and Traffic Plan comprising the Road, Rail and Metro-rail networks. There is a need to explore other options and possibilities such as, Light Rail/Tramway/Mono-rail systems, the objective being optimal use of the existing road network and make best use of the available space by following measures:

- Expansion and restructuring of the existing network through expressways, arterial roads, elevated distributors and relief roads with a view to creating-alternate access ways and reducing congestion on the existing roads to the extent possible Urban Relief Roads are also to be identified to reduce congestion as an additional or alternative link roads, wherever possible.
- Planning of new road network in such a manner as to prevent possibilities of future congestion by modifying road sections to accommodate road side parking, and space for widening, expansion and provision of grade separators, etc.
- Planned and targeted expansion of the metro-rail network.
- Expansion and strengthening / restructuring of the Ring Rail System.
- Developing an integrated relationship between the road, rail and metro-system to provide for seamless multi-nodal transport, through provision of additional stations, park and ride facilities, introduction of single multi-modal ticketing, etc.
- Development of a comprehensive parking policy in line with the broad aims of the plan for transportation mentioned earlier, including measures for linking new vehicle registration with owner parking facilities.

- Establishment of a quick and efficient transport network between the NCR and the NCT of Delhi.
- Provision of directional Goods and Passenger terminals with adequate infrastructure.
- Provision of arrangements for by-pass of through National Highway traffic without having to pass through the city.
- Review of the licensing policy and systems, and effective arrangements for training of drivers / transport operators.

Today Delhi is emerging as a borderless urban continuum of Haryana and UP. Simultaneously Delhi is also emerging as global city of the 21st century. Hitherto, transportation planning in Delhi aims at minimizing the gap between demand and supply. The mobility related problems of the vast majority of the population relating to pedestrians, cyclists, public and private modes of transport all over the city have been relegated to back-burner. In this context, the following are the objectives of transport planning:

- *Efficiency:* Providing an efficient and affordable transport system.

- *Equity:* Providing equal accessibility to all sections of the population.
- *Environment:* To ensure protection of the urban environment and minimizing the pollution by the transport system/fuels.
- *Energy:* Conserving energy in moving the people.

It is well known that about two-third of the SPM causing air pollution in Delhi is contributed by vehicular traffic. The pollution continues to impair the health of the residents. It is necessary to develop alternative fuels and "Factor-4" technologies, which include celectricity/battery, CNG, propane and solar energy. These objectives should be translated into quantifiable goals ensuring the following:

(*i*) Economical, fast and safe commuting between the place of origin and destination.

(*ii*) Accessibility to all areas for all sections of society.

(*iii*) Least generation of transport related pollution.

(*iv*) Energy efficiency

(*v*) Safety to all sections of the road and transport users

The basic objective of transport planning should be transport conservation, which calls for review of land use concepts and systems of transportation. This requires radical change in the concepts of land use by offering higher level of mix of communications, housing, jobs, recreation and transportation.

Radical problems need radical solutions. We cannot solve the problems with the same thinking by which those have been created. As such, there is a need to adopt innovative solution evolved by lateral thinking. Some of the strategies could be the following:

- Recognising the fact thai the growth of metropolitan city seems to be irreversible optimal use of existing road network and full development of right of ' way by removing all impediments.
- To establish transport systems and networks in the NCR so that the distance " between Delhi to any corner of the NCR can be covered within 2 hours.

- To Improve and achieve efficient movement, road network needs to be restructured to have expressways, arterial roads, district distributors and access roads. This requires that critical areas are identified and Urban Relief Roads are developed as alternative link roads.
- As an innovative strategy, alternative network through elevated/underground/tube 'roads can be thought of, which will ease the movement of tho traffic and reduce air pollution.
- Rationally located, identified and designed passenger and goods terminals on the basis of directional need to be developed with adequate infrastructure. The infrastructure should cover transfer, storage and interface modes and the related facilities.
- To encourage energy conservation and environmental protection, an integrated and multi-modal transport system has to be developed. The main mode being the Mass Rapid Transit System (both Road and Rail) and supportive modes i.e., public buses, Intermediate Passenger Transport (IPT), Non-motorised Transport (NMT) and private vehicles, there is a need to make the provisions for all the modes.
- To ensure that parked vehicles are not a hindrance to the movement of vehicles on distributors and arterial roads, proper parking and provision of additional parking spaces including multilevel facilities may be encouraged.
- Bus terminals in all directions, preferably for each division, near MRTS stations or strategic locations need to be developed.
- Intermediate Passenger Transport and Non-Motorised Transport should be encouraged taking into consideration their potential as environment friendly and low coot transport.
- Parking is emerging as a major problem associated with urban development. There should be two pronged strategy - (*a*) to augment parking capacity and supply (*b*) Demand management and fiscal measures.

- Since the city is witnessing unprecedented growth of vehicles, it is necessary to explore the options like time zoning concepts, auction of car registrations, mandatory certification of parking space, incentives for use of public transport etc.
- Provide long lasting good-quality roads.
- Provide good traffic management and road furniture.
- Construct roads on optimum life cycle cost analysis.
- Provide funds for adequate maintenance to improve public transportation.
- Introduce long term performance based rehabilitation and maintenance contracts through PPP for road and parking infrastructure.
- Training of traffic police, advocacy, lane discipline etc..

Keeping in view the diverse physical form, a single mode of transport can not effectively serve the needs of the city. Accordingly, an integrated multi-modal transport system suitable for the overall structure of the city and at the same time interlinking various sub-structures is proposed. It is envisaged that the future transport system shall consist of a mix of rail and road based system which may include MRTS, ring rail, dedicated rail corridors for daily commuters, light rail, bus, high capacity bus on a select number of corridors.

Delhi is planned on a ring-radial pattern with a hierarchical road network. Broadly, the road network is designed for regional, intra-city and local traffic for the urban traffic. The roads are classified taking into account the land use pattern and the road system hierarchy with recommended right of ways as follows:

- National Highways : 90-100m
- Arterial Roads : 60-95m
- Primary Roads : 45m
- Primary all purpose roads : 30m
- Sub Arterial Roads : 24m
- Primary Collector : 18-24m
- Secondary Collector : 13.5-18m
- Local Streets : 9-13.5m

The ratio of the registered vehicles to urban road length which was 88 vehicles per km in the year 1990, had increased to 131 vehicles per km in 1999. The total urban road length has increased by 4,400 km in the last decade and was about 26500 Km in the year 1988-89. In spite of roads occupying 21% of the total area of the city, the continuous increase in vehicular traffic on major arterial roads is resulting in lowering of the journey speed, congestion, intersection delays and significant pollution level especially during the peak hours. The total number of registered vehicles on Delhi's roads has reached a staggering 35.51 lakhs by 2004. The share of two-wheelers is about 63% in the total vehicles. In order to reduce congestion on the existing roads, it is proposed to identify some additional/ alternative link in the immediate vicinity. Such links are called as Urban Relief Roads. These can be along drains (including their covering) or identification of a new alignment or upgradatlon/strengthening of an existing road, alignment etc.

Transportation policy and planning have been concerned with moving people by mass transport, modernization and introduction of new systems of transport. Construction of bridges, flyovers, widening of roads, metro etc. have been pursued during the last two decades. The net result is to sustain and subsidise inefficient and loosing public transport undertakings which consequently encourage personal transportation. As such, the paradox of transport policy has been that very ills that it should have resolved.

This has also relegated para-transport and traditional modes into background. Classical case is of the bicycles in Delhi which declined from 30% in 1970 to 7% in 2001. The surveys indicate drastic reduction in the volume of the cycle traffic in the cities whereas there has been phenomenal growth of light-fast vehicles.

Communications and land-transport synergy provide viable substitutes for transportation. As such, transportation policy is to be linked with telecommunications, electronic mail, video conferencing, radio-paging, mobile-phones, computer networking. E-mail etc. as the alternatives to physical movement. Likewise there is a need to redesign the system of goods movement. Containers and computers can very effectively avoid unnecessary goods movement.

To optimise the existing transportation infrastructure and corridors, various proposals have been mooted, such as given below :

– Double decking of Ring Road

– Development of relief roads, missing links, NH-2 Bye-pass, new bridges on River Yamuna, circulation tracks along the nallas/canals, etc.

– New links with peripheral/NCR Expressways.

– Interlinking of Commonwealth Games venues, airport and transport nodes.

– Development of multi-level and underground parking lots.

It is worthwhile to examine the option of going underground for the above mention transport infrastructure, keeping in view the following constraints and potentials :

- Land in Delhi is becoming scarce, and subterranean space can multiply its availability.
- Overhead flyovers and roads are often aesthetically offensive, disturb the heritage and generate noise.
- Tunnels deal with dense and fast traffic in more efficient manner.
- Tunnels can go below the buildings and existing services networks. The length of travel corridors can be shorter than the roads, reducing the costs, time and fuel consumption. The experiences of other countries show that a 2 km tunnel in congested urban areas has the potential to cut crossing time by 15 minutes in peak hour. It may lead to a saving of over 10 million litres of fuel a year.
- Environmentally tunnels and underground corridors are more sustainable and compatible.
- A tunnel can connect existing roads in congested areas. Flyovers eat into substantial surface land for the approaches. Tunnels do not violate the skyline and are ideal for heritage enclaves noise pollution is confined to below the ground.

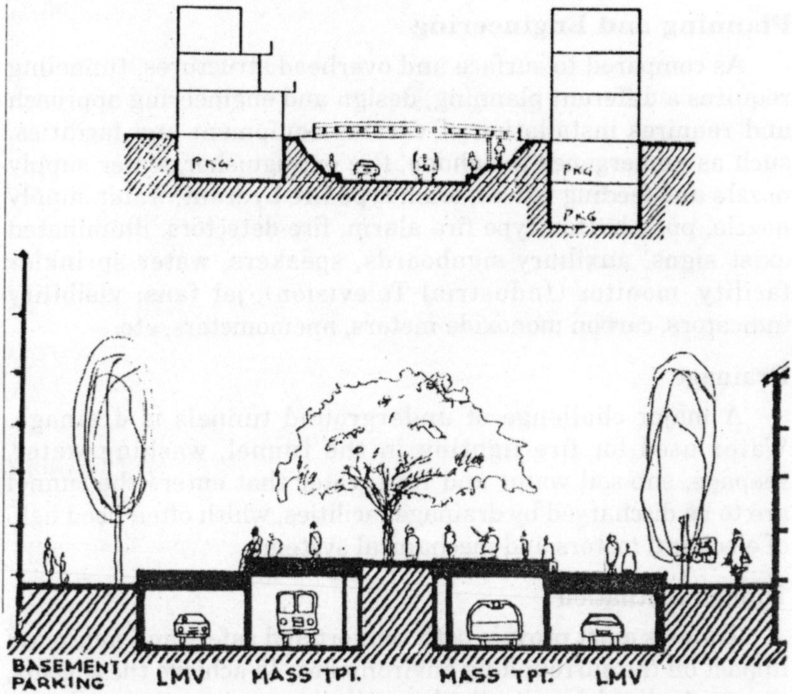

The use of subterranean space provides tremendous scope to deal with the urban transport problem and restoring the ground to the people. Though initially expensive, the major transport networks linked with parking. Should be planned underground. Vehicular roads may be dipped by 1.5 m below ground level, which will reduce noise any yield additional space for the people.

- Structurally tunnels are safer in case of an earthquake, as compared to overhead structures. There is a need to formulation the planning and design standards and norms the underground corridors, parking and tunnels.
- The major problem with tunneling could be the costs. As a thumb-rule, constructing a tunnel is three times costlier than a flyover.
- Tunnels also need maintenance overheads and power. The exhaust for fumes and round-the-clock lighting require electricity. Security is another major concern, and underground structures need guarding against subversives and anti-socials.
- It is necessary to explore the BOT and PPP options for meeting the costs and also to bring in the latest technology.

Planning and Engineering

As compared to surface and overhead structures, tunneling requires a different planning, design and engineering approach and requires installation of various equipment and facilities, such as - emergency telephone, fire extinguisher, water supply nozzle and feeding valves, foam type fire hydrant, water supply nozzle, push button type fire alarm, fire detectors, illuminated exist signs, auxiliary signboards, speakers, water sprinkler facility, monitor (Industrial Television), jet fans, visibility indicators, carbon monoxide meters, anemometers, etc.

Drainage

A major challenge of underground tunnels is drainage. Water used for fire fighting in the tunnel, washing water, seepage, sub-soil water and rain water that enters the tunnel are to be discharged by drainage facilities, which often need help of electrical motors and mechanical systems.

Tunnel Ventilation

Tunnels must provide both comfort and safety and minimum impact on the surrounding environment. To achieve these goals, the centralized longitudinal ventilation system with exhaust ducts can provide separate gas exhaust for each direction of traffic. Exhaust gas equipment should be installed in the ventilation building. Exhaust gas sucked from the tunnel is filtered by the dust prevention devices and noise from the operation is minimized with sound absorbers so as to reduce the impact on the surrounding environment.

Remote Monitor/Control Equipment

To automate the management and operation of exhaust fan and jet fan of the tunnel facilities and to save man power, the remote monitor/control equipment should be installed in a central control room which monitors and transmits control signals.

Power Supply

To ensure a reliable power supply for the tunnel facilities, the power supply/distribution facilities should have a dedicated, local power generation facility, besides city power network.

Tunnel Lighting

Low pressure sodium lamps provide good visibility for drivers, and high pressure sodium lamps can be added at the entrances to the tunnel so that the drivers' eyes quickly adjust to the tunnel lighting.

Exhaust Fan

To keep the concentration of soot, smoke and carbon monoxide in the tunnel within the tolerance limits, the proper amount of ventilation air conforming to the traffic conditions, exhaust gas from the tunnel are discharged by exhaust fans, while absorbing fresh air from both ends of the tunnel. In the event of fire in the tunnel, exhaust fans help to remove smoke with the wind velocity kept at a specified level.

Jet Fan

Jet fans are to be provided to correct the balance of wind pressure if disturbed inside the tunnel close to the exhaust outlet. It also serves to assist the exhaust fan operation and to remove soot and smoke in the event of fire in the tunnel.

Visibility Indicator

Using the transitivity of the light, this instrument measures the concentration of fumes, soot and smoke contained in the exhaust gas in the tunnel and to control the amount of the air to be discharged by the exhaust fan.

Anemometer

The anemometer measures the velocity and direction of the wind according to the traffic volume, vehicle speed and ventilation air, to control the amount of the air to be discharged by the exhaust fan.

Emergency Rescue and Relief

In case of accident and emergency, the tunnel should provide for removal and storage of accidental vehicles, cranes, ambulance and security vehicles, medical aid, close circuit video/ cameras, public address system and other facilities. In case, the tunnel is closed for longer periods, there should be a contingency plan to allow the movement of traffic on the surface.

The backbone of urban dynamics is its transportation structure and system. While the Indian Metros are aspiring to become 'world class', it is necessary to break new ground and find new paths. The translation of new dreams and ideas into reality requires meticulous planning, together with financial, administrative and institutional reforms and support of the citizen, business and industry.

KO
SARI NIKET
FANCY WED
KATRA SH
JAIN
VEG
HOTEL
CORNER
CHANDN
CHANDNI CHOWK: 55

17

PARKING POLICY, PLANS AND PRACTICE

It's not the plan that's important, it's the planning.

— Dr. Gramme Edwards

Parking is one of the critical problems being faced by the India cities. This is becoming serious due to distortions in land use, encroachments, longer trip lengths, higher private vehicle ownership, poor public transport and easy financing of private vehicles. With the phenomenal increase in personalized motor vehicles, there is an acute shortage of parking space. In the absence of adequate parking facilities, valuable road space is being used for parking.

There has been an increase of about 90 per cent in overall growth of registered vehicles during 1991-2001 at an average annual compound growth rate of about 6.7 per cent. Though buses constitute only 1.2 per cent of the total number of vehicles, they cater to 60 per cent of the total traffic load. Personal vehicles - cars and scooters - though more than 93 per cent of the total number of vehicles, cater to only around 30 per cent of the travel demand. While two-wheelers still constitute about 65 per cent of the vehicle fleet, the size of passenger car fleet has increased at a much higher rate than that of two-wheelers. According to estimates 164 passenger cars on average are registered per day as compared to 117 two-wheelers.

Passenger cars are increasing at a faster rate than two-wheelers and private vehicles constitute 90 per cent of the vehicle fleet.

Compared to other Indian cities, Delhi has the highest number of passenger cars per thousand people and is next only to Chennai in case of two-wheelers. But going by numbers of these two categories of vehicles, as well as total vehicles, the vehicle population exceeds the combined number of vehicles in Mumbai, Chennai and Kolkata.

Growth of vehicular population in Delhi

Vehicle category	*Decadal growth rate (in %)**			*As percentage of total vehicles#*			*Average numebr of vehicles registered per day*
	1974-83	*1983-92*	*1992-2001*	*1983*	*1992*	*2001*	
Cars, Jeeps, Station wagons	75.92	222.21	109.18	20.45	22.42	26.64	164
Two-wheelers	182.34	196.40	69.34	66.53	67.10	64.53	117
Auto rickshaws	75.66	177.35	29.58	3.62	3.42	2.52	
Taxis	61.80	34.36	71.70	1.19	0.55	0.53	
Buses	157.81	81.33	105.35	1.67	1.03	1.20	
Goods Vehicles	113.97	146.25	47.26	6.54	5.48	4.58	
Total	139.86	193.85	70.81	100	100	100	

Source :

* Calculated from statement showing the Registered Population of Vehicles in Delhi's provided by the office of the State Transport Authority, Delhi, and Motor Transport Statistics of India.

\# Website of the Transport Department oif the Government of NCT of Delhi.

Motorisation in Indian Metropolises

City	*Passenger cars* (2000)*	*Cars/1000 peuple#*	*Two-wheelers (2000)**	*Two-wheelers/1000 people#*
Delhi	8,69,820	63	21,84,581	158.50
Mumbai	3,03,108	17.12	4,07,306	23
Chennai	1,99,848	47.40	8,48,118	201.17
Kolkata	2,65,477	20.58	3,34,649	25.94

Source:

* Anon 2002, Motor Transport Statistics of India 1999-2000, Transport research wing, Ministry of Road Transport and Highways, Govt. of India, New Delhi.

\# Calculated on the basis of motor transport statistics and population of the cities.

The basic approach should be to conserve transport thereby to curb the need of demand of parking. A multi-pronged approach comprising of the following, should be adopted:

(*a*) Establish a close range and inter-relationship between place of residence, work centres, social infrastructure/ facilities.

(*b*) Promoting mass transport for which a cellular hierarchy system is proposed in terms of rail, MRTS, bus network, etc.

(*c*) Restrictive and selective mixed land use, for which potential of parking revisions is of critical importance.

(*d*) Optimum density and development controls for a compact and integrated city form.

(*e*) Stipulated mandatory parking norms for various land uses.

The Master Plan for Delhi stipulates parking norms, however, actual experience has shown that:

(*a*) the provisions relating to parking within the plot area are normally not adhered resulting in vehicles spilling over on to the roads and adding to congestion; and

(*b*) the norms themselves appear to be considerably on the lower side keeping in view the actual vehicle use, both in terms of the multiple vehicle ownership in the same family and the pattern of individual private vehicle use.

Various suggestions have been made in this regard. In a report submitted to the Supreme Court by the Environment Pollution (Prevention and Control) Authority for the National Capital Region; it has been suggested that the approach should be focused more on demand management (restricting vehicle numbers) through parking control and pricing rather than only on increasing of supply of parking for the growing demand. The Environment Pollution (Prevention and Control) Authority (EPCA) for National Capital Region (Bhurelal Committee) in its report to the Supreme Court suggested the pedestrianisation of the market areas and encouraging the use of public transport to curb the use of private vehicles by making it both expensive and difficult for them to ply. The Committee underlined the need to hike parking fees in Chandni Chowk, South Extension, Connaught Place, Karol Bagh and other areas and to launch a drive to remove the encroachments from public roads.

DUEIIP Recommendations

Delhi Urban Environment and Infrastructure Project (DUEIIP) while formulating vision for Delhi-2021 stated that increasing parking demand together with limited parking supply and absence of a Parking Policy is an impediment to the smooth flow of traffic, specially in and around major commercial areas/ activity centres. It is pointed out that parking pricing is a major tool for environmental improvement accompanied by provision of park and ride facility, additional parking supply in critical areas with optimal private sector participation, employers participation in transport demand management and stringent controls in zoned areas are key policy issues. The DUEIIP recommended the following proposals for planning and evaluation:

- Park and ride system with supplementary transit systems.
- Underground parking facilities at selected areas.
- Surface parking with modern management techniques.
- Imposition of higher parking charges accompanied by restriction on movements and re-organizing traffic circulation.

The policy highlights short term, medium term and long term strategies for parking and terminals:

(*i*) Short Term Measures

- Establishment of differential parking norms and guidelines based on public transport services.
- Appropriate pricing with respect to real cost to discourage use of personalised vehicles.
- On street parking in critical areas should be banned and on street parking in residential areas to be priced.

(*ii*) Medium Term Measures

- New developments and regularisation of illegal activities to be approved through traffic impact assessment.

- Encourage private parking facilities and terminals in facilities areas on BOT basis.
- Provision of parking facilities in critically deficient areas with introduction of park and ride systems.

(*iii*) Long Term Measures

- Actions to continue to reduce parking demands.
- Discouraging higher FAR/ground coverage in congested areas.

The Government of Delhi alongwith the Delhi Development Authority, MCD and Delhi Traffic Police worked out a parking policy, salient features of given below:

- There is need to check addition of vehicle population.
- Need for differential rates of parking making surface parking expensive.
- Parking charges on hourly basis and differential parking rates, parking charges be fixed keeping in view the parking congestion in different areas.
- Front setback of commercial (Mixed Use) plots be surrendered to local body and utilized for parking.
- Misuse of parking in commercial areas be charged for creating additional infrastructure.
- Spaces should be created for second hand car market.
- Staggering of market closing days.

- Proposal to set up parking lots, including underground and multi-level structures with modern technology.
- Restrictions of cars in certain areas accompanied by restriction of sale of four wheelers.
- Provision of comfortable, modern and efficient transport to curve the use of private transport.
- Banning road side parking in congested areas.
- Pedesrtrianising shopping areas.

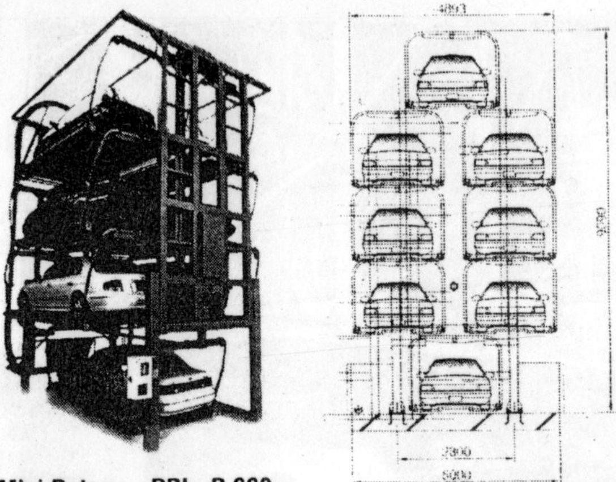

Mini Rotary • RRI - R 800

- Haphazard road parking may not be allowed.
- Motorist to pay corridor pricing or to have a license to enter a particular area for example work place.
- Good alternative public transport be provided.
- While identifying parking lots suggestions of the RWA/ shopkeepers be taken and advantages and risks may be considered.
- Introduction of market holiday off on different days may be explored.
- In congested shopping areas, differential rate of parking fee be imposed as a deterrent.
- Efforts may be made to retrieve planned and designated parking spaces.
- Setting up second hand car markets may be examined.

To make parking facilities commercially viable with effective parking pricing, 25 to 30 per cent of the space in multilevel parking sites is allowed for commercial use.

Rationalisation of parking fees is an important factor. The provision of parking facilities involves considerable costs that should be legitimately passed on to the users. Parking restriction is one of the most powerful mechanisms to restrict the use of cars, because accessibility is directly affected. The full cost of creating parking lots must be factored in an recovered from the users. The users must be charged for the cost of the land occupied by the cars and the investment made to create them. The MCD has proposed to levy a parking charge on all commercial (annual basis) and non-commercial vehicles (one time at the time of registration) plying in Delhi. This one-time levy may be counter to the idea of regulating parking as it legalizes the misuse of the parking space, with a one-time payment.

Strengthening Public Transport Systems

A multi-proposed, multi model public transport system has been proposed that will help the shift of car users to such systems. It includes high capacity bus system and electric trolley bus system, besides metro and other modes of public transport:

The transport plan comprises of the following:

(*i*) Phase-I and Phase-II Delhi Metro Development Plan - 130 Km.

(*ii*) Integrated Rail-Bus Transport along three routes - 51.20 Km.

(*iii*) Rapid Bus System along five corridors - 98 Km.

(*iv*) Electric Trolly Bus System along two routes - 32 Km.

(*v*) Light Rail Transit System for Walled City.

(*vi*) To provide park and ride system by half hour shuttle service.

(*vii*) Purchase of 2000 low floor new buses.

(*viii*) Purchase of 1000 deluxe and air-conditioned buses

(*ix*) Development of parking facilities (including in DTC depots).

The impact of metro transport system operated by DMRC is encouraging. This has reduced the use of personalised modes. The following corridors have been completed:

(*i*)	Shahdara-Tri Nagar-Rithala	- 26 Km
(*ii*)	Vishwavidyala-Central Secretriat	- 7 Km
(*iii*)	Barakhamba Road-Dwarka Sub-city	- 28 Km
	Total	**- 61 Km**

The following corridors have been identified for Phase-ll, to be completed by 2010:

(*i*)	Vishwa Vidyalya-Jahangirpuri	– 7 Km
(*ii*)	Central Secretariat-Qutub Minar	– 11 Km
(*iii*)	Barakhamba Road-Indraprastha NOIDA	– 9 Km
(*iv*)	Connaught Place - Dilshad Garden	– 14 Km
(*v*)	Anand Vihar ISBT – Yamuna Vihar Depot	– 6 Km
(*vi*)	Shahdara-Seema Puri	– 6 Km
(*vii*)	Kirti Nagar-Nangloi	– 15 Km
	Total	**– 88 Km**

The DMRC is providing large parking areas at Metro Stations and also linking them with the bus system. Apart from providing Park and Ride facilities with reference to integration between the Road and Metro Rail/ Rail Transport systems such facilities would also need to be provided with a view to reducing the problem of parking on main arterial roads in the context of identified work and activity centres which may not be directly connected by the MRTS and to encourage use of public transport.

Public Parking

The major effort will, however, have to come through the creation of public facilities in designated commercial/work centres and other areas and corridors where significant commercial activity has developed by way of mixed land use. In the context of the latter, it would also need to be linked to pedestrianisation within the identified areas. In the above background following steps would be necessary:

(*i*) All existing areas of concentration of business / commercial activity, where absence of adequate parking and congestion is visible, should be identified and listed, and based on studies of vehicle volumes specific projects for multi level parking, using the latest available technologies should be formulated and implemented in a time bound manner.

(*ii*) Major corridors along which commercial activity has grown over the years by way of mixed land use with/ without authorisation should be identified and taken up for redevelopment with a major objective being the identification and development of open areas for parking, green development and pedestrianisation.

(*iii*) In all new commercial/business/industrial centres, adequate parking on the surface as well as below and above the ground must be provided. Revised norms in terms of Equivalent Car Space (ECS) are being provided and would need to be strictly adhered to and enforced.

(*iv*) The development of multi level parking facilities may be taken up, wherever, feasible in a public private partnership framework, with private sector investment and involvement, for which incentives may be provided by way of land use and FAR etc.

(*v*) Liberalised provision of basements for parking and enforcing the use of basement for parking.

(*vi*) Stringent provisions by way of fine and other penal actions need to be invoked for violation of land use and parking rules.

(*vii*) A graded parking fees structure should be evolved as of measure of parking demand management, and encouraging use of public transport.

(*viii*) Serious consideration should be given to evolve a policy linking registration of new vehicles to availability of owner parking facilities.

(*ix*) All encroachments on land earmarked for public parking should be removed. However, public parking areas may be used for second hand car bazar on payment basis only during holidays subject to meeting requirement/conditions of the concerned authorities.

Parking Facility in DTC Depots

The use of DTC terminals and depots for development of public parking alongwith parking of DTC buses, private buses and chartered buses, should be explored.

Underground Parking

Based on the site feasibility, parking facilities can be created under the open spaces without disturbing the green areas on the surface and surrounding environment.

Parking in Residential Areas

Over the years a large number of the residential areas have also been experiencing severe problems of vehicular congestion and shortage of parking space. Most of the parking is, in fact, being done on the road, which significantly reduces the carriageway width. The problem has been exacerbated by the traffic congestion generated by schools in gross residential use areas. Some measures required to alleviate the problem, to some extent, will be as under:

(*i*) All the encroachments on residential streets in the form of kitchen gardens/roadside private greens, large projections/ramps, etc. need to be removed.

(*ii*) The road cross sections may be redesigned wherever possible to accommodate planned car parking along residential streets, and also create more surface movement space.

(*iii*) Other options, in selected areas, such as creation of underground parking below parks and open space will also have to be considered.

(*iv*) The RWAs will have to be called upon to participate in this process by raising contributions from the residents on the basis of objective criteria such as number of cars owned, etc.

(*v*) The problem of congestion arising on account of the traffic generated by schools have to be specifically addressed, and the main responsibility for putting up the required additional facilities has to be borne by the schools themselves. Policy guidelines will have to be evolved for this purpose. Master Plan for Delhi-2021 has proposed that front boundary of schools and such institutions to be built after leaving 6 mt. setback along the road for buses/visitors' parking.

Parking Standards

Parking being one of the utilities is permitted in all use zones except in ridge/regional park, developed recreational areas and parks as per the approved layout plan. Parking standard have been prescribed in each use premises. The standards given are in Equivalent Car Space (ECS) which include parking for all types of vehicles, i.e. cars, scooters, cycles, light and heavy commercial vehicles, buses etc. Parking adequacy statement/ study for large projects like Stadia, Shopping Malls, Multiplexes will be desirable.

Multi-Level Parking

Multi-level parking facility is to be preferably developed in the designated parking spaces or in the commercial areas transport nodes, public-semi public facility, institutional areas, etc. with the following Development Controls:

(*i*) Minimum Plot Size-1000 sqm (however, specific proposal, which are technically feasible and viable, could be considered on a cases by case basis for smaller plots by the Authority.)

(*ii*) In addition to the permissible parking spaces (ECS) on max. FAR, 3 times additional space (ECS) has to be provided for parking component only.

(*iii*) Max. FAR permitted: 100 (for commercial use).

(*iv*) Maximum ground coverage, FAR, height and setbacks could be relaxed subject to technical viability and feasibility.

(*v*) In case of comprehensive schemes, development controls including height shall be as per approved scheme.

(*vi*) Number of basements - No limit subject to adequate safety measures.

Institutional Framework

The constitution of a Unified Metropolitan Transport Authority has been recommended in the National Transport Policy (2006) for planning and development of an integrated transport system and for implementation and enforcement of policies framed in this context. A parking authority should be a part of the Unified Transport Authority, who will be responsible for coordinating the roles of various transport and parking agencies.

PARKING NORMS AS PER MPD - 2021

S.No.	*Use*	*Use Premises*	*Permissible Equivalent Car Spaces (ECS) per 100 sqm of floor area*
1.	Residential	Residential Group Housing	2.0
		Plotted Housing (Plots above 165 sqm)	2.0
2.	Commercial	Convented Local Shopping Community Centres, District Centres	2.0 – 2.4
		CBD, Wholesale, Warehousing, Cold Storage and Oil Depots, Hotels, etc.	3.0
3.	Industry	Manufacturing and Service Industry	2.0
		Flatted group industry	2.0
4.	Government	Government Offices	1.8

5.	Public & Semi Public Facilities	Nursing Home, Hospitals	2.0
		Education and Research - College, University & Public Schools	1.33
		Socio-Cultural, Distributive and other Community Facility Centres	2.0
		Communications Post/ Telegraph/ Telephone Centres	1.33
		Religious Centres Police Station/ Fire Station/Disaster Management Centre etc.	1.33

* In case of parking facilities in the mixed land use areas, pooled parking areas shall be identified by RWAs and cost of development of such parking places shall be payable by the beneficiaries to the concerned authorities.

* In case of misuse of parking area within a premises/plot the same shall be liable to be taken over by the DDA/Local Body.

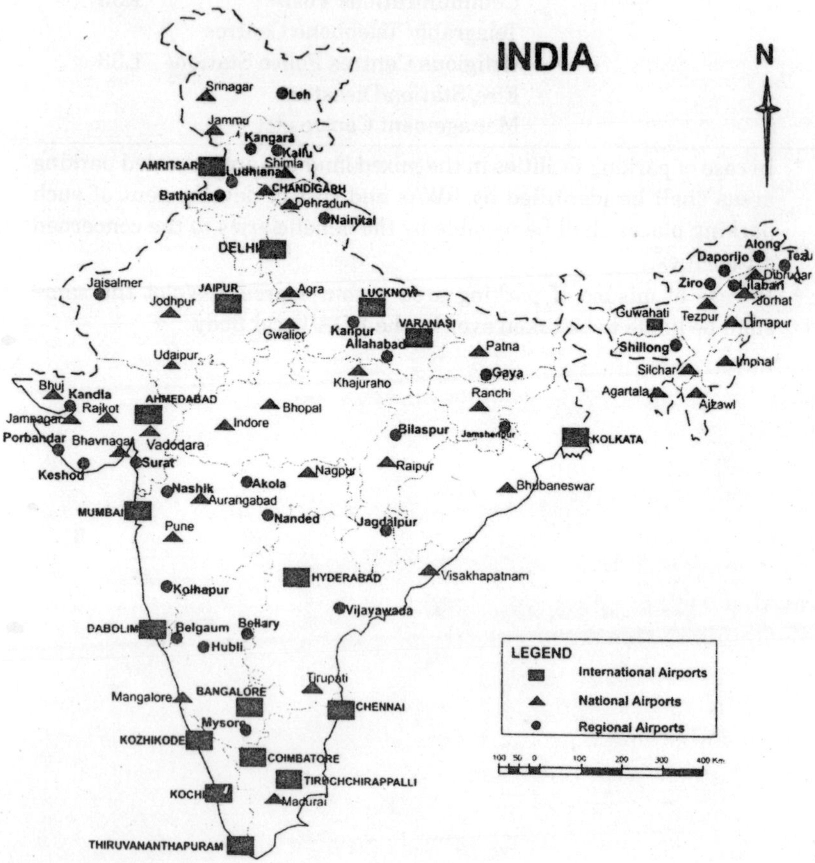

: International, National and Regional Airports of India

18

ENVISIONING THE INDIAN AIRPORT

Make not little plans; they have no magic stir men's blood and probably themselves will not be realized. Make big plans; aim high in hope and work, remembering that a noble, logical diagram once recorded will never die, but long after we are gone will a living thing, asserting itself with ever-growing insistency.

— Daniel H. Burnham, architect (1846-1912)

India has a network of 449 airports, out of which 122 are passenger traffic airports controlled by the Airports Authority of India (AAI). Of these 11 are international airports. The air services policy was liberalized in 1994 towards an open skies policy. The total passenger traffic handled by the Indian airports in 2001-02 was over 40 million, while the cargo traffic handled was around 854,000 tonnes. There has been immense traffic growth over the past three decades. The passenger traffic at the international airports (Mumbai, Delhi, Chennai and Kolkata) has grown from 5.7 million in 1972 to 28 million in 2000. Most air traffic is handled at these four airports. They together account for as much as two-thirds of total passenger traffic and almost four-fifths of total cargo traffic in the country.

Recent initiatives of the government include deregulation of the domestic airline markets, inviting private participation in the development of airport infrastructure and modernization of the air traffic system. The Government of India has drafted a new Civil Aviation Policy that aims at:

- Improving the development and regulation of civil aviation including the operation of air transport services to meet the needs of the people for safe, secure, regular, efficient and economic air transport;
- Establishment of the Civil Aviation Authority;

- Continued adherence by India to the Chicago Convention, the Tokyo Convention, The Hague Convention and the Montreal Convention, including the Montreal Protocol;
- Commitment of India to the convention for unification of certain rules relating to international carriage by air, signed at Montreal on 28 May, 1999.

Over the last few years, there have been significant changes in India's bilateral air services policy. Recognising the need to enhance the capacity for international traffic, the government has re-visited or entered into bilateral agreement with a number of countries. As a result, the capacity on international routes has gone up to approximately 3.3 million seats per annum. Considering the astronomical sums required for modernization and upgradation of airports at Mumbai (Rs.10,000 crores), Bangalore (Rs.1600 crores) etc., the government has proposed privatization of projects so as to utilize state resources in the most optimal manner. According to the Ministry of Civil Aviation:

> "The truth of the matter is that public funds for development of airports are getting more and more scarce and private sector involvement has, therefore, got to grow. There is a definite worldwide movement from monopoly state ownership of airports to corporatization, in the first phase, with the final aim of privatization of ownership and management. India has to be a part of this global transition."

The policy statement further mentions that "it would be best to keep all the options open in respect of the management of airports or parts of airports. These could be on Build-Own-Transfer (BOT), Build-Own-Lease-Transfer (BOLT), Build-Own-Operate (BOO), Lease-Develop-Operate (LDO), Joint venture, Management Contract or Wrap-around Addition basis. In each individual case, the exact pattern could be negotiated, depending on the circumstances."

Besides the financial and functional efficiency objectives, the policy seeks to introduce of state-of-art air traffic, security and related services; and also provide multi-modal linkages.

The government has allowed 100 per cent FDI in airports. FDI up to 74 per cent are approved through the automatic route.

Under the policy of enhancing the role of the private sector in improving the efficiency of the airport infrastructure, four of the largest international airports at Delhi, Mumbai, Chennai and Kolkata have been opened up for private investment in building new facilities. Two new airports at Hyderabad and Bangalore have also been taken up through private sector participation.

Apart from the International airports, there are plans to revamp 35 non-metro airports, including Ranchi, Bhopal, Trivandrum, Nagpur, Indore, Trichy and Coimbatore. All 35 airports have been divided into groups of five airports each so that some of the non-profitable airports can be clubbed with the profitable ones.

Technical, legal and financial advisors have been appointed to conduct techno-economic feasibility studies of the airports and come up with an appropriate model based on the viability of each project. The cost of revamping the 35 airports is expected to be around Rs.5,000 to 6,000 crore. Work on the airports is likely to be completed by 2008-2009. Unlike airports in Delhi and Mumbai, modernization of these airports will not follow the PPP model. However, Government of India is seeking private partnership for city-side development such as retail, hotels, car parks, malls and other non-aeronautical ways of revenue earning.

Classification of Airports

The airports in India are classified in the following manner :

***(i)* International Airports** : These are declared as international airports and are available for scheduled international operations by Indian and foreign carriers. Presently, Mumbai, Delhi, Chennai, Calcutta and Thiruvananthapuram are in this category.

***(ii)* Customs Airports** : These have customs and immigration facilities for limited international operations by national carriers and for foreign tourist and cargo charter flights. These include Bangalore, Hyderabad, Ahmedabad, Calicut, Goa, Varansi, Patna, Agra, Jaipur, Amritsar and Tiruchirapally.

***(iii)* Model Airports** : These are domestic airports which have minimum runway length of 7500 feet and adequate terminal capacity to handle Airbus 320 type of aircraft. These can cater to limited international traffic, if required. These include Lucknow, Bhubaneshwar, Guwahati, Nagpur, Vadodara, Coimbatore, Imphal and Indore.

(*iv*) **Other Domestic Airports** : All other airports are covered in this category.

(*v*) **Civil Enclaves in Defence Airports** : There are 28 civil enclaves in Defence airfields.

To develop the capacity of airports in accordance with the future projections, it is proposed to reclassify the airports as follows :

(*a*) **International Hubs** : This category will be that of 'International Hubs' which cover airports currently classified at 'international airports' and those eminently qualified to be upgraded as such. These would at present cover Delhi, Mumbai, Chennai, Calcutta and Thiruvananthapuram. Airports at Bangalore, Hyderabad, Ahmedabad, Amritsar and Guwahati can be added to the list. International Hubs would be used for dispersal of international traffic to the hinterland. In these airports, the facilities shall be of world class standards, including convenient connections to international and domestic passengers, airport-related infrastructure like hotels, shopping areas, conferencing and entertainment facilities, aircraft-maintenance bases, etc.

(*b*) **Regional Hubs** : Regional hubs will act as operational bases for regional airlines and also have all the facilities for model airports, including the capability to handle limited international traffic. The identification of Regional Hubs will be made on the basis of origin-destination surveys, traffic demand and the requirements of the airlines, State Government will be closely associated as co-promoters of regional airlines.

(*c*) **Other operational airports** : These will be developed so as to be cost-effective on the basis of individual needs to meet the requirements of traffic handled by them. Airports serving State Capitals will be given priority.

2-4-6-8 Syndrome

It is a coincidence that the rates of growth of GDP and air traffic (6 to 8% per annum) have been running almost parallel during last decades. India's traffic growth reflects a pattern, what can be called 2-4-6-8 syndrome, the figures indicating respectively the annual growth rate of the population, rail/bus traffic, private cars and air traffic.

There is a growing realization to make public transport attractive, with the long-term effect of improving quality of life cities, country-side and the hinterland and saving depleting energy resources. Considerable efforts are required to achieve successful transport interchanges. It is not only the public transport vehicle and its service which counts, it is the whole journey that involves a traveller transferring from one route or mode to another. The airports provide an excellent opportunity to integrate intra-city and intercity modes of transport. These can also trigger the development of a vast region by opening it up. Coordinated inter-modality strategy plans can present the opportunity to reduce substantially large road traffic.

Planning, Design and Development

While embarking upon the modernization and privatization, it is equally essential to understand the concept of an international airport as a social, economic and transport hub bringing together the railways, highways and bus stations. Pre-planning and the development of design ideas, supportive to the replacement of private transport by sustainable public transport will pay dividends. All have a part to play- the airlines, transport operators, local and central authorities, developers, investors and designers, but it is the vision of a planner which will act as a catalyst to both the process and the product.

The process:

- Proactive planning strategy and programme
- Design and Development alternatives.
- Social benefits.

The product:

- Safe, comfortable, world class interchange bringing together key mobility functions.
- Improved public transport, accessible and attractive to all.
- Airport as a sustainable thriving public space.

Planning attempts to interface the locational, physical, transport, social, legal, management, financial and other aspects into a composite whole. It strives to strike a balance between conflicting demands – passenger comfort versus security controls, commercial opportunity versus environmental sustainability, service with speed versus mandatory procedures. Most important is to develop an orientation, a vision and ideas as the basis of planning. There is a need to reimagine the airport and develop lateral thinking to evolve out of box ideas.

Reimagining the Future Airport

When I first landed at the New York, J F K Airport in the early seventies, my immediate reaction was-future is now, Utopia is here! The architecture of Eero Saarinen and other celebrated architects, interiors as art gallery, the mono-rail, Greyhound buses, smooth and rapid check-in and check-outs that time made the airport appear like a dreamland. Today in 2006, Indian airports still give a primitive, sad and serious look, creativity squeezed out by over-riding procedures, safety regulations, pre-dominant public sector controls and the new concepts bogged down by mental blocks (such as free trade is evil and fun is funny, financial planning is the ultimate planning and PPP management is a panacea for all kinds of problems). It is a never-again opportunity to make a turn-around by re-imagining and developing certain wild ideas. Such ideas could be –

- Airport as the Gateway to the Future
- Airport as a self contained and integrated city
- Airport as the hub of city network
- Airports (helicopters) for everyday commuters

The central idea of an airport is its role as an interchange of mobility, services, functions and networks. The backbone of planning for the future is the radical transformation of infrastructure systems. Energy, water, waste management, sanitation, mobility and information networks need to be planned on the basis of future growth patterns and physical and environmental potentials, alongwith price-based signals enabled investment and technology choice. The extensive use of IT and biotechnology would enable the airport complex to evolve and adapt with its metabolism networked to the surrounding ecosystems. This requires the widespread application of eco-technology and changes in institutions, management and governing regulations and the principles. There is an urgent need to focus upon the improvement in energy services. This involves using 'factor 4' technologies and de-centralised generation alternative and renewable energy sources, such as solar energy, wind turbines, biomass-based energy generation, gas and clean coal for thermal power, the grid CNG and hydrogen as the major energy carriers, need to be explored. The concept of energy efficiency begins with Zero-fossil Energy Development (ZED), which should be incorporated as the basis of planning.

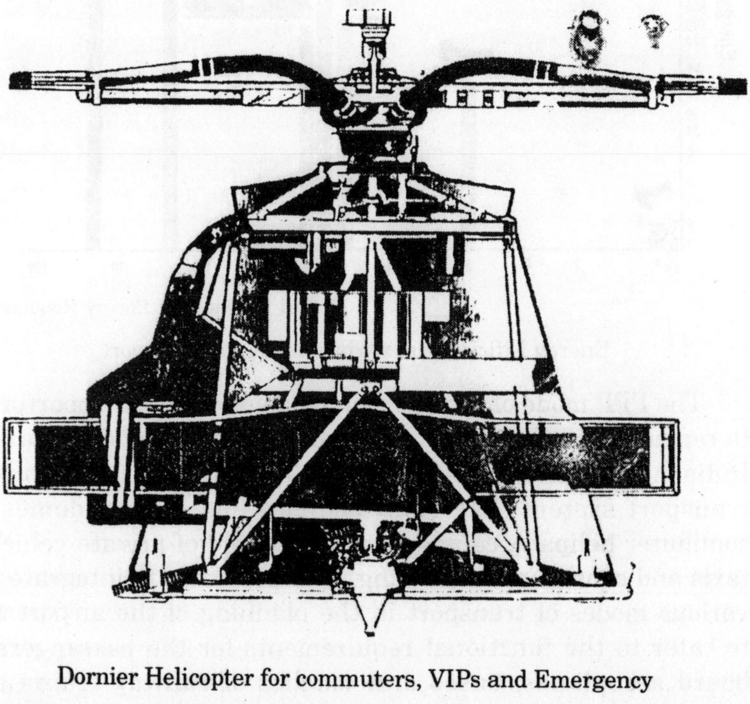

Dornier Helicopter for commuters, VIPs and Emergency

Resource saving technologies and processes is the starting point for environmentally responsive planning. For eco-efficiency factor four provides a valuable tool. As a rule of thumb, if a certain level of resource use is defined as a baseline, reduction of use by a factor x (say half) implies a reduction of the load on ecosystems by the same factor. At the same time enhancing the efficiency factor for technology and operations (say twice) gives a 'Factor-4' efficiency. A specific efficiency factor may be an abstract target, but successfully increasing efficiency requires knowledge of local ecology on which to base the technologies and processes used. Planning along the lines of Factor-4 in actual implementation produces very tangible results and improves on the limited carrying capacity and conservation of natural resources.

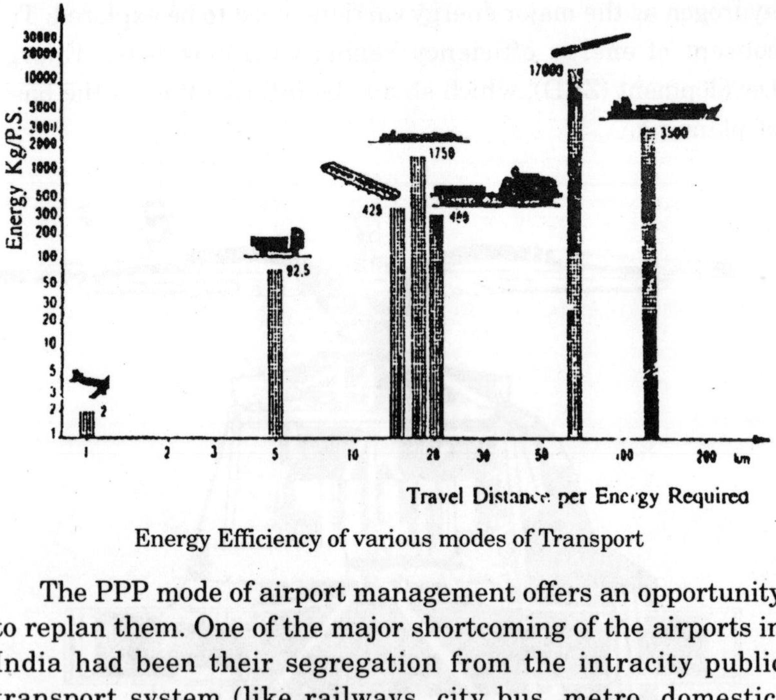

Energy Efficiency of various modes of Transport

The PPP mode of airport management offers an opportunity to replan them. One of the major shortcoming of the airports in India had been their segregation from the intracity public transport system (like railways, city bus, metro, domestic/ commuter helipad), causing undue demand of private vehicles/ taxis and consequently parking. It is necessary to integrate the various modes of transport in the planning of the airport and to cater to the functional requirements for the passengers to board aeroplanes, buses and coaches of railway trains and transfer among them. The development of benchmarks and parameters is a pre-requisite to address integrated planning:

Aero-train

- Space standards.
- Organisation of transport networks and integration of various modes
- Segregation of Incoming and outgoing traffic, Cargo and passengers, Visitors, customers and officials, Public and private vehicles
- Passenger Information System (including touchscreen, internet, phone, tourist, hotel, transport, etc.
- Security
- Border, Customs and other controls.
- General legislation.
- Commercial opportunities, community, cultural and social facilities, passenger accommodation and amenities
- Terminal operator's requirements.
- Transport operator's requirements.
- Parking and traffic control
- Needs of passengers with reduced mobility.

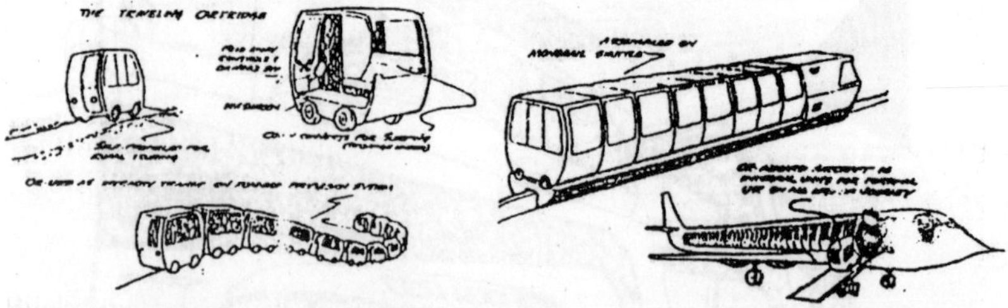

Buckminster Fuller's proposal for computerised personal transport using personal cabins. Passengers type their required destination into a computer at a station, insert their card and are driven automatically to their appropriate plane, which the cabin enters.

Source: Baldwin's Bucky Works. John Wiley & Sons Inc.

One of Alden's early sketches showing the automatic vehicle switching, on deand, into a station to allow passengers to interchange with a long-distance train. *Source: William Alden.*

- Infrastructure Services and utilities (roads, communications, water supply, power, solid waste, fire, police, drainage, disaster management, etc.)

It is essential that the services and utilities are planned with flexibility to keep with fast changing technology. These should incorporate intelligent controls and 'state of the art' maintenance system.

Space standards are variable and subjective. The objective solution is to work out the norms from the concept of level of service. For many passengers the criterion by which terminals such as airports are judged is the walking distance between one mode of transport and another. Although there is an inevitability about the length of a railway station platform or an airport pier, design can mitigate the strain of walking distance by providing passenger conveyors. The checking of passengers and their possessions requires the installation and manning of suitable

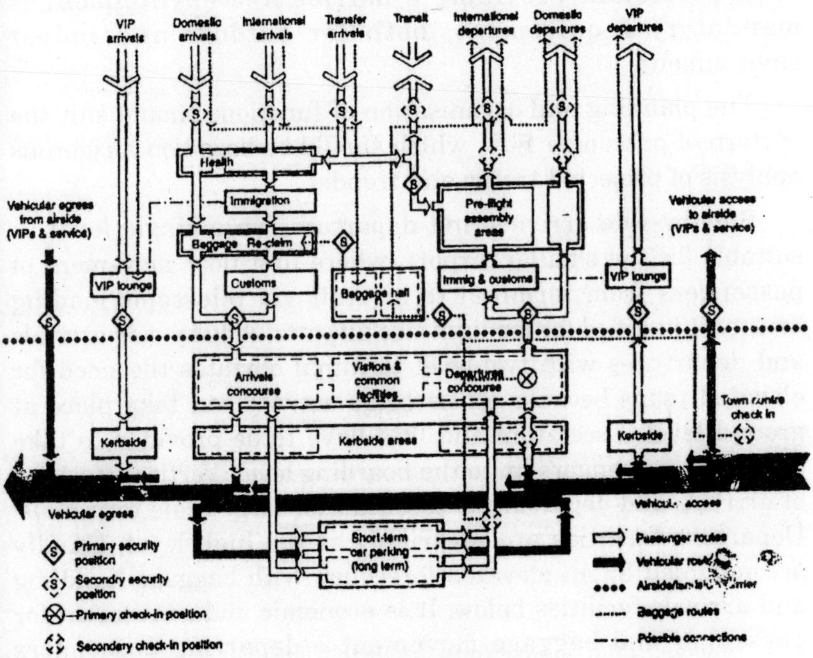

Passenger and vehicular flow patterns for an international plus domestic terminal.

equipment and the strategic location of the check point in order to ensure that the procedure is carried out in the most efficient manner.

Integrated Public Transportation should be the basis of design of the future airport. Networked just-in-time public transportation systems, such as hypertrams and guided hyper-buses could be the least cost and low ecological footprint solutions. High speed intercity rail line, air transport and the containerization with radio tagging of goods enable automated rapid goods movement across different levels of aggregation. Piggybacking on the passenger network should be integral component of airport network planning.

For efficient use of space, which is always at a premium in an airport, grade separated corridors, multi level parking and subterranean space for circulation and parking should be explored. Transport systems are intimately linked to pollution control, including noise, which should be a major determinant of Airport Plan. Providing a barrier free environment is mandatory requirement, both for outdoor and indoor environment.

The planning and organisation of functions should suit the pattern of passenger flow, which should be based on a rigorous analysis of projected traffic and trends.

Side-by-side arrivals and departures on a single level, is suitable for the smaller airport, where first-floor movement of passengers from terminal to aircraft via telescopic loading bridges is justified for medium size airports. Side-by-side arrivals and departures with two-level terminal obviates the need for elevated roads because all kerbside activity can take place at ground level. Escalators and lifts have to be provided to take departing passengers up to the boarding level. Vertical stacking of arrivals and departure is essential for large-scale terminals. Departure facilities are invariably at the high level, usually accompanied by an elevated forecourt, with baggage handling and arrivals facilities below. It is economic and convenient for passenger and baggage movement – departing passengers arrive at an elevated forecourt and move either on the level or down a short distance.

While the Indian economy is all set to integrate itself into the global economy, the modernization of airport infrastructure is at the threshold of a major take-off. Recognizing the fact that this is crucial for sustainable development of the Indian economy, trade and tourism, it is necessary to develop the Indian airports as the 'Gateways to the Future'. This calls for a vision based approach and planning based on radical ideas. The new civil aviation policy has already opened a window and if this opportunity is not grabbed, it would be catastrophic for the country and for the aviation sector too.

River Yamuna in Delhi, 1857

19

INTERLINKING OF RIVERS

At a certain point...- very recently in historical terms – we started worrying less about what nature can do to us, and more about what we have done to nature. This marks the transition from the predominance of external risk to that of manufactured risk.

— Giddens, 1999

Total annual water availability in Indian rivers is 4,000 billion cubic meters (BCM), out of which utilizable water is only 1,122 billion cubic meters, indicating a huge wastage of the water resource. The precipitation in our country is erratic and uneven leading to frequent floods and droughts. The rivers are mostly fed by the monsoon precipitation, which occurs during 4 months. However lack of the storages results into frequent flooding and it discharge into the sea. There are large disparities in the water availability in various river basins, which varies from 182 Cum in Sabarmati basin to 1068 in Kaveri, 2500 in Mahanadi and 3082 cum. in Narmada basins. As a result, similar disparities are visible in water available per hectare of cultivable area.

India is moving fast to join the club of water stressed nations. The per capita availability of water is reaching fast towards the threshold of 1000 cubic metres per person, which is the bottomline for water-stress condition. According to the forecast of the Ministry of Water Resources and Agriculture Ministry, by 2025, 11 river basins including the Ganges will be water deficit, threatening 900 million lives.

The average run-off in the river system of India has been assessed as 1,869, cubic kilometre. Of this, the utilisable portion by conventional storage and diversion is estimated as about 690

km^3. In addition, there is substantial replenishable groundwater potential in the country estimated at 432 km^3. The per-capita availability of water at the national level has reduced from about 5,177 cubic metre in the year 1951 to the present level of 1,869 cubic metres.

The Conception of a National Water Grid

India with **2.3% of world's land area,** occupies second place in the world with **11.7% of world's arable area** and first place in the world with **21.8%** share of **world's irrigated areas.** It indicates that the water use in our irrigation system (which uses 90% of freshwater withdrawals), is quite wasteful and inefficient.

India's eternal paradox is that while some parts of the country suffer from floods, at the same time many parts suffer from the drought. The programme on interlinking of rivers is based on the premises that the water that becomes surplus during the monsoon in some of the river basins can be transferred to reservoirs from where it can be released through link canals to the water scarce areas. This would reduce the intensity of floods and bring water to water scarce regions.

TIMELINE

1839	:	Sir Arthur Cotton proposed a plan to interlink Indus river for inland navigation.
1972	:	K.L. Rao, then Minister for Irrigation and Power, prepares proposal for national water grid. His proposal, called the Ganga-Cauvery link stretches across 2640 km, from Ganga to the South.
1977	:	Captain Dastur proposes construction of 4,200 Km. long Garland Canal across the Himalayas, 9,300 Km. long Southern Garland canal and pipelines to connect the two near Delhi and Patna.
1980s	:	Government prepares National Perspective Plan with the Peninsular component as the priority.
1982	:	National Water Development Agency set up to prepare detailed plans for project
2002	:	Task Force set up by government

River Basins of India

For integrated development and management of water resources, basin being the basic hydrologic unit, it is essential to know the water potential basin-wise. The country is having a large network of rivers, which have been divided into twenty river basins comprising twelve major basins having drainage area exceeding 20,000 square kilometer (sq.km). These are (1) Indus, (2) Ganga-Brahmaputra-Meghna, (3) Godavari, (4) Krishna, (5) Cauvery, (6) Mahanadi, (7) Pennar, (8) Brahmani-Baitarni, (9) Sabarmati, (10) Mahi, (11) Narmada and (12) Tapi.

The remaining medium rivers (with drainage area from 2000 to 20,000 sq.km) and minor rivers (with drainage area less than 2000 sq.km) are combined together to make eight composite river basins for the purpose of planning and development. These are (1) Subernarekha, (2) East flowing rivers between Mahanadi and Pennar, (3) East flowing rivers between Pennar and Kanyakumari, (4) Area of Inland drainage in Rajasthan Desert, (5) West flowing rivers of Kutch and Sauarashtra, including Luni, (6) West flowing rivers from Tapi to Tadri, (7) West flowing rivers from Tadri to Kanyakumari, and, (8) Minor rivers draining into Bangladesh and Myanmar.

India – River Basins

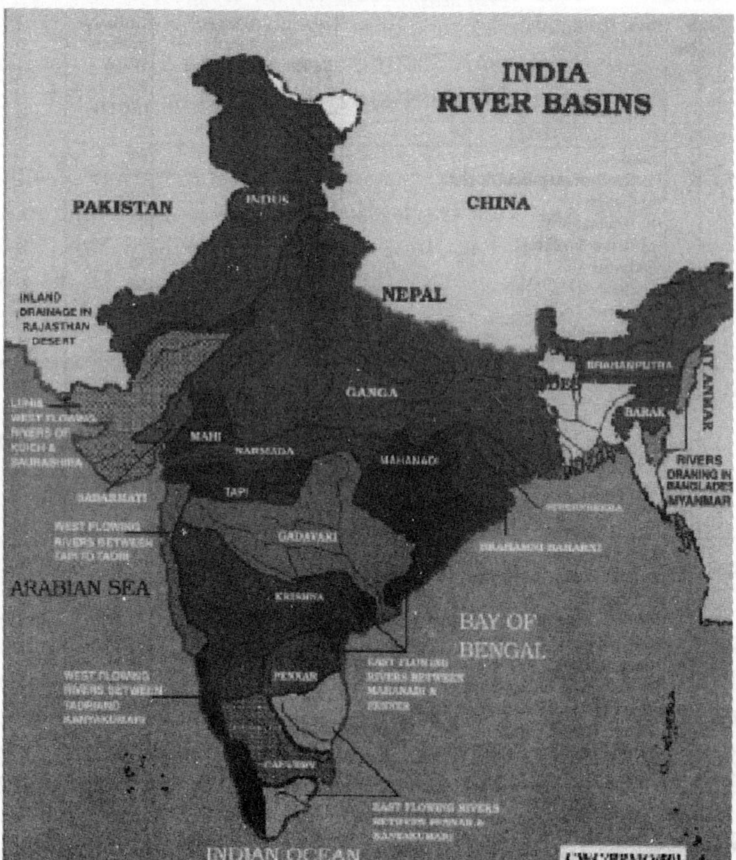

The issue of number of river basins has been examined by National Commission for Integrated Water Resources

Development (NCIWRD) and the Commission has considered 24 basins in the country for the purpose of assessment of water availability.

Basin-wise Storage in India (in Billion Cubic Metre)

S. No.	Name of the River Basin	Catchment Area (sq km)	Average Annual Flow (BCM)	Live Storage Capacity		
				Completed Projects	Projects under Construction	Projects under consideration
1	2	3	4	5	6	7
A MAJOR RIVER BASINS						
1.	Indus	3,21,289	73.31	13.83	2.45	0.27
2.	(*a*) Ganga	8,61,452	525.02	36.84	17.12	29.56
	(*b*) Brahmaputra and Barak	2,36,136	585.60	1.09	2.40	63.35
3.	Brahmani & Baitarni	51,822	28.48	4.76	0.24	8.72
4.	Mahanadi	1,41,589	66.88	8.49	5.39	10.96
5.	Godavari	3,12,812	110.54	19.51	10.65	8.28
6.	Krishna	2,58,948	78.12	34.48	7.78	0.13
7.	Pennar	55,213	6.32	0.38	2.12	
8.	Cauvery	81,155	21.36	7.43	0.39	0.34
9.	Tapi	65,145	14.88	8.53	1.01	1.99
10.	Narmada	98,796	45.64	6.60	16.72	0.47
11.	Mahi	34,842	11.02	4.75	0.36	0.02
12.	Sabarmati	21,674	3.81	1.35	0.12	0.09
B COMPOSITE RIVER BASINS						
1.	Subernarekha	29,196	12.37	0.66	1.65	1.59
2.	West flowing rivers of Kutch Saurashtra including Luni	3,21,851	15.10	4.31	0.58	3.15
3.	West flowing rivers from Tapi to Tadri	55,940	87.41	7.19	2.66	0.84
4.	West flowing rivers from Tadri to Kanyakumari	56,177	113.53	10.24	2.31	1.70
5.	East flowing rivers between Mahanadi & Pennar	86,643	22.52	1.63	1.45	0.86
6.	East flowing rivers between Pennar & Kanyakumari	1,00,139	16.46	1.42	0.02	
7.	Area of inland drainage in Rajasthan	60.00	Neg.	0.00	0.00	0.00
8.	Minor river basins draining into Bangladesh & Myanmar	36.202	31.00	0.31	0.00	0.00
	Total		**1869.35**	**173.73**	**75.42**	**132.32**

Note

1. Projects having alive storage capacity of 10 million cubic metre and above only are included.
2. An additional storage capacity of 3 billion cubic metre (proxy.) is estimated to be created through Medium Projects each having a capacity of less than 10 million cubic metre thus making a total live storage capacity of 177 billion cubic metre in completed projects.
3. Totals may not tally due to rounding off.

Source: National Commission for Integrated Water Resource Development (NCIWRD)

National Perspective Plan

The National Water Policy underlines the need for making water available to water short areas by transfer from other area including transfers from one river basin to another, based on a national perspective, after taking into account the requirements, of the areas/basins. The Ministry of Water Resources had prepared in 1980 a National Perspective Plan for development of country's water resources, disregarding political boundaries of States.

The National Plan is in two parts namely, (i) development of Peninsular Rivers which is entirely within the control of the Central and State Government, and (ii) Himalayan Rivers. These two components are proposed to be linked by Mahanadi.

Thc Himalayan Component

This envisages construction of dams, diversion works and canals to transfer water from surplus eastern rivers towards deficit central, western and southern regions. The National Water Development Agency (NWDA) took up 11 Himalayan links for study. These include Manas-Sankosh-Tista-Ganga link to transfer Brahmaputra waters to Eastern Ganga Basin. This link envisages high dams on Manas and Sankosh and very large canals running through densely forested as well as populated areas cutting across major drainages and the narrow strip of land north of Bangladesh. Other links proposed are Kosi-Ghagra, Gandak-Ganga, Ghagra-Yamuna and Sarda-Yamuna to supplement the supplies of Ganga and Yamuna and to further transfer water west to Rajasthan and Gujarat.

The Penisular Component

The link from Mahanadi would require construction of Manibhadra dam that would submerge 45,900 ha. of agricultural land and displace 91,000 people. It is facing opposition from Orissa which however, does not accept that there is surplus water in the Mahanadi. The Mahanadi-Godavari link would be 9,390 km long and cut across east-flowing drainages, though it involves no lift.

Godavari is joined by two major tributaries, Indravati and Penganga downstream of the major storage at Shri Ramsagar. Even after meeting downstream basin requirements Godavari has surplus water in this reach which can be stored in the available dam site of Incharmpalli. In spite of the displacement involved the benefits, including to those to be rehabilitated from low yield unirrigated farming to high yield irrigated land deserve an objective assessment and demand a high priority. After irrigating about 11.5 lakh hectares of dry land between Godavari and Krishna, there will still be about 3 lakh cubic metre of water available, which can be transferred to Cauvery Basin and relieve it from occasional shortage. It may also help to resolve the dispute between Tamil Nadu and Karnataka.

The Development Plan calls for cooperation of India, Nepal, Bangladesh and Bhutan. The Himalayan and Peninsular River Plans would add to the presently estimated ultimate irrigation potential, besides providing large quantum of hydro-power and flood control. Development and transfer of waters on inter-State and international rivers will require diplomatic, political and strategic initiatives by the Government in formulating an acceptable plan and its financing.

As most of the major rivers in India are inter-State in character having catchments/watersheds in two or more States, no integrated development on water resources is possible without inter-State co-operation. Even in those cases where the tribunals set up under the Inter-State Water Disputes Act, 1956 have given their final awards, implementation and operationalization of these awards become difficult if the participating States do not cooperate. Most of the arrangements for sharing river waters and co-operating on joint projects were mutually reached by the states themselves. Mediation by the Central Government was also sometimes neccessary. There are currently 58 independent agreements: 39 for joint projects and 19 for the sharing of river waters.

However, specific tribunals had to be set up under Section 3 of the Inter-State Water Disputes Act, 1956 to resolve inter-State water disputes when the issues were highly contentious or water shortages serious enough that negotiation by the relevant parties, by itself, proved inadequate. So far, five river tribunals have been established and awards of three tribunals - Krishna (1976), Godavari (1979), and Narmada Water Disputes Tribunal (1979) have been finally delivered. Ravi-Beas Tribunal and Cauvery Water Disputes Tribunal are still continuing. The project is facing several hurdles as given below:-

- Absence of Consensus among co-basin states to transfer of surplus waters.

- Construction of dams in India, Nepal and Bhutan requiring International agreements.
- Construction of dams involving environmental issues like submergence of forest
- land and habitations. Manas-Sankosh-Tista-Ganga link passes through Manas, Raidak and Buxar Tiger Reserves and Gaburbasra Reserve Forest. Ministry of Environment and Forest, GOI has not granted permission for surveys and investigations.

The Proposals

Considering the availability of surplus flows in the Brahmaputra and its tributaries, the alternatives for transfer of surplus water from Brahmaputra to Ganga outlined in the National Perspective Plan, are as follows:

Option 1 : Jogighopa (Brahmaputra)-Farakka (Ganga) link through Assam, Bangladesh and West Bengal by gravity.

Option 2 : Brahmaputra-Ganga link through Manas-Sankosh-Tista-Ganga (Farakka) by gravity.

Option 3 : Brahmaputra-Ganga link with lift from Jogighopa upto Tista and then by gravity upto Farakka (Jogighopa-Tista-Farakka link).

Option 1, that is, the proposed link canal from Jogighopa to Farakka via Bangladesh is the shortest compared to the other alternatives of National Perspective Plan being only 324 km in length while the others are 457 km and 440.53 km respectively. Further, *entire flow will be through gravity.* However, about 1/3rd of the link canal will pass through Bangladesh which requires consent and cooperation of Bangladesh Government. For working out option 1, diplomatic channels need to be opened up with Bangladesh, because this is the cheapest and best option which also provides flood control benefits in the Bangladesh portion of the Brahmaputra valley. All the options, however require the following :

To minimize displacement of people transfer of water by *tunnels* should be explored to the maximum possible.

Donor States should be helped in developing infrastructure, like small and big hydro reservoirs.

The characteristics of the river link proposal:

- Building Dams for storage of water
- Construction of link canal systems
- Transfer of water mostly by gravity from surplus basins to deficit basins / areas
- Pumping of water where necessary (confined to max. depth of 120 M)

Main Issues

- Consensus among 'Donor' and 'Donee' States.
- Reengineering the irrigation management for efficiency.
- Re-defining 'surplus monsoon run off' so that the surplus can be diverted.
- Defining and calculating the normal average flood within and outside flood plain zoning areas to determine excess, unnatural flood waters for diversion.
- Identification of a pilot projects for linking Southern and Western States of India with Ganga-Brahmaputra Basin.
- Water surplus /^deficit studies of basins based on current usages and projected future usages
- A definition of 'surplus' incorporating:-
  (*a*) Basin capacity based on current, emerging and future use.
  (*b*) Basins capacity plus surplus monsoon runoff plus surplus monsoon spillover as floods.
  (*c*) Definition of minimum flow, average flow (non-monsoon and monsoon season).

Critical Management Issues

- Integrated Flood Control and Drought Management
- Water Management on ecological basis
- Adequate quantity of water to be made available for water-deficit basins
- Demand side management through efficient management, planning, technology and institutional, legal framework

- A combination of macro and micro scales of irrigation and water storage.
- A comprehensive water conservation strategy including financial and regulatory reforms (such as user pay and polluter pay principles)

The following Table indicates the impact matrix for various option of river basin development for water augmentation:

Impact matrix of River basin development

Development option	*Geomorphological Impact*	*Possible Effect*
Dam construction	• Soil erosion active • Helocene/historical erosion • Soil erosion controlled at source • Seismic danger	Sedimentation in upland basins/dams Sedimentation from stores Degradation of sediment stores Submergence of forests & habitations Ecological consequences
River regulation	• Dam above alluvial zone • Dam with flood control/hydropower • Dam near coast	Channel change below dam Habitat effects via floods/bed structure Coastal erosion
Land-use development	• Land on slope/ active tectonics • Land on active/ semi-active stores • Floodplain land • Changes in water quality and pollution	Insert failure unless small scale Changes to hydroloogy release sediment Loss of habitat/ spontaneous regularion
River linking & Canal networking	• Buffer strips • Re-vegetation of riparian zone • Intercept existing drains • Reduction in erosion • Restoration of	Political/adminis-trative disputes Huge financial overheads Need to conserve heritage Acquisition of lands Micro-climatic impacts

Development option	*Geomorphological Impact*	*Possible Effect*
	meanders, riffle, pool sequences • Aquifer protections • Tehabilitation of submerged settlements	
Water storage in Micro-structures	• Irrigation, flood management, drainage linked planning • Restoration of local flora and fauna • Aquifer protection	Seasonal/rain dependence Small financial overheads Participatory process and community control

During the recent years, the environmental, social and human impacts of large artificial storage and changes in river hydrology and morphology have been the subject of intense debate and disputes. It is essential to consider these aspects carefully during planning and management of river basins and evolve the broad guidelines:

Guidelines for River Basin Management

1. Preservation or improvement of the spontaneous functions fulfilled by the river by:
   - (*a*) Restoring erosion/sedimentation processes, through countering increased silt loads caused by upstream erosion (improvement of watershed management).
   - (*b*) Preserving genetic diversity through conserving natural areas and threatened species.
   - (*c*) Preserving the self-purifying capacity of the river through combating pollution (water-treatment plants at source, anti-pollution measures).
2. Conservation of the natural values of the river basin by:
   - (*a*) Preventing deterioration/destruction of natural resources, by means of legislation (including compulsory environmental impact assessments) directed towards industrial development impoldering schemes and drainage activities.

(*b*) Establishing reserves in the most vulnerable ecosystems, with surrounding buffer areas.

(*c*) Establishing environmental education programmes.

(*d*) Initiating programmes to promote sound, durable exploitation of ecysystems (particularly fisheries, herding and forestry).

3. Conservation of the river basin's extensive-exploitation functions by:

(*a*) Guaranteeing the protection of productive zones, such as floodplains, estuaries and lakes, by allocating appropriate quantities of water and by means of the programmes mentioned in para 2.

(*b*) Implementing reforestations schemes for supply of firewood, in relation to sound watershed management.

4. Development of sustainable intensive exploitation functions by:

(*a*) Drawing up a water allocating plan for the entire river basin, to achieve a better match between water demand and supply; this should give due consideration to the water requirements of the spontaneous functions, natural values and extensive exploitation functions.

(*b*) Developing small-scale projects, e.g., irrigation, fishponds, forestry.

(*c*) Improving product processing, sales and marketing, e.g., by making better use of the river as a transport route.

(*d*) Ensuring that detailed plans for the above objectives are thoroughly checked against the other criteria within the framework of an environmental impact assessment procedure.

5. Improvement of the overall health situation in the river basin by:
   - (*a*) Combating water-borne diseases.
   - (*b*) Improving the food situation, both quantitatively and qualitatively.
   - (*c*) Establishing a drinking-water programme for rural areas, with the objective of making clean, healthy water available for the whole population.
   - (*d*) Ensuring that detailed plans for the above objectives are thoroughly checked against the other criteria within the framework of an environmental impact assessment procedure.
6. Guiding principles for regional planning:
   - (*a*) Work not against the environment.
   - (*b*) Start work from the existing situation, i.e., existing infrastructure, technical know-how, perceptions of subsistence security, cultural needs, etc.
   - (*c*) Protect the authentic evolution of local culture, institutions and know-how.
   - (*d*) When underkaing action or introducing social change, prefer those actions involving decision-making at the lowest possible level.
   - (*e*) Assess the carrying capacity of extensive agricultural and water-use systems, as well as their present value.
   - (*f*) Assess the required inputs for intensive systems of land and water use and their value if a growing number of people are to be fed.
   - (*g*) Intensify or introduce intensive land and water-use systems at locations with the best soil and superior climatological and market conditions.

(*h*) Preserve, develop and utilize nature's spontaneous functions.

(*i*) When planning reserves for species or ecosystems, endeavour to make these as large, as varied and as interconnected as possible.

(*j*) Preserve rare species and ecosystems in their authentic ecological setting, giving due consideration to the long-term effects of isolation.

(*k*) Avoid land-use and water-use systems exhibiting irreversible dependence on a single crop or market (especially narrow or foreign markets), also on the input side.

Displacement and Rehabilitation

Displacement as a sequel to hydel work and barrages has brought in its trail an atrophy of adversities. This is particularly tough on the poor and even more so on the landless. Interlinging of rivers will inevitably bring about widespread displacement of forests and habitations. The entire matter, therefore, deserves a fresh look, particularly in the context of riverine interlining projects.

This, however, is not a plea to cry wolf or to stall such projects to a halt. No, not that. On the contrary, the phenomenon of displacement needs to be woven as an integral part of the project itself and understood in a much wider prespective. Simultaneously the strategy of rehabilitation needs to be perceptive and well conceived and may largely precede implementation and be executed with finesse and sincerity. The people's participation may also be enlisted.

The acquisition laws, a legacy of foreign rule, are autocratic and in many cases heartless and lean heavily against the poor and the landless. Rehabilitation so far in case of river valley projects has been half-hearted, defective and desultory—this, again, does not provide for the landless, artisans, labourers and women. The porous and defective land laws, on the other hand, militate against the oustees, favour the well-to-do and are prone to corruption. This has, naturally, given rise to popular resistance movements not only in India but also abroad.

The story of neglect and heatlessness in this regard should not be woven in brazen indifference. The screams of the *vox populi* will in that case become both strident and resonant—in India and China, Europe and North America, and elsewhere in the world. The State will have to take care to ensure that riverine interlinking projects do not falter on grounds of displacement and rehabilitation. These factors are as important as project planning itself.

Many of these projects, as in the past, are likely to flounder on the anvil of displacement and rehabilitation. This has happened even for the hydel projects and flood control strategies. Damodar Valley and Narmada Valley projects are two telltale examples. It may, therefore, be appropriate to comment on this problem in anticipation, particularly because interlinking projects will involve massive displacement and rehabilitation.

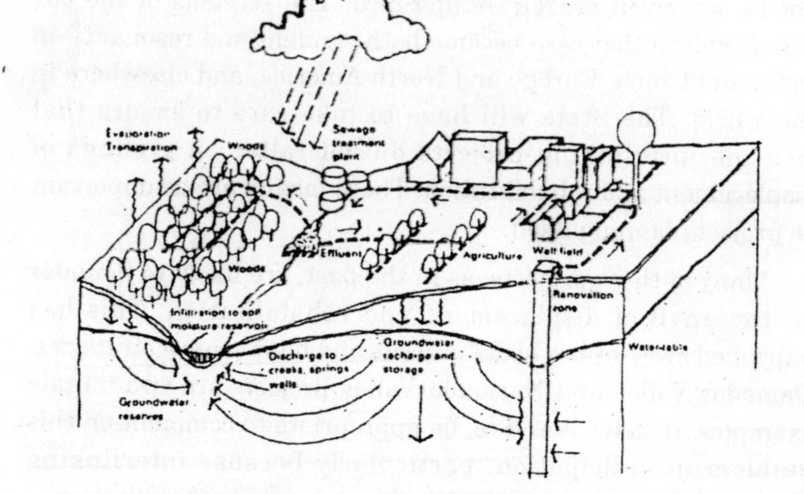

The Waste Water Renovation and Conservation Cycle

Solar Aquatics Treatment System

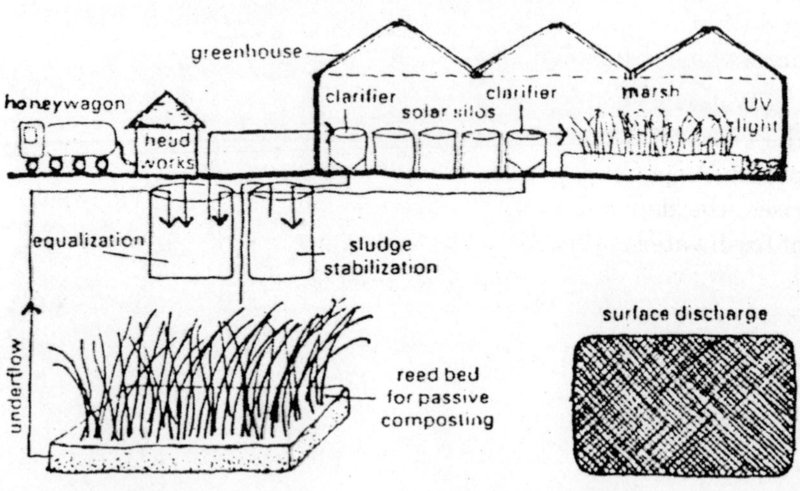

20

WATER HARVESTING AND CONSERVATION

Zig-zag is the way to success. A straight line leads to failure.

— Masai Proverb

Water is literally the source of life on earth. About 70 per cent of the earth is water, but most part of it is ocean. Practically, only 3 per cent of the total water available on earth is freshwater. Out of the 3 per cent, only 1 per cent is accessible surface freshwater whereas the rest 2 per cent is locked away in the form of ice caps and glaciers in the Polar regions, far distant from human habitation. The 1 per cent surface freshwater is regularly renewed by rainfall and other means and thus available on a sustainable basis and easily considered accessible for human use.

Water is the biggest crisis facing the world today. In India the crisis in terms of spread and severity affects one in three people. As population grows rapidly and use of water per person rises, the demand for freshwater goes up. Besides, the supply of freshwater is threatened by pollution.

Sources of Water

Source	*Percentage*
Oceans	96.5
Ground Water	1.70
Soil moisture	0.001
Glaciers and Permanent snow	1.74
Lakes – (Fresh and salt water)	0.013
Rivers	0.002
Atmospheric	0.001

Water Crisis in India

Water is clearly the single largest problem facing India today though once upon a time it had been a water-rich society. Rainfall is uneven across the length and breadth of the country and not uniform throughout the year. About 90 per cent of its annual rainfall occurs during the summer monsoon, which lasts from July to September whereas the rest of the months the country gets barely a drop of water. In India, every summer on an average, 91 districts are drought-affected while 40 million hectares in 83 districts are submerged in floodwaters. Besides, a peculiar problem also manifests in some parts of the country such as in Cherrapunji which has abundant rainfall in the rainy season (11,000 mm) and is the wettest place on earth but which faces acute shortage of water during the rest of the year. Between Cherrapunji's (Assam) 11,000 mm and Jaisalmer's (Rajasthan) 200 mm rainfall, on an average India receives 1,170 mm annual precipitation.

India receives an annual precipitation (snowfall and rain) of around 4,000 billion cubic meter (bcm). Of this, the run-off-accessible water is 1,869 bcm, of which barely 690 bcm is used. Nearly 1,179 bcm (roughly two rivers the size of Brahmaputra) of water drains into the sea, much of it in the rainy days (around 100 days) that define India's wet season. Adding 432 bcm of ground water with 690 bcm runoffi accessible water, the total real availability of water in India is 1,122 bcm for the billion-plus population of the country.

National Water Resource Potential

Precipitation	4000	BCM
Average Runoff in Rivers	1869	BCM
Utilizable Surface Water	690	BCM
Replenishable Ground Water	432	BCM
Total Water Availability	1122	BCM
Transfer from Surplus Basins	200	BCM
Irrigation Potential	140	Mha
Hydro-Power Potential (L)	84000	MW @ 60%
Hydro-Power Potential (S)	10000	MW

Rapid population growth and increasing water consumption for agriculture, industry, municipalities and other areas have strained Indian freshwater resources. Nearly 90 per cent of the water required for irrigation is met from ground water resources. The rest 7 per cent and 3 per cent the country spends for industrial and domestic purposes, respectively. In many parts of our country chronic water shortages, loss of arable land, destruction of natural habitats, degradation of the environment, and widespread pollution undermine public health and threaten economic and social progress. According to a survey report published in India Today, (June 9, 2003) while 12 major Indian cities require 14,000 million litres (mlt) of water a day, they get only 10,000 mlt. The shortfall of 4,000 mlt is what Mumbai needs everyday, and is enough to fill 4 lakh water tankers. Similarly, since the 1970s and 1980s the governments and municipal councils have developed and established water purification plants and pipelines to the house, without addressing the real issue of source of water supply. Rapid pace of urbanization in India has led to drying up of traditional water sources like tanks and lakes. In Bangalore, for example, out of 262 tanks, about 181 have dried up; in South Delhi, tubewells are now routinely dug at a depth of over 200 meters; and in and around Chennai, water is being mined and pumps are being dug 3 to 6 meters deeper every year. Ground water levels have plunged in 206 districts in our country. The Ministry of Water Resources estimates that the demand of water in top 35 Indian cities/metros is expected to double to 12,906 million cubic meters (Mcm) as the population of these cities shoots up from 107 million (2001) to 202 million in 2021, while water availability stays at the 2001 level. The results are, these excess population will be vulnerable to water-wars. According to a forecast by the Ministry of Water Resources, by 2025 eleven river basins including the Ganges will be water deficit, threatening 900 million lives.

Rainwater Harvesting

India drains a total volume of 400 million hectare metres of rain water of which hardly 100 million hectare meters is retained in the soil. The remaining water runs off, carrying with it fertile soil. The amount of water available per person in India is decreasing steadily – from 3450 cu.m in 1951, it fell to 1250 cu.m in 1999. This according to the Ministry of Water Resources, is expected to decrease further to 760 cu.m per person in 2050.

This gravity of water crisis in recent years does not need any new invention, but reinventing our own water wisdom. Looking back traditional practices provide clues and a pragmatic approach to handle the impending water crisis.

Traditional Water Harvesting Practices

Over the centuries a range of techniques to harvest every possible form of water, from rainwater, steams, rivers and flood water had been developed in India. In Meghalaya, a 200 year old system of tapping steam and spring water for irrigating plants by using bamboo still exists. The "kundis" of Rajasthan are unique structures which look like huge saucers and are used for collecting rain water to meet the needs of local villagers and their animals. In Rajasthan, particularly, Jodhpur, traditional water system still exists and village people maintain their traditional water systems even after they started getting piped water. The villagers that neglected their traditional systems and relied solely on piped water sources faced scarcity under drought conditions, particularly when the canals dried up. An ironic contrast of water management are Jaisalmer and Cherrapunji – Jaisalmer gets 100 mm of annual rainfall while Cherrapunji gets 1500 mm. Yet Jaisalmer was able to collect enough water for itself until recent years, while Cherrapunji, the wettest place on earth, faces a drinking water shortage.

In the desert towns of Rajasthan roof top water harvesting was a common practice. The sloping roofs of the houses were used to collect the rainwater, which was taken through a pipe into underground 'tanka' (tank), sometimes as big as a room built in the main house or the courtyard . This would not only meet the drinking water needs of the households, but also for cooling the rooms built next to the tank. Another traditional rainwater harvesting system in Rajasthan was the kund, a simple saucer shaped structure, having about 50 feet diameter whose sides were plastered with lime and ash. As water would naturally flow down to the centre along all the sides, a tank was built at the center to collect and store the water. A dome shaped cover was put on the top, which was plastered with mud. The kund had two or three openings from which rainwater could enter. Besides the kundas, the tanks or ponds were constructed in the depressions to store rainwater. Apart from the tanks, there were small reservoirs (Augor or Agar), with the Aav or Payatams (channels) that fed the reservoir. They were wide and shallow so that water velocity was low to avoid or reduce silting of the pond. Khurra or stone pieces placed strategically within the Aav reduced the velocity further. The tanks were stepped to receive the maximum water, the lower portions were known as Neshta and were constructed in lime and stone to withstand water pressure. This portion received the first rainfall, which were sometimes reinforced. The embankments are regularly repaired before the rainfall.

Shallow wells in the form of Baoli or Chuher were sometimes dug within the tanks or in low lying areas to supplement the surface accumulation. The reservoir was planned and constructed taking into account the actual and projected demands of the community. Various sections of varying heights ensured supply throughout the year. Measuring rods with different coding indicated the quantum of water available at different points within the reservoir. Usually, the tanks were constructed 20 Basis or Purush deep, one Purush being roughly 1.8 meters. For large tanks small islands were created in the middle to absorb the wave energy and to protect the mud embankments. Shrines were constructed on these islands to contribute to the waterbody's sacrosanct status and minimise its misuse. The catchment areas, the channels feeding the reservoir, the reserves and the outlets for irrigation or drainage were integral parts of the water harvesting system. Pani Panchayat or water societies created by electing members from the community were responsible for water management, together with arid agriculture. Special festival days were earmarked for repairs and desilting, in which the entire community participated.

The Approach

In order to adopt appropriate measures for augmenting ground recharge, it is necessary to spread water harvesting techniques by construction of check dams and percolation tanks, besides direct injection methods utilising the abandoned structures available in large numbers in the hard rock region.

Before undertaking direct recharge into such abandoned structures, suitability of the structure for receiving recharge and also the quality of source water should be thoroughly examined to confirm the technical feasibility. Rain water harvesting and ground water recharge can be dovetailed with watershed development programmes aimed at soil and water conservation by arresting the run-off. This involves evolving an action plan at local level, with the following objections:

- Arresting ground water decline and improving its accessibility
- Benefiting water quality in aquifers
- Preventing surface water run-off during monsoons
- Enhancing availability of surface water at a specific place and time
- Reducing power consumption
- Conserving urban waste water

To achieve the above objects the Key Action Areas would be the following:

- Practicing and implementing rain water harvesting and ground recharging through local bye laws.
- Organising mass awareness campaigns through hand-outs, posters and community level involvement.
- Motivating communities to participate in shramdan camps for cleaning ponds, tanks, wells and borewells; and reutilising them for ground water storage.
- Financial support for construction of check dams and creation of catchment ponds.
- Recycling waste water subject to quality and dual piping system.
- Recharging industrial effluents after treatment.

Alongwith water harvesting, it is also necessary to adopt the practices of Water Conservation and Recycling, as given below:

- Redesigning cisterns/tanks/reservoirs for conservation of water, e.g. traditional 3.5 gallon toilet cistern can be replaced by a 5 to 7 litres one with equal effect.
- Using urban waste material effluents after suitable treatment for horticulture etc.
- Recycling of waste water
- Conserving monsoon water in Johads, check dams, percolation tanks, village ponds etc. and their regular desilting.
- Using existing or defunct wells and tubewells for purpose of recharging and rainwater harvesting.

In order to conserve available water, and harvest rain water to the maximum extent possible, the following are the critical measures:

- Leak detection and water supply network maintenance and rectification.
- Rain water harvesting, through in-situ tanks check dams etc.
- Controlling indiscriminate extraction of ground water
- Recharging of aquifers
- Meters to be installed along trunk mains and for bulk consumers and tariff review.
- Percolation structures, wherever suited, be encouraged in open grounds and road side will help recharge bore-wells and provide water for gardening, car washing etc.
- Mandatory system of roof-top rain water harvesting.
- Recycling and reuse of treated waste water
- Soft parking, landscape and pavements filled with pebbles and coarse sand to allow percolation.

Rain water falling on roof can be collected and injected into ground water through various structures, such as given below:

Root Zone System

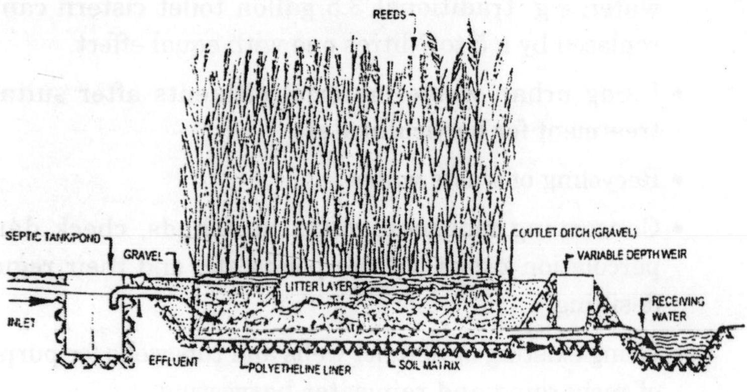

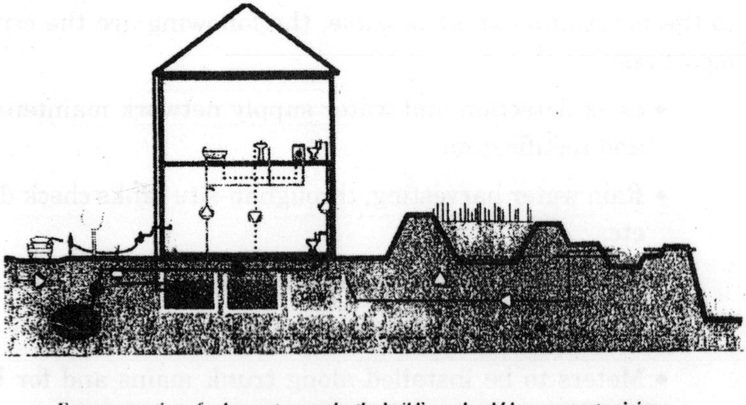

For conservation of urban water supply, the buildings should have separate piping systems for drinking water, for washing/showering and for re-circulating grey water.

- Reviving the Abandoned Dug Wells
- Reusing Abandoned/Running Hand Pumps
- Recharge Pit
- Recharge Trench
- Gravity Head Recharge Well
- Recharge Shaft

Urban planning should dovetail watershed management, the drainage concept should be based on and arresting the run-off.

It should ensure the conservation of natural valleys, water bodies and acquifers. The concepts of 'zero run-off drainage', with retention ponds, sediments traps and balancing lakes should be adopted, with a segregated wastewater disposal system. A green network overlapping the blue network would protect the ecology of acquifers, as also provide a pleasant environment. Simple methods of site planning, which incorporate porous/semi permeable paving, drop inlet/down pipe, sediment trap, retention ponds, etc. will contribute in maintaining ground water table. This is necessary if we want to avoid the impending water catastrophe looming over urban India.

The city should have variety of open spaces (a) about 2 sq. m per person at housing area level (tot-lots, having parks, courts), 2 sq. m per person at neighbourhood level (play ground, neighbourhood parks etc.), 2 sq. m at zonal and district level, 2 sq. m at city level, totalling to about 8 to 10 sq. m per person.

21

THE CONCEPT OF BIO-DRAINAGE

The next Big Thing may be a whole lot of little things – call it ecological pointillism.
— Richard D. Parsons

Indiscriminate and unprecedented urban growth during recent decades has created ecological hazards, trampling upon the nature countryside. Rains and floods in Mumbai and many other cities every year claim huge loss of lives, health and property and disrupt normal life. Such events manifest horror of destruction of ecology and natural drainage by unregulated developments. The rainfall of 944 mm recorded at Santa Cruz on 26 July 2005 was the highest within 24 hours in Mumbai and more than the 844 mm recorded in Cherapunji in 1910. The gravity of the situation has been compounded by projects like the Bandra-Worli Sea Link, which pinched the mouth of Mithi River that drains the bulk of Mumbai's excess water out into the Arabian Sea, at Mahim.

The Mithi River originates in the overflowing water from lakes of Tulsi, Vihar and Powai and also from the ridges, valleys of hills of Borivali. The actual source of the Mithi River is at the L&T factory at Powai (Vihar Village). The catchment area is around 10,800 ha. Suburbs such as Jogeshwari, Goregaon, Malad and Dahisar - all relatively young north-western suburbs - discharge sewage straight to the sea without mandatory treatment. Thus, in a very conspicuous manner, legal obligations have been ignored by the authorities, which has had stark effects on the local ecology. Mangroves, which act as the city's sponges, have shrunk from an area 23,500 ha in the Greater Mumbai area (in 1924) to only 16,000 ha in 1994. An additional 1000 ha of mangroves are estimated to have been destroyed in Mumbai by 2000, many of them in violation of the

Coastal Regulation Zone (CRZ) Rules, 1991. According to a 1995 study, over 15,600 ha in Mumbai acts as watershed or drainage basins for the streams that flow into the four big creeks in the city. Most of these basins have now been built upon with roads, buildings and slums, particularly in Jogeshwari to Kandivali and in areas around Mithi River.

More than 55% of city's population, 11.9 million, are living in slum areas and hutments (1,25,000 nos). The Bandra Kurla complex had been developed over 300 ha of mangrove land. Similarly, the basins in the western suburbs that flow into the Malad creek have been built upon without accommodating the natural drainage pattern; thus the overflow has flooded the nearby areas. In Ghatkopar, where the streams once flowed along the expressway, the Mithi River has been reduced to a narrow nullah. The illegal encroachments and reclamation near the Mithi River have occurred during several decades and have added to the deluge. At no point have these encroachments been inconspicuous; nor has any obvious action been taken to reduce or remove them. The flooding of July 2005 also affected in areas such as Dahisar, Borivali, Mulund, Thane, Kalyan, Navi Mumbai and other areas of Mumbai and its surroundings through which the Mithi River does not flow. Mumbai's stormwater network is more than 70 years old and hence requires improvement and upgrading, as recommended by consultants Watson and Hawksley. The stormwater drainage network is surveyed by the Storm Water Drains Department before every monsoon and the necessary work is required to be carried out, which includes desilting of stormwater drains. Unprecedented and indiscriminate developments along drainage channels have made these measures ineffective or impossible.

The present storm water drainage (SWD) system in the city is about 480 km in length. It is capable of handling rain intensity of 25 mm per hour at low tide. There are 107 major outfalls in the city that drain into Arabian Sea directly, four at Mahim Creek and four at Mahul creek. There are 29 out-falls in western suburbs draining directly into sea while 14 drain into the Mithi River which ultimately joins Mahim Creek. In the eastern suburbs, 14 out-falls discharge into Thane Creek while six discharge into Mahul Creek. One of the most heavily polluted storm water drains, which is known as Mithi River (15 km long and is narrow in the initial stretch and is about 10 m wide but at Bandra Kurla Complex it is much wider), is responsible for polluting Mahim Creek.

As a part of the Rs. 1200 Crore drainage and flood control plan, the Mumbai Municipal Corporation (MMC) has worked out the plans to reduce the flooding spots from 47 to 13. The state government decided in 1999 to ban the use of plastic carrier bags below the thickness of 20 microns in Mumbai and 15 other municipalities, but this has hot been enforced. The state government and the MMC have identified weak spots on the roads and bridges all over Mumbai and carried out preventive maintenance work. For systematic maintenance of roads and drainage the task of preparing a maintenance manual has been taken up in 2005, which is under progress. The drainage system is designed as per the guidelines of Indian Roads Congress (IRC). As a medium-term measure for Mumbai, the Government of Maharashtra has set up a Mithi River Development Authority and the Mumbai Municipal Corporation has been asked to implement the Brihan Mumbai (Greater Mumbai) Storm Water Disposal (BRIMSTOWAD) Report to improve the drainage system in the suburban areas.

The major goals of the project are to lay new drains to augment the carrying capacity of the existing drains, training of watercourses, deepening and widening of nallas (rivulets). This project will take 12 years to complete and will cost Rs. 616 Crores at 1992 prices. The Central Power and Water Research Station, Khadakwasla, has given recommendations for rainwater holding and discharging capacities. A survey of Dahisar and Poisar rivers is being conducted by the Water and Power Consultancy Services, an undertaking of the Government of India, New Delhi and Indian Institute of Technology (IIT), Mumbai is working out an Action Plan for the environmental improvement of Mithi River and its surroundings. There is an urgent case to protect the remaining mangroves, creeks and green areas, and to restore the original drainage basins, water channels and culverts in the reclaimed areas, such as the Bandra-Kurla Complex, Essel World and many others.

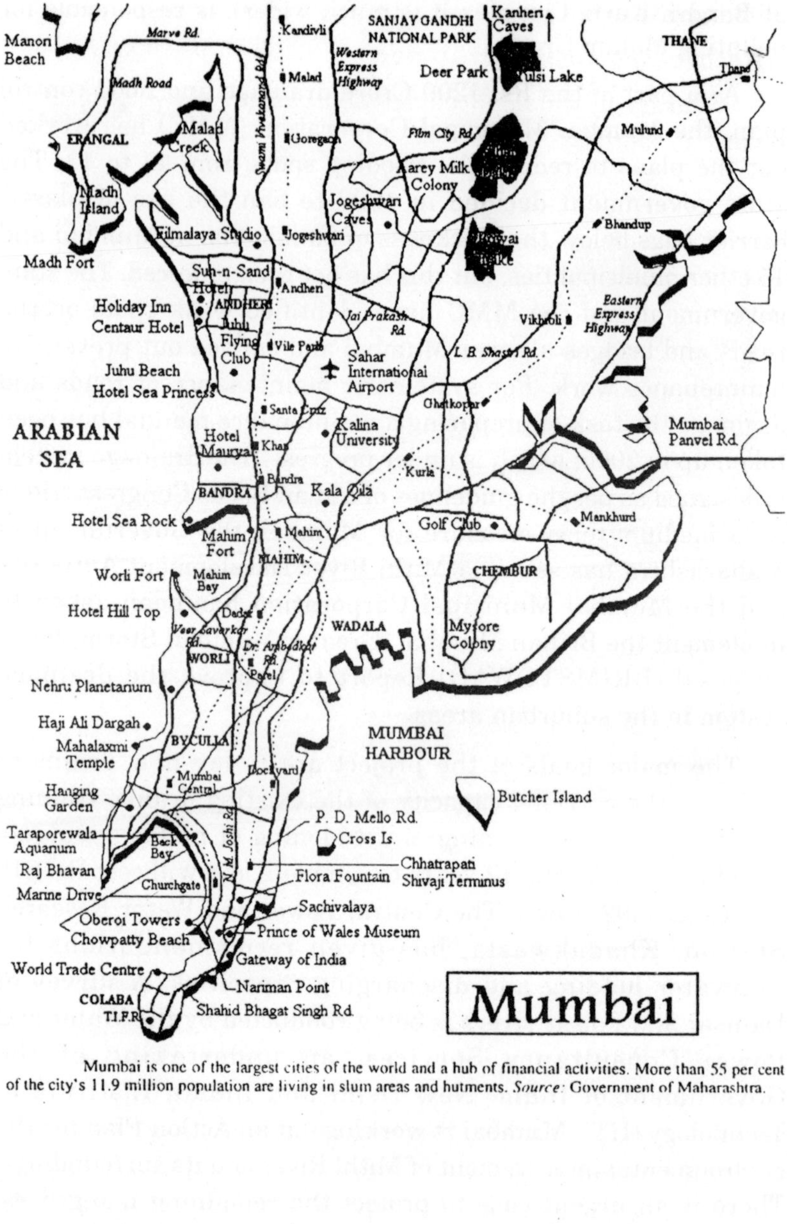

Mumbai is one of the largest cities of the world and a hub of financial activities. More than 55 per cent of the city's 11.9 million population are living in slum areas and hutments. *Source:* Government of Maharashtra.

Ecological factors should be the basis of future planning and development of Greater Mumbai (and any other Indian city), in order to avoid future catastrophes.

Rethinking urban drainage

The storm water in the urban areas usually originates from various sources:

15 km long Mithi River discharges at Mahim Creek.

- Water originating from rural and suburban areas flowing through the urban zones.
- Water originating from the adjacent urban areas.
- Surface water from rivers and the other streams flowing under extremely high levels near the areas considered. Water can enter the city either through streets and open areas or through the underground sewer network.
- Water from overtopping or breaking of dykes.
- Water from rising ground water levels.
- Water from the rainfall.

Large scale flooding may disrupt water supply and sanitation systems and result in diseases and epidemics. In poorly drained areas with inadequate sanitation, urban runoff mixes with excreta, spreading pathogens around communities and increasing risks to health from various water-borne diseases. This is common in the Indian sub-continent; and has been a feature of the floods in New Orleans after hurricane Katrina (September 2005). Infiltration of polluted water into low-pressure water supply systems can contaminate drinking water and is frequently a source of gastro-intestinal disorders.

Storm Water Management Strategies

A well-coordinated and balanced combination of both structural and non-structural measures is required as part of the long-term flood mitigation strategies. Examples of different types of non-structural storm-water management strategies are summarised in table 1.

Table 1. Natural drainage basin of Mumbai

Site No.	*Basin flowing into*	*Area (km^2)*	*Built up area (%)*	*Length of stream (km)*
1.	Vasai Creek	8.98	43	23.58
2.	Vasai Creek	27.2	10	81.2
3.	Manori Creek	37.44	18	95.69
4.	Malad Creek	16.56	49	35.4
5.	Malad Creek	24.21	50	40.49
6.	Mahim Creek	42.07	54	86.81

Natural Drainage Channels

In the Indian sub-continent, a large number of natural drainage channels wind their way across settlements on their way to the rivers and sea. A few are in good shape whereas many are carriers of polluted water with certain stretches having become open lavatories. While the sewage water can be piped in the centre of channel, other undesirable activities would be prevented with the provision of alternatives such as community toilets and fencing barriers.

Existing water channels (nallas) in urban areas can be used to provide continuous on-channel recharge of groundwater, to transfer water from these channels to various storage sites and also to store water from the channels with the help of sluice gates. Continuous recharge would take place through deep holes on the channel floor. This would be a complex exercise that requires computer modelling of channel capacities, transfer mechanisms, storage capacities, flood prevention and system operations.

The channels once filled with water thus could constitute urban waterways. Their cleanliness would be maintained with the use of root zone system, mosquito weed, guppy fishes to consume mosquito larvae and aeration. The channel would be shaped, landscaped and deepened to increase the water storing capacity wherever possible. Their banks would be the green lungs of the city. While serving the primary function of on-channel groundwater recharge they would also modify the micro-climate. The use of groundwater together with on-channel recharge would also be possible. Their use for urban water sports, recreation, floaters, floating offices, waterborne transport (with sluice gate barriers) should be integrated in the system.

Typology of flood types, characteristics and effects

Flood type	*Characteristics of flooding and effects*
Type A	Localized flooding caused by inadequate drainage of stormwater runoff, which can happen virtually every time it rains, where the provision of drainage infrastructure is poor. The main effects of these events are related to a deterioration in environmental health conditions, especially water-borne diseases.
Type B	Flood events of this type occur less frequently than type A floods, but affect larger areas. The effects may include temporary disruption to transportation systems and inconveniences to city life. These events contribute to the propagation of water-borne diseases and can cause structural damage.
Type C	Large-scale inundation causing widespread disruption and damage affecting communities and businesses throughout cities. These events are infrequent and often reach a dramatic scale of the effects and structural damage; e.g. inundation of New Orleans (September 2005).

Source: Adapted from Cairn Cross S. and E.A.R. Qnano (1991), Surface Water Drainage for Low Income Communities. WHO/UNEP.

Flooding problems and strategies for control

	Flooding problems strategies
Flood avoidance	Preventive responses which aim to ensure that flood problems are avoided.
Flood mitigation	Immediate responses to flood warnings before a flood, and the course of action to take during a flood to reduce risks.
Flood recovery	Action to be taken after a flood event to enable communities to recover from the impacts of a flood event.
Solid waste management	Control of solid waste to avoid blockages (such as plastic bags, packaging) and reduction in hydraulic capacity of the drainage system.
Pollution mitigation	Reduction in the discharge of pollutants into the storm-water drainage system.
Vector control	Improved practices to reduce vector transmission of diseases related to urban drainage and flooding.
	Stormwater management options
Natural catchments	Natural channels Streams Water courses
Partly sewered	Man-made ditches Open channels Sewers
Combined sewer systems	Open channels Combined sewers Overflows Treatment facilities
Fully separated sewer system	Separate sewers and trunk Sewers Treatment facilities Outfalls
Advanced drainage systems	Separate sewers Trunk sewers Infiltration ponds and source Control storage basins etc.

Source: WHO.

It has to be admitted, however, that such historical examples as Venice and the city of Castres, in France, do not indicate such an idea to have been accepted. The notion that a stream can take excreta and the domestic and industrial pollutants of citizens is very deep-seated. For such an idea to work in India, legislative measures are as necessary as active educators. The precedents are, however, not very encouraging. Nevertheless, the proposal needs to be considered.

Concept of Bio-drainage

Bio-drainage is an ecological option for controlling water logging, flooding and salinity, combined with recharging of ground water aquifer and plant physiology. Bio-drainage is an option for urban drainage, which seeks adaptation of water channels for green corridors and siting of roads, buildings and housing with the following basic principles :

- To reduce flooding, and ensure ability of existing primary and secondary drainage channels to handle storm run-off by defining drainage easements.
- These drainage easements will be determined by the 25 year floodplain (an area, which had inundated anytime during last 25 years) but a minimum vegetation easement of undisturbed forest and undergrowth must be respected: 45 to 90 m for primary drainage channels and 20 to 30 m for secondary drainage channels.
- In order to minimize erosion and siltation, there must be a legal and enforceable prohibition on clearing of ground cover, shrub undergrowth or trees within drainage easements.
- Existing channels should be enhanced where necessary with berms (side barriers) and create natural swales (water holding depressions) by introducing layered plantings of native vegetation. It is necessary to provide adequate storage of run-off in impoundments or temporary water storage ponds.
- In order to retard run-off and to enhance recharge, it is proposed to build check dams in swales over permeable soils to enhance recharge. Install trickle tubes in impounded areas to permit even flow.

Zero Run-off Drainage

The concept of bio-drainage is based on two principles. First, the segregation of rainwater from urban waste water disposal, so that it can be used for recharging of aquifers, irrigation, etc. Second, the principle of zero run-off drainage by way of complete retention of rainwater into the area by creating retention ponds, lakes and storage. This was the concept behind the creation of a network of lakes for flood/rainwater discharge, which had been prevalent in the ancient cities, for example Udaipur, Lucknow, Bhopal, Alwar, Jaipur and Pushkar- Ajmer. The present method of draining of storm water through masonry drains entails huge costs and effort, which also endangers the groundwater aquifer. The age old system of having a pond in the low lying area not only solved the drainage problem, but also provided a multi-purpose source of water recreation, cattle rearing, fishing and improvement for the micro-climate.

The prevalent drainage system having open drains to direct the entire discharge of surplus water and rainwater into the river (or sea) has created a serious problem of lowering of the underground water table, as with an ever-increasing number of tube wells being dug in the urban areas, the water table is gradually going down. The increasing population of greater Mumbai and consequent construction reduces the green and open areas and natural drainage channels become the first target of constructors. The system of zero run-off with small pondages not only results in huge financial savings, but also helps in maintaining the ecological balance and underground water reserve. This concept requires segregation of the storm water and wastewater drainage network and landscape development of drainage channels as green corridors. In other words, blue network planning (that is river, water streams and drainage channels) should synchronize with green network planning (parks, trails green belt/corridors).

A well planned system of small lakes, balancing ponds and porous paving can lead to avoidance of the construction of huge storm water drains. Possible advantages include:

(1) An efficient and effective drainage system which will increase ecological sustainability.

(2) Availability of self-sustaining greenery, recreational and water reserves for recreation, boating, fishing, etc.

(3) The enrichment of the underground aquifer, stabilizing and increasing the level of the underground water reserves, with continual replenishment.

(4) An economic and ecological process of development of the area in terms of human settlements.

(5) A source of water for the lean periods, especially for horticulture and agriculture.

(6) Savings in terms of the cost of constructing medium and major drains and culverts.

Retention Systems

The possible retention systems and their descriptions are given below:

(1) Low area drain (soakaway, in English landscaping terms): Water collects at the lowest part of the site. It is generally designed as an extension of the lawn where the soil can become highly saturated during rain. After heavy rainfalls it can take up to three days for the water to drain away. Visually the area under drain functions like a lawn and can be used a green trail.

(2) Ditches and swales: These can also be grassed or planted with water-loving plants and laid out with rocks. The ecological value of ditches and swales is higher since they provide a habitat for animals. Ditches will form temporary water features after rainfall. They take up less space than a low area drain. They are permanent features and cannot easily perform a different function when dry. Swales can form part of a surface water collection network that feeds into a pond.

(3) Permanent retention ponds: These are permanent water features that have a higher amenity value than the above options. Ponds require more space than ditches as water levels needs to fluctuate and more water is permanently retained on site. Retention ponds can be well supplemented with reed-bed filtration systems prior to discharge into a local river. They score

slightly higher than ditches and swales in environmental terms as they combine aesthetic values with new habitat creation and filtration.

(4) Underground collection cistern: This is the most expensive option with the lowest environment rating and also limited capacity. Its strongest point is the minimal space required. Water is collected and slowly discharged into the groundwater through a sand and gravel pit. Filtration is therefore minimal and water quality inferior to that of the other systems.

The suitability and advantages of each system depends on the topography concerned and the aims of the development in each case. The land-take necessary (the site area required for natural drainage systems) depends on the depth of the drain, which in turn depends on the local soil and slope. The approximate land-take is a percentage of the total site area to be drained and.forms a rough guide, to enable the planning of natural drainage system. The exact land-take for a natural drainage system relates to the actual quantity of scaled land on site and the degree of impermeability of materials used.

Measures proposed

It is necessary to conserve and maintain those streams mangroves, lagoons and wetlands that have survived urbanization by preventing encroachments. This requires a deliberate policy upheld by the local authority and the state government with the full rigour of the law. The Mithi River is the only major natural waterway running through Mumbai. There is an intrinsic relationship among drainage, land use planning and ecology, which should be organized and coordinated so that the demands of growing population, housing, drainage and water supply are met without comprising the ecology. There is a need to strike a balance between natural surface drainage and creating new drainage corridors. A network of canals should be considered to act as drainage system and also to retain rainwater for recycling during drought periods. The storm water network, BRIMSTOWAD, must protect the city's chronic spots - Nana Chowk, Slater Road, Hindmata cinema (Dadar East), King's Circle, Milan Subway (Santa Cruz), Kurla Car Shed, Postal Colony (Chembur) and Indira Steel Yard

(Mulund). Such network could be planned under the major roads, and should link up with the Mithi River. The Bhandup aerated lagoon, Versova Lagoon and Ghatkopar lagoon can also be connected with the rainwater drainage system. There is a need to take care not to mix up sewage and wastewater with the canal network and to have built in to the plan a system of pumping (wherever necessary), regular oxidation and root-zone cleaning and filtration of storm water, together with restoration of mangrove plantations. This requires a comprehensive planning of diversion canals and drains, removing obstructions from storm water drain including their widening and deepening.

A geographic information system (GIS), computer mapping and simulation facility would provide baseline data and a correct picture of the deluge and the potential danger areas. GIS in recent years has emerged as a valuable forecasting tool, especially because of its ability to create complex digital maps with voluminous data. Accordingly, a detailed plan of all the waterways in the city, with details of cross-sections, longitudinal profile, drainage basin and catchment areas of each of the gutters, creeks and rivers should be produced.

A network of high-tech holding tanks can be built beneath the city's open spaces, such as Mahalaxmi Race Course, among the island city's largest open areas. When the tide is out, its contents can be discharged through gravity or assisted by pumps. There should be pumping stations at the floodgates to move storm water in the catchment area, when high tide prevents natural drainage.

Indian cities frequently face the problem of flooding caused by poor drainage, additionally there are also problems off severe shortage of water, especially before the monsoons. This is largely a consequence of adoption of borrowed concepts of urban drainage, together with indiscriminate and unplanned developments in the natural drainage channels. There is an urgent need to resort to the ecological concept of bio-drainage, which is a combination of controlling the urban flooding and water-logging and arresting the run-off and conservation of precious rainwater for dry seasons.

Shahjahanabad - 1873
Source : Survey of India

Gateway to Jama Masjid, Delhi-1795, Aquatint by Thomas Daniell

22

CONSERVATION AND REDEVELOPMENT OF INNER CITY

Designing a dream city is easy, rebuilding a living one takes imagination.
— Jane Jacobs

The cityscape of a typical Indian city is the combination of the traditional, inner or core area, post-independence/planned developments and unauthorised/unplanned peri-urban growth. While the plans and development usually focus upon greenfield areas, the other two categories are often left to posterity and uncontrollable market forces. This is largely because of the complex nature of the core areas, characterized by the intermixing of land uses, amorphous, high density urban fabric, perennial shortages of services, utilities, open space, parking and community facilities, narrow roads and traffic congestion, demographic heterogeneity, predominance of low income group population, socio-cultural and religious diversity, lack of clear land titles, together with progressively deteriorating buildings and services. The jurisdictions of service agencies and local bodies are often overlapping and their functions are disjointed. The planning approach, based on the assumption of conventional controls and government as the main player, has not succeeded in addressing the problems of such areas, divorcing them further form the mainstream of development process. Delhi presents an excellent case study of inner city conservation and heritage.

The Master Plan for Delhi-2021, notified in February, 2007, reviews the approach and the planning strategy for the traditional, core areas of Delhi.

Shahjehanbad

Shahjehanbad the old Delhi, the medieval capital, built by Shahjehan in 1638, remains one of the most beautiful and graceful cities in the Orient. In 1803 the British arrived in Delhi. The British and the natives lived side by side within the Walled City. After the war of 1857, the British attitude had been hostile and over one-third of the city was razed to ground. The city came to be seen as "dark, unhealthy and congested". The Walled City was perceived as a 'useless maze' and its surroundings as "heterogeneous patches of dirty hovels."

The transfer of Imperial Capital from Calcutta to Delhi in 1912 furthered the process of devaluation of the Old City. The New Capital's Hausmannian vistas and imperial scale dwarfed the Walled City and brought immediate and direct comparisons. During 1920s, the concept of 'congestion' crystallized into 'slums'. After the independence (1947), the slum clearance continued to be the main agenda in dealing with the Old City, around which cities were developed from time to time, including Lutyens' Delhi. The Walled City has an area of 569 Hectares (Ha) with a land-use break up as given below:

Land use Pattern in Walled City

Land Use	*Area in Ha.*	*Percentage*
Residential	181.00	31.8
Commercial	66.80	11.7
Warehousing	22.43	3.9
Manufacturing	9.60	1.7
Transport, Utilities	131.70	23.1
Parks and Open Spaces	96.87	17.0
Public and semi public use	41.90	7.5
Govt. and semi-Govt.	18.70	0.3
Total	569.00	100.0

There is high concentration of commercial activity within the Walled City, covering 17% of the land. Major open areas include Gandhi Ground (in front of Railway Station) and open space in front of Jama Masjid, which together cover an area of 59 ha.

There is a declining population trend during the 1991-2001 decade. The shifting of residential population from the Old City is due to conversion of residential premises for commercial uses.

The other factors are deteriorating and out-dated facilities, change in social composition and space requirements, blighted environment etc.. The invasion of many other activities has further deteriorated the area.

Population trend in Walled City (Shahjehanabad)

Year	*Delhi*	*Shahajanabad*	*% of Col. 3 to 2*
1951	17,44000	38,1000	21.84
1961	26,59000	4,20,000	15.79
1971	40,66000	4,09000	10.05
1981	62,20000	3,62000	5.81
1991	93,70000	3,50000	3.73
2001	1,37,83000	2,62,000	1.90

The residential densities vary from 400 PPH to 2000 PPH with Maliwara and Dariba Kalan as the most congested. The overall density works out to about 436 PPH.

Traditionally, the Walled City had been a provider of major housing stock to the population of Delhi, however since 1971 the residential population started to decline. The social pattern is of cohesive residential groups in traditional housing areas, in the form of Katra (residence enclosing a central courtyard) and narrow streets. It primarily caters to the poor living in rented accommodation. Shahjehanabad, the Central Business District of the metropolitan Delhi has about 7.05 per cent of commercial enterprises of Urban Delhi.

Enterprises in Delhi and Shahjehanabad - 1998

No.	*Area*	*Number of Enterprises*
1.	Delhi	685852
2.	Delhi (Urban)	656325
3.	Shahajanabad	46256

One fifth of wholesale markets of Delhi are located in Shahjehanabad, which acts as a regional distribution centre.

Distribution of Enterprises and Employment

No.	*Area*	*Employment*	*Enterprises*	*Employment per Ent.*
1.	Delhi	3500872	685852	5.10
2.	Delhi (Urban)	3415104	656325	5.20
3.	Shahajanabad	196475	46256	4.25

Physical and Social Infrastructure: Many of the houses in Walled City are still without individual water supply and latrines. The service networks require up-gradation. There is a general deficiency of the schools, health facilities, park, etc.

The multiple modes of slow moving, fast vehicles, NMVs, including rickshaws, operating on the narrow right of ways of roads with high pedestrian activity and the concentration of wholesale business make the movement in the Old City very difficult. Traffic is also generated by the Railway Station. The movement of traffic is made difficult by encroachments, building projections and electric poles, as well as spill-over of activities mainly of informal trading. The Metro is now functional in the Walled City, which is somewhat reducing the volume of individual vehicles and bus movement.

Physical conditions

A primary survey was undertaken by a Committee set up by the Ministry of Urban Development and Poverty Alleviation for Urban Renewal of Walled City. The Survey was conducted to ascertain the ground realities of physical conditions and use of properties along important roads. The following are major findings.

It is observed that the total number of the properties surveyed at the selected stretches of the walled city is 2334 and among them only 108 (4.6%) properties are with ground floor construction while 793 (34%) properties, have G+1 floor construction whilo (44%) properties have G+2 floors construction. Further, 369 (15.8%) properties have G+3 floors construction while the remaining properties i.e. 36 (1.6%) have construction beyond third floor.

The major and well known markets include food-grains market in Naya Bazar, Kirana, Dry Fruits and spices market at Khari Baoli, paper market at Chawri Bazar, Iron and hardware markets at Chawri Bazar, Ajmeri Gate and Lal Kuan area, cloth market in the Katras of Chandni Chowk, motor spare parts market at Mori Gate and Kashmiri Gate area, electrical market in Bhagirath Palace and diversified retail trades spread along the streets of the Walled City. The major shares of enterprises in Shahjehanabad involved in other activities are storage and ware-housing, real estate business, etc. The enterprises in Delhi are concentrated mainly in retail trade, manufacturing and repairing, service activities, transport and wholesale trade, etc. Near about 45 per cent of the enterprises in Shahajanabad were engaged in retail trade, while 15.62 per cent in wholesale trade, 12.1 per cent in manufacturing and repairing and 13.02 per cent in service activities. .

Enterprises in Delhi by Type (Non-agricultural)

S.No.	*Activities*	*Delhi Urban Nos. (percentage)*	*Shahjehanabad / Old Delhi Nos. (percentage)*	*% of Shahjehanabad to Delhi Urban*
1.	Manufacturing & Repairing	120175 (19.35)	5926 (12.81)	4.70
2.	Electricity, Gas & Water	10.17 (00.16)	27 (00.06)	2.65
3.	Construction	7890 (01.21)	123 (00.27)	1.56
4.	Wholesale Trade	36515 (05.60)	7224 (15.62)	19.78
5.	Retail Trade	218778 (33.54)	20676 (44.71)	9.45
6.	Hotels and Restaurants	29111 (04.46)	1845 (03.99)	6.34
7.	Transport	46461 (7.12)	1374 (02.97)	2.96
8.	Storage & Warehousing	6339 (00.97)	861 (01.86)	13.58
9.	Communications	10764 (01.64)	650 (01.41)	6.04
10.	Financial, Insurance, Real Estate Business	28324 (04.34)	1519 (03.28)	05.36
11.	Community, Social and Personnel Service	140826 (21.60)	6024 (13.02)	4.25
	Total	652203	46849	7.09

Source: GNCTD Year Book, 2000.

Nearly 6 per cent of the existing employment of Delhi in Urban Delhi is working in Shahjahanabad with an average of 4 persons per enterprise as compared to 5 persons per enterprise in rest of Delhi, This may be due to wholesale activities requiring less workers.

Major Findings

- All the surveyed stretches show intense commercialization and there is virtually no residential use on the ground floor.
- The stretch from Red Fort to Fatehpuri comparatively has higher number of construction beyond second floor.
- 'The presence of commercial use above ground floor indicates that the properties are being converted from residential commercial use.
- Stretches of Red Fort - Fateh Puri, Chitli Qabar to Jama Masjid and Chitli Qabar Chowk to Tiraha Bairam Khan have shown construction upto fourth floor.
- Properties along the Nai Sarak are in vary dilapidated condition. There is rampant encroachment as the properties have extended by adding pillars/ columns. This has severely hindered the pedestrian movement.
- In Chawri Bazar area, there has been reckless addition and alteration of properties and commercialization of upper floors is intense.
- The stretch from Chitli Qabar to Chowk Tiraha Bairam Khan shows that none of the properties have commercial use above ground floor while residential use is found in upper floors upto the fourth floor.

Karol Bagh

Karol Bagh had been originally a suburb of the Walled City. It is bounded by Rohtak road in North, Pusa road in South, Faiz Road in east and Ramjas Road in West. The population of this area as per Census has been computed as 71,098 persons. The total area of sub-zone B-2 (Karol Bagh area) is about 320 hec.

The built up area generally consists of buildings with courtyards and service lanes and has developed over a period as congested locality lacking the community facilities. Some residential area has 2-3 storied buildings with little better spaced service lanes, Bungalows are relatively recently developed on bigger size plots. Some of the bungalows along Pusa Road and Ajmal Khan Park are in good condition. There are some single or double storied blocks of government quarters in north western portion of the zone near Dev Nagar. In the Regarpura area basties have come up at Satnagar, and Rameshwari Prasad Nagar, etc. The planned area had a unique character as the physical development of buildings was based on a planning framework. Most of the residential buildings have similar character with compound wall, gates narrow front margin, balconies, and rounded edges at corners, ground plus one storey development and internal courtyards. Most of the buildings display a great deal of variety.

This area being located near the New Delhi Railway Station and Connaught Place has been a natural centre of commercial growth. The main commercial and shopping centre of Karol Bagh area is Ajmal Khan Road serves as a Central Business District. Almost entire Ajmal Khan road starting from Pusa Road upto Original Road has been commercialized. There are few markets also namely, Gaffar Khan Market, D.B. Gupta Market and Krishna Market. The majority of the existing commercial area caters to retail business. There is only one big established park i.e. Ajmal Khan Park measuring about 8.0 ha., besides smaller parks and play spaces in residential areas.

Pahar Ganj and Old Subzi Mandi Area

This area is also part of the Special Area of MPD-2021 and is covered under the Slums Act. Paharganj is part of Planning Division-A (A-1 & 2 sub-zones) and Old Subzi Mandi falls in Planning Division - C (C-4 - C-7 sub-zones). The total area is 190 ha (Paharganj 87 ha and Old Subzi Mandi is 103 ha). Both were mostly developed during and after colonial times. The density has increased multifold especially after the Partition of the Country in 1947. The road pattern is irregular with high level of mixed use along the road arteries. Due to its proximity to New Delhi Railway Station, Paharganj has many ancillary uses. The residential density ranges more than 1000 persons per hec. with fairly small size of plots, generally having at least 3 stories.

Built Heritage

Delhi is a historic city whose remnants are spread right from Mehrauli to Shahjahanabad. Large number of monuments are scattered all over Delhi. The built heritage of Delhi is an irreplaceable and non-renewable cultural resource. Besides being part of life for many, it has educational, recreational and major tourism potential. It enhances Delhi's environment, giving it a unique identity and character. It encompasses culture, lifestyles, design, materials, engineering and architecture.

Surveys conducted by the Archaeological Survey of India in 1911 identified 1321 historical monuments, sites and buildings. Out of these, 170 monuments have boon declared as protected. In addition MCD, NDMC and State Archaeological Deptt. have published lists of Heritage Buildings.

While preparing any layout plans, these should be suitably incorporated. In case of major monuments it is necessary that the surrounding area should be identified in the layout/detail plan, and should have building controls in relation to height, material and spread of the monuments.

It is stipulated to formulate "Special Development Plans" for the conservation and improvement of listed heritage complexes and zones. Alteration or demolition of any building is prohibited in the listed heritage complexes and zones without the prior approval of the Competent Authority.

The Government of India amended Building Byelaws 1993, vide Clause 23 and inserted a chapter on 'Conservation of Heritage Sites including Heritage Building, Heritage Precincts and Natural Feature Areas". The development plans and building schemes are required to conform to these provisions.

Review of Planning Approach

The Master Plan for Delhi-1962 had recommended a three pronged strategy of Urban Renewal, comprising of redevelopment, rehabilitation and conservation of the unique character of the Old City. With this broad outline, the Old City was divided into conservation, rehabilitation and redevelopment areas. It was also proposed to de-densify the densities from 1000 Persons per Acre (PPA) to 250 PPA. Adopting lower space standards for facilities was proposed. There was phased program for shifting non-conforming land uses. But the only schemes that could be implemented were Jama-Masjid complex, Turkman Gate and Dujana House.

Development of Shahjahanabad, Pahar Ganj and Subzi Mandi areas was undertaken largely under the Slum Improvement and Clearance Act, 1956, whereas Karol Bagh was under MCD jurisdiction. The Slum Department undertook on ad hoc basis up-gradation of services and provision of certain facilities, like night shelter, etc.. The municipal services of waste disposal, maintenance of roads, public spaces etc. vested with the MCD. Water supply and sanitation has been the responsibility of the Delhi Jal Board (DJB). There were about 3500 evacuee properties/katras which were being managed and controlled by the Slum Department. These were transferred by Ministry of Rehabilitation for utilization under the slum clearance program.

The Master Plan for Delhi-2001 (MPD-2001) projected the concept of 'Special Area Plan'. It stated that the old built up areas with peculiar problems shall be dealt under special regulations, as given under 'Development Code'. The Special Area of 2600 Ha., has been sub-divided into (i) Urban Renewal Area (Walled City), (iii) Urban Renewal Area (Karol Bagh), (iv) Other Urban Renewal Areas, and (iv) Specific Use Zone Areas.

The policy of conservation and revitalization in case of traditional areas like Walled City, required: (*i*) shifting and delimitation of non-residential activities, (*ii*) up-gradations of physical and social Infrastructure, (*iii*) conservation and revitalization of historical building and (*iv*) revitalization of residential areas. The Plan designated the old inner city areas as Special Area with special regulations Urban Renewal schemes were to be prepared indicating clearance areas with subsequent plans for redevelopment. The buildings were to be constructed in same style and form as existing, i.e. maximum ground coverage and Floor Area Ratio (FAR) are to be same as for residential plots in plotted developments.

Acts and Regulations

There are two major Acts that have significance in relation to the core city areas. These are Rent Control Act, 1958 and Slum Areas (Clearance and Improvement) Act, 1956. Other Acts are:

(*a*) Ancient Monument (Preservation) Act 1904, (*b*) Delhi Fire Prevention and Safety Act, 1986, (*c*) Wakf Amendment Act, 1984, (*d*) Delhi Urban Art Commission Act, 1973, (*e*) Delhi Municipal Act, 1957 and Delhi Development Act, 1957, (*f*) Regulations under Building Byelaws.

1. Rent Control Act, 1958: According to this Act, the rent is frozen in old and low rental premises constructed prior to 1955. For post 1955 buildings the rent is agreed between landlord and tenants. The operation of this Act has aggravated the problem of decay. The Act should be so amended so that landlords and tenants both benefit through it.

2. Slum Area (Improvement & Clearance) Act, 1956: The Walled City and its extensions are notified slum area under section 3 of the Slum Area (Improvement and Clearance) Act, 1956. As per Census 2001 the population in this is computed as 2,61,652 persons. The population of Paharganj and Subzi mandi areas is 27843 persons. Provision of minimum basic civic amenities by the Slum Department with Plan funds as available with Grants-in-aid from the governments. At present MOD is incharge of the maintenance of infrastructures, as well as garbage removal. Although the Slum Act under sections 4 & 5 specifies the cost of improvement works or provision of services is to be recovered from the owner/occupier, but in Delhi it is not being followed.

Under Section 9 of the Act, the dangerous property/ buildings can be demolished. A stock of 21394 re-housing flats/ tenements had been provided on license fee through Plan Funds to the evictees of the Walled City and its extension area, However, with effect from June 1989 these are being provided on leasehold or freehold basis also. Govt. of India discontinued Slum Clearance Scheme in June 1989 and areas which were earlier notified in ward I to XV and XVIII were denotified in March 1990.

The lands cleared under this scheme had beeh utilized as urban renewal and redevelopment program in Turkman gate scheme, Dujana House Scheme Phase I and II, flats under Ajmeri Gate scheme and facilities likes schools, multi-purpose facility complexes, night shelters, open/green lung spaces, etc.

Under section 19 of the Act no proceedings against eviction of tenant can be filed without permission of the Competent

Authority. Before granting or refusing permission to the owner after hearing both the parties (owner and tenant) the Competent Authority considers:

(*a*) Whether the tenant is able to obtain alternative accommodation within his means? High court order has held 10-12% of the income as affordable amount as house rent.

(*b*) Whether eviction is in the interest of improvement and clearance of slum?

(*c*) Any other factor prescribed.

The Act has a provision under section 9 to clear the slum area while making alternative accommodation arrangement. If this is not complied by tenants before six weeks, the Competent Authority can demolish the structure.

Planning and Building Regulations

Permission for construction/re-construction of buildings in Walled City and its extensions including Paharganj and peripheral areas that are Slum Notified areas is given by MCD as per the policy guidelines issued on 10.8.89. NOC for applying for sanction of plans was to be issued by Slum and JJ Deptt., except for areas/structures which are specified in the Guidelines. These guidelines were derived on the basis of Interim Structure Plans and Zonal Plans. The documents, clearances and fees that are to be submitted is specified in the guidelines. The land use has to be as per Master Plan/Zonal Plan. Basement is not permitted except in Public & Semi Public uses and transport use. NOC is to required for (*a*) Heritage Control Zonos and listed identified buildings (*b*) one property depth along the specified roads/streets (that are major commercial spine), (*c*) Important road junctions, (*d*) Residential areas identified by the Heritage Conservation Committee, (*e*) existing wholesale godowns and warehousing premises, (*f*) public & semi-public uses and adjoining premises.

City Area Policy of the municipal corporation of Delhi stipulates building control for plots of 50 sq.yds. and above. Front, sides and rear set backs are specified in relation to road widths, size and floors. For reconstruction the building plans are required to be sanctioned by MCD in accordance with development controls and mixed use policy.

Issues and Problems

The present framework of planning, development and enforcement has not been successful in the conservation of heritage, urban renewal, legitimate property tenure, titles and transfers, infrastructure upgradation, financial mobilization, development rights, etc. On the other hand, indiscriminate or non-application of the Acts has proved counter-productive in economic and physical regeneration of the Special Area. For example, the whole of Walled City has been notified as Slum under the Slum Areas Act, 1956, but neither the legal framework, nor the present organizational structure have been able to control unauthorized reconstruction of historical havelis/ buildings or in taking up meaningful redevelopment of dilapidated, degraded and dangerous areas. The plans of shifting of wholesale trade, noxious industries and hazardous trades have by and large remained on the papers. The encroachment on public lands, particularly road right of ways continues unabated. There are unending and plethora of legal disputes regarding property ownership, tenancy, misuse, licencing and other issues. In order to address effectively to the emerging issues and the need of conservation and regeneration of the Special Area, it is necessary to review the existing planning and regulatory framework, organizations and procedures and evolve a new framework.

The existing road widths are narrow, the plots are almost 100% built up, with odd shapes and in an unorganized manner. These require a participatory local area planning, so as to mutually resolve the issues of ownership/multiple tenancies.

A fresh look is required to be given with a view to arrest the decline and dilapidation of the inner city and to improve its functioning. While there is a set of guidelines for urban renewal in the Master Plan, it is dependent upon the government/local body's initiative and a people centred approach is lacking. It is, therefore, necessary that a clear approach is evolved, with safeguards for maintaining the original charm and heritage, keeping in view the following issues:

Land and Land Use Planning:

- Disputes in land title, jurisdiction and baseline data.
- Proliferation of non-conforming Wholesale Trade/ Markets, industries and informed Sector of Trade.

- Spatial congestion, lack of open spaces.
- Encroachment on public lands, parks etc.

Urban Renewal:

- Non-preparation of Urban Renewal Plans.
- MCD/Government as the major initiator, lack of participatory planning.

Building Controls

- Proliferation of unauthorized construction.
- Non approval and delay in sanction of building plans.
- Ambiguity in planning and building controls.
- Multi-tier, Multi-departmental Controls/Permissions.

Traffic and Transportation Management

- Traffic congestion, narrow roads, slow moving traffic lack of parking, squatting on roads/ paths.

Conservation of Heritage

- Loss of heritage buildings and areas.
- Lack of data/documentations of heritage buildings.
- Reduction in property value by planning controls.

Infrastructure Services

- Lack of physical infrastructure services.

Public Facility and Conveniences

- Lack of social infrastructure.
- Lack of public amenities and conveniences.

Enforcement

- Non-enforcement of Land Use and Planning Proposals/ Regulations.

Legal Framework

- Complex legal framework, tardy procedures, court cases and disputes.

Management and Financial Issues

Proposed Approach

The experience of four decades of interventions in the 'Special Area' requires rethinking about the need for certain basic systemic changes, as well as to evolve the strategies that will trigger a process of renewal and regulations that will give a 'pride to tho citizen for having a unique city of heritage value and give a new lease of life'. These antique areas should be upgraded with improved services, accessibility and facilities and a risk free environment for which the following strategies are proposed:

Land Use Planning

- Introducing the concept of local area planning, whereby landuse and planning parameters are to be determined on the basis of detailed urban design schemes, based on the characteristic of specific area.
- Development of GIS/Spatial Data Infrastructure (SDI) and making Digitized Base Maps/Property Maps available on Web-site.
- To decongest the Old City and to shift traffic generating activities like wholesale trade, noxious industries and hazardous business, develop counter-centres in the form of:
    - Integrated Freight Complexes at the peripheral locations of Delhi.
    - Development of Truck Terminals, vehicle repair workshops, Old Car Markets, Motor parts market at the periphery of Urban Delhi.
    - Noxious/Polluting Industries are hazardous trade are to be shifted from the Special Area in time frame by a set of incentives (providing alternative plots, tradable FAR, etc.) and disincentives (non-renewal of trade/industry licenses etc.) within a time frame.
    - The enterprise that vacates the premises can use the existing premise for residential/ conforming activity.
    - All unauthorized occupations and encroachments from Government properties/Katras public land should be removed for their planned development for social infrastructure and open space.
- A major issue of land use planning had been who is to prepare the local area redevelopment plans? As a basic principle, the concerned land owning/jurisdictional local

body has to initial and coordinate this task. There is a need to work out a mechanism to develop the concept of local area planning. A Committee under Commissioner, MCD on 'Making Building Bye-laws Work for Delhi - Policy Agenda and Legislative Intentions' (July, 04) suggested the following reform process:

- Building Bye-laws should be developed at different levels
- Building Bye-laws should be prepared in the context of Local Area Plans
- Rationale underpinning of building bye-laws should be clearly documented
- Local Authority (MCD) should focus on Local Area Plans and the MCD should be mandated to plan and undertake development
- The jurisdiction of tho MCD should be clarified
- Time limits should be specified for preparing and revising Local Area Plans
- Flexibility should be provided for delineating planning boundaries.

The Local Area Plans for Special Area should be initiated by land owners, local leaders, developers and consultants.

Planning Framework

- Area based renewal approach specifying "Protected Areas", conservation/heritage zones.
- Private developers and residents may be encouraged to undertake conservation of heritage and redevelopment guided by planning controls, allowing internal flexibility of space and use.
- FAR incentives for those who maintain the heritage control.
- The concept of Transferable Development Rights (TDR) and Accommodation Reservation have been introduced, whereby land required for provision of essential public facilities to be handed over to the local body/government, the owner is given full permissible FAR.

- When land is to be surrendered for widening of roads or any other public facility, the equivalent FAR should be permissible to the owner/developer either to use on same plot or added tothe TDR component.
- A new set of development controls for land use, FAR and parking, removing unnecessary controls and replacing building permission by planning and block approvals.
- Budgetary and infrastructure support be given to the developer, so that the narrow streets get widened and modern infrastructure services get extended.

About 50 per cent of the Inner City will be soon within 8 to 10 minutes of walking distance from Metro Stations. Hopefully, this will release some congestion from already choked roads and reduce the parking demand. This will also provide opportunity (*i*) to pedestrianise some of the roads in tho Walled City and other are, (*ii*) to redevelop areas along metro corridors, (*iii*) to upgrade infrastructure services, and, (*iv*) to improve interface between land use and transportation. Improved accessibility will facilitate and encourage decentralization of trade from Old Delhi. A new pattern of economic corridors can emerge by planned interventions and incentives and disincentives which may be built-in within the planning framework. The influence zone of 500 meters on both sides of metro corridor should be area specific.

This way the process of area by area renewal and redevelopment would trigger a process of decongestion and conservation, releasing heavily built up area for open space/ greenery, upgradation of social-physical infrastructure and shifting out of hazardous, inflammable and noxious activities from the Old City. The incentive of additional FAR, alongwith other measures like liberalization of land use and time bound approvals would motivate the owners and residents to adopt the route of planned development.

The proposals, like clearance and rehabilitation of the core areas, often termed as 'slums', have time and again proved to be a case where the cure is worse than the disease. The replacement of traditional, organic and Indigenous form of high density housing in the Old City by formal, planned, modern apartment blocks stands as its testimony. It is a mute edifice which reminds that the plans were wrong and the people were right.

The concerns of the externals for improving the living conditions of the traditional settlements had always been pigeonholed under the physical manifestations, like slums, overcrowding, blight and sub-standard. The evaluation by the persons having borrowed perceptions had been contradictory with the reality and its complexity. None of the priorities of officials agencies, such as decongestion, open space, aesthetics, land use zoning, building bye laws and physical accessibility figure among the main issues of the community. This is a clear expression of separation of planning programmes from cultural roots, social needs and realistic considerations. There is a need to abandon such concepts and to evolve more participatory and realistic strategies based on a deeper understanding of historical, social and cultural aspects of city building.

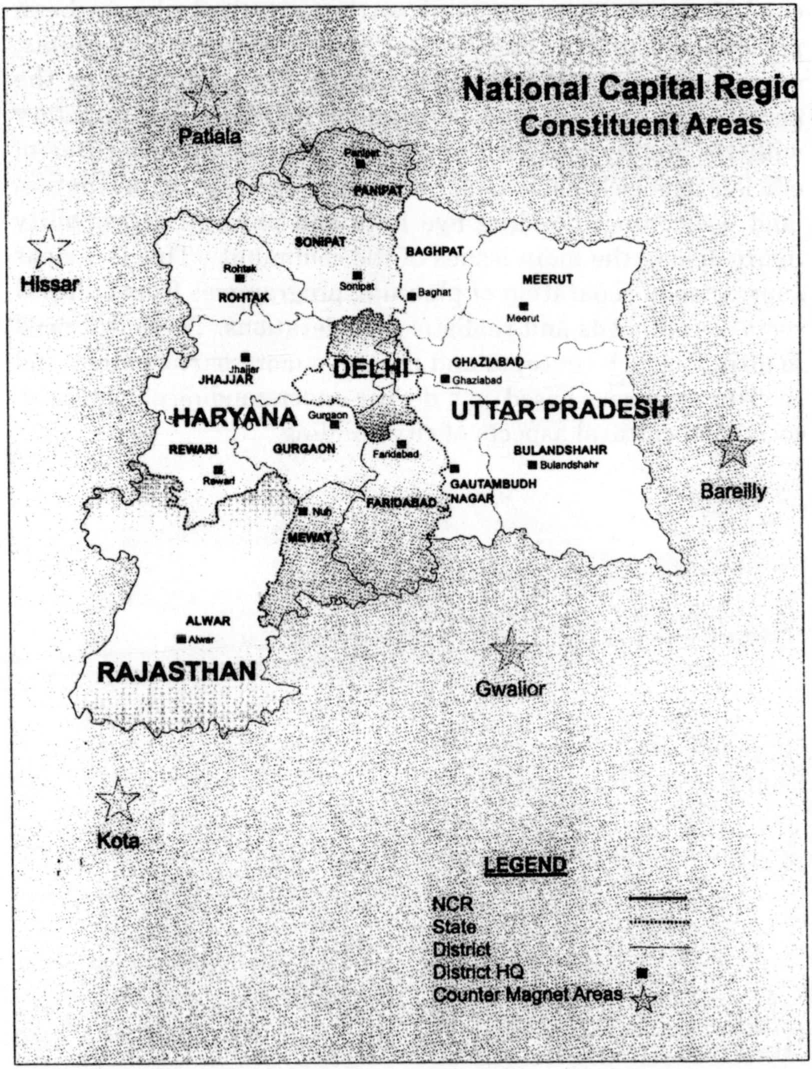
National Capital Regio
Constituent Areas
Patiala
Hissar
Panipat
PANIPAT
SONIPAT
Rohtak
ROHTAK
Sonipat
BAGHPAT
Baghat
MEERUT
Meerut
Jhajjar
JHAJJAR
DELHI
GHAZIABAD
Ghaziabad
HARYANA
Gurgaon
UTTAR PRADESH
REWARI
Rewari
GURGAON
Faridabad
BULANDSHAHR
Bulandshahr
GAUTAMBUDH
NAGAR
Bareilly
Nuh
FARIDABAD
MEWAT
ALWAR
Alwar
RAJASTHAN
Gwalior
Kota
LEGEND
NCR
State
District
District HQ
Counter Magnet Areas

23

A SUSTAINABLE VISION FOR THE NATIONAL CAPITAL REGION

A plan is a list of actions arranged in whatever sequence is thought likely to achieve an objective. — John Argenti

The 1991-2001 Census indicates that the growth rate of population of Delhi is reducing (46% growth during 1991-2001 as compared to 51.5% during 1981-91) whereas the population growth of fringe areas of NCT of Delhi accelerated 3 to 4 times of population growth rate of Delhi. This is largely due to competitive approach adopted by the fringe areas like Noida, Gurgaon, etc. The population projections based on Census should act as a broad guideline, but need not be over-emphasised in the preparation of Regional Plan. There is a need to adopt an alternative approach, which should be sustainable, integrating the economic, physical and environmental potentials.

There is a need for serious rethinking so as to adopt a more pragmatic approach, where the State governments, Local Bodies and Private Sector provide the incentives for the development of the settlements/areas, which are appropriate and environmentally sustainable for balanced growth of the region.

This requires some basic structural changes in the policies and regional planning approach, as well as the institutional structure. It will be worthwhile to start with a bottoms-up approach, rather than continuing with a top-down approach.

Basic Framework

It will be more pragmatic if the development activities are undertaken by the, National Capital Region Planning Board (NCRPB) itself in collaboration with the concerned State governments and Urban Local Bodies (ULBs). NCRPB would also be in a better position to mobilize resources for development through Planning Commission, MOUD, MORD, HUDCO, Financial Institutions, proposed Urban Development Finance Corporation, National Bank for Agriculture and Rural Development, LIC, market borrowing, NHB, International Finance grants etc. Since about 90 per cent of NCR area is rural, Ministry of Rural Development should be mobilized as a major partner in the planning, development and financing of the NCR.

A Regional Plan is all embracing, overlapping different sectors, organizations, State Governments and departments. The present hierarchical command structure cannot respond to the exigencies of planned development. It is suggested that special organizations to deal with the specific targets, such as, transport, trade and commerce, financing and taxation, development and conservation of greenery, forests and agriculture, infrastructure services (water supply & power), waste management, industry and employment generation, etc. may be constituted. These can comprise of concerned Ministries/Departments of the Central/State Governments, private sector and experts. The creation and corporatisation of such bodies will add to capacity building and mobilize the Central/State Governments and private sector resources in the process of planned development.

So far the focus of NCR plan had been to decongest and decentralize Delhi. It is necessary to redefine the goals and lay more emphasis on development, regeneration and other opportunity zones, rather than restrictive approach. This will need mobilizing the ULBs and DDA to operate beyond their administrative boundaries/NCTD, who can collaborate in taking up various projects outside Delhi for development of opportunity areas, work centres, industries, wholesale markets, etc.

The new regional plan should invent and open up new opportunity areas, which offer better prospects and provide incentives to people, business and industry to shift themselves by choice.

Vision 2021

Before we embark upon the goals, objectives and process, it is necessary to dwell upon the Vision-2021 which will define what we aspire the NCR to be.

In 21st century lifestyles, all the people in the NCR are above poverty line and are engaged in productive work and leisure. Local networks work in parallel to global networks, sharing resources and a sense of belonging and support. Both absolute and relative poverty reduce and gap between urban and rural lifestyles is minimal. Social networks provide continuous family support and cultivate self-help with basic needs met at marginal cost by city/regional consortiums. Healthy lifestyles are widespread, supported by environmental best practices at work and home. Community-based paramedics help to deliver integrated self-help positive and preventive health. Crime rates, social tensions fall rapidly with preventive measures and widespread social networks. A multi-cultural system of facilities meets the people's needs with focus on the women, old, young and disabled/handicapped. Education becomes more integrated and responsive, schools are pro-active, eco-centres providing self-development through practical skills, and pupils and their families have personal advocates for self-directed project-based learning. Community action and the voluntary sector expand through new social network for social and environmental services. Most decision-making is open and interactive with digital tools at the neighbourhood level. The sustainable development continues the leading agenda - the creation of new visions and social networks, bringing together public, private and community sectors.

In the National Capital Region 2021 Vision for lifestyles, communities, public services and social strategy, an outline of few key themes can be as below:

- Poverty reduction and focused rural development.
- Urban renewal and regeneration.
- Region of plenty and no shortages of services.
- Ecological and sustainable development.
- Cohesion, self-help, green economy.
- Cultural diversity and individual empowerment.
- Integration and coordination of public services.
- An open, flexible civic society, which heals its divisions and nurtures its people.

All the above fit together in a composite vision of how lifelstyles and public services could change positively in all aspects. Superimposed on these aspirations would be the trends and dynamics, of demographic, cultural and social change. This suggests that the conventional menu of 'local communities' should not be the only theme on the agenda, and that we should not ignore the opportunities and pressures brought by globalisation and liberalization - the internet, the media, businesses and employment interest groups, cultural and religious network and so on. The challenge is not to return to some Arcadian myth but to invent viable futures for new problems and opportunities.

Policy Zones

As per the present practice, the policy zones imply physical delineation of NCR comprising of NCR area, DMA and NCTD. The policy zones should cover and define the following:

Physical

- Area delineation,
- Land use zones.

Functional Policy Zones

- Land Policy,
- Industries and work centres,
- Traffic & transportation,
- Financing,
- Infrastructure/municipal services,
- Waste management,
- Redevelopment & regeneration,
- Opportunity zones etc.

Environmental Zones

- Potential water areas,
- Zoning atlas for industries,
- Waste recycling/management areas,
- Forests and greenery.

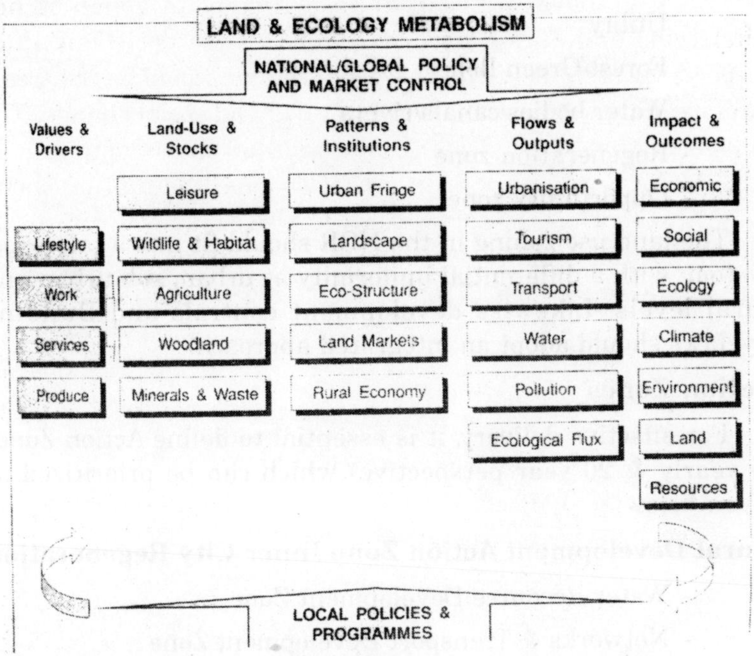

Action Zones

Land use zoning at Regional Level had to be different than what is practiced in urban planning. Land use zoning should comprise of the following hierarchy and categories:

(*a*) Regional land use

(*b*) Metropolitan/Sub-urban

(*c*) Urban land use zoning

(*d*) Land use premises.

Regional land use zones will provide a broad structure, within the framework of which sub-regional and urban plans should detail out the land uses.

The land use zones at Regional Level may comprise the following:

- Urban
- Sub-urban
- Rural/agriculture
- Transport

- Utility
- Forest/Green Belt
- Water bodies/canals/rivers
- Regeneration zone
- Opportunity zone.

The land use zoning in the NCR should fit into a telescopic system, with a differential uniformity at urban, sub-urban and rural levels. Likewise development controls and Building Byelaws should adopt an integrated approach.

Action Zones

For effective delivery, it is essential to define Action Zones (5 yearly & 20 year perspective) which can be prioritized as given below:

Rural Development Action Zone Inner City Regeneration

- Water Resource Development Zone
- Networks & Transport Development Zone
- Opportunity Zone
- Value Addition Zone
- Waste & Pollution Control Zone.

Approach to Regional Plan

The system of regional planning and management should include the following:

- The introduction of short and medium-term, Integrated Action Planning which complements comprehensive long term development objectives.
- Simplification of procedure and integration of the management of development schemes.
- Better utilization and increase of the revenue base for local bodies.
- A new urban land policy to match with the National Urban Housing and Habitat Policy, whereby the local authorities act as the facilitators to harness the resources of private sector.
- Upgrading technology in infrastructure services, transportation, construction and recycling.

- Exploring new options for financing of infrastructure, land development, housing, conservation, environmental improvement and slum/JJ rehabilitation.
- Adoption of Multi-year Investement Planning to match priorities of state budget/5 year plans with urban projects.
- A new approach towards Development Controls, mobilizing private sector in land assembly, provision of services and community facilities and adoption of concepts like Accommodation Reservation, Transfer of Development Rights (TDR), Excess Condemnation, etc.
- Networking with international and national urban programmes, e.g. Citynet, Healthy Cities, UMP, Training and Education.

The exercise of Regional Plan - 2021 should be based on the following premises:

- To develop a programme of partnership between concerned State Government, Local Bodies, Development Authorities and Industry to spearhead regional development which would in turn catalyze economic growth.
- To suggest priority areas to provide largest possible impact in the shortest possible time with the primary objectives of improving the quality of life in the region.
- The need for a new initiative and integration so as to adopt a uniform planning approach, standards and procedures.
- Common platform where issues of greater regional importance may be resolved by a common forum.
- Shared objectives, where Govt. and Business/Private Sector work together in a programme of partnership.
- Practical implementable solutions which act as vehicles to promote economic growth.
- Government - Local Body - Private Sector interface & cooperation.
- NCR as integrated environmental, economic and planning zone.

- Infrasturcture services, particularly power & water supply.
- Urban Financing Strategy.
- Development of land, infrastructure services & housing.
- Reforms in legislation and adoption of a uniform system of Urban Planning Legislation for the NCR.
- Urban environment & management.
- Demand driven development on a coalition basis.

Land Policy

An integrated but differential land policy should be worked out keeping in view the factors of equity, employment, ecology, enforcement and efficiency. The mobilization of private sector can be a major consideration in the land policy. The land policy should be differentiated on the basis of potential of development opportunity and directed urbanization.

Major Goals

- Integrated sustainable development and directed urbanization
- Open up new avenues and opportunity zones

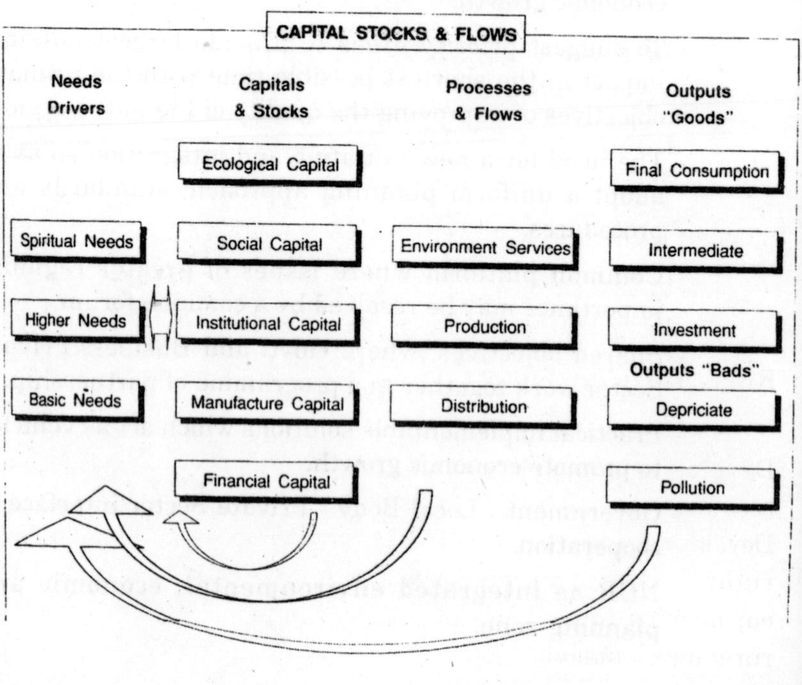

- Increasing empoloyment to accelerate economic development and poverty alleviation
- Value addition
- Spur larger investments from public, private and foreign sector
- Promote a better quality of life for the people in Delhi and the NCR.

Planning Objectives

- To meet the functional needs by development of opportunity areas in the NCR.
- Economic growth and employment generation.
- To achieve a high level of efficiency in services delivery and maintenance.
- To improve the environment
- Rural development focus.
- To create a beautiful urbanscape.
- To preserve heritage and conservation, regeneration of old settlements.
- Integration among economic growth, physical development and environmental improvement.
- Transition from centralized system to a decentralized partnership approach.
- People oriented planning.

Rural Development

A major focus of the NCR Plan should be Rural Development, which has not receievd much attention and resource during last decades. The Union Ministry of Rural Development and concerned State governments can be mobilized right from the planning stage for working out a policy, earmarking funds and framing and implementing schemes of rural development.

There is a need to evolve the SMART (Specific, Measurable, Action Oriented, Realistic and Timely) targets of Rural Development, which should include the following:

Municipal Services

- Water Supply
- Sanitation/Sewerage
- Electricity/Street Lighting
- Solid Waste Management
- Drainage

Pucca Roads

Regional Bus Terminal

Rainwater Harvesting

Social Infrastructure

- Education
- Health/Dispensary/Hospital
- Police Station
- Post Office, Bank, Ration Shop, etc.

Sustainability Agenda

The environmental sustainability is emerging as a major issue and mainstay of the development. It is, therefore, necessary to develop an Environmental Information Base for the NCR and involve concerned organizations such as CGWA, CPCB, DPCC/SPCC, NGOs, etc. in this task.

Water is perhaps the most critical issue and the Regional Plan should be based on the potential of water resources. The measure for its conservation, harvesting and recycling should be extended and made mandatory in the entire NCR. The Government of India have recently notified certain mandatory provisions in this regard for Delhi, which should be extended in the NCR.

A region-wide environmental management aims to link the environment, social, political, economic & financial system into a strategic management. A pro-active environment stratergy

ENVIRONMENT-ECONOMY-SOCIETY

Human Needs & Demand Mangement

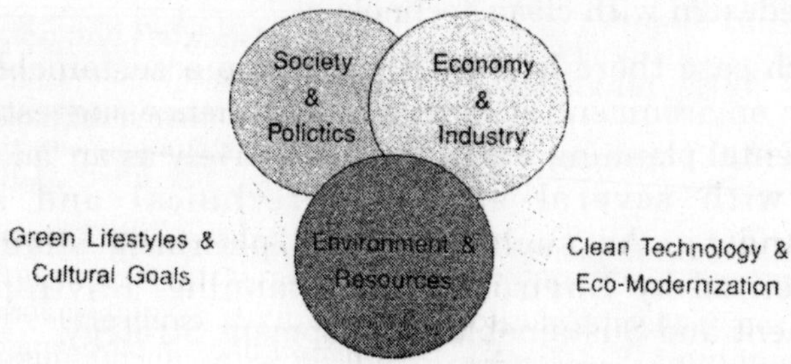

SUSTAINABLE BALANCE

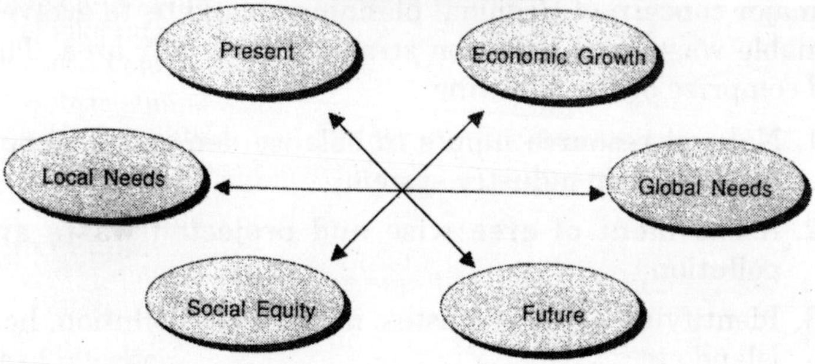

LADDER OF LOCAL SUSTAINABILITY

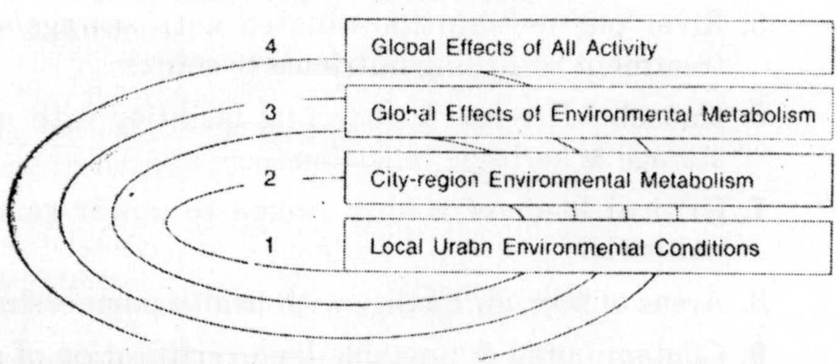

would seek positive links between individual policies and programmes and integrated development scenarios for the region and all its components. In practice there are many gaps in methods and techniques:

- Gaps between 'specifics' (products, firms or impacts) and 'systems' (spatial or functional);

- Gaps between the environmental goals and the 'means' in business and policy performance;
- Gaps between end-of-pipe abatement and complete redesign with clean technology.

In each case there is a need to develop a sustainable and pragmatic environment system. The experience suggests that environmental planning works more effectively as an 'adaptive' process with several stages of technical and social understanding. As such, land use planning should be complemented by Environmental Planning, Environment Management and Sustainable Development Strategy.

Waste and Pollution Control Strategy

A major concern of Regional planning should be to evolve a sustainable waste and pollution strategy, as its key area. This should comprise of the following:

1. Natural resource inputs to balance demand & supply to closed loop industry system;
2. Assessment of area wise and projected waste and pollution;
3. Identifying areas of wastes, noise, dust, pollution, heat island etc.;
4. Neighbourhood-based recycling & materials management in closed loop cycles;
5. River partnership coordinated with sewage/effluent treatment returning nutrients to source;
6. Household re-use & recycling facilities with internal storage & kerbside collection
7. Critical loads of acidity linked to power generation industries;
8. Areas of poor air quality with health partnerships;
9. Contaminated & unstable land certification of derelict lands for its regeneration; and
10. Quality management strategy linked to transport & industrial emissions.

Added Value

Tnere is a need to value addition of the 'sustainability' agenda, which focusses on integrated long term strategy:

- Integrated environmental management and best practices within the NCR framework.
- Innovative industrial commercial and residential clusters or villages.
- Long-term approach within Regional Plan framework.
- Coordination of economic development with local markets and public services.
- Evolving an Economic Value Metabolism.

Opportunity Areas

Development of opportunity areas can become the generators for the restructuring of the NCR. Success may come through working with the remains of the industrial landscape rather than sweeping them away completely. There are no certain solutions to the re-invention of the nature and function of the city in these areas. There is rather a wide-open opportunity for exploring new and creative urban environment for working and living. Such opportunity areas can be the following examples:

1. Zones of intra-modal road-rail transfer, local distribution networks, smart logistics & pipeline movement.
2. Industrial ecology, energy via CHP and heat cascades, integrated materials, waste emissions and effluent management, low impact transport modes.
3. Green growth poles for investment, innovation, technology transfer, green supply chain and distribution markets.
4. Innovative living-working villages, cultural focus, mixed tenures, courtyard layouts, public transport, urban greening and water features.
5. Local community economic development via business training, innovation, public services and intermediate economy programmes.
6. Leisure, sporting & cultural magnets as generators for confidence, investment and infrastructure support.
7. Corridors to rebuild connectivity of damaged landscape.

Regeneration Areas

The regeneration of old cities, inner areas and other developments can be a viable way to improve the quality of life in the NCR and revitalize its economic, social and environmental potential. Regeneration areas are dynamic zones of opportunity, which attract the best and most creative development, as vital parts of the future region. For business there are multi-mode freight interchanges, and industrial ecology networks for integration of energy and waste flows. For local communities there is work, training and leisure in a diverse range of environmentally friendly enterprises. New urban communities are building residential-commercial villages around dynamic watersides and townscapes with ecological transport and leisure facilities.

The Regional Plan should identify potential regeneration areas comprising of urban, rural and natural assets, which need to be regenerated, conserved or redeveloped. The community and private sector can be mobilized and incentivised to take up local regeneration projects.

Bridging Gap Between Planning and Implementation

The experience indicates that in spite of elaorate plans, there are serious gaps in the implementation. This is largely due to administrative and management bottlenecks, vested interests, political intervention, etc. The concept of CQT (coordination, quantum, time) analysis and focus on action planning, Management Information System (MIS), and monitoring of programmes can help in performance orientation. The plans should, however, be simple and result oriented. The programmes should spearhead balanced and affordable services, which catalyse planned development. Priority areas should be worked out so as to deliver the services in the shortest possible time, with a sense of competition between public and private sectors. The planning approach, standards and procedures should be evolved on the basis of realistic assessment, and should be implementable.

Action planning should dovetail urban development, revenue generation, institutional organisation, capacity building, multi-year programme and technology upgradation. The priority of the projects can be fixed on the basis of community demand and importance from development point of view. During the last few years, the cost of infrastructure development has increased disproportionately. It is necessary to review the concept and costing of land, housing and service and evolve low cost development of land and services. For proper implementation, mandatory performance management system and MIS should be developed.

Urban infrastructure is a critical area, which requires much more focus in planning, development and management. The activity of services planning should be a determinant of the spatial form. The concept of self supporting community with decentralised services should be evolved to reduce the dependence on the centralised municipal services. This will facilitate formation of self contained neighbourhoods and development of captive sewerage, power supply, solid waste management and water supply system. Under Build-Own-Operate system private sector may be allowed to provide services. In this way new technology and innovative systems can be introduced to replace obsolete, environmentally inappropriate systems of waste management, power generation and water supply.

The standards of infrastructure services need to be reviewed which may be based on realistic assessment of demand and affordability. There may be differential standards for services according to the character of area and stage of development.

Coalition among the industry, business and the Govt./ NCRPB should be the basis of demand driven development. In this way a new dimension of relationship of corporation and competition will be introduced in the pursuit of better Delhi. The system of tendering on maximum rates should be done away if we want the NCR to become an area of excellence. HUDCO and CIDCO have developed alternative contracting approaches, which are cost effective and ensure time bound development. These should be explored for possible use in the case of NCR.

Proposed Settlement Pattern 2021

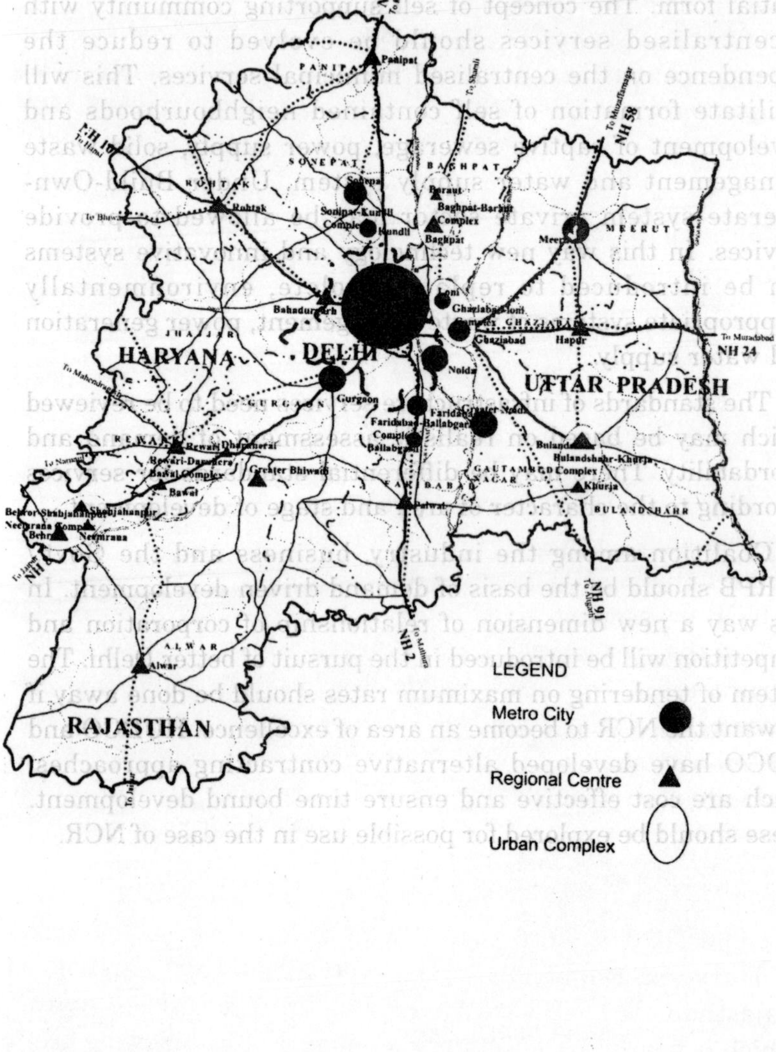

24

STRATEGIC PLANNING FOR THE NATIONAL CAPITAL REGION

Good plans shape good decisions. That's why good planning helps to make elusive dreams come true. — Lester Robert Bittel

Delhi, the national capital, is today emerging as a sprawling conurbation. It attracts people from all over the country and its footprints extend much beyond the borders of Delhi. As many of the problems of the city emanate from the areas beyond Delhi, the solutions also lie beyond its geographical frontiers. Realising this, a regional approach has been adopted for the balanced development of National Capital Region (NCR).

In 2001, NCR accommodated a population of 3.70 crores. This accounts for 3.6% of the total population of the country. In 2021 this will be around 6.40 crores. The urban component of NCR population in 2001 was about 2 crores, accounting for 55% of the population. The rest, nearly 1.7 crore, i.e., 44% live in rural areas. NCR has a higher density in comparison to other areas of the country which is 1202 persons per sq. km. against all India average of 324 persons in 2001. Delhi has the highest concentration of people in the country at 9292 persons per sq. km.

Sprawl and Population

The NCR around the NCT of Delhi covers 7 districts of Haryana, 5 districts of Uttar Pradesh and 1 district of Rajasthan. The NCR covers an area of about 33,578 sq.km., which is nearly 1% of country's area, as per the following break up :

- NCT Delhi - Covering 1483 sq. km. accounts only for 4.4% of the total area of the NCR but contains about 37% of NCR population. 56% of the workers are migrant from outside Delhi. The rate of net migration to Delhi had been around 17 per 1000 population. Population of Delhi (137.82 lakh in 2001) is projected to increase to 230 lakh in the year 2021 with the following projected work force.

Projected Work Force for Delhi-2021

Agriculture, etc.	0.8 percent
Industry	21.3 percent
Construction	7.1 percent
Trade & Commerce	30.2 percent
Transport, Storage & Communication	7.4 percent
Other services	33.2 percent
Participation Rate	**38.1 percent**

- Haryana - Covers about 13400 sq. km. which accounts for 40% of the total area of the NCR, but contains only 23% of the NCR population. Haryana contributes 12% in migration to Delhi.
- Uttar Pradesh - Covers about 11000 sq. km. which is 32% of the total area of the NCR and has 31% of total population of the NCR. U.P. contributes 50% of migrants to Delhi.
- Rajasthan - Covers about 7800 sq. km. which accounts for 23.32% of the total area of the NCR, but only 8% of NCR population. Rajasthan contributes about 6% of migrants to Delhi.

The NCR has 110 towns and cities. Actual and assigned population of various components of the NCR, Delhi, DMA Towns and Priority Towns has been given in the Table.

The planning structure in NCR comprises of the following levels :

- Regional Plan
- Sub-Regional Plans for Central NCR/Delhi
- Master Plans - Undertaken by different States
- Zonal Plans
- Local Plans, Projects and Sectoral Plans, which are prepared by the concerned local body/land owning agency.

Urban Settlements in NCR, 2001

	Class I 100,000 +	*Class II 50,000-99,999*	*Class III 20,000-49,999*	*Class IV 10,000-19,999*	*Class V 5,000-9,999*	*Class VI Below 9,999*	*Total*
Haryana Sub-region	8	0	6	14	5	1	34
UP Sub-region	7	9	16	22	8	1	63
Rajasthan Sub-region	1	0	3	2	3	0	9
NCT-Delhi	1	0	0	1	2	0	4
NCR	17	9	25	39	18	2	110

Analysis of the Assigned Population RP-2001 and Actual Population 2001 of Delhi, DMA and Priority Towns

Name	*Actual Population*			*Decadal Growth (%)*		*Assigned Population*	*Actual Population (RP=2001) (Pop. as % of assigned Pop.*
	1981	*1991*	*2001*	*1981-91*	*1991-01*		
NCR	19018909	26446180	37033214	39.05	40.03	32500000	113.95
NCT-Delhi	6220406	9420644	13782967	51.45	46.31	11200000	123.06
NCR excl. NCT Delhi	12798503	17025536	23250247	33.03	36.56	21300000	109.16

DMA Towns							
1. Bahadurgarh	37488	57235	131924	52.68	130.50	200000	65.96
2. Faridabad	330864	617717	1054981	86.70	70.79	1000000	105.50
3. Gurgaon	100877	135884	229243	34.70	68.70	700000	32.75
4. Ghaziabad Incl. Loni	297429	548320	1089180	84.35	98.64	1100000	99.02
5. Noida	37000	146514	293908	295.98	100.60	550000	53.44
6. Kundli						150000	
Total	803658	1 505670	2799236	87.35	85.91	3700000	75.66
Regional Centres/Priority Towns							
1. Panipat	137927	191212	261675	38.63	36.85	500000	52.34
2. Rohtak	166767	216096	294537	29.58	36.30	500000	58.91
3. Palwal	47328	59168	100528	25.02	69.90	300000	33.51
4. Rewari	51562	75342	100946	46.12	33.98	110000	91.77
5. Daruhera	5266	10848	18890	106.00	74.13	75000	25.19
6. Meerut	536615	849799	1 167399	58.36	37.37	1550000	75.32
7. Hapur	102837	146262	211987	42.23	44.94	450000	47.11
8. Bulandshahr	103436	127201	176256	22.98	38.56	500000	35.25
9. Khurja	67119	80305	98403	19.65	22.54	300000	32.80
10. Alwar	145795	210146	265850	44.14	26.51	500000	53.17
11. Bhiwadi	1729	15285	33830	784.04	121.33	115000	29.42
Total	1366381	1981664	2730301	45.03	37.78	4900000	55.72

Source: NCRPB (2004), Regional Plan, 2021.

All these plans should synchronise and harmonise into an integrated development framework. It has been stated by Ministry of Urban Development (MOUD) in the *guidelines for the preparation of MPD 2021* that :

> ... the growth of DMA towns has resulted in deflecting some of the accretions that would have otherwise occurred to Delhi's population. However, a stronger effort is needed to check the growth of migration to the national capital in the future. The National Capital Region Plan has to be much

more dynamic. The harmonisation of tax rates among the NCR States needs to be carried forward into economic and industrial linkage policies. Transportation linkages (including suburban rail links and byepass expressways) have to be built. The synergy between the NCR plan and Delhi Master Plan has to be strengthened.

The Regional Plan-2021 has proposed development through following four Policy Zones :

- NCT Delhi (1483 sq km)
- Central National Capital Region (excluding NCT Delhi) (2000 sq km)
- Highway Corridor Zone (500 m belt on either side)
- Rest of the NCR (27063 sq km)

The Delhi Metropolitan Area (renamed as Central NCR), as defined in Regional Plan-2021, measuring about 2000 sq. km. comprises the notified/controlled development areas of contiguous towns of Ghaziabad, Loni, NOIDA, Gurgaon, Faridabad, Bahadurgarh and Kundli and the extension of the Ridge in Haryana.

Proposed Metro Centres, 2021

	City / Complex	*Proposed Population (in lakh)*	
		2011	*2021*
1.	Faridabad	16.00	25.00
2.	Gurgaon	4.50	16.50
3.	Ghaziabad (incl. Loni)	19.00	30.19
4.	Noida	6.00	12.00
5.	Sonepat-Kundli	3.50	10.00
6.	Surajpur-Kasna (Greater Noida)	7.00	12.00
7.	Meerut	15.00	22.00

Source : NCRPB (2005), Regional Plan, 2021

To restrict the galloping growth of the Capital City, restrictive policy on the employment generation has been proposed as given below :

- Only such new Central Government offices which directly serve the Ministries of the Government of India be located in Delhi.
- Existing offices of public sector undertakings within Delhi should be encouraged to shift, whereas new offices of the public sector undertakings, to the extent possible within their operational areas, should be set up outside Delhi.
- Industrial growth in Delhi should be restricted to small scale with emphasis on units which require skill, less of manpower and energy and are non-nuisance and clean and largely subserve Delhi's economy.
- Legal and fiscal measures should be adopted to restrict employment in industries and distributive trade.
- Major regional transport corridor and communication network needs to be strengthened to enhance economic development within the region and decentralisation of distributive trade.
- The defined natural features such as forests, wildlife sanctuary, ridge, river Yamuna and water bodies should be conserved and kept free from any urban development.

Floating Populace and Commutation

The RITES research report (1999) revealed that a large amount of commuters visit Delhi everyday for employment, education and other purposes. As much as 20 lakh inter city passenger trips per day are contributed by those who come from outside Delhi. A majority of commuters coming from National Capital Region travel by bus (50 per cent) followed by private modes (30 per cent) and rail (20 per cent) in 1998. About 2 million passenger trips are made daily between Delhi and the neighbouring towns which indicate the influence of commutation in the development of Delhi. Therefore, till the development of appropriate regional transport is taken up vigorously, the avenues for reducing the immigration and population growth of Delhi may not practically succeed.

Hierarchy of Settlements

The following six-tier hierarchy of settlements is proposed in the Regional Plan-2021:

Proposed Six-Tier Hierarchy of Settlements

Hierarchy Level	*Population*
Metro Centre	10 lakh and above
Regional Centre	3 to 10 lakh
Sub-Regional Centre	0.5 to 3 lakh
Service Centre	10,000 to 50,000
Central Village	5,000 to 10,000
Basic Village	Below 5,000

As per the 2001 census, in the NCR outside Delhi already three towns/complexes namely Ghaziabad-Loni Complex, Faridabad and Meerut have crossed the million (10 lakh) population mark. The Metro and Regional Centres as given below, are located in the CNCR and the rest in the NCR :

Metro and Regional Centres in Central NCR (DMA Towns)

- Ghaziabad-Loni Complex
- NOIDA
- Faridabad
- Gurgaon
- Sonepat-Kundli Complex
- Bahadurgarh

Metro and Regional Centres outside Central NCR within NCR, (Priority Towns)

- Meerut
- Hapur

- Greater NOIDA
- Bulandshahar-Khurja Complex
- Baghpat-Baraut Complex
- Panipat
- Rohtak
- Palwal
- Rewari-Dharuhera-Bawal Complex
- Alwar
- Greater Bhiwadi
- Behror-Shahjanpur-Neemrana Complex

Some of the cities in the Delhi Metropolitan Area have shown a promise of growth 'potential and adopted innovative strategies of development. The foremost among these is Gurgaon which is emerging as a 'Millennium City'. Covering an area of about 10,000 ha., it was planned for a population of 7 lakh in 2001, and 37 lakh in 2021. The biggest advantages that Gurgaon has exploited is the proximity to Delhi and international airport and the absence, of river bridges. This has led to the positioning of a large number of international corporate offices, shopping malls, housing and call and data centres in Gurgaon.

The role of the private sector is very important in effecting this change for which the credit goes to a pro-active policy of the government, allowing the private sector to consolidate land for township development. Haryana Government pursues the policy of joint sector development under Haryana Development and Regulation of Urban Areas Act, 1975 which enables the private sector to assemble land under Government license. They have to make private contributions to Haryana Development Authority for off-site infrastructure. Part of developed land is mandatory to be reserved for EWS and LIG housing and institutional plots are to be provided by developer free of cost.

While granting a license for development by a private developer under Haryana Urban Development and Regulations of Urban Areas Act, 1975, a condition of alloting 20% of the number of plots in the colony to EWS category of persons having a family income upto prescribed limit (Rs. 2500 per month) by draw of lots, is imposed through a bilateral agreement of the colonizer with the Haryana Government. Such plot sizes vary from 50 to 125 sq m each. In case of group housing colonies, the licensee is required to construct EWS flats not less than 200 sq. ft. each to the extent of 15% of the total number of flats sanctioned. However, this is not enough and needs to be reviewed in the light of National Urban Housing and Habitat Policy, 2007, which stipulates minimum 15 percent of total permissible FAR or 25 per cent of dwelling units, whichever is higher, for EWS housing.

GURGAON

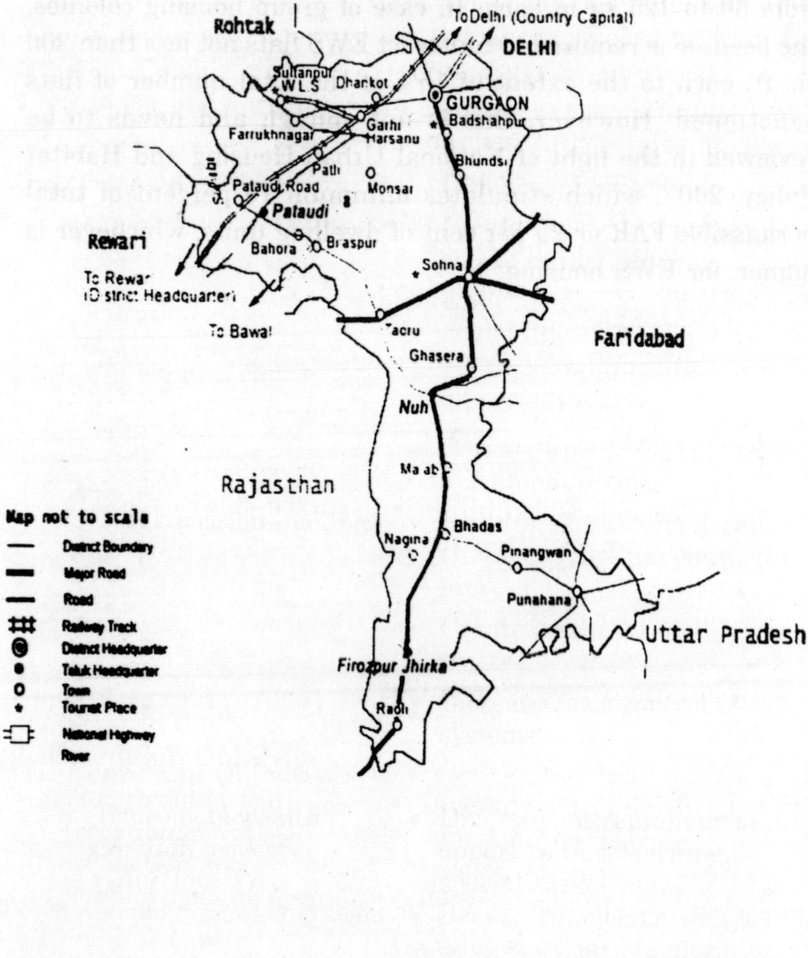
Rohtak
ToDelhi (Country Capital)
DELHI
Sultanpur
W.L.S
Dhankot
GURGAON
Badshahpur
Garhi Harsanu
Farrukhnagar
Bhundsi
Patli
Monsar
Pataudi Road
Pataudi
Rewari
Bahora
Biaspur
Sohna
To Rewari (District Headquarter)
To Bawal
Tauru
Faridabad
Ghasera
Nuh
Rajasthan
Bhadas
Nagina
Pinangwan
Punahana
Uttar Pradesh
Firozpur Jhirka
Raoli
Map not to scale
District Boundary
Major Road
Road
Railway Track
District Headquarter
Taluk Headquarter
Town
Tourist Place
National Highway
River

DELHI
MAJOR URBAN DEVELOPMENT PROJECTS

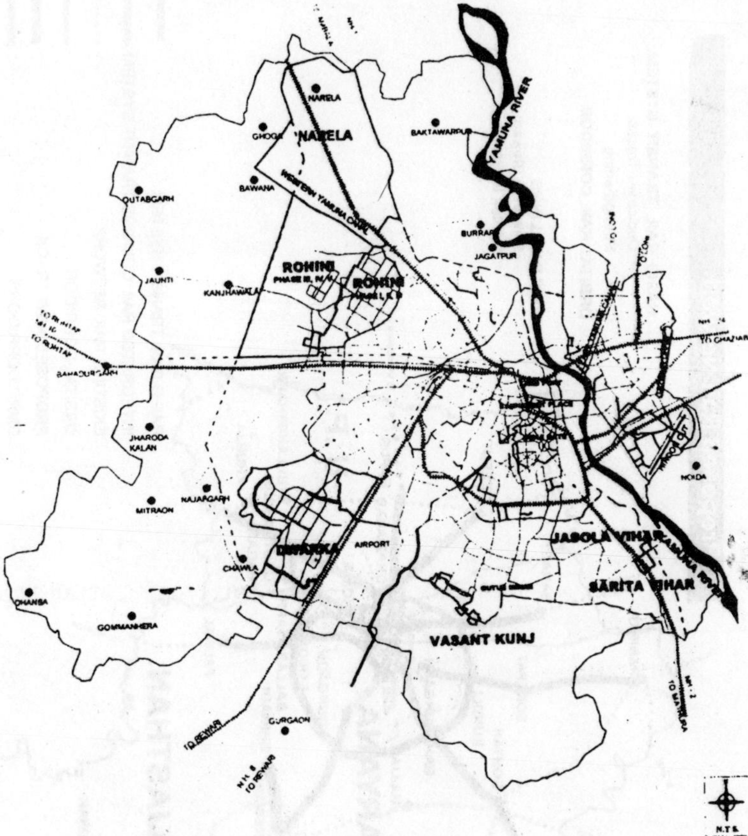

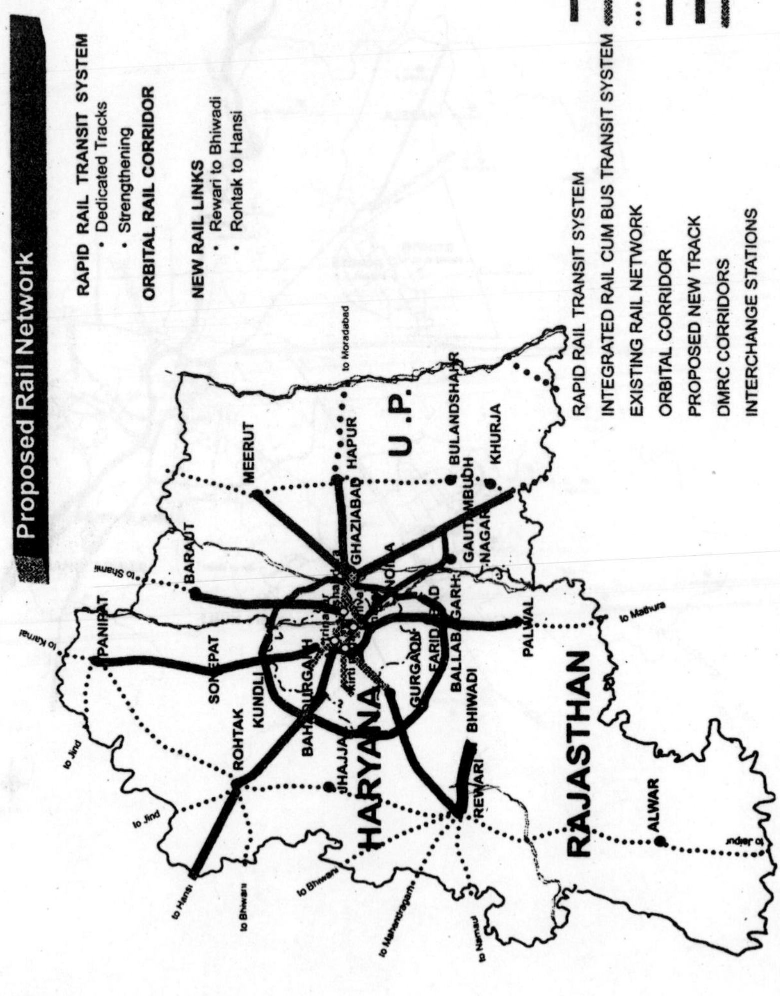

Proposed Rail Network
RAPID RAIL TRANSIT SYSTEM
· Dedicated Tracks
· Strengthening
ORBITAL RAIL CORRIDOR
NEW RAIL LINKS
· Rewari to Bhiwadi
· Rohtak to Hansi
RAPID RAIL TRANSIT SYSTEM
INTEGRATED RAIL CUM BUS TRANSIT SYSTEM
EXISTING RAIL NETWORK
ORBITAL CORRIDOR
PROPOSED NEW TRACK
DMRC CORRIDORS
INTERCHANGE STATIONS
PANIPAT
SONEPAT
KUNDLI
ROHTAK
BAHADURGARH
JHAJJAR
HARYANA
GURGAON
FARIDABAD
BALLABGARH
BHIWADI
REWARI
PALWAL
RAJASTHAN
ALWAR
BARAUT
MEERUT
GHAZIABAD
HAPUR
U.P.
BULANDSHAHR
KHURJA
GAUTAMBUDH NAGAR
NOIDA
to Karnal
to Shamli
to Moradabad
to Mathura
to Jind
to Hansi
to Bhiwani
to Mahendragarh
to Narnaul
to Jaipur

Proposed Road Network

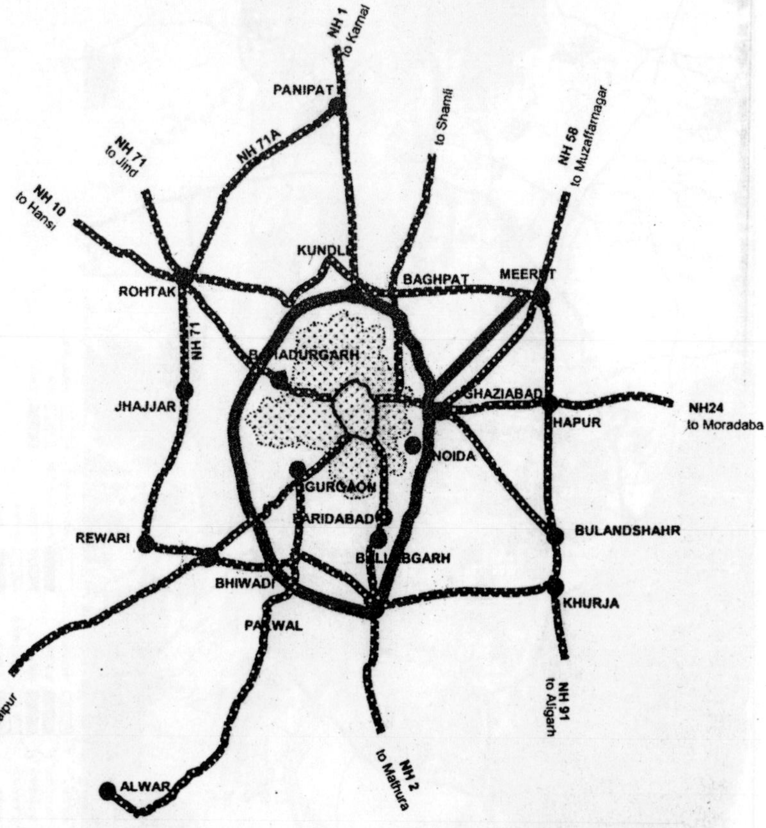

PRIMARY ROAD NETWORK

EXPRESSWAYS

(Conceptual Alignments)

- Western Peripheral Expressway
- Eastern Peripheral Expressway
- Ghaziabad Meerut Expressway

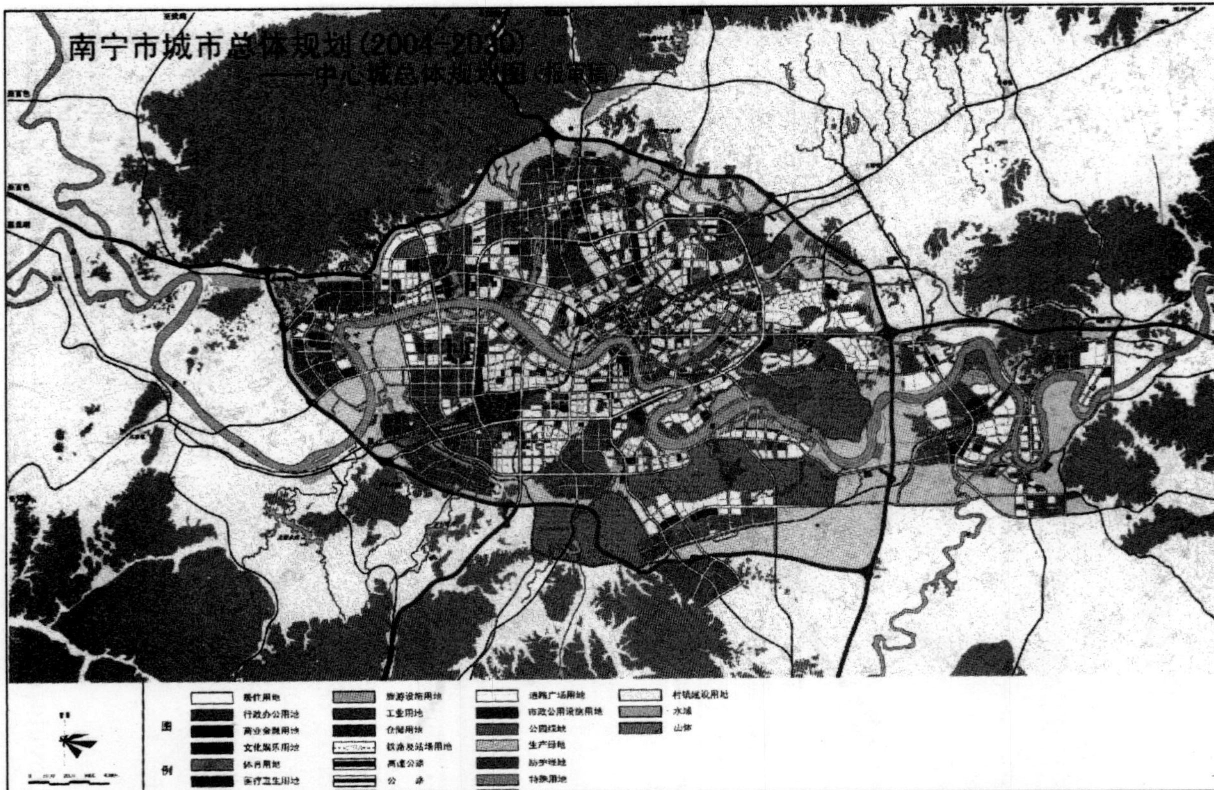

Comprehensive Development Plan of Manning (2004-20)

25

SUSTAINABLE DEVELOPMENT IN CHINA

sus.tain.able adj (ca. 1727) 1: capable of being sustained 2 a: of, relating to, or being a method of harvesting or using a resource so that the resource is not depleted or permanently damaged <~ techniques> <~ agriculture> b: of or relating to a lifestyle involving the use of sustainable methods <~ society> – sus.tain.abil.i.ty n

— Merriam - Webster (1994)

Nanning (population 1.5 million) is one of those provincial cities that provide an insight into just how fast China is developing. It showcases how new affluence, development and sustainability could go hand in hand. Nanning is called the 'Green City of China', and boasts of providing 10.5 sq.m. of parks for every citizen which is also the norm for housing. Nanning is well known for its beautiful environment, greenery and high-quality air. In Nanning, architecture acts as the bridge between the man and nature.

Guangxi is the only region in China that enjoys the coastal open-up policy, China's Western Development policy and the policy of regional autonomy for minority nationalities, which have triggered the development of Nanning Hi-tech Development Zone, China-ASEAN Commerce & Trade Town and China-ASEAN Economic Park. Nanning is located within the economic zone of Nanning, Guiyang and Kunming, and the economic zone of the Ban-pearl River Delta, with its north linking the hinterland of China and the south opening up to the coastal zones. It has a highly developed transportation network of express ways, railways, air services and waterways.

Development Planning

Development of Nanning, like other major cities of China, is guided by a comprehensive Development Plan (Master Plan).

The emphasis of the plan is the development of regional infrastructure, which includes the classification, spatial planning and joint modes of development. The main contents of spatial development plan are dedicated to the protection of ecological and environmental resources. The implementation mechanism of spatial planning relies on the governance of regional spatial development. As China is undergoing rapid urbanization and a transitional period of economic take off, the urban areas are faced with competition from home and abroad, the influx of rural population into cities, the problem of limited land and related ecological problems. In order to achieve the objective of sustainable development, the concept of spatial planning provides the basic guidelines and direction. The principles of planning and development are based on the following "ten transformations":

1. From regional development to internationalization.
2. From economic objectives of planning to sustainable development.
3. From centralized growth to the decentralized and competitive development.
4. From the 'follow up' planning to "leading" type of planning
5. From spatial-economic relationship to the networks, materials, economic, social and cultural inter-relationships.
6. From the focus on the growth poles to the concept of equitable growth, which include the inner-city.
7. From the traditional land use structure to the network model composed of the hierarchical structure and space networks.
8. From the model of urban land use and development controls to the model of economic development with ecological balance through resources and spatial managements.
9. From the pursuit of the government as the developer to the pursuit of collaboration and coordinated development.

10. From the macro-control policies to strategic approach of urban development management.

Flagship Projects - Emergency and Disaster Response Centre

Nanning City Emergency Response Centre (CERC) is the first of its kind in China, which provides an integrated emergency service to city with a command coordination and combined action of different departments. Digitization and networked technology has been used to build a unified command platform and information network platform which offer comprehensive emergency rescue services under one roof, including Police, Fire, Medical emergency, Traffic, besides a Mayor Hotline. Travel complaint system, judicial assistance system and price complaining system are also being included. The Centre aims at building an emergency response management platform to deal with severe disasters, which may have a widespread influence.

The unified emergency response system in Nanning provides response within 5 seconds, which comprises of the following components and system structure.

Emergency Receiving and Event Reports – Handling citizen emergency calls 24 hours a day with the aid of computers.

Emergency Dispatch – Collects first-handed information and makes it possible for unified commanding and dispatching.

Emergency Status Control – Dispatches various city-level resources for emergencies and of the specific situations on a specialized commanding platform.

Radio Dispatch Communication – Covers entire area of Nanning (about 10029 square kilometers) and enables dispatchers to hold simultaneous talks with field units via voice and data radio. Each console for watch command, dispatchers and other emergencies is provided with wireless dispatch terminals.

Unattended Stations' Centralized Remote Control – Monitors far-end equipments' status and performance.

Traffic Control – Monitors traffic status on major roads 24 hours a day.

Simultaneous Satellite Transmitted On-site Pictures – Transmits real-time field images to the CERC.

Data Inquiry – Inquiries related data information system via desktop as well as police vehicle terminals.

Automatic Vehicle Locating – Displays accurate location of assigned vehicles from police, traffic police, fire and first aid.

Records of Incidents – Keeps voice and data records of each single event for later trace.

Mobile Emergency Communication Vehicles – Serves as a command center at the scene of occurrence and provides emergency communication in the areas beyond Smart zone radio coverage.

Display of Incident Status – Real-time incident status can be displayed on the video wall by projection devices.

Safety Guard – Advanced video monitor, door/gate control and identification system.

System Control – Enables system controls via computer terminals, which are linked to relevant sub-systems.

Redevelopment and Rehabilitation of Slums

Nanning City is engaged in an evolutionary and continuing cycle of urban renewal and rebuilding its old dilapidated, slum areas. This work is mainly spearheaded by the City government. An example of such project is the rebuilding of the shanty neighborhood in Donggouling. The neighbourhood had poor quality, unplanned buildings, inadequate public utilities and adverse living environment. Most of the houses had asphalt felt and asbestos roofing with poor structural quality, without sewerage and piped water supply.

In 2001 under the principle of "people first, environment first and sustainable development", the Municipal Government started the rebuilding project to improve the infrastructure and living environment of the shanty neighborhood through cooperative way of financing. Two relocation communities with community facilities, squares, parks, roads and services have been built, housing 724 families (2,540 people). The resettlement of another 1452 households, involving a population of about 6000 has been planned.

The following are the basic guiding principles adopted for redevelopment and Slum Rehabilitation Schemes:

- Provision of minimum habitable area of 10 sqm per person or a minimum 30 sqm dwelling size.
- Provision of about 10 sqm of green/play area, community plaza. If land is not sufficient, such facilities are created by grade separation, rooftops, or even over the roads.
- Ground + 5 floors walk-up apartments, with density of around 400 dwelling units per Ha.
- Mandatory provision of community facilities, services and utilities as per norms by the municipal government.
- Cost of land is usually not included in the apartment cost charged from the residents. Soft loans are available for financing of housing.
- The neighbourhood is maintained jointly by the Residents' Cooperative and municipal/service agency.

Apart from Slum Rehabilitation, large scale affordable housing projects are undertaken for middle and low income families, so that quality of life of such families keeps pace with the economic development.

Housing for the Disabled

Nanning Xinyang Paper Factory was built in 1958 as a State-owned welfare enterprise to settle a large number of the disabled living in the area. Among its 504 employees, 237 were disabled. The factory faced with fierce market competition and suffered losses and most of the disabled lived in a very inhuman, unserviced environment, with poor housing. After closure of the factory, the worst hit were the disabled, who lost their source of employment and also shelter. Nanning City initiated a strategy for improving the living conditions of the disabled. The land under the factory was divided into 3 parts, one part was auctioned for commercial use and the funds were used for rehabilitation housing for workers, including the facilities. One third of the area was used for the living quarters for the disabled and other workers by building 6 storied residential buildings. Remaining area was retained for the revival of the derelict factory. Each dwelling units has 2 rooms and is gross-subsidized through commercial use of part of the land. A visit to the housing project indicates a strong sense of community activity among the residents, who are looked after by the city state as well as their own community.

The South Lake Square

Nanning is known as a Green City. There is much emphasis on development and maintenance of the greenery. Major roads are lined up with flowering shrubs and trees and are often developed as the boulevards. The City has beautiful gardens, parks and river-front. One of the flagship landscape projects is the South Lake Square. It comprises of a Fantastic Tree Garden, South Lake, Water Screen Film and Integrated Water Scenery Project. The Fantastic Tree Garden covers an area of 38.23 hectares. It is characterized with open grasslands, large and exotic trees. There is a "March 3rd Merry Song Plaza" in the center with a terse style and imposing magnificence. The array of woods and the forest with shady trees creates a fairytale environment. More than 870 large tree (25 indigenous and subtropical species) have been planted in the garden.

The South Lake Xincheng Water-screen Film and Integrated Water Scenery Project serves as a cultural and recreational facility. It is a combination of water-screen film, laser beam projection and music fountain. It is always crowded with people and is a flagship project to promote Nanning's brand of "Green City of China".

The Nanning Lang Dong Wastewater Treatment Plant

With ever increasing shortage of water in urban centres, there is no way except to recycle the waste water. Nanning has taken such a step well in time and the Nanning Lang Dong Wastewater Treatment Plant is the first such modern project built in the City. The wastewater processing equipment has been imported from France, which uses conventional activated sludge processing technology. The plant serves a catchments area of 30.5 sq.km. and a population of 350,000. Its designed processing capacity is 260,000 cubic meters of water per day. The Nanning Lang Dong Waste Water Treatment Plan handles waste water of the City before it is ushered into the parks, South Lake or discharged into the River. As such, the plant plays an active role in improving the environment by conservation and recycling of waste water.

At local levels new housing areas and major projects install their own waste water processing system to ensure that waste water is processed before it is discharged into the city drainage system, open space or the River.

Wastewater Recycling Plant

Affordable Housing for Low and Middle Income Groups

26

TURNAROUND OF MUMBAI: LESSONS FROM SHANGHAI

Planning lies with men; success lies with heaven.

— Chinese proverb

During the last decades there have been two major policy changes, which have a direct bearing on urban development:

- **Democratic Decentralization**

  The Constitution (Seventy-third and Seventy-fourth) Amendment Acts, 1992 provide for gradual devolution and localization of development and decision making functions. These amendments provide for preparation of district and metropolitan development plans. The preparation of development plans envisages integration of investments and a participatory process.

- **Globalization and Economic Liberalization**

  During early nineties, the Government of India adopted the policy of economic liberalization and reforms in tune with the era of globalization of the world economy. Together with legislative and regulatory reforms, the review of land infrastructure and urban policies have been the subjects of market orientation, privatization, public-private partnership and low subsidy regime. As a result private sector investments and resources, including Foreign Direct Investment (FDI), are being increasingly mobilized for urban sector in India.

Mumbai and Shanghai

The above phenomena have not been confined only to India. China has been almost a parallel, where the policies of economic liberalization and FDI in real estate sector had been embarked almost at the same pace as in India. As such, Mumbai and Shanghai, the financial capitals, as well as the largest cities of India and China respectively, provide an interesting case study.

The development of diversified market-based financing models in both India and China had been accelerated by opening up the infrastructure sector and creating a competitive market environment for urban infrastructure investment and financing where the role of the government had been mainly to encourage, regulate and guide capital flows. Earlier during 1990s, the country had invested heavily in the development of socially beneficial projects of sanitation, provision of basic amenities, etc., which gave no returns. Given the huge population of the country and the maintenance that such infrastructure requires, these projects did not really make a mark on increasing the quality of life of the local population substantially.

With liberalization, the governments and local bodies began to look at the cost recovery of infrastructure investments. Having realized the need for efficient project management and expertise in such projects to be financially viable, the government started opening up the sector to private and joint sector agencies.

Changing Trends

With the arrival of overseas players to Indian markets, the trends began to change. Soon the metros saw a mushrooming of businesses and global enterprises. The IT and BPO companies transacted most of their businesses over the state-of-art communication lines and internet technologies. Their requirements were of huge space where various functions of their business could be housed under one roof. The suburbs of the main cities began developing with leading IT and BPO companies willing to shift their bases to areas like Vashi, Bandra-Kurla and Andheri in Mumbai; Pune and Nashik, and to other regions like NOIDA and Gurgaon. Such suburbs offered a better life both by default and design providing corporates with world class commercial towers and skilled employees. Following the development of commercial complexes, the companies which shifted base to these townships began to look for residential real estate. This led to the development of residential complexes where, unlike in the central city areas, land, power, and other basic facilities were better.

As the drivers of development, the urban centres today are essentially comprise of the tertiary sector employment. However, there is not much improvement of the standards of living of the local population in the emerging urban centres. The corporates are enabling decongestion of cities by taking their working staff with them out of the city. However, the first generation of suburban boom is waning and the development in terms of finances, investments, businesses and employment is slowing down. This will have to be pushed by the local bodies, who have to seriously review the strategies of sustained development together with how the local population can be benefited from growth.

Reports indicate that migration towards the metro areas will slow down considerably over the next decades. It is important for the local bodies to take stock of the situation and to work towards offering all sections of population a basic standard of living and amenities. It is time to redirect the process of urbanization which is predicted to be top heavy, led by a few metros percolating down to the smaller settlements in a wider region.

Lately, Central and State Governments have approved the development of two major townships - New Gurgaon and Greater Noida as a major step towards decongestion of city. There is no doubt that both Mumbai and Kolkata will have to follow suit.

Brihan Mumbai

Known as the financial capital of India, Mumbai is the largest city in India. It has witnessed continuing and substantial development during last three centuries. Mumbai is a man-made city, largely reclaimed from the sea. It was mainly developed by the European colonialist for trade, which it perpetuates even today. Industry and trade has prospered and fortunes were made in this 'City of Gold'. Every day thousands of people arrive in the city hoping to find their pot of gold or to realize their 'dreams'.

During the twentieth century, Mumbai's transformation into a megacity proceeded apace. Mumbai continued to grow both literally and metaphorically. It emerged as one of the biggest industrial complex on mainland Asia.

After independence, Mumbai witnessed a runaway growth. To cope with the growing demands, the administrative boundaries of the city were enlarged twice, in 1952 and 1957 by incorporating the suburban areas. From just 0.81 million population in 1901, Mumbai crossed 16.3 million count in 2001. From an island city of few square kilometers, it has grown into a conurbation running to a length of hundred kilometers in various directions. Brihan Mumbai is a district and the capital of Maharashtra state. On one hand it claims as one of the biggest film making cities in the world and on the other it has the distinction of having the largest slum, Dharavi.

Mumbai Metropolitan Regional Planning Board (MMRPB), established in 1967, prepared a Regional Plan for Mumbai area. Mumbai Metropolitan Regional Development Authority (MMRDA) was set up in June 1975 to direct balanced development of the region, covering an area of 4156 sq km, 20 urban centre and 1174 villages. It proposed development of a counter-magnet, that is New Mumbai, which has been planned for population of 2 million. It envisaged a poly-centred development with a series of nodal centres along a mass transportation corridor. One such node which has already been developed is located at Vashi near Thane Creek Bridge. It connects Mumbai near Chembur. This township is having a population of 1,00,000.

Mumbai's contribution in national economy is immense. Alone it accounts for 20% of the total employment in India's organized industry. Of the entire state of Maharashtra, Mumbai alone provides 54% of industrial employment, 88% of joint account companies and 62% of productive capital. The status of Mumbai as the financial capital of the country is vindicated by the fact that it is contributing 10 per cent of the nation's total employment, 33 per cent of income tax, 60 percent of custom duties, 20 per cent of central excise and is handling 40 per cent of India's foreign trade. It also receives 50 per cent of international air-passengers. Its contribution to the state domestic production is nearly 40 per cent.

The population of Mumbai increased from 2.96 million in 1951 to 16.36 million in 2001. To cope up with the growing demands of its economic activities and mammoth population, the mega-city is growing both vertically and horizontally. As a result it is getting more and more congested. The residential density, i.e., the population per sq. km. of the Mumbai urban conglomeration in 2001 was estimated at 40,956 persons.

Vision Plan

During the seventies, a vision plan for Mumbai was charted out by Charles Correa, who proposed development of a string of nodes tied by a railway corridor with a view to decentralize and shift the development activities to New Mumbai, Vashi-Belapur and Kalamboli. The New Mumbai was placed under City and Industrial Development Corporation (CIDCO). The draft development plan for New Mumbai was approved in 1979, under which a series of urban centres were proposed. These were intended to be linked by railway and road routes. The population projected for these centres varied from 1,00,000 to 2,00,000. The site included a portion of the New Port envisaged to be developed by the Port Trust at Nhava Sheva. Major access to New Mumbai is through the railway links and a motor bridge constructed over Thane Creek. Initially, the execution had been slow. Due to non-development of the rail-road links, the industries stuck largely to the existing areas along the railway lines. After two decades, the new city is emerging as a real counter-magnet and many industries, commercial offices and other work centers have started functioning.

New Interventions

Traditionally the lifeline of Mumbai's growth had been the availability of local railway facility to the commuters. Accordingly the decision to extend the commuter railway line from Mankhurd to Belapur providing direct link between New Mumbai's CBD and Chhatrapati Shivaji Terminal (Victoria Terminus) has accelerated its growth. The development of a new port at Nhava-Sheva by the Government of India has resulted in increase in jobs and spurt in construction activities. As a strategy of accelerating development, the CIDCO initiated a major market intervention programme. It includes massive construction of 65000 dwelling units for various income groups with hire-purchase facility, together with creation of social infrastructure like schools, hospitals, shopping centres, police stations, fire stations and other religious, sports and cultural activities.

In view of the usual initial difficulty faced by various organizations in building and development of their own facilities, CIDCO started with development and construction of certain priority projects which were later handed over to the concerned organizations. These included bus service, which was later transferred to BEST and State Transport Corporation. It also developed and built railway stations integrated with supermarkets and various other facilities. This has been a new phenomenon. For a development authority, taking up construction projects, which are conventionally within the jurisdiction of other departments, has been a bold initiative which has accelerated the pace of development. Acting as a lever, this has in turn attracted huge investments from the private sector in various fields such as industry, warehousing, trade, offices, housing, etc.

CIDCO took up several initiatives through privatization, which include maintenance of sewerage pumps, and water pumps, meter reading and billing, maintenance of parks and gardens, collection of CIDCO's service charges, etc. CIDCO has given the responsibility of collection of its service charges to the Senior Citizens Club to whom it pays one per cent as commission. SPARC, Mumbai alongwith Mahila Milan have taken up the schemes of slum upgradation and rehabilitation in various parts of Mumbai.

Vision Mumbai

Transforming Mumbai into a world-class City is a report prepared by McKinsey and Company, which has triggered a series of projects. These amounting to more than Rs. 200,000 crore, include transport-related projects (Mumbai Metro Rail, the Bandra-Nariman Point Sealink and Sewri-Nhava Sealink with estimated cost of Rs. 31,000 crore.) Some other projects are proposed to be taken up under the Jawaharlal Nehru National Urban Renewal Mission. Vision Mumbai involves re-shaping of parts of the city, which has emphasized slum rehabilitation and recycling of surplus land in the textile mills. There have been several court cases and controversies about the proposals, with the allegation that it is the vision of corporate business, the financial and real estate groups and not that of the people of Mumbai.

A six-lane, 22 km. long Mumbai Trans Harbour Sea Link project of the Maharashtra State Road Development Corporation Ltd. (MSRDC) has been planned across Sewri to Nhava Sheva in Navi Mumbai. Scheduled to be completed by 2010, its cost is estimated to be about Rs.4000 crores. It will connect Mumbai and New Mumbai reducing the commuting time from 2 hours to 45 minutes.

Shanghai

Shanghai is not only the largest city of China, it is also one of the largest in the World and has a population of over 16 million. According to the World Bank, it is likely to have nearly 24 million inhabitants by 2015 and would be the fourth largest urban agglomeration in the world after Tokyo, Mumbai and Lagos. Shanghai is the financial and trade centre of China. It began economic reforms in 1992. Shanghai's tax contribution to the central government is around 20-25% of the national total. Shanghai today is the biggest and most developed city in mainland China.

The City Planning Law of the People's Republic of China (1990) envisages to control the size of big cities and rationally develop medium and small cities. The City Planning Law of 1990 encourages regional planning so as to arrange for regional infrastructure in an integrated way and to clearly define the urban system. It gives stress to ecological balance, economic growth and environmental protection. It also stresses on integrated development of newly built areas and inner city redesigning.

A decade ago, the town of Suzhou (about 100 km inland and on the highway connecting Shanghai to Nanging), was a recipient of induced growth with a Singapore consortium as a main partner. It was part of a strategy to disperse new growth over a wider region rather than just Shanghai. Today with Shanghai opened for promotional growth, Suzhou is a competitor and not a partner for regional employment generation.

The City Planning and Management Regulations of Shanghai (Land use and Building Management, 1994) identify three areas of growth: (a) the Central Area within the inner circle (the old metropolitan area and part of Pudong); (b) the area between the inner and outer perimeter (roughly the extended metropolitan area composed of ten urban districts) and, (c) the rest of the municipal area (outside the outer perimeter). The floor area ratio (FAR) and coverage are laid down per plot in each of the three zones. In Shanghai, buildings below three storeys are deemed to be low rise (R_1); between four to eight storeys are deemed to be multi-storeyed (R_2) and nine storeys and above as high rise (R_3). The main land uses are residential (R_1, R_2, R_3); commercial (Administration, Commercial/Banking, Cultural/Entertainment, Sports/Stadia, Health, Education/ Research); Manufacture (non pollutant, medium pollutant, very pollutant); warehousing (normal and dangerous/hazardous); Municipal Utilities (water, power, gas, transport, communication, sanitation, construction sites) and Greens (public and protected). Minimum plot sizes are specified (500 sqm. in low rise residential zones, 1000 sq.m. in multi-storeyed residential/ commercial zones, 2000 sq.m. in high-rise residential zones and 3000 sq.m. in high rise commercial zones). There are provisions for the development of plots smaller than that specified. Distances to be left between buildings (both within and adjoining plots) is based on air and light planes. This determines building heights. Thus in large plots, as in Pudong, very tall buildings are possible.

Transport and Infrastructure

Transport and physical infrastructure is receiving greater financial assistance in Shanghai. The bicycle still dominates (Shanghai is the biggest manufacturer of bicycles in the world) but the motor car and other personalized motorized vehicles are on the increase with major roads making the inner city's historical environment increasingly characterless. Two major mass rapid rail corridors - below ground in about a north-south and east-west axis is growing to help in a modal split that favours mass transit alongwith the bus. The inter-urban and intra-urban transport systems also seem well integrated with the main railway station on the mass transit routes. The two airports would also be so connected over the next decade. In this process and with the bicycle having limitations (in terms of journey to work beyond 5 to 8 km each way), the work and home places are increasingly being separated through increased trip length. The physical infrastructure in terms of water, drainage, sewerage, electricity, gas and telecom seem to be keeping pace with maintenance assured through regular collection of user charges.

Districts and Counties

Shanghai Municipality spread over 6340 sq km. is divided into twelve urban districts and ten suburban counties. The terrain is mainly flat between 3 to 5 meters above mean sea level and it has an intricate network of canals and waterways. Large areas are subject to subsidence and to control this, water replenishment is through recycling rather than tapping underground sources. The plan now under revision gives stress to an integrated multi-modal traffic-cum-land use cum services plan as spearheaded by SUPDRI and which has ensured the completion of the inner perimeter ring road and its north-south axis largely as elevated expressways. The east-west axis is now nearing completion. The outer surround line or outer ring road is also under rapid execution and is complete in key segments - all at ground level. These expressways would accordingly redefine the inner and extended city boundaries. The inner ring road crosses the Huangpo river at two points and more connections, including one road connection and one intra-urban rapid rail transit corridor, is under construction by tunneling under the river bed. Thereby the new extension of Pudong to the East gets integrated as Shanghai's contiguous growth.

Pudong Extension

The Pudong New Area Master Plan was prepared by SUPDRI. By 2000, Pudong would have the main airport, new port facilities, a free trade zone, export processing zones, financial and trade zones, a Hi-tech park, major sports and cultural centres, a large seashore tourism zone, an agro-industrial zone, a large wild life park and several residential parks. Pudong has thus emerged as perhaps the largest city extension project in the world with services, transport and built space programmed for integrated development on government owned land through primary and secondary markets.

China's land market operates in urban areas as a system comprising :

- Primary markets for the sale of the rights to the use of state-owned lands whereby land use rights are sold to developers and users by public auction, bid or agreement by land administering departments on behalf of the state. This type is considered to be monopolistic.
- Secondary markets for the transfer of the rights to the use of state-owned lands on which developers and administrators carry out development, sales and transfer operations after they have acquired land-use rights according to law. This type is considered to be competitive.
- Financial transactions through leasing, mortgaging and transfer of rights on use of land and buildings with full insurance to reduce risks.
- A special land market to serve the needs of foreign nationals.
- Consultancy in terms of information, brokerage, valuation, registration and arbitration—all essential for an efficient market mechanism.

Investment

Since 1992, accelerated financing reforms and increased investment in urban infrastructure have helped in urban turnaround. As a result, several key projects have been completed, including 4 bridges and 3 tunnels crossing the Huangpu river, connecting the east and west parts of Shanghai; expressways and urban elevated road network; three rail transit lines totaling 125 km in length; Hongqiao Airport extension and Pudong International Airport construction; an integrated' sewerage system; water supply facilities upgrading and water resource protection; and large-scale public green area developments, etc. By the end of 2004, the per capita road area, public green area and net living space in Shanghai have undertaken a dramatic rise compared with 1990s, as indicated in the Table, give below:

Comparison of Urban Infrastructure Development Between 1990 and 2004

Item	*1990*	*2003-2004*
Road Area (m^2 per capita)	2.28	12.3
Rail Transit (km)	0	12.5
Living Area (m^2 per capita)	6.60	14.2
Green Area (m^2 per capita)	1.02	10.0
Waste Water Treatment Rate (%)	0	65.3

Shanghai has taken on an entirely new look. Sustained double-digit economic growth for 16 consecutive years since 1992 proves that effective investment in infrastructure has not only directly improved the living standard and investment climate in Shanghai but has also stimulated China's national economic growth.

By 2004, foreign direct investment in Shanghai had risen to US$ 11.7 billion, and the FDI sum-up from 1992 to 2004 reached US$ 85.0 billion; Shanghai government's fiscal receipts have risen to RMB 359.17 billion by 2004, among which the municipal fiscal revenue is RMB 111.9 billion.

The approach to urban infrastructure financing in Shanghai is explained hereinafter:

- **Diversification of financing sources**

  Under the planned economy, government fiscal input had been the only source of financing for urban infrastructure development. The first part of Shanghai's strategy for diversification of infrastructure financing was the establishment of governmental investment corporations, such as Shanghai Chengtou Corporation (Urban Development Investment Corporation), with a mandate to initiate new financing approaches, including bond issuance, concession management, and capital market financing, etc. As the biggest governmental investment corporation in Shanghai, by the end of 2004, Shanghai Chengtou Corporation mobilized more than RMB 140 billion of direct investment in urban infrastructure. The second was to leverage limited governmental investments to attract loans from both international and domestic lenders. The loans from the World Bank, ADB, the German Government, and the Dutch Government for the construction, respectively, of the Shanghai Sewerage Project and the Hongqiao International Airport have been mobilized.

- **Land as a resource**

  Since the 1990s, Shanghai has taken lead in land leasing and has generated revenues of over 100 billion RMB in the past 13 years, which have been injected in urban infrastructure and housing complexes.

- **Developing multiple market-based investment models**

  For revenue-generating projects, such as expressways, urban water supply works, waste-water treatment facilities, etc., investments have been encouraged and attracted from international partners, domestic enterprises, and private investors, through concession contracts, BOT, initial public offerings, joint ventures, etc.

Lessons from Shanghai

As soon as you land in Shanghai, it is difficult to escape making a comparison between the Indian cities and Shanghai. The broad tree-lined roads with magnificent buildings on either sides, cleanliness and absence of slums in Shanghai make a marked difference between cities of the two countries. Most of the roads have bicycle lanes, which are well used. In spite of the huge crowds, there is no chaos and disorder. There is a great sense of civic discipline. The city is proud of its past while modernizing itself and keeping pace with the future. Hunger, poverty and begging seems to be vanishing. There is no shortage of water, power and other services. The digital maps of the city are freely available on the websites. Going a little deeper one discovers that these achievements have been possible by genuine simplification of investment and development process. One hardly hears of political interference in Shanghai. Decentralisation of decision-making, focus on infrastructure development and autonomy of various local bodies have been the key factors in creating a competitive environment. There is plenty to learn in metropolitan planning and management from Shanghai.

Lately there is a chorus that Mumbai should be developed as a Shanghai. While this is a laudable idea, the path to it is tough and arduous. Nevertheless there is, in any endeavour to transform Brihan Mumbai into a parallel of Shanghai, plenty to learn from the example of the Chinese metropolis. There are many lessons to learn and imbibe from Shanghai.

Renewal Missions

The Government of India has embarked the Jawahar Lal Nehru Urban Renewal Mission designed to meet the challenge of urban development, covering the cities with a population of over a million (and some towns), with an initial outlay of Rs. 50,000 crores. Access to the resources of the Urban Renewal Fund by the State Governments is contingent on the fulfillment of the core obligations and reforms based on a well worked out strategy for development of selected urban centres tied up with national and international investments.

The sustainability of infrastructure and urban projects depends on the success of developing and implementing a strong techno-financial and techno—legal regime based on viable rates of return for private sector participation. The techno-financial and techno-legal regime should support each other so that a conducive and sustainable environment is maintained for constant investments in the sector.

Decentralization

Approaches to infrastructure development have traditionally been considered 'large solutions' to 'large problems' with centralized infrastructure as the norm. Whether it is telecommunications, power distribution or water supply, there has been limited success of government efforts to effectively reach these areas. This is unlikely to be any different with the growing involvement of the private sector on account of the perceived market risks. There are several problems facing the development and financing of infrastructure projects. The challenges that need to be addressed to enable decentralized and smaller scale infrastructure projects to become a reality are the following:

- *Technology viability:*

  One of the constraints facing infrastructure projects is the low level of technology as sophisticated technologies backed by R & D may not be affordable.

- *Financing packages:*

  Decentralized projects normally require the risk mitigation, as is required for larger infrastructure projects. The normal financing packages and institutions that are available at the local level often do not have the capacity to assess and finance these projects.

- *Policy issues:*

  Policy and regulatory issues are not often conducive to enabling decentralized development on a commercial basis. Issues such as licensing requirements, linkages to larger facilities, etc., need to be conducive to enable such development.

Policy Initiative

Various multi-disciplinary issues require policy, legal and institutional changes. There is need to have a credible regulator to promote a competitive culture in the sector within the framework of meeting social obligations. The setting up of a regulatory authority for decisions related to fixing tariffs, quality of service, etc., is necessary so that after privatization of power, water and other urban services, fall in quality of service does not take place. The constitution of the Utilities Commission to safeguard the public interest in the delivery of urban services such as power, telecommunication, roads, etc., deserves serious consideration. This could be done through State level Regulatory Bodies, which may decide upon the nature of tariff and deal with other service related regulations. Various components of urban planning and development will require well crafted Special Purpose Vehicles which can substantially leverage funds and augment resources by ensuring commercial viability to service debt. Multi-tiered local bodies should evolve a strong planning process, based on consensus, consultations and interactive process. Accordingly, capacity building efforts should be undertaken towards developing a strong planning and management structure in the local bodies and city authorities for a techno-legal financial nexus towards achieving a Public Private Partnerships (PPP) mode of development. Capacity building efforts have to aim at achieving the interrelated principles of transparency, efficiency, mutual understanding and partnership. This requires a change in role of the urban professionals - from controller to catalyst of change, from office manager to organizer and from technical expert to facilitator. This also involves redefining the outsourcing procedures and the participatory process, which synthesizes the financing/economic, spatial, technical and institutional aspects of city development.

It is easy to talk about transforming Brihan Mumbai into a second Shanghai. It is more difficult to plan, programme and execute the journey. We have discussed the development of Brihan Mumbai - how it has come about - more or less as a natural process over time, with some planned sectoral developments from time to time.

Thereafter we have discussed how Shanghai has developed to one of the greatest planned metropolises of the world as a parallel case in point.

It is therefore a natural corollary that we should endeavour to draw lessons from Shanghai—if any serious endeavour has to be made to develop Mumbai into a planned and orchestrated megalopolis comparable to Shanghai.

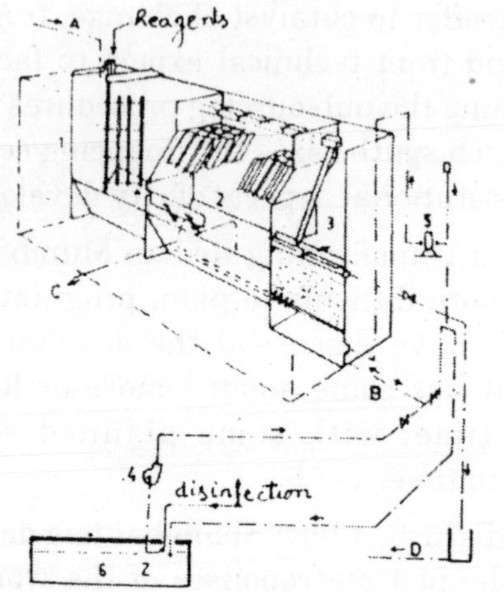

1. Flocculation Unit
2. Clarifier
3. Filter
4. Raw Water Pump
5. Air Blower
6. Treated Water Tank

A Raw Water Inlet
B Treated Water Outlet
C Sludge Draw-off
D To Drain

COMPACT WATER TREATMENT UNIT

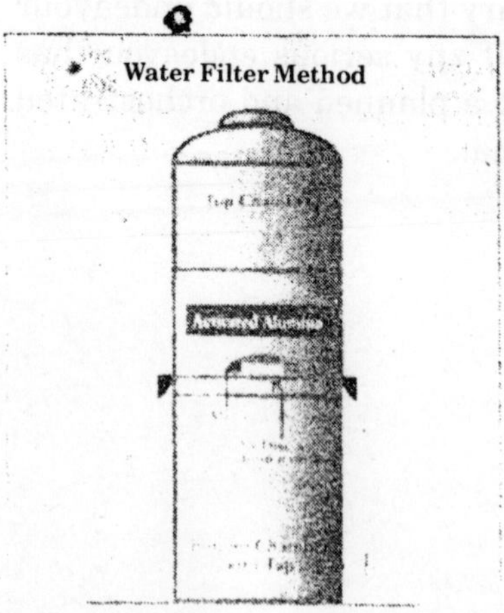

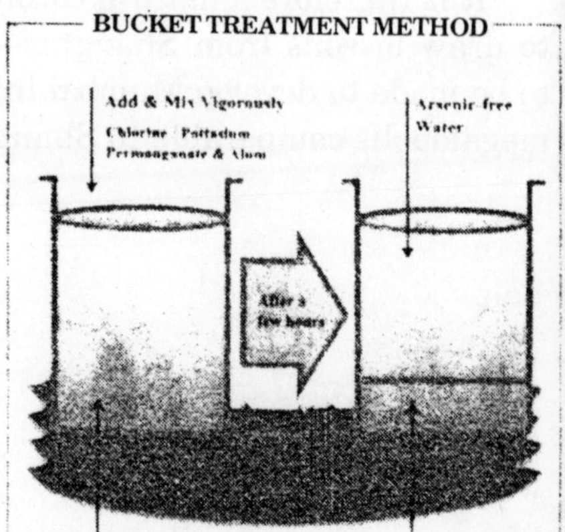

27

A ROADMAP FOR SUSTAINABLE RURAL DEVELOPMENT

A good plan is like a road map: it shows the final destination and usually the best way to get there. — H. Stanely Judd

India is an agrarian country with about 72 per cent (about 80 Crores) of its population in about 5,75,936 villages. The villages are inhabitated by the rural poor with agriculture as their predominant occupation. They are largely small and marginal farmers, agricultural labourers, artisans and scheduled castes and scheduled tribes. A large number of rural people (about 30 crore) are still living below the poverty line and often face the basic problem of survival, viz., jobs, poverty, hunger, shelter, ill-health and disease. By the year 2015, India's population may surpass that of China. Dr. M.S. Swaminathan, credited with the 'Green Revolution', has warned of a coming famine. The increasing unemployment in the rural sector is likely to have serious ramifications on India's socio-economic and political balance. Today, we often witness serious contradictions – an aeroplane, a sign of progress and power and a bullock cart dragging in a slushy and deeply rutted kaccha road. We can not afford to loose the focus of rural areas and make them subservient to the urban life. The hi-tech should be blended with indigenous practices in a manner that it eradicates poverty, disease, inequality and provides basic human needs such as, water, roads, medical care and literacy. Value addition to agro-products is very crucial in this respect. The planned development of rural areas should envisage provision of 'urban' facilities and services, including work centers, agro-industry, hospitals, schools, piped water supply, sanitation, housing, recreational facilities etc., which can be clustered into viable units or 'cities in the field'. These can also be the centers of learning of new technologies of computer, space, telecommunication etc. From the pre-independence era of Mahatama Gandhi, every government after the Independence of the country in 1947, has committed itself to rural development. The UPA Government at the centre announced a Common Minimum Programme (CMP), according to which the following are the commitments:

Panchayati Raj: "It will be ensured that all funds given to states for implementation of poverty alleviation and rural development schemes by panchayats are neither delayed nor diverted. Monitoring will be strict. In addition, after consultations with states, the UPA government will consider crediting elected panchayats with such funds directly. Devolution of funds will be accompanied by similar devolution of functions and functionaries as well. Regular elections to panchayat bodies will be ensured and the amended Act in respect of the Fifth and Sixth Schedule Areas will be implemented. The UPA government will ensure that the gram sabha is empowered to emerge as the foundation of panchayati raj."

Women and Children: "It will be ensured that at least one-thirds of all funds flowing into panchayats are earmarked for programmes for the development of women and children. Village women and their associations will be encouraged to assume responsibility for all development schemes relating to drinking water, sanitation, primary education, health and nutrition."

Infrastructure: "The highest priority is attached to the development and expansion of physical infrastructure like roads, highways, ports, power, railways, water supply, sewage treatment and sanitation.

Drinking Water: "Providing drinking water to all sections in urban and rural areas and augmenting availability of drinking water sources is an issue of the topmost priority. Harvesting rainwater, desilting existing ponds and other innovative mechanisms will be adopted."

The 73rd Constitutional Amendment Act, 1993

73rd Constitutional Amendment Act is a landmark event in the field of rural development, by which the Panchayats and Gram Sabha got constitutional status in 1993. Women, SCs, STs and OBCs got reservations in decision-making at PRIs level. Schedule XI containing 29 items was laid down for devolution of powers to PRIs. The District Planning Committee was proposed for preparing plans for economic development and social justice at district level.

The Eleventh schedule by which 243 G defines the scope of rural development, which is quite comprehensive and is often taken as the basis of preparing Five Year and Annual Plans and programmes by the Central and State Governments. As such, the same, as given below, has been adopted in this paper, as the scope of amenities and services for rural planning. The Eleventh Schedule (Article 243 G) of the 73rd Constitutional Amendment Act, contains a list of the amenities and facilities, which cover the following:

1. Agriculture including agricultural extension.
2. Land improvement, implementation of land reforms, land consolidation and soil conservation.
3. Minor irrigation, water management and watershed development.
4. Animal husbandry, dairy and poultry.
5. Fisheries.
6. Social forestry and farm forestry.
7. Minor forest produce.
8. Small-scale industries including food processing industries.
9. Khadi, village and cottage industries.
10. Rural housing.
11. Drinking water.
12. Fuel and fodder.
13. Roads, culverts, bridges, ferries, waterways and other means of communications.
14. Rural electrification including distribution of electricity.
15. Non-conventional energy sources.
16. Poverty alleviation programme.
17. Education including primary and secondary schools.

18. Technical training and vocational education.
19. Adult and non-formal education.
20. Libraries.
21. Cultural activities.
22. Markets and fairs.
23. health and sanitation including hospitals, primary health centers and dispensaries.
24. Family welfare.
25. Women and child development.
26. Social welfare, including welfare of handicapped and mentally retarted.
27. Welfare of weaker sections and in particular the SCs/STs.
28. Public distribution system.
29. Maintenance of community assets.

There are a number of Central and State Governments programmes and projects for each of the above subjects. The Central Government has recently announced a new Twenty Point Programme (TPP-2004), which overlaps the provisions of rural amenities and services. The salient programmes of the Central Government under each head are given below:

1. AGRICULTURE (INCLUDING DAIRY, POULTRY AND FISHERY)

Intensive Agriculture District Programme

- Launched in 1960-61, intensive agriculture district programme (IADP) was started to expand food production based on a package of irrigation, seeds, pesticides, credit and technical assistance.
- Comprehensive Crop Insurance to farmers against calamity and loss of crop.
- Kisan Credit Card and Life Insurance Cover to Kisan Credit Card holders.
- Kisan Mitra (Twenty Point Programme-2004)
- Agriculture Insurance – Crops and livestock

- Agro Clinic (Kisan Call Centre)
- Water shed development and Rain water harvesting
- Dry land farming
- Promotion of horticulture, floriculture, aquaculture and dairying
- Marketing and infrastructural support to farmers
- Irrigation facilities (Including minor and micro irrigation)
- National Programme for Desert Areas and Drought Prone Area
- Land Reforms
- Distribution of surplus land to landless SC/ST families
- Compilation and computerization of land records
- Waste Land Development Programme
- Debt relief and clearance of dues to farmers
- Promotion of Commercial Agriculture
- Effective functioning of agricultural cooperatives

2. LAND

- Integrated Rural Development Programme (IRDP)

The sector-wise rural development programmes were sought to be integrated in a package through the Integrated Rural Development Programme (IRDP) launched in 1976-77, which directed at formulation of District Development Plan. Basic criteria for identifying the districts were economic backwardness, development potential, acute unemployment, presence of basic infrastructure and scientific and technical institutions extension services.

- Tribal Area Development Programme (TAD)
- Border Area Development Programme (BADP)
- MP Area Development Scheme
- Prime Minister Gramodya Yojana (2000)
- Nationwide programme to computerize land records.
- Kshetriya Vikas (TPP-2004)

With a view to redress regional imbalances through fiscal, administrative, investment and other means, the programme titled Kshetriya Vikas has been launched in 2004, which covers various aspects, such as:

- Surplus Land Distribution (TPP-1986)
- Flood Control
- Prevention of erosion
- Creation of productive assets
- Financing

3. IRRIGATION AND WATER MANAGEMENT

- New Watershed Development Projects taken up to develop 62 lakh hectares of wasteland/degraded lands.
- Pumpset Energisation Scheme (TPP-1986)
- Desert Development, Drought Prone/Arid Prone Watershed/Wasteland Development Programme (1999)

4. SOCIAL FORESTRY AND MINOR FOREST PRODUCT

- Tree Plantation Programme (TPP-1986)
- Paryavaran Sanrakshan evam Van Vridhi (Twenty Point Programme – 2004)

This covers plantation and conservation of forests, identification of air and water pollution, pollution of rivers and their prevention.

5. SMALL SCALE/VILLAGE/COTTAGE INDUSTRIES

- Deendayal Hathkargha Protsahan Yojana (TPP – 2004)
- Babasahib Ambedkar Hastshilpa Vikas Yojana (TPP – 2004)
- Modernisation of Village Industries (TPP-2004) : (*i*) Khadi Village and Cottage Industries, (*ii*) Small Scale Industries, (*iii*) Handicrafts, (*iv*)Sericulture, (*v*) Handloom, (*vi*) Coir and Jute, (vii) Rubber, (*viii*) Cashew, (*ix*) Food processing, (*x*) Leather, and (*xi*) Pottery

6. RURAL HOUSING

- Shelter for all by 2007 – Construction of 25 lakh houses per year in rural areas.

- Apna Ghar (Twenty Point Programme – 2004) : Apna Ghar covers Rural Housing, Indira Awaas Yojana and Valmiki Ambedkar Awaas Yojana.
- Basti Sudhar (TPP – 2004) : With a view to paying particular attention to the needs of slum dwellers the programme of Basti Sudhar would cover seven basic amenities and housing for slum dwellers.

7. DRINKING WATER

- **Safe Drinking Water** by 2004 for all villages. 87.9% villages fully covered and 10.9% partially covered so far. Sector Reforms in 62 pilot districts with an outlay of Rs.1800 crore is under implementation.
- **Shudh Peya Jal (Twenty Point Programme – 2004):** Providing drinking water to all and augmenting availability of drinking water sources is an issue of the topmost priority. Harvesting rain water, desilting existing ponds and other innovative mechanisms are to be taken up and monitored.

8. RURAL ROADS

- Pradhan Mantri Gram Sadak Yojana providing on all weather road to all rural habitations with a population of 500 by the year 2007. 21,000 projects already taken up.
- Rural Infrastructure Development fund (RIDF) corpus with NABARD for creating infrastructure in rural areas increased to Rs.5000 crores.

9. RURAL ELECTRIFICATION AND NON-CONVENTIONAL ENERGY SOURCES

- Bio-Gas Plants (TPP-1986)
- Village Electrification Scheme (TPP-1986)
- Awasthapna Vikas (TPP-2004)

The Awasthapna Vikas (Infrastructure Development) envisages giving the highest priority to the development and expansion of physical infrastructure, like Power, Coal, Steel, Railways, Ports, Shipping and Telecommunications, Cement, Fertilizer, Petroleum & Natural Gas, Civil Aviation, Rural and Urban Roads, Electrification, Solar Energy, Integrated Rural

Energy Programme, Water Supply, Sewage Treatment, Sanitation, Interlinking of rivers, and irrigation.

- Accelerated Rural Electrification Programme covering the following:
  - Electrification of Villages
  - Electrification of Hamlets
  - Electrification of Dalit Bastis
  - Electrification of Households
  - Bio-gas Plant
  - Solar Energy for (i) Water heating, (ii) Solar cooking and (iii) Air heating
  - Integrated Rural Energy Programme

10. POVERTY ALLEVIATION

- Jawahar Gram Smridhi Yojana (GSY-2002)
- **Sampoorna Grameen Rozgar Yojana** – outlay of Rs.10,000 crore per annum – provides 100 crore mandays of employment with food security. 50% of funds earmarked direct to Panchayats.
- **Swarnjayanti Gram Swarozgar Yojana** providing sustainable income to rural poor through Self-Help Groups. 14 lakh Self – help groups, one in each habitation.
- **Massive Food for Work Programme** introduced in calamity affected States. 25.13 lakh tons of food grains valued at Rs.2353 crores released.
- Employment Assurance Scheme (2002)
- Antyodya Ann Yojana (2000)
- Employment and Food Bank
- Garibi Unmoolan (Twenty Point Programme – 2004)
- The National Common Minimum Programme (NCMP) lays down that a National Employment Guarantee Act will be enacted to provide a legal guarantee for at least 100 days of employment to begin with on asset-creating public works programmes every year at minimum wages

for at least one able-bodies person in every household, which include:

(*a*) Kisan Mitra

(*b*) Shramik Kalyan : With a view to ensure the welfare and well being of all workers, particularly those in unorganized sector, including the Social Security for Agricultural and Unorganised Labour, Minimum Wages Enforcement (including Farm Labour), Prevention of Child Labour and Women Labour.

- Prime Minister Rojgar Yojana (TPP-2004)

Increasing employment potential in service industries viz. (*i*) Information Technology enabled services, (*ii*) Trade, (*iii*) Transport, (*iv*) Tele-communications, (*v*) Finance and (*vi*) Tourism.

11. EDUCATION, TECHNICAL/VOCATIONAL EDUCATION/NON-FORMAL EDUCATION AND LIBRARIES

- **Vidyadeep (Twenty Point Programme 2004) :** The Vidyadeep Programme includes Sarv Shiksha Abhiyan, education guarantee scheme and non formal education, Mid-day Meal Scheme, literacy rate, and financial assistance to poor students for professional education.

12. CULTURAL ACTIVITIES, MARKETS AND FAIRS

- **Community Development Programme (CDP)** was launched in 1952 to establish an appropriate data base for village development plans and programmes to improve village community life.

13. HEALTH FAMILY WELFARE AND SANITATION

- Immunisation of Children (TPP – 1986)
- Total Sanitation campaign launched in 200 districts. Project cost Rs.1195 crores.
- Asistance of Rs.10,000/- to the family of deceased bread earner under National Family Benefit Scheme.
- **Jan-Jan Ka Swasthya (TPP-2004) :** Jan-Jan Ka Swasthya Programme envisages Health Care for the Poor (Sub Centres/Primary Health Centres/Community Health Centres), Immunisation of Children, Disease

Prevention (Blindness, Leprosy, Malaria, TB, AIDS and Goitre), National Scheme for Health Insurance for the poor, and Sanitation Programme.

Chhota Pariwar (TPP-2004) : The Government has targeted high fertility districts (150) for population control programme, which includes the following:

- Child survival and safe motherhood programme
- Supplementary nutrition (Mother and Children)
- Universalization of ICDS Scheme
- Functional Anganwadis in every settlement

14. WOMEN AND CHILD DEVELOPMENT, SOCIAL WELFARE

- Bhagyashree Child Welfare Policy for girl child, Rajrajeshwari Mahila Kalyan Bima Yojana for women, Janashree Bima Yojana for Labour in Unorganised Sector, Khetihar Mazdoor Bima Yojana for agricultural labours & Shiksha Sahyog Yojana for education allowance to poor children.
- Decentralisation and devolution of powers, funds and functions to the Panchayati Raj Institutions with mandatory reservation for women.
- Balika Smridhi Yojana
- National Maternity Benefit Scheme
- Stree Shakti (TPP – 2004) : The programme launched in 2004, covers micro financing. Rashtriya Mahila Kosh, Balika Samridhi Yojana, Kishori Shakti Yojana and Women Participation in Panchayats, municipalities, state legislatures and Parliament.

15. SOCIAL WELFARE OF WEAKER SECTIONS/ SC/ST/YOUTH

- National Old Age Pension Scheme provides social security

to 44 lakh destitute persons above 65 years. 10 Kg. Free foodgrains per month to identified poor under Annapurna Scheme. Under National Maternity Benefit Scheme Rs.500/- to women below poverty line during maternity.

- Social Security Scheme
- **Anusuchit Jaati, Jan Jaati, evam Alpsankhyak Shashaktikaran (Twenty Point Programme – 2004):** This covers the issues of reservation quotas assistance to primitive tribal sub-groups, ownership rights to tribals, and promoting modern and technical education among all minorities.
- **Yuva Shakti (TPP-2004) :** The Yuva Shakti programme covers the items like National Service Volunteer Scheme, National Service Scheme, National Cadet Corps, Nehru Yuva Kendra, Youths – sports and cultural development.
- **Samajik Suraksha (TPP-2004) :** To provide social security to the weaker sections of society, this programme aims at rehabilitation of the handicapped, National Policy on older persons for providing health and shelter, vocational training, reforming social/juvenile delinquents, alcoholics and drug addicts.

16. PUBLIC DISTRIBUTION SYSTEM

Upbhokta Jaagran (TPP-2004) : To make the consumer more aware, to ensure food and nutrition security, and to bring about improvements in the food storage facilities, the Upbhokta Jaagran programme, which includes the following, has been launched in 2004:

- Consumer court cases
- Jagriti Shivir Yojana
- Strategy for food and nutritional security: (i) Nutrition Programme for mother and children (boys/girls), (ii)

Targeted Public Distribution system, (iii) Anthodhya Anna Yojana, (iv) Annapoorna Scheme, (v) Construction of additional storage facilities, (vi) Establishing Grain banks in cronically food scared area, (vii) New Strategy for food and nutritional security and (viii) New Ration Card issue for BPL families/others

17. PANCHAYATI RAJ

- Conducting timely Panchayat Elections
- Devolution of funds and functions
- Transfer of functionaries to Panchayats for local administration
- **Kriyasheel Prashaasan (TPP-2004) :** The programme – Kriyasheel Prashaasan aims at improving governance and responsiveness of the public administration, covering items like simplification of procedure, delegation of authority, enforcement of accountability, Redressal of Public Grievances, and Transparency in decision making, Development of Technology for e-Governance, versatile on-line information system for citizens, civic administration and municipal corporation, Development and upgradation of website of Ministries and State Governments.
- **Sheeghra Nyay Prakriya (TPP-2004)** : To expedite disposal of court cases the Sheeghra Nyay Pakriya programme has been launched for monitoring the pendency of court cases and expansion of legal aid services.

The Reality

In spite of numerous laudable programmes and huge investments, the reality of rural livelihood is rather dismal. There is a continuous distress migration to the cities and most of the villages lack the basic amenities and services, like a pucca road, transport, communications, drinking water supply, power, sanitation, health center, irrigation facility and jobs for survival and sustenance. The power is concentrated in the hands of few and the village administration is by and large urban-centred. The concepts of citizen empowerment, participatory governance and decentralization are often confined to the seminars and papers. The decision-making is often piecemeal, disjointed, ad-hoc, motivated and lacks an overall perspective. A lion's share of subsidies is eaten up by the administration/establishment structure and their salaries. The programmes are too many, so are the departments involved in each one of them. There is often overlapping and lack of clarity about the organizations and their accountability. The programmes too often exceed the time and financial allocations and the facilities including housing built up by the government bodies have often remain unoccupied. This leads us to identification of the pertinent issues involved in rural development, as given below:

Issues

- Lack of clear goals, objectives and targets
- Lack of benchmark and quantifiable standards
- Abstract and disjointed programmes without a coordinated spatial dimension
- Lack of strategic interventions and time frame
- Gap between plans/programmes and implementation
- Urban centred, multi-layered and multi-tiered rural administration and lack of accountability
- Complex procedures and obsolete legal frame
- Lack of funds, bulk of expenditure booked for establishment and salaries

The Approach

- Evolving Smart targets (Specific, Measureable, Action-oriented, Realistic and Timely)

- Setting up the benchmarks for amenities and services
- Preparation of the development plans at policy, strategic and operational levels, and exploring a need based approach for clustered hierarchy of facilities
- Strategic planning for priority projects, areas and sectors in a timeframe
- Action Planning and participatory management
- Institutional/organization framework/Governance
- Legal framework and procedural reforms
- Financial Planning and harnessing the potential of private and community sectors

Planning of the Rural Areas is essentially comprised of the following levels:

1. Policy Goals
2. Strategic objectives
3. Action Plans
4. Projects

So that all these fit into a comprehensive frame-work, a matrix structure can be developed relating the planing levels with the following action areas:

(*a*) Focus Areas/Priority Sector, based on the characteristics and potential of a particular region/district/village.

(*b*) Benchmarking of standards, levels and norms

(*c*) Time frame for achieving the targets/accomplishing the activity

(*d*) Key organization/departments responsible

(*e*) Financial resources

(*f*) Monitoring and feedback system

Towards A Needs Based Approach

Participatory learning with the target groups provides useful clues towards adopting a 'needs based approach'. The needs of the rural population can be categorized in the following priorities:

1. Survival: Freedom from hunger and malnutrition, food security, agriculture and employment, credit facility
2. Supportive: Shelter, drinking water supply, power, transport, sanitation etc.
3. Transformational: Education, literacy, skill development, environmental upgradation and access to information.
4. Empowerment: Equal access to resources, including land, finance and services, justice, participation in decision making, etc.

It is observed that with a little external support, the rural poor are often capable of meeting their survival needs. The organized sector has a vital role in helping the rural poor in meeting these needs. The experience indicates that the supportive needs really help the rural poor in climbing up the economic ladder. The provision of basic services and facilities in the rural context is a major concern. As such the rural amenities and services be grouped under the above heads and the priorities of planning, development and investments can be worked out. Based on participatory rural learning, the viable distances for these amenities and facilities can also be worked out (which will vary according to public transport facility, topography and characteristics of potential areas). This leads us to a system of clustering of the facilities into a conceptual hierarchy of rural settlements (such as 'cities in green field', urban centers, growth centers etc.) which can be developed according to the potential of either the existing settlement or as the new areas.

The Process

Keeping in view the ground truth situation and understanding, the following steps are necessary in the process of rural planning:

1. Mission Statement and Objectives (mainly derived from 11th schedule, Article 243 G and 20 Point Programme-2004)
2. Translating the above into regionwise SMART Goals and Targets (specific, measureable, action-oriented, realistic and timely).
3. Baseline information and participatory learning at district, taluk and village settlement levels
4. Identifying the issues and Key Action Areas
5. Conceptual framework with respect to policy options, strategic planning, benchmarks and standards
6. Evaluation of planning options, by SWOT analysis, financial implications, cost benefit analysis, feasibility and viability assessment.
7. Development of Plans at District, Taluk and settlement levels, strategies of development, disaggregated into sectoral plans fcr various amenities and services.
8. Resource Planning and Governance:
    - Shared governance and decentralisation
    - Identifying key issues vis-à-vis resource assessment
    - Empowerment of the community.
    - Participatory Action Planning

Implementation Planning

- Matrix structure for integrated implementation
- GIS/MIS, computerisation, information sharing and participatory monitoring

- Capacity building and networking
- Legal, institutional and financial framework.

The entire superstructure of rural planning and development rests on the three pillars of-

- Organisation/institutional structure
- Finance
- Legal frame

No plan, however good, can be implemented unless it is supported by the people and stakeholders, who have to participate at all levels of decision making and implementation.

The Government with its avowed commitment to rural development has resorted to the conventional "programme" approach, which has serious shortcomings in achieving its objectives and has the danger of reducing the laudable mandate into mere exhortations. It is time that a more professional, participatory planning approach is evolved, which should be accompanied by supportive governance, organization/administrative structure, fiscal and legal/procedural reforms to induce a holistic approach towards the development of the rural areas.

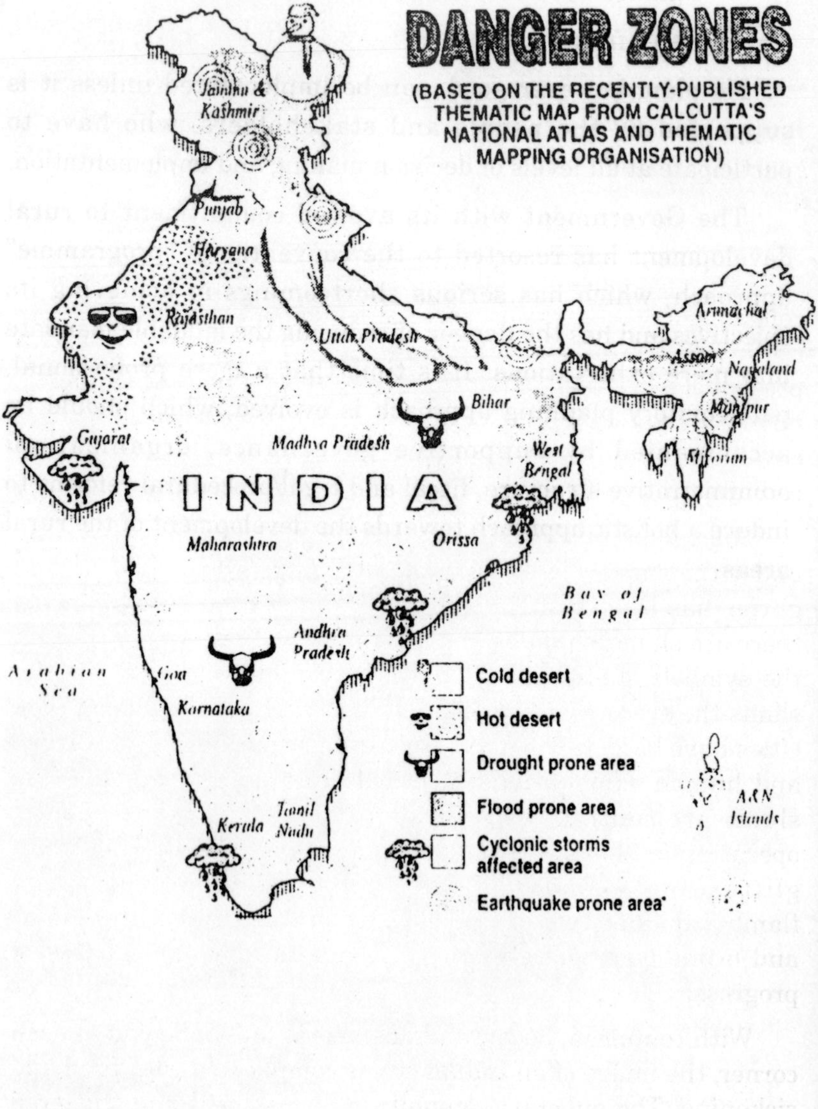
DANGER ZONES
(BASED ON THE RECENTLY-PUBLISHED THEMATIC MAP FROM CALCUTTA'S NATIONAL ATLAS AND THEMATIC MAPPING ORGANISATION)
Jammu & Kashmir
Punjab
Haryana
Rajasthan
Uttar Pradesh
Arunachal
Assam
Nagaland
Manipur
Mizoram
Bihar
West Bengal
Gujarat
Madhya Pradesh
INDIA
Maharashtra
Orissa
Bay of Bengal
Andhra Pradesh
Arabian Sea
Goa
Karnataka
Kerala
Tamil Nadu
A&N Islands
Cold desert
Hot desert
Drought prone area
Flood prone area
Cyclonic storms affected area
Earthquake prone area

28

FRAGILE PLANET—DEADLY CITIES

Burn down our cities and leave our farms, and your cities will spring up again as if by magic; but destroy our farms and the grass will grow in the streets of every city in the country.

— Williams Jennings Bryan

The myth that the cities are the melting pots of various religions, cultures, castes, races and classes lies shattered. The notion that cosmopolitan cities are most liberal, open and progressive has been unveiled by the fact that political interests, poverty and degradation have been giving birth to the criminals, mobsters, religious fundamentalists and street level corruption.

The image of the cities in India had been of filthy slum under the shadow of imposing skyscrapers. Their glamour and glitter has been skin deep-along the major roads only. Inside there are slums, shanties and insanitation. The towers had been the symbols of elitism, affluence, luxury and power, while the slums-the eyesores, testifying to ever-oozing puss of squalor. The cities have become the nerve centres of crime, smuggling, drugs and human exploitation, including children and women. The slums are controlled by ruthless gangs and mafia outfits, operating in nexus with the politicians and officials. The gloss, glitter and glamour of big business and industry and flamboyant lifestyle of upper crust pretend that the squalor and crime were merely unreal, temporal and natal pains of progress.

With confusion, decay, unemployment and upheaval at each corner, the image of an Indian city is complicated, cluttered and sickening. The pulsing anonymity of its vastness and scattered spaces is remote, mysterious and frightening. In fact, these manifest 'inhumane' settlements, that anticipate and even create the crimes and wickedness. The misery of being poor in a metropolis is the penalty which provokes and punishes the crime.

Mahatma Gandhi, who lived in a much more peaceful era, could see that urban environment could generate crimes and the city as metaphor of hell. In a secular inferno of a city crimes thrive with turbulent misery. People swallowed by its immensity and deranged by the alienation of their great city, pursue self destructive obsessions. The city appears as a huge portfolio of visual paradox and aphorisms. Sheer size of a city reduces it to an administrative abstraction and a conglomerate of districts and zones.

The effectiveness of frequent riots in the cities is not so much to the rioters as to their political resolution, more than anything else. A city, as a concentration of poor people, is the locus of political power which articulates their lives. They demonstrate, make riots or insurrections, flare up and vandalise. Its frequency and effectiveness depends on the urban structure, how easily the poor and youth can be mobilized, how vulnerable the centres of authority are to them and how easily they may be suppressed. These are determined partly by sociological, partly by urbanistic and partly by technological factors.

The cities represent the paradigm of social organization. The human destiny is intimately tied up with the darkening fate of their amorphous urban structure. The physical form and manifestation of a city may eliminate certain problems and inconveniences, but power politics and technical ingenuity create as many hazards as they may eliminate. Social situations entailed by new conveniences create new danger of riot, restlessness and wilder excesses of civilized anomie. The order and immutable regularity of a city could provide a mnemonic metopher.

New Delhi, the new capital designed by Edwin Lutyens, provides a classical example of conscious urban structure, evolved on the considerations of safety and security. Its location towards the south of the Walled City was itself a major determinant of securing the new city from the natives. The monumental grid of New Delhi was related to its major function, that is the government axis. The flanking and overlapping hexagonal system was local and residential. The monumental grid of royalty, encompassing the Viceroy House and the Central Vista was secured by the hexagonal grid of residential area. The role of the people in public activities had been that of participants as an admiring and applauding audience. The processional Rajpath flanked by the Central Vista had the Vicerory's palace on one end and India Gate on the other. The desire of the rulers to impress of their folio-de-grandeur is manifested by wide, symmetrical and grand avenues and layout. To secure the royalty and ruling elite from the dangers of native population, a city wall in the form of office complex was built all along Asaf Ali Road. Another tier of security fencing was in the form of the elevated embankment of railway line, with only two underpasses, viz., Minto Bridge and Harding Bridge. In the event of an insurgency or a mutiny, the army could be deployed along the railway track and the gates could be closed. Further, the segregation of rich and poor working population within the new capital was systematically maintained towards the south and north of the Central Vista. These barricades ensured ample security for the alien rulers. An unintended effect of new and wide avenues had been provision of an ideal location of popular movements, mass demonstrations and processions.

Notions and Reality

The planning and growth of the cities, including Delhi, in the post-independence era, had been by and large enormous and uncontrolled. The planners had their own notions on the sociological aspects of city planning. It was believed that the old cities, slums and high densities were the symptoms of crimes. As a result, large resettlement and mass housing projects were taken up in the new areas. The whole population was divided and distributed in terms of income groups. The land use zoning system was widely adopted for functional segregation of activities. The pattern of functional segregation and single function zoning was based upon the idea of exclusion of undesirables - often from the residential areas.

The pattern of functional segregation by land use zoning has led to development of sterile and geographical separation of classes. Mass housing and transport have further disintegrated the city as a potential riot centre. Many educational complexes, rehabilitation and large rehousing schemes have been seen as accumulation of potential rioters, particularly those near the major business centres. The universities in the midst of urban concentration are evidently more dangerous than those on the outskirts. Large and dense concentration of poor and homogeneous community areas are more vulnerable than the suburbs with a mixed population.

According to the National Crime Records Bureau (NCRB), Delhi had the highest number of crime (20.7 per cent) among major cities in India (1999), followed by Mumbai (11.5 per cent) Chennai reported the highest incidence of violence against women, while Lucknow has the distinction of recording the lowest number of cases. Of the 4 supermetros, Calcutta emerges as the safest city in relation crime against women. Ahmedabad recorded the least violent crimes among ten cities.

Crime in Major Cities

City	*Violent Crimes*	*Crimes against Women*
Delhi	4,289	2,428
Mumbai	1,823	1,253
Jaipur	1,817	697
Bangalore	1,643	1,170
Pune	1,369	N.A.
Patna	1,202	N.A.
Kanpur	1,111	861
Kolkata	971	N.A.
Lucknow	847	644
Ahmedabad	042	728

Source: National Crime Records Bureau, 1999

Crime and Insecurity in Delhi

According to Delhi Human Development Report, 2006, published by the Government of Delhi, public safety has emerged as a major concern of the residents. The Public Perception Survey 2005 reveals that:

- Only 19 per cent of the people feel that the city is safe.

- One-third of the respondents rate levels of personal safety as poor.
- Half the respondents feel that the city is not safe for women.
- Only 6 per cent of respondents feel that the workplace is highly secure for women employees.
- Nearly 90 per cent of respondents feel that public transport is not safe for women commuters.
- Only 24 per cent felt that Delhi Police is doing good or very good work.

Crime statistics for Delhi (refer Annexure-1) point to the unusually high incidence of crime in the city. Delhi leads the four metropolitan cities of India in crimes against women. For every 100,000 persons, there are fourteen crimes against women in Delhi. In Chennai, it is 7, and in Mumbai and Kolkata, it is 4. The greatest deterrent to crime reportage, especially in cases of crimes against women, stems from deficiencies in the delivery of justice, delays in police and court proceedings and low conviction rates.

The perpetration of crime against women is alarming. In 2001, for instance, Delhi recorded 381 cases of rape - more than one every day. In addition, the city registered 113 dowry deaths, 502 cases of molestation and 90 cases of eve teasing. The safety of women cannot be adequately represented merely by statistics on crimes as a large magnitude of insecurities and violence that women face remains outside the purview of such reports. The survey reveal that only 19 per cent of the people feel that the City was safe. A significant proportion (33 per cent) rated the level of personal safety as 'poor'. Almost half of the respondents felt that the city was not safe for women. New Delhi, followed by Central and South Delhi districts were considered to be relatively safer than the other six districts. JJ resettlement colonies were rated as being 'least safe', followed by JJ clusters and rural areas. Urban villages were rated as the safest in the city.

The elderly and the aged constitute an extremely vulnerable group of people in Delhi. Growing every year in numbers, 'senior citizens' constitute around 5 per cent of Delhi's population. They are increasingly confronted by financial insecurity, loneliness, physical insecurity and absence of effective support structures. Large number of children work as domestic servants, in dhabas (roadside cafes), in shops and other occupations. Instances of exploitation and abuse are commonly reported. Many live off the streets with little protection from exploiters. Most at disadvantage among working children are girls. The girls are forced to help out with harsh household chores. According to a survey, there are around 102,000 disabled persons in Delhi. Of these, nearly one-third - 36 per cent - are women. Several disability-related concerns remain insufficiently addressed including ease of physical access in public spaces, inclusion in educational facilities, opportunities for employment and self-employment, and eliminating social stigma associated with certain kinds of disabilities.

Public Perception Survey 2005 of the GNCTD, reveals that the lowest income groups facing considerable economic insecurity also felt most unsafe in the city. Most women in Delhi do not feel safe either in their workplace or while commuting. Only 6 per cent of respondents felt that the workplace was highly secure for women employees. Around 45 per cent of respondents felt that the workplace was not at all safe for women. 90 per cent of respondents felt that public transport was not safe for women commuters. Only 24 per cent felt that Delhi Police was doing 'good' or 'very good' work, 40 per cent felt that the performance was average, and around 31 per cent felt that the performance of the Delhi Police was 'poor' or 'very poor'. The Public Perception Survey reveals that only one-fourth of the respondents felt that Delhi Police was doing good work while more than one-third felt that Delhi Police was not doing enough to protect women in the city.

The factors that make Delhi unsafe are common to other cities as well. These include:

- A poor urban environment - dark or badly lighted streets, derelict parks and empty lots, badly maintained public spaces, inadequate signage, lack of public toilets.
- Empty streets at night because of early closing of shops and businesses or lack of a tradition of street life.

- Poor public transport and rude, unhelpful behaviour of bus drivers and conductors.
- Insufficient presence, unresponsive and aggressive attitudes of police and civic authorities.
- Isolation from neighbours and lack of community life.
- Traditional notions of privacy and refusal of the police to intervene in situations of domestic violence.
- Ideas and beliefs about appropriate behaviour, leading to reluctance to protest in cases of public violence.
- Lack of respect for women and women's rights, leading to cases of violence being ignored or trivialized by the general public or authorities.

Hazards of Travel

The number of people killed on Delhi's roads has been steadily increasing, which in 2004 was 1812. The main reason for higher fatalities is unsafe crossing of road and heavy movement of commercial goods vehicles. Half the fatalities (748) in 2004 were by commercial vehicles. A major reason for increasing accident has been increasing vehicular density on Delhi roads.

No of vehicles, Road Length and People Killed on Delhi Roads

Year	*Vehicles (lakh)*	*Road length (kms)*	*Population (lakh)*	*People killed in accidents*
1971	2.17	8380	43	NA
1981	5.61	15490	62	1072
1991	19.23	22487	94	1778
2001	35.89	25948	137	1842
2004	44.00	25948	160	1812
2011*	60.00	27000	1820	

*Projected

Most Dangerous Roads	*People Killed*
Ring Road	182
Outer Ring Road	104
GTK Road	78
Rohtak Road	60
Najafgarh Road	50
BM Road	39
Mathura Road	32

Source: Traffic Police (2005)

Ongoing Approaches

The approach to urban safety has been mainly through legal framework (a plethora of complex laws on all kind of crimes, violations and unsafe practices exist in India), and their enforcement through the executive (Police, Government Departments) together with the intervention of the judiciary. Isolated para-legal, community based and non-governmental attempts have, by and large, failed to make a dent in the problem in providing a strong safety-net in an institutional manner. These include the following:

- Neighbourhood watch groups, community mapping and safety consulting & counselling
- Tourist and Women Police
- Community Scouting, Surveillance, Volunteering and Training
- Use of Amateur radio, telecast, electronics, surveillance videography (CTV), GIS and Satellite imagery
- Drug / HIV / Trauma & Legal Assistance
- Mother and Child Centres, Creche, Anganwari, Stress Relief Clinics
- Old Age Centres
- Facilities and amenities for Special Persons

It is necessary to examine closely the prevailing concepts of city planning, land use zoning, slums, infrastructure services and energy efficiency, together with equitable access to urban services, amenities and resources. A basic need is to facilitate employment generation in the cities along with reducing the need for travel by a close home-work relationship and decentralization. All those factors impinge upon the safety and security of the people. A greater degree of safety can be achieved through city planning and design of public spaces and by promoting social and gender integration.

Planning Reorientation

In the wake of the changing scenario, there is a need to have a fresh look at the concepts of planning. This needs vision and bold action, beyond the conventional planning notions, such as population control, regional planning, eradication of slums, hierarchical formation of communities, development satellite towns, low density development and the like. In fact one of the best example of inter-communal integration after the independence of the country is witnessed in the selective development of the old empires, like Lucknow, Bhopal, Hyderabad and Jaipur as the new capitals of newly formed states. A strategy of population redistribution and development could be tried in terrorists threatened and vulnerable States and cities. The strategy has to be preventive rather than being curative. As such the distribution of population and growth are to be redirected so as to maintain a sensitive balance between homogeneity and hetrogenity. For this planning action alone may be grossly inadequate, but has to be imbued with the political apparatus.

In this context, it may be worthwhile to consider moving the capitals out of the megacities. As the centres of power and politics, these not only demand high security, pre-empting the general needs of the common man, but continuously generate riots, processions and disturbances. A capital city should be an exclusive seat of the government, rather than being a hotch-potch of industry, services, business, sports, education and health.

At the city level there is a greater need to integrate land use activities, different communities, vocations, professions and income groups in a composite manner. The urban structure has to be evolved keeping in view the geographical features combined with the man-made form to provide a safe and manageable form. The security has to be built-in and self-managing, rather than being dependent upon the security, police force and outside help. For this, in the urban context, "decentralization", "homogeneity and hetrogenity" are the keywords. Planning as sociological function should adapt to the demand of safe and manageable cities. Physical planners are required not to know 'about[1] the society but to know 'the' society.

Reinforcing the central parts of the urban areas while integrating their economic, political and cultural dimensions can contribute to better urban organization and vibrancy, with the much required access of disadvantage social groups. Many cities and urban areas offer possibilities of creating a polynucleated and polycentric structure as the prime generators.

Several research findings have highlighted the negative economic, social, and environmental impacts of the urban sprawl. The famous Kenworthy and Newman curve has shown that cities with a low density have much higher energy and social costs. A coherent spatial policy should encourage the revitalization of existing inner areas. High priority needs to be given to the upgradation of the infrastructure and security. At the same time, there is a need to promote a higher level of mixed use, in place of single use zoning.

In many communities, current development patterns mandate a separation of land uses. Conventional suburban development - which is primarily low-density, single-use development - is a significant departure from the way towns were built in the early 20th century. During that time, land uses were more integrated, enabling many people to walk to a corner store, school, or work. Where once walking to school as a child was the standard practice, today land uses and other changes in development patterns combine to make walking or bicycling the mode of transportation.

A mix of land uses provides a more diverse population and a wider commercial base to support public security of an area by increasing the number of people on the street. Furthermore, a mix of land uses helps streets, public spaces and retail stores again become places where people meet, thus helping to revitalize community life.

Multi-dimensional Issues

Ongoing fragmented, compartmentalized and sectoral jurisdictions have failed to tackle the problem of urban safety and security. Besides city planning, there is a need to adopt a unified approach to the various aspects of safety, embracing the following in a composite and comprehensive manner:

- Cultivating Safety Culture and Behaviour
- Environmental Health & Safety (including pollution control, safe drinking water, disposal & management, sanitation, noise control, reducing carbon emission and toxins, climate change, etc.

- Occupational Health and Safety
- Safety against violence, crimes and human abuse
- Travel and Transport Safety
- Safety from Disaster, fire and emergencies
- Energy Safety
- A Holistic Action Platform

At every step it is required to prepare action plans with respect to risk reduction, insurance and management, review the safety laws, norms and standards and adopt the practices of safety audit, controls, protocols and monitoring. The dictionary meaning of 'safety' is 'freedom from danger'. As such, a safe city or habitat should ensure freedom from all kinds of dangers. According to UNDP (1994) 'Human Security' means 'Safety from such chronic threats' as hunger, disease, repression and protection from sudden and hurtful disruptions in the patterns of daily lives, whether in homes, jobs or community'.

Cultivating Safety Culture and Behaviour

The components of safety culture are the following:

(*i*) Workplace environment : The state of the workplace environment, such as, means of access, physical plant safety, house-keeping, safe place of work.

(*ii*) Competence & Training : The competence and training of those involved including the ability to understand, apply and respond to safe systems of work.

(*iii*) Motivation & Behaviour: The development of motivational and behavioral influences including the use of more direct strategies to identify unsafe behaviour and attitudes and to motivate employees.

Safe behaviour strategies are aimed at cultural change. Encouraging desirable behaviour, by acknowledging such behaviour is necessary. Evidence indicates that one of the most powerful methods of encouraging safe behaviour is to provide social rewards in the form of praise or recognition. A hallmark of behaviour based safety programmes is safety incentives or safety awards programmes.

Environmental Health and Safety

According to a World Health Organisation (2007), four million children under the age of five die every year, due to environmental hazards including polluted air or water, or exposure to chemicals. Poisonings, acute respiratory infections, diarrhea diseases and malaria carried by mosquitoes which thrive in dirty water account for most of the toll. About 30% of illnesses and deaths in children due to disease can be attributed to environmental factors. Environmental hazards include a wide range of causes and effects, such as:

- Ozone Depletion
- Global warming and climate change
- Water Pollution
- Air Pollution including Sound Pollution
- Toxins and Wastes
- Radioactive Pollution

In order to restrict the damage to the environment caused by the anthropogenic activities and thereby retard the process of climate change, it becomes absolutely essential to abide by various policies, plans and protocols for environmental protection, so that the development is sustainable. This includes the following actions:

- Reduce the discharge of pollutants, attain environmental quality standards as early as possible in order to secure a pleasant and clean environment.
- Reduction of nitrogen oxide and carbon emissions.
- Install denitrification equipment, incineration plants, promote use of low-emission cars, restraint the volume of car traffic.
- Promotion of measures to improve the quality of water.
- Reduction of car noise and promote the use of electric cars.
- Tackle global environmental problems through technical cooperation.
- Support environmental protection activities conducted by civic organisations.

- Develop urban environment improvement projects, such as, recycling of used paper, utilisation of urban exhaust heat and planting greenery.
- Helping citizens to review lifestyles and environmental awareness, educate and train leaders of environmental protection activities, hold exhibitions, conduct studies and surveys.

The concept of Environmental Impact Assessment is emerging one of the most important tools in the overall planning of a development project. It helps in identifying the adverse impacts, which can be mitigated at an early planning stage and helps to achieve a sustainable development.

Occupational Health and Safety

Occupational Health and Safety is defined as 'conditions and factors that affect the well-being of employees, temporary workers, contractor personnel, visitors and any other person in the workplace'. The International Labour Organisation has contributed to the development of vast knowledge on occupational safety and health measures over decades. It has published the 'Guidelines on Occupational Safety and Health Management System ILO-OSH-2001, International Labour Office, Geneva'. The Bureau of Indian Standards (BIS) has published various standards on the subject. OHSAS 18001 : 1999 is an Occupational Health and Safety Management System Specification developed by a number of international co-operating organizations.

Many organisations are seeking certifications for QMS (ISO9001), EMS (ISO 1400). OH&SMS (OHSAS 1800). Seamless integration of these diverse management systems into one coherent system is necessary as a policy. A common holistic framework provides opportunities for continually improved performance through underlying Risk Management principles (Activity - Risk - Effect) in each management area - Quality, Environment, Occupational Health and Safety.

Safety Against Crimes, Violence and Human Abuse

Government of Delhi jointly with Jagori and Centre for Women's Development Studies, New Delhi have recommended the following for making Delhi a more secure city:

Infrastructure:

- Improve urban infrastructure - lighting, signages, pavements, and parks.
- Signage in all public places giving details of helpline numbers and persons to be contacted in case of harassment.
- Provisions of clean and well-lighted toilets in all public areas.
- Ensure adequate infrastructure in resettlement colonies, particularly affordable and clean toilets and drinking water points.
- Provide night-shelters for homeless women.
- Ensure services for mentally ill women and women with disabilities.
- Sensitization of bus drivers and conductors and signage on buses.

Services for women facing violence:

- Improve the quality of services, including helplines, medical facilities, legal aid units, shelter homes and counselling centres.
- Enforce government guidelines on prevention and redressal of sexual harassment at the workplace.
- Disseminate information on government commitment to women's safety and available services.
- Training for women in self-defence.

Community action:

- Strengthen community-level womens's organizations.
- Gender sensitization for resident Welfare Associations to enable them to respond to cases of domestic violence in their areas.
- Collaboration between Resident Welfare Associations and women's organizations.

Media:

- Sensitization of media persons to issues of women's rights.

- Formulation of a code of ethics in reporting cases of violence.
- Public campaigns on women's safety.
- Dissemination of information on available infrastructure and services.

Police:

- Training for police to equip them to deal sensitively and appropriately in cases of violence and violations of women's right to safety.
- Recruitment and placement of women police officers in each police station.
- Collaboration with women's NGOs for helpdesk in police stations.
- Increase the number of PCR vans and police personnel.
- Collaboration between senior officials and women's organizations to monitor and address violence against women - women's organizations could be invited to regular monthly review meetings taken by Police Commissioner.
- Review of the functioning of the Crimes Cell to ensure that it responds appropriately to the needs.

Safety & Welfare of the vulnerable population:

- Development of a health structures.
- Promote 'Community Health Promotion with the help of RWAs / Public & Private Sector.
- Building a desirable environment for all children through the coordination of the entire society, families, schools, communities, administration, etc.
- Strengthening the functions of the child raising centres, maternity centres, mother care centres, etc.
- Enable disabled people to live in the community.
- Subsidize medical expenses improvement of emergency signaling systems, install communications equipment at household level for physically disabled people.
- Housing for disabled people with home care services.

- Community welfare centres for disabled people.
- Promotion of housing measures, welfare / recreational centres, home help services, nursing homes & life care for elderly people.
- Build model institutions to conduct comprehensive services for people suffering from senile dementia - from counseling to nursing and building of welfare-medical institutions, including hospitals for elderly.

Safety of Structures and Construction

Ensuring safety of structures and persons at work is a complex matter and there is no "one solution". Nearly all accidents and the resulting losses at work are preventable. This calls for continuing monitoring and innovation research both in collecting information about where things have "gone wrong" and where accidents have occurred, and also in gathering information about where matters have gone particularly well and a high performance has been achieved in safety. It is often the non-adherence to safety norms and the lack of the preventive measures that lead to accidents at construction sites. A major area of focus should be to check and retrofit the non-engineered buildings, mostly existing in the inner city, old areas, villages and unauthorized colonies.

There is a need to focus on strategic issues of how to prevent and avoid accidents on sites and preventive measures to be taken during the work. Experience shows that often construction accidents are poorly investigated and while the primary cause of the accident is usually obvious, exactly why the situation was allowed to develop and accident happen is often much more difficult to determine.

Safety during construction requires ensuring stability of structures, as well as safety of the work force and the machinery at site. Adequate steps should be taken to prevent such mishaps or failures and to contain its aggravation, at construction site, power project, roads, rails, buildings, mines, embankment, coastal erosion or any other projects.

Safety may be endangered due to geological failures, landslides, embankment failures, flooding, earthquake or other natural disasters, human and machine failures, and lack of adoption of safety norms/carelessness, leakage of gases or radio-active radiations. Safety in tunnels and cavities may be endangered due to sudden rock falls, water and or gas inflows, geological failures, inadequacy of ventilation, etc. Failures at excavation sites may take place due to slope failure, inflow of water, inadequate measures taken during blasting, etc.

During recent past, India has experienced a number of destructive earthquakes, floods, tsunami and other disasters. The recent trends and field research about seismo-electro-magnetic earthquake precursors indicate that these are manifested about 15 to 25 hours before the occurrence of any major to large earthquake (magnitude $M \geq 6.5$ or so). If advance information is available, it is possible to reduce the death toll during earthquake and other disasters.

Travel and Transport Safety

Annually more than eighty thousand lives are lost on Indian Roads due to traffic accidents. With less than 1 per cent of the world's vehicle population, India accounts for 6 per cent of world's road accidents and 10 per cent of world's road fatalities. With rapid growth in vehicle ownership ambitious road development plans, and India having one-sixth of the world's population, the road transport demand is growing very fast; and therefore the consequent safety hazard is likely to be a potential threat to the entire community.

Road safety problem in India, which has grown to disaster proportion, is not only a socio-technical problem, but has created a serious public health issue. Road Safety Audits are seldom undertaken. The countries which have been able to successfully reverse the trend, tackled it through structured programmes as part of national mission. Multiplicity of modes in transport and low level of education, incompatibility of the road use behaviour make the problem extremely complex, and it requires innovative solutions. A serious effort by thorough scrutiny of the existing and planned road infrastructure, safety audit and strengthening and revamping the institutional framework for targeted levels of road safety is the first step towards ameliorating the situation. A proper accident data record system is a pre-requisite.

There is a need for a holistic action plan and implementation of an effective management system to make a breakthrough in such a huge problem. In urban areas it is essential to ensure road safety, streamline road traffic and reduce traffic accidents through the promotion of the improvement of roads with emphasis on space for pedestrians, and through the upgrading of traffic control capability. Immediate needs are:

- Safety oriented planning and engineering specifications, norms and practices.
- Improvement of sidewalks, cycle tracks, underpasses & overpasses.
- Upgrading of traffic control systems - introduce multi-functional and sophisticated new systems including signal control.

Safety from Disasters, Fire and Emergencies

Natural disasters, such as earthquake, hurricane, floods, landslides, volcano eruptions cannot be prevented. However, by prudent planning and preparedness to meet and organize the relief measures, it is possible minimize the loss of property and human lives to a great extent. It is essential to establish support systems to deal with major disasters, including the organization of information, assistance and training. Fire, traffic accidents, outbreak of infectious diseases, collapse of structures, stampede etc. are some of the man-made disasters. The loss due to these disasters is manifolds-loss of human lives, loss of property, disruption in the daily life. These disasters take place mainly due to the carelessness of the man, improper planning and not observing the preventing measures. There is a need to adopt safety standards, alongwith inculcating safety behaviour and practices to minimize such risks.

Fire prevention steps are to be built in at the design and planning stage and in the layout of the building/plant, and process control. Elimination of fire hazard should be ingrained in the handling of fires, explosives and process operating instructions, as well as maintenance and engineering practices. Besides these safeguards, the education and continuous training regarding the elimination of fire hazards, is an important element for the effective management of fire safety.

Land Use and Town Planning are the important aspects of disaster mitigation, prevention and management. According to the Indian Seismic Zone map, Delhi is placed in Seismic Zone IV, which means high damage risk zone. In the past, several earthquakes of Richter magnitude 5.5 to 6.7 have occurred in the National Capital Territory of Delhi. Two major lineaments, namely Delhi-Haridwar ridge and Delhi-Muradabad faults pass through the territory, both having potential of generating earthquakes of the magnitude upto 6.5 to 6.7 in future. Such natural and man made disasters neither can be prevented nor predicted. However, with the technological advancement to some extent mechanism can be developed to mitigate the after effects of the disaster. Areas of vulnerability can be identified and necessary measures can be proposed by the concerned agencies. The concerned local bodies should keep updating the building byelaws to safeguard against disasters and ensure effective and impartial enforcement. Following policies and strategies for disaster management are proposed :

Pre-Disaster Preparedness

(*i*) (*a*) Micro-zonation surveys should be referred for land use planning and be considered while preparing the Zonal Plans and Layout Plans.

- Seismic micro-zonation for selected areas having high growth rates should be taken up on priority.
- On the basis of vulnerability studies and hazard identification, which includes soil conditions, probable intensity of earthquake, physiographic conditions of the area, fault traces, etc., local level land use zoning and planning should be undertaken.

(*b*) Building bye-laws should incorporate the aspects of Multi-Hazard Safety and Retrofitting.

- Priority should be given to public buildings (such as hospitals, educational, institutional, power stations, infrastructure, heritage monuments, lifeline structures and those which are likely to attract large congregation) for their ability to withstand earthquake of the defined intensity.

- Suitable action should be taken for retrofitting and strengthening of structures identified as vulnerable as per earthquake manuals and National Building Code. A techno-legal regime has to be adopted for provisions on Multi-hazard safety aspects.

(*ii*) The nodal agency for disaster management should identify vulnerable areas such as areas with high density and poor accessibility in the city and propose suitable measures. Proposed Disaster Management Centres should be established in every zone to deal with the disasters, including bio-chemical and nuclear disasters.

(*iii*) Sensitize people, particularly school children, about after effects of disaster.

(*iv*) Make people aware through media campaigns and advertisements about emergency procedures and location of emergency shelters etc.

Post Disaster Management

It has been observed that any disaster is generally followed by break down of communication lines and disruption of essential services. Therefore, the key communication centres should be protected from natural disasters, i.e. flood, fire and earthquake etc. and services restoration should be taken up on top most priority. Necessary setup should be created in each of the concerned department for such eventualities.

Energy Safety

Promote effective use of resources, promote energy saving at facilities and promote area air-conditioning to realize an energy-efficient city.

- Promoting the utilisation of exhaust heat at incineration plants and sewerage treatment facility.
- Promote use of non-conventional sources of energy.
- Replace coal based power generation to CNG / non-polluting alternative fuels.
- Observe strictly safety controls and instructions.
- Check transmission and distribution losses.

- Incentivise decentralised power generation and energy conservation.

A Holistic Action Platform - City Emergency Response and Safety Centre (CERSC)

Since safety and security are multi-dimensional issues and require multi-pronged actions, the priority should be to set up a City Emergency Response and Safety Centre in every city / district. The objective of City Emergency Response and Safety System is to establish a common platform to provide instant response, rescue and relief to the citizens by coordinated action of different departments. Digitisation and networked technology are applied to build up a unified command platform and information network platform, which offers comprehensive emergency rescue services including police, fire, medical emergency, traffic and others. It may also include travel complaints, judicial assistance and price complaining system. Besides, it also aims at building an emergency response management platform to deal with natural and man-made disasters.

After 61 years of free India, while we have launched missiles, sent rockets in space and India has joined the club of nuclear powers, we are far from the freedom from dangers. The prevailing fragmented, territorial and sectoral approaches have failed to ensure safe living to the citizens, particularly in the urban areas. This is the time to take stock of the issues of safety and security in our cities and rethink how we can make the life of the people, the habitat and Indian settlements more safe. In the pursuit of an integrated approach towards the "Safety First" objective and to address the wide ranging issues, problems and concerns on a sustainable basis, it is proposed to make a beginning with the establishment of City Emergency Response and Safety Centre in every Indian City.

Annexure-1

Crime Statistics for Delhi

(*Source: Delhi Human Development Report 2006, Govt. of NCT Delhi*)

- Delhi ranks first among thirty-five cities for crimes against children and 6th in the whole country.

- Delhi contributes to
  - 24.4 per cent of all-India crimes; the contribution of Mumbai is 8.8 per cent
  - 24.4 per cent rapes
  - 33.7 per cent kidnappings
  - 17.6 per cent dowry deaths
  - 13.3 per cent molestations
- Delhi accounts for 4.8 per cent of crimes against children - as against the national average of 1 per cent.
- The national average for child rape is 0.2 per cent. But in Delhi it is 1 per cent.
- Delhi accounts for 9.2 per cent of all kidnapping. The average for 35 cities is only 2.1 per cent.
- Delhi reports the highest abduction rate among women - 6.2 per cent - in the country.
- Delhi has the highest number of cases pending against policemen - 22.2 per cent.

Crime incidence in Delhi: 2004

District	*Crimes against women*	*Total crimes*	*Per cent Crimes against women*
North	165	3418	4.82
North-West	775	9840	7.87
Central	169	3335	5.06
New Delhi	80	2651	3.01
East	500	5528	9.04
North-East	401	3896	10.24
South	641	9672	6.62
South-West	356	5932	6.00
West	431	7343	5.86
Delhi (Total)	3543	53,623	6.60

Source: Delhi Police.

Types of crimes committed against women is Delhi: 2004

Districts of Delhi	*Rape*	*Kidnapping Abduction of women & girls*	*Dowry deaths*	*Molestation*	*Sexual harassment*	*Cruelty at home*	*Crime against women*
North	23	55	06	21	05	55	165
North-West	124	203	29	129	23	267	775
Central	27	41	01	44	12	44	169
New Delhi	08	11	01	34	15	11	80
East	62	125	13	82	06	212	500
North-East	67	120	18	46	06	144	401
South	96	175	21	130	40	179	641
South-West	79	68	11	59	13	126	356
West	58	79	24	46	09	215	431
Delhi	551	881	126	601	130	1254	3543

Source : Delhi Police.

Disposal of Indian Penal Code (IPC) cases by Delhi Police : 2004

Total no. of cases for investigation (including pending cases)	102,959
Charge found false/mistake of fact, etc.	642
Among cases where investigation was completed : Total	49,761
- Final report true submitted	20,663
- Charge sheets were submitted	28,456
No. of cases pending investigation at the end of year	52,979
Pendency (percentage)	51.5
Conviction rate (%)	49.7

Source : Delhi Police.

Disposal of IPC cases by Delhi Courts : 2004

Total no. of cases for trial (including pending cases)	165,167
No. of cases in which trials were completed:	11,295
Of which convicted cases	5618
Acquitted or discharged	5677
Pending trial cases at the end of year	153,872
Pendency (percentage)	93.2
Conviction rate (%)	49.7

Source : Delhi Police.

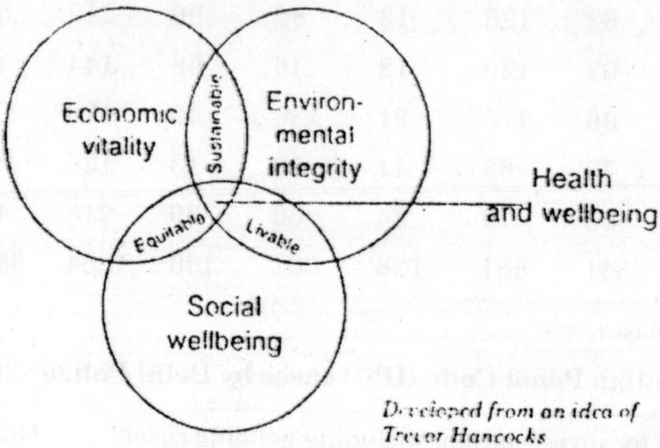

Developed from an idea of Trevor Hancocks

Human health is the ultimate purpose of creating a liveable, equitable and sustainable development, which depend upon the integrity and interface among Economic, Social and Environment factors

29

BUILT ENVIRONMENT FOR THE ELDERLY

There are some people, who live in a dream world, and there are some who face reality; and then there are those who turn one into the other.
— Douglas H. Everett

With the overall improvement of health, the elderly population in India is continuously increasing. Around 8 per cent of the population, that is one out of every 12 persons in India is a senior citizen (age plus 60 years). A total elderly population of around 80 million makes India an ultra-age society. Care of the elderly is a moral and ethical responsibility of the society for which built environment has a major role to play.

By and large in Indian cities, the planning, development and management of built environment manifest indifference towards the elderly, which is reflected by the following:

- Hostile and aggressive traffic
- Lack of sensitivity, concern, civic sense, safety and security.
- Changing attitudes and values, general apathy towards the aged.
- Inappropriate and inconvenient buildings.
- Landscape and road development unsuitable for the weaks, disabled and the aged.
- Encroachment on footpaths, public spaces and parks.
- Lack of transport, health and other facilities for the older persons.

- Planning and building regulations overlooking the needs of the older persons.

National Policy for Older Persons

The Government of India in January 1999 announced a National Policy on Older Persons. The policy identifies principal areas of intervention, such as, Financial Security, Healthcare, Nutrition, Shelter, Education, Welfare, Protection of Life and Property of Older Citizens. The Policy provides for a broad framework of collaboration and cooperation both within the government as well as between governmental and non-governmental agencies. An important thrust in the policy is on active and productive involvement of older persons and not just their care. The National Council for Older Persons (NCOP) has been constituted to operationalise the policy.

The National Policy on Older Persons, recognizes shelter as a basic human need, and commits that the stock of housing for different income segments will be increased. It stipulates that housing schemes for urban and rural lower income segments to earmark 10 per cent of the houses/house sites for allotment to older persons. This includes Indira Awas Yojana and other schemes of the government. Earning persons will be motivated to invest in housing so that they have no problem of shelter when they grow old. This requires speedy development of land for housing, time bound provision of civic services and communication links, availability of loans at reasonable rates, easy repayment installments, time bound construction schedules and tax relief.

Development of housing has to be a joint endeavour of public and private sectors and requires participation of Government housing agencies, civic authorities, housing finance institutions and private sectors.

Basic Needs

The basic needs of the older population in a developing country like India are the following:-

- Independence/freedom from wants income, housing, health, water, sanitation, communications, privacy, security and physical mobility.
- Participation, Social and Civic Needs

Integration in the society and family, opportunity to serve the society, recreation, education etc.

- **Care**

  Access to community care, health care, institutional, social & legal services.

- **Self fulfillment**

  Facility to pursue development of potential of older people in educational, cultural, economic, spiritual, political and other activities.

- **Dignity**

  Respect and equality regardless of age, gender, caste or creed, freedom from physical, financial and mental dependence.

Meeting the housing and basic needs of older people in urban and rural areas will be a tremendous challenge to the governments and to civil society in the coming decades. Turning ideas into reality implies great financial costs and transfer of resources.

Built Environment

The built environment of the older persons includes the following areas of concern:

(*i*) Housing

(*ii*) Health & community facilities

(*iii*) Services and transport

(*iv*) Open space, recreation and outdoor environment

Corresponding to the policy, strategic and operational levels of interventions, a set of comprehensive parameters and guidelines can be worked out for the needs of the older persons:

General Guidelines

- Provide helpline and home-help service assistance to older people in managing, maintaining and improving their existing homes.
- Provide community centers offering day care service, library, hobby rooms, games, catering service, etc.

- Make neighbouhoods more attractive for older people and ensure improved physical and social planning.
- Consult older people to identify their specific needs in housing design, services and domestic equipment.
- Ensure personal security and safety, provide Emergency Signaling System.
- Design dwellings to ensure greater flexibility of use by all ages and handicapped persons.
- Make existing neighbouhoods and dwellings more easily accessible.
- Encourage a social network within the local community.
- Make available opportunities to utilize the potentials and capacities of older people.
- Link housing with income generation by the older persons.
- Introduce reverse mortgaging arrangements to release some of the equity tied up in a house.
- Nursing and medical care visits to be provided for bed-ridden elderly people on regular basis.

Health and Community Facilities

With the theme of 'Adding Life to the Years', in place of conventional 'Adding Years to Life', the aspect of health is becoming increasingly important for both older persons and society at large for the lifelong enjoyment of active and affluent lives. This requires launching of a health promotion movement for the older persons with the united efforts of the Government local bodies and the private sector in a bid to advance the health-promotion activities and the creation of an environment to support such activities. There is a need to identify the need of the older people and work out norms for the development of facilities for health promotion. Besides public health centers, it is also necessary to identify the voluntary agencies and facilitate them in promoting health facilities. For spreading the awareness, Citizens' Councils on Health Promotion can be constituted to further health promotion activities on a local basis. These can serve as the centers of health promotion activities in communities.

For dissemination of information, education and awareness of health promotion, health festivals and other relevant events can be very helpful. Model health promotion projects at the community level, including the conduct of health campaigns and the preparation of manuals for the health promotion movement can be regularly taken up by the government/local bodies. Yoga, meditation centers, indigenous health systems and lifelong sports facilities should be promoted for healthy living of older people. 'Life Plaza' can be established in every city to support health promotion, nutrition and provide information with regard to indigenous systems of health.

A comprehensive approach will be to design a system comprising of norms and standards for health and community facilities. Construction of geriatric hospital facilities, including nursing homes for the elderly should relate to easy accessibility. Health facilities should include nutrition, recreation and other support for the elderly.

Besides health facilities, the development of special community facilities for serving the elderly is equally important. For an environment of convenience, a system of essential facilities and services should be evolved integrating the community, accessibility, transport and housing with the facilities. A system for supporting elderly people's life will comprise of the following provisions at various levels:

City Level

- Comprehensive social welfare centres
- Silver Human Resource Centre/Training Institutions
- Institutions for protecting the rights of mentally disabled and the elderly suffering from senile dementia.
- Medical care information centres
- Rehabilitation hospitals
- Medical Health Centres
- Geriatric hospitals, nursing homes

Local Level

- Information counseling, household services
- Community welfare services for elderly people

- Emergency communication
- Health centers, health consultation stations, Health check-up and counselling.
- Clubs, sports and swimming pools
- Home care service centers for elderly people

Housing Level

- Welfare equipment
- Rehabilitation
- Disease prevention
- Treatment, nursing
- Emergency communication
- Clinics
- Hobby Centre
- Community Hall
- Medical care visits for elderly people

Older people can, and already do, make a significant contribution to society in a variety of ways. It is necessary to provide support and expand contribution in both scope and scale. This will help provide a sense of value and purpose, which is so essential for older population. The role of older people in the voluntary sector of the society is of increasing importance. A variety of organizations foster the use of such skills. The greater involvement of older people in society is one of the many ways in which they can remain busy, productive and active. They can be involved in teaching, in school management, either paid or as volunteers. This serves the purpose of increasing contact between the generations and passes on the skills and experience of the older people, as well as improving computer literacy for the older people.

Recent advances in technology, such as, computer assisted service provision (telephone banking, ordering of goods and services, on-line advice systems, etc.) are helping to break down the barriers and enable the physically weak older people to be productive. The older people can be more involved and also do productive work through the internet and computer operations.

For this, facilities should be provided at housing level and also make the older people conversant with the use of such facilities.

Services and Transport

For a livable habitat, a healthy environment plays a major role for the elderly. As per WHO, environmental sanitation is a health related package, which should include the following:

- Safe disposal of wastes (human, solid, liquid and gaseous waste).
- Safe drinking water
- Personal hygiene
- Clean house and pollution free indoor and neighbourhood.
- Barrier free, safe movement of the elderly.

It is essential to adopt the environmental and physical norms and standards for various services. The system should be based on participation by the older people. Stand-by arrangements and Complaint redressal mechanism should be integral part of the service delivery. The pricing of various services should be affordable. It is observed that often elderly persons go for payment of bills, or lodging complaints with the service agencies. They should be provided with minimum facilities and their standing in a queue for more than 5 minutes should be avoided. At housing level 24-hour service centers should be provided, managed by trained personnel.

Open Space, Recreation and Outdoor Environment

The Older persons invariably need clean and green ambience for health. Besides city level, greenery/parks, about 10% to 15% of the area should be planned for neighbourhood parks and playgrounds within the residential areas. A system of landscaped linkages connecting various activities in a city or neighbourhood should be provided where people can go for long walks without interruption of vehicular traffic. The parks and open space should provide a sense of oasis and shelter from oppressive climate. Green belts also act as noise buffers and can be utilized as wind breakers. These also reduce the pollution, dust and high SPM levels present in the urban atmosphere.

Urban transport usually contributes nearly two-thirds of the total air pollution in the form of suspended particulate matter. This is causing a serious threat to the environment and health of the people. The objective should be to provide access to people and places by 'green' modes of urban transport. These include walking, bicycling, intermediate public transport modes, exclusive bus ways, dedicated mobike tracks, CNG powered vehicles, trains, etc. Inherent with this is the aim to curtail the need for commuting and to shorten the distances by various strategies, such as, decentralization of work centers, urban form, and by telecommunications, electronic mail, mixed land use zoning etc. The alternative modes of transport need not be high cost and high technology solution, but there are several low cost options, which can be explored. Polluting and life endangering transport modes have to be discouraged, while environment friendly modes need to be given the center-stage. An important consideration of public transport should be easy access and mobility with comfortable boarding and embarking for the older people and handicapped. Bus stops, vehicle design and facilities like toilets; public telephones etc. should be carefully and sensitively designed so as to meet the needs of the aged.

Noise is emerging as a major pollutant and irritant in the Indian cities. Its high intensity is constant source of pain and disturbance and cause of health hazard. Against a permissible level of 50 to 60 dB (A), the sound level in Indian cities often exceeds 80 dB (A). Faulty and leaking silencers, over-use of horns and vehicles plying on rough roads accentuate noise level from the traffic. Besides this, the noise from commercial and industrial activities in residential zones, unabated use of sound amplifiers, generator sets and firecrackers often disturb the peace of the sick, old and all others.

Besides civic sense and enforcement, land use planning, landscape and green buffers and building design can immensely contribute in reduction of noise levels. It is not desirable to locate residential areas of the old persons along major arteries. By proper land use planning, such as, location of public, semi-public and commercial activities along major transport arteries, a buffer can be created for residential zone. The green buffer with thin leave trees, land formations, mounds, embankments, etc. would provide effective barriers to transmission of noise.

Barrier Free Environment

A major consideration in the planning and design of outdoor and indoor environment should be that people with disabilities and older persons with arthritis could move around without much difficulty. This means that level differences shall be evened out to enable people in wheel chairs to move about without help from others. This also requires that:

- Paths and pavements shall be flat, uniform and slip-free.
- Orientation points and guide routes must be provided for usually disabled people.
- Paths and pavements shall be free from unnecessary obstacles.
- Information and warning signs must be understandable, clear and well lit.

Operational Aspects

Alongwith a strategic plan of action, its implementation is most crucial. This involves a number of interlinked activities, as given below:

- Identifying the priorities and evolving processes.
- Identifying the institutions/NGOs/CBOs and their roles
- Estimates, sources of finances.
- Time frame and mechanism of implementation.
- Management and maintenance aspects
- Coordination and project monitoring
- Raising awareness, sensitivity and evolving mechanism, facilitating participation, consulting and counselling
- Measures for capacity building and training of organizations, government departments and individuals.

The experience has demonstrated the need of adopting a facilitating approach by harnessing the resources, skills and energies of the community, NGOs and private sector. It is necessary to involve and support them with a view to leverage and converge the efforts of the voluntary bodies/NGOs, CBOs, private sector and individuals in the pursuit of a more livable, comfortable and healthy built environment for the older persons.

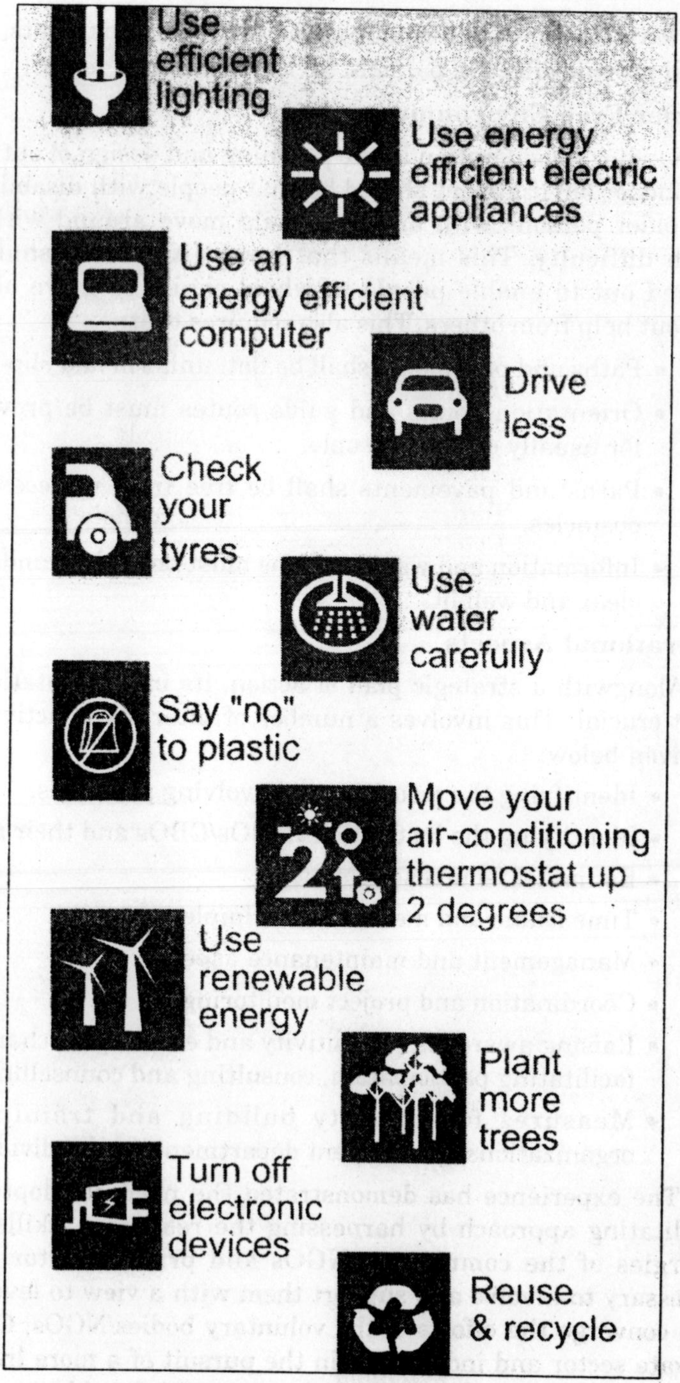

Use efficient lighting
Use energy efficient electric appliances
Use an energy efficient computer
Drive less
Check your tyres
Use water carefully
Say "no" to plastic
Move your air-conditioning thermostat up 2 degrees
Use renewable energy
Plant more trees
Turn off electronic devices
Reuse & recycle

ACRONYMS AND ABBREVIATIONS

ADB	Asian Development Bank
AIILSG	All India Institute of Local Self Government
Approx.	Approximate
AUWSP	Accelerated Urban Water Supply Programme
BAU	Business As Usual
BMTPC	Building Materials and Technology Promotion Council
BOD	Biological Oxygen Demand
BOLT	Build, Operate, Lease and Transfer
BOOM	Build Own Operate Maintenance
BOT	Bild, Operate and Transport
BPL	Below Poverty Line
BSUP	Basic Services to the Urban Poor
c.c.	Cement Concrete
CBO	Community Based Organisation
CBOs	Community Based Organisations
CCTV	Closed Circuit Television
CDP	City Development Plan
CDS	Community Development Society
CDSs	Community Development Societies
CETP	Common Effluent Treatment Plant
CPCB	Central Pollution Control Board
CPHEEO	Central Public Health and Environmental Engineering Organization
CPWD	Central Public Works Department
CSMC	Central Sanctioning and Monitoring Committe
Cu.m.	Cubic metres
dB(A)	decibel (Absolute)

DDA	Delhi Development Authority
DEFF	Delhi Environment Funding Facility
DFID	Department for International Development (U.K.)
DJB	Delhi Jal Board
DMA	Delhi Metropolitan Area
DMRC	Delhi Metro Rail Corporation
DoED	Department of Education
DoEF	Department of Environment and Forest
DoLBD	Department of Land & Building Department
DoNER	Development of North Eastern Region
DoTr	Department of Transport
DoUD	Department of Urban Development
DPCC	Delhi Pollution Control Committee
DPRs	Detail Project Reports
DSIIDC	Delhi State Industrial and Infrastructure Development Corporation
DTC	Delhi Transport Corporation
DUAC	Delhi Urban Art Commission
DUEIIP	Delhi Urban Environment and Infrastructure Improvement Project
DVB	Delhi Vidyut Board
DWCUA	Development of Women and Children in Urban Alleviation
EG	Enforcement Group
EIUS	Environmental Improvement of Urban Slums
EPA	Environment Protection Agency
EPCA	Environment Pollution (Prevention and Control) Authority
ESP	Electro Static Precipitator
ETP	Effluent Treatment Plant
EWS	Economically Weaker Section
FAR	Floor Area Ratio
GDP	Gross Domestic Product
GIS	Geographical Information System
GNCTD	Government of National Capital Territory of Delhi
GNP	Gross National Product

GoI	Government of India
GSDP	Gross Sectoral Domestic Product
GT Road	Grand Trunk Road
ha	hectare
HD/LD PE	High Density/Low Density Poly Ethylene
HFI_S	Housing Finacne Institutions
HIW	Hazardous Industrial Waste
HUDCO	Housing and Urban Development Corporation
ICE	Information Communication and Education
IDG	Infrastructure Development Group
IDSMT	Integrated Development of Small and Medium Towns
IFFAD	International Fund for Agricultural Development
IGA	Income Generating Activities
IHSDP	Integrated Housing and Slum Development Programme
INTACH	Indian National Trust for Art and Cultural Heritage
JBIC	Japan Bank for International Co-operation
JJC	Jhuggi - Jhompari Cluster
JNNURM	Jawaharlal Nehru National Urban Renewal Mission
kg	kilo gram
khs	kilo grams
KL	Kilo Litres
KLD	Kilo Litres Per Day
KW	Killo Watt
Leq	Level equilvalents
LMC	Ludhiana Municipal Corporation
Lpcd	Litres per capita per day
LPG	Liquid Petroleum Gas
MCD	Municipal Corporation of Delhi
MCL	Municipal Corporation of Ludhiana
MDG	Millennium Development Goals
MGD	Million Gallon Per Day
MLD	Million Litre Per Day
MM	Mahila Milan

m m	milimetre
MML	Margin Money Loan
MNP	Minimum Needs Programme
MoEF	Ministry of Environment & Forest
MoHUPA	Ministry of Housing and Urban Poverty Alleviation
MoRly	Ministry of Railways
MoUDPA	Ministry of Urban Development Poverty Alleviation
MPD	Master Plan for Delhi
MRTS	Mass Rapid Transit System
MSW	Municipal Solid Waste
MTAs	Market and Traders Associations
NAAQM	National Ambient Air Quality Monitoring
NAAQM	National Ambient Air Quality Monitoring
NBCFDC	National Backward Classes Finance and Development
NCM	National Commission for Minorities
NCOP	National Council for Older Persons
NCR	National Capital Region
NCRPB	National Capital Regional Plannign Board
NCT	National Capital Territory
NCTD	National Capital Territory of Delhi
NDMC	New Delhi Municipal Council
NGC	Neighbourhood Committee
NGO	Non-Government Organisation
NHGs	Neighbourhood Groups
NHHP	National Housing and Habitat Policy
NIUA	National Institute of Urban Affairs
NPOP	National Policy for Older Persons
NRY	Nehru Rojgar Yojna
NSDF	National Slum Development Programme
NSTFDC	National Scheduled Tribes Finacne and Development Corporation
O & M	Operation and Maintenance
OBCs	Other Backward Classes
PMCU	Project Management and Co-ordination Unit

PMIUP	Prime Ministry's Integrated Urban Poverty Eradication
PPG	Policy Plannign Group
PPP	Public Private Partnership
PPPs	Public Private Partnerships Programme
PPW	Public Participation Window
PSP	Private Sector Participation
PTG	Public Transport Group
PWD	Public Works Department
RCC	Reinforced Cement Concrete
RIAP	Revenue Improvement Action Plan
RITES	Rail India Technnical and Economic Services
RTI	Right to Information Act
RWA	Residents Welfare Association
SCA	Special Central Assistance
SCs	Scheduled Casts
SEWA	Self Employed Women's Association
SHASU	Scheme of Housing and Shelter Upgradation
SHC	Social Housing Corporation
SHGs	Self-Help Groups
SJSRY	Swarna Jayanti Shahari Rozgar Yojana
SLNA	State Level Nodal Agency
SME	Small Medium Enterprises
SO_2	Sulphur Dioxide
SPARC	Society for Promotion and Area Resource Centre
SPM	Suspended Particulate Matter
Sq.m.	Square metre
SSI	Small Scale Industry
STEP	Support to Training and Employment Programme for Women
STP	Sewage Treatment Plant
STP	Strategic Transport Plan
STs	Scheduled Tribes
SUME	Scheme of Urban Micro Enterprises
SUWE	Scheme of Urban Wage Employment
SWM	Solid Waste Management

TBL	Triple Bottom-Line
TCPO	Town and Country Planning Organization
TCSs	Thrift & Credit Societies
TINP	Tamil Nadu Integrated Nutrition Projcct
TMG	Traffic Management Group
ToR	Terms of Reference
TRIFED	Tribal Cooperative Marketing Development Federation of India Limited
TSM	Transport Systems Management
UAs	Urban Agglomerations
UBS	Urban Basic Services
UBSP	Urban Basic Services for the Poor
UCD	Urban Community Development
UDD	Urban Development Department
UFW	Un-accounted For Water
ULB	Urban Local Body
UNCHS	United Nations Center for Human Settlements (Now Un-Habitat)
UN-HABITAT	United Nations - Human Settlements Programme
UPA	Urban Poverty Alleviation
USEP	Urban Self Employment Programmes
UTs	Union Territories
UWEP	Urban Wage Employment Programme
VAMBAY	Valmiki Ambedkar (Malin Basti) Awas Yojana
WB	World Bank
WTP	Water Treatment Plant

CHRONOLOGY - BUILDING BYE-LAWS AND MASTER PLAN FOR DELHI

1959	Building Bye-Laws for Delhi framed under Punjab Municipal Act, 1914 and U.P. Building Control Operations Act, 1954.
1962	Delhi Master Plan 1961-81 Notified
1.5.1965	Authority Resolution for delegation of powers to MCD for sanction of Bldg Plans in Development Area.
1967	Builiding Bye-Laws for Delhi 1959 modified.
8.6.67	Authority Resolutions 444 for disposal of bldg. applications.
18.12.68	Authority Resolution 315/68 for sanctioning of Bldg. Plans by DDA.
21.10.78	Authority Resolution 171/78 for approval of layout plans.
1983	Unified Building Bye-Laws. 1983 framed under Section-57 of Delhi Development Act, 1957 (and also Section-346 of DMC Act, 1957 and section-260 of NDMC Act. 1994).
1.8.90	MPD-2001 notified, resulting in major changes in Development Controls/BBL-83.
1990-92	Public Notice dated 10.5.90 issued by MCD under Section 483 of DMC Act, 1957 compounding 20% (upto 450 sq ft.) excess covered area and 2 ft. infringement of set-back (10% extra coverage and 1 ft. set-back in future).
	Similar Public Notice issued under DMC Act by Delhi Administration (LSG Deptt.) on 13.12.90 and in August. 1992.
	Revised Public Notice dated 27.8.92 issued by MCD under section 483 of DMC Act:

	-1% excess FAR as one time compounding.
	Upto 5% excess FAR as one time compounding.
	More than 5% to be demolished, recurring fine double the land rate.
18.6.91	Authority Resoulution 72 for simplification of procedure for CGHS/Govt. Bldgs.
19.9.91	Authority Resolution 92/91 for sanction of Bldg. Plans under MPD-2001.
11.5.92	Notification of 13.12.90 withdrawn by GNCTD-8(2)90/LSG.
27.5.92	Delhi High Court in CWP 3461 (1999) directed Govt. of India to reframe BBL.
18.8.92	Authority Agenda 113/92 to condsider GNCTD & MCD notifications.
1.9.92	A Sub-Committee under Pr. Secy. LSG, GNCTD constituted.
19.9.92	DDA Public Notice under Section 11(A) of DD Act for excess coverage.
17.10.92	DDA Public Notice under Section 11(A) of DD Act (10 modifications).
Aug 1993	Draft BBL submitted to Delhi High Court.
15.12.93	GNCTD appointed commitee under Chief Secretary, to consider proposed increase in FAR by 25%.
Sept 1994	Delhi High Court directed to notify BBL under DMC Act within 3 months.
28.11.94	Authority agenda 11/94 dated 28.11.94 approved the porposed amendments in MPD-2001.
15.5.95	MOUA&E issued notification for 39 amendments in MPD-2001.
August, 95	Report of Committee under Chief Secy GNCTD appointed by GNCTD (Dec. 93) on construction of an additional floor finalized.
25.1.95	Draft BBL published inviting obections/suggestions by MCD; 314 objections/suggestions received.
10.2.97	Sub-committee under AC(E). MCD to examine objections/suggestions.
6.8.97	Part-I report submitted by Prof. V.K. Malhotra.
Nov., 97	MOUA&E accepts recommendations of Malhotra Committee (except Part-II and Farm Houses).

4.12.97	GNCTD notification for constitiution of Malhotra Committee.
Dec., 97	Constitution of Committee under Addl. Secy. (UD).
25.5.98	Public Notice inviting objections/suggestions from public under section-11(A) of DD Act.
23.7.98	Final Gazette Notification issued by MOUA&E.
27.7.98	Government order for levy on additional FAR (Rs. 1550/-per sqm.).
25.9.98	Revised order for levy on additional FAR charge (Rs. 450/-).
1998	Malhotra Committee report on Amnesty scheme for regularization of unauthorized constructions in plotted development and Farm Houses.
7.6.2000	MOUD Gazette Notification with respect to no plot housing can be converted into group housing.
7.8.2000	MOUD Gazette Notification for min. farm house area as 1 Ha.
2.3.2001	Gazette Notification regarding safety from earthquake.
28.7.2001	Gazette Notification regarding Rainwater harvestings.
21.11.2001	Gazette Notification for replacement of C&D forms.
27.11.2001	MOUD order for operationalisation of Notification dated 23.7.98 without additional dwelling units.
22.1.2002	Gazette Notification regarding stacking charges.
6.3.2002	Gazette Notification regarding parking norms for Group Housing.
28.8.2002	Gazette Notification regarding Barrier-free Environment for Public Buildings for Disabled.
July, 2003	Guidelines for MPD-2021 issued by MOUD & PA.
12.12.2003	Supreme Court orders - Stay on notification dated 23.7.98 withdrawn.
24.8.04	Authority Resolution 42/2004 for delegation of powers to Architects for residential plots upto 500 sqm.
16.3.05	Gazette Notification-Draft MPD-2021, published inviting objections/suggestions from the public.
8.4.05	Public Notice issued in Newspapers.

28.7.05	MCD prepares Draft Bldg. Regulations for Delhi.
14.12.05	Delhi High court in CWP 458/2003 orders MCD to remove unauthorized construction/encroachments/ misuse.
14.2.06	MOUD sets up a committee under Sh. Tejender Khanna, Former L.G. to examine various aspects of unauthorized constructions and misuse.
16.2.06	Supreme Court order (1A No. 22 in WP(C) No. 4677/ 1985 to stop misuse of premises on 80 ft wide and above roads/sealing.
16.2.06	High Court order (WPC 4582/2003) regarding village Lal dora, unauthorized construction etc.
16.2.06	Sealing of residential premises for misuse commenced in compliance of the order dated 16.2.06 of the Supreme Court of India in the matter of "M.C. Mehta Vs. UOI & otheres" (IA. No. 22 etc. in WP. (Civil) No. 4677/1985).
28.3.06	Gazette Notification on Mixed Land Use issued.
13.5.06	Tejender Khanna committee submits its report to MOUD.
19.5.06	The Parliament enacted the Delhi Laws (special provisions) Act. 2006, wherby sealing/demolition activities were stayed for a period of one year w.e.f. 19.5.06.
20.7.06	Proposed amendments in MPD-2001 finalised by MOUD for processing under section 11A of DD Act. 1957.
22-23.7.06	Public Notice issued inviting objections/suggestion within 30 days.
	About 2500 ojbetions/suggestions received.
23.8.06	Board of Enquiry & Hearing notified in Gazette.
25.8.06	Public Hearing of objections/suggestions.
7.9.06	Final Gazette Notificaiton for modification of MPD-2001 issued for Mixed Land Use, and authorized the local body to notify those stretches of roads where large scale commercialisation has taken place, as 'commercial/ mixed land-use/pedestrian shopping streets' (except in 'A' and 'B' categories of colonies as per the House Tax categorization).

15.9.06	The Municipal Corporation of Delhi identified and notified 2183 stretches of roads as commercial/ Mixed land-use/pedestrian streets vide Gazette Notification dated 15.9.06 (Delhi Govt. Notification).
22.9.06	Gazette Notification of modification of MPD-2001 for norms for residential plots issued.
Oct. 06	Small shops (upto 20 sq.mtrs.) of 24 categories, catering to the daily needs in residential areas on the recommendations of the Monitoring Committee formed by the Supreme Court of India, except in 'A' & 'B' categories of colonies, exempted from sealing.
20.11.06	DDA (levy/charges for Residential Development) Regulations, 2006 notified.
Jan., 07	Draft MPD-2021 approved by the Delhi Development Authority.
7.2.2007	MPD-2021 notified in Gazette of Inida (Extraordinary), No. 125.

MUNICIPAL HISTORY OF DELHI

1824	First improvement and development agency set up as the Town Duty Committee.
1863	First Municipal Committee for Delhi constituted under Act XXVI of 1850.
1881	Municipal Committee Passed Building Bye Laws.
1892	Introduction of piped water supply.
1895	Construction of Sewer in Chandni Chowk.
1901	First Notified Area Committee for Mehrauli formed.
1910	Survey of city carried out on behalf of the Municipal Committee which brought out detailed map of the city.
1913	Notified Area Committee for Civil Station formed.
1916	Establishment of New Delhi Municipal Committee.
1916	Notified Area Committee for Shahdara formed.
1924	Notified Area Committee for Red Fort Area formed.
1925	Delhi Joint Water and Sewerage Board constituted.
1937	Establishment of Delhi Improvement Trust. (DIT)
1938	Cantonment Board constituted.
1950	Delhi Road Transport Authority set up.
1951	Delhi State Electricity Board constituted.
1957	Delhi Municipal Corporation Act enacted. Delhi water supply and sewage disposal committee, Delhi electricity supply committee and Delhi Transport Undertaking transferred to MCD.
1957	Establishment of Delhi Development Authority
1966	Delhi Metropolitan Council constituted.
1971	Delhi Transport Corporation (DTC) created.
1992	GNCTD Act enacted.
1993	Legislative Assembly set up.
1996	Constitution of Delhi Vidyut Board.
1997	Constitution of Delhi Jal Board.
2002	Privatisation of Electricity Supply as Delhi Vidyut Board ceases to exist.

CHRONOLOGY : VILLAGES IN DELHI

1908 The boundaries of village settlements determined during land settlement by Revenue Department.

1912 Acquisiton of village lands in Delhi began under Land Acquisition Act, 1894, with shifting of capital from Calcutta to Delhi.

1948 East Punjab Holdings (Consolidation & Prevention of Fragmentation) Act.

1954 Delhi Land Reforms Act, 1954 notified for use of agriculture land, extension of village boundaries, etc.

1957 Delhi Municipal Act provides for declaration of villages as 'urban villages' under section 507(a).

1959 Large scale acquisition of agricultrual land for urban development begins.

1959 Delhi Municipal Corporation gives concession to permit setting up of cottage industry within the villages and allows power connections.

1960 Delhi Land Holdings (Ceiling) Act.

1962 Delhi Master Plan recommends that village settlements overtaken by urban development should be redeveloped and integrated into the neighbourhood, 23 villages identified on fringe to relocate villagelike industries and for development as Urban Villages.

1963 Municipal Corporation decides that unless development works are complete in Urban villages, building permission is not required.

1972 Delhi Land (Restriction and Transfer) Act, 1972 notified.

1982 Delhi Administration issues policy statement laying emphasis on promotion of small scale industries consuming less power. 56 types of non-polluting industries identified, which can run in residential area.

1983 Govt. of India approves the scheme to provide basic amenities to 90 urban villages in Delhi at an estimated

	cost of Rs. 206.73 milion, with central grant of Rs. 183.3 million, balance by levying 'village development cess' @ Re.1/ sq. yds. on areas planned and disposed of by DDA. Village beneficiaries were to pay for individual water supply, electricity and sewerage connections.
1987	The work related to planning and development of villages transferred to Delhi Municipal Corporation.
1990	Perspective Plan of Delhi - 2001 identifies 106 villages within urbanizable limits.
1993	73rd constitutional Amendment Act, 1992.
1994	111 villages notified as 'urban'.
1997	68 villages in Urban Extension (Rohini, Dwarka & Narela) for notifications as urban.
2007	Master Plan for Delhi - 2021 notified providing the policy framework for redevelopment of villages and mixed use regulations.

CHRONOLOGY : RIVER YAMUNA ZONE IN DELHI

1977-83
- DDA requests the Central Water & Power Research Station, Pune (CWPRS) for model studies on River channelisation.

1984
- High Powered Committee constituted by Lt. Governor

1985
- Report submitted by High Powered Committee recommends utilising 40 ha. of land for institutional purpose.
- Irrigation and Flood Department, Delhi Administration submits project report on river channelisation.
- Ministry directs DDA for 3D model on River Channelisation.
- CWPRS submits interim report.

1986
- Second interim report submitted.
- A comprehensive report prepared (on channelisation, pollution abatement and environmental improvement). Report discussed by Advisory Council under Lt. Governor.

1987
- Ministry of Environment & Forests agrees to participate in the project.
- DDA directed to take action for pollution abatement and environmental improvement of bathing ghats and preparation of action plan for pollution control.
- DDA submits report on socio-economic survey of all properties near Nigambodh Ghat.

1989
- Inland Waterways Authority submits report on navigational feasibility to Lt. Governor.

	• 3500 ha in river bed declared as Development Area.
1991	• CWPRS submit draft final report
1992	• An NGO files a petition WP 537/1992 in SC for enforcement of measures to stop pollution of River Yamuna
	• DWSS&DU submits action plan on river cleaning
1993	• Cabinet approves Yamuna Action Plan.
	• CWPRS submits final plan
	• MoU signed between UP, Haryana, Rajasthan, Himachal Pradesh and Delhi . It was agreed that a minimum flow of 10 cumecs would be maintained.
1994	• Exercise on identification and mapping of land ownership
	• Supreme Court took suo moto notice of an article 'and Quiet flows Maily Yamuna' and a case filed against CPCB and others.
1995	• Concept plan for land utilisation of 490 ha approved by DDA.
	• CWC/Yamuna Committee Govt. of India gives clearance to the plan for pocket-III (260 ha). & allotment of land to "Bochasanwasi Akshar Purshottam Sanasthan"
	• Change of land use of 28 ha. of land at Madanpur Khadar from 'Agriculture & Water body' to 'Commercial' (IOC Bottling Plant) approved vide Resolution no 90/95 dt.11.9.95.
1997	• Change of land use of 26.0 ha of land near near Jaitpur from agriculture & water body to manufacturing (M-2) notified on 1.09.97
	• The Authority vide resolution no. 170/97 dated 23/12/97 decides a study on Environment Impact Assessment by NEERI.
1998	• Change of land use of 4.04 ha of land near Rajghat thermal power station form 'Agriculture & Water body' to 'Manufacturing (M -2)' notified vide notification no K-13011/12/91-DDIB dated12.03.98

- SC appoints a Committee headed by former Cabinet Secretary to look into the river pollution
- High Powered Committee constituted by the Union Ministry of Env. & Forest to determine minimum flow of current.
- MoEF constitutes a High Powered Committee headed by Member, Planning Commission on the issue of minimum flow

1999
- A report on 'Initial Environmental Examination of development plan in river Yamuna stretch between new Railway bridge and proposed ILFS bridge' submitted by NEERI to DDA.
- Development Plan for stretch between new Railway bridge and ILFS bridge prepared.
- Change of land use of 42.5 ha of land from "Agricultural and water body" to "Public and Semi Public Facility" notified on 21.9.99

2000
- Change of land use of 4.0 ha of land near Nangla Machi from 'Agriculture & Water Body' to 'Manufacture (M -2)' notified vide notification no. K-13011/12/91-DDIB dated 12.10.2000.

2001
- NEERI submits draft report on Environmental Management Plan for Rejuvenation of River Yamuna'.
- Change of land use of 14.21 ha of land at Madanpur Khadar Resettlement Colony from "Rural use Zone" to "Residential" notified on 18.04.2001

2002
- NEERI submits revised report on 'Environmental Management Plan for Rejuvenation of River Yamuna'.
- Wazirpur Bartan Nirmata Sangh files petition against jhuggi clusters in Delhi HC

2003
- Change of land use of 51.9 ha of land near Shastri Park from "River Bed/Green" to Transportation (MRTS) notified on 5.11.2003
- High Court directs removal of jhuggies from the River Bed in WP(C) no 2112/2002

- High Powered Committee constituted under Secy, MOUD, submits its Yamuna Action Plan to Supreme Court of India

2005

- Change of land use of 6.0 ha of land near Shastri Park form "Agriculture & Water Body" to "Commercial" notified on 25.04.2005
- Delhi High Court appoints Yamuna Removal of Illegal Encroachment Monitoring Committee headed by Justice (Retd.) Usha Mehra.
- Change of land use of 37.0 ha. & 1.05 ha of land from 'Agriculture & Water Body' to "Residential & Public & Semi-Public Facility' respectively *approved by Authority vide resolution no.19/ 2005 dated 29.3.2005.*

2006

- Usha Mehra Committee (in WP(C) 689/2004 dated 29.3.2006) directs no construction within vicinity of 300m on either side of Yamuna River
- On 11.8.2006, in WP(C) no2112/2002 & CMS 5294/2006,6310/2006, 8740/2006 Delhi High Court directs construction of Ring Road and Kalindi By-Pass.
- Change of land use of 16.5 ha of land from Agricultural & Water Body/Recreational' to 'Residential (11.0 ha) and commercial (5.5 ha.) for Common Wealth Games Village Complex notified vide Gazettee Notification no SO.1321(E) dated 18.8.2006
- DUAC 'Imagining Delhi' proposals cover the Conservation and Rejuvenation of Yamuna.

2007

- Delhi Master Plan 2021 notified on 07.02.2007 vide Gazette Notification no.SO.141(E)
- Proposed Signature Bridge on River Yamuna approved.
- Constitution of River Yamuna Authority, under the Lt. Governor, Delhi.

2008

- Draft Zonal Development Plan of Zone 'O' published for inviting public objections/ suggestions.

BIBLIOGRAPHY

Asian Development Bank, *"Reducing Poverty in Urban India"* Final Report, June 2001, (Technical Assistance No. 3480) Government of India, NIUA, New Delhi.

Baross, P. (1983), The articulation of land supply for popular settlements, Third World Cities, Select Books, Singapore.

Baross, Paul, 1978, Analysis of Housing Production Systems, Bandung, Indonesia, Open House, 1994.

Benninger Christopher, 1994, Poverty Alleviation in Cities, Development Network, Oct.-Dec.

Billand, C.J., 1990, Delhi Case Study : Formal Serviced Land Development, RHUDO, USAID, New Delhi.

Banerjee, B. (1986). *Rural to Urban Migration and the Uraban Labour Market,* Himalaya Publishing House, Delhi.

Burton, J. (2000), The Development Challenge: Poverty and the Environment. Note on Urban Poverty by DFID India. prepared for the 2000 Development Forum. Delhi.

Batley, Richard (2000), Urban Governance and the Poor. Paper prepared for DFID India Urban Poverty Workshop, March 2000.

Benjamin, S. (2000) Economic Development for the Poor in Urban Areas. Paper prepared for DFID India Urban Poverty Workshop, March 2000.

Baud, Isa and Hans Schenk (ed) (1994). *Solid Waste Management. Modes, Assessments, Appraisals and Linkages in Bangalore.* Delhi: Manohar.

Cross, J.C. (1998), "The Informal Sector" Encyclopaedia of Political Economy, Philip O'Hara (ed.), Routledge, London & New York.

Chaplin, Susan (1999). Cities, Sewers and Poverty : India's Politics of Sanitation, *Environment and Urbanization.* Vol. 11. No. 1, April.

Chand Himal, *"Urban Informal Manufacturing Sector: A Study of the Border Districts of Punjab, Jammu & Kashmir and Rajasthan"* Centre for research in Rural and Industrial Development, Chandigarh, 1997.

Corporation of Cochin and DFID (1996). Urban poverty Profile Study. Cochin Urban Poverty Reduction Project - Design Phase. Corporation of Cochin and DFID, India report.

Data Base Unit Research Division, *"Selected Statistical Data on Indian Higher Education - 1 (data for 1993-94 to 1995-96)"* Association of Indian Universities, New Delhi, January 1997.

Directorate of Economics and Statistics, *"Delhi Statistical Hand book, 1981, 1986, 1991, 1997, 2001,* Government of NCT of Delhi.

Directorate of Economics and Statistics, *"Report on Classification of Employees in Delhi Government. & Autonomous/Local Bodies 1999"* Government of N.C.T. of Delhi.

Directorate of Economics and Statistics, *"Report on Unorganised Manufacturing & Repairing Enterprises and household Consumer Expenditure in Delhi, NSS 51st Round (July 1994-June 1995) State Sample, June 2001"* Government N.C.T. of Delhi.

Directorate of Employment and Training, "Employment Review (April June 1997)" Ministry of Labour, Government. of India.

Dupont Veronic, Tarlo Ema, Vidal Denis ed. *"Delhi Urban Space and Human Destinies",* Manohar Publications, New Delhi, 2000.

Department for International Development (1997), Eliminating World Poverty : A Challenge for the 21th Century; White Paper on International Development. HM Stationary Office London.

Department for International Development (1999), India Country Strategy Paper, DFID: Delhi.

Dawson, J., and Oyeylnka, B. (1993), "Structural adjustment and the urban informal sector in Nigeria" ILO World Employment Programme Research Working Paper WEP 2-19/WP65, Geneva.

Dessing, M. (1990), "Support for Microenterprises: Lessons for sub-Saharan Africa" Africa Technical Department Series, World Bank Technical Paper No. 122, The World Bank, Washington, D.C.

De Soto, Hernado (1989). The Other path : The Invisible Revolution in the Third World, New York, Harper & Row.

Dupont (V), Mitra (A), 1995. "Population distribution, growth and socio-economic spatial patterns in Delhi. Findings in Delhi. Findings from the 1991 census data" Delhi, Demography India, Vol. 24 No. 1 & 2, January-June, pp. 101.132.

Dupont (V), Tingal (D.), 1997, 'Residential and economic practices of pavement dwellers in Old Delhi' Institute of Economic Growth, Working Paper Series, No. E/186/97, Delhi.

Dreze, Jean and Sen, Amartya, 1996, India-Economic Development and Social Opportunity, Oxford India Paperbacks, New Delhi.

Delhi Development Authority (2007), Master Plan for Delhi-2021. New Delhi.

Economic Census of Delhi, 1998 to 2005, Govt. of NCT Delhi, New Delhi.

"Economic Survey 2001-2002", Economic Division, Ministry of Finance, Government of India.

"Employment and Unemployment in India 1993-1994," Fifth Quinquennial Survey, NSS 50th Round (July 1993-June 1994), National Sample Survey Organisation, Government of India, March 1997.

"Employment and Unemployment in India 1999-2000 (part 1)," NSS 55th Round (July 1999-June 2000), National Sample Survey Organisation, Government of India, May 2001.

Franks, J.R., (1994), "Macroeconomic policy and the informal sector" In Rakowski, C.A. (ed)" : Counterpoint : The informal sector debate in Latin America, State University of New York, Albany, Chapter 6.

Fraser, Nancy (1995), 'From Redistribution to Recognition. Dilemmas of Justice in a 'Post-Socialist' Age'. *New Left Review,* August, 1995.

GoI, MOUD (1999). *Draft National Slum Policy,* New Delhi.

GoI, MoUAE (2007), *National Urban Housing and Habitat Policy,* New Delhi.

GoI, MoDU (1988), *Report of the National Commission on Urbanisation.* New Delhi.

GoI Planning Commission (1983a). *Report of the Task Force on Shelter for the Urban Poor and Slum Improvement.* New Delhi.

GoI, Planning Commission (1983b). *Report of the Task Force on Management of Urban Development,* New Delhi.

Gopinathan, P.K. and V.L. Srilatha, (1998). 'Measuring Poverty' *Economic Times,* 19.7.98.

Greenwood, M.J. (1971), "A Regression Analysis of Migration to Urban Areas of a Less Developed Country : The Case of India" *Journal of Regional Science,* Vol. 11, No. 2.

Harrjs, J.R., and M.P. Todaro (1970), "Migration, Unemployment and Development : A Two Sector Analysis" *The American Economic Review*, Vol. LX. no. 1.

Gupta (D.B.), Kaul (S), Pandey (R.), 1993, Housing and India's Urban Poor, Har Anand Publications, New Delhi.

Gita Dewan Verma, 2000, Slum Upgrading, Architecture + Design, Jan-Feb., Page 109-11, New Delhi.

Government of India (1999). Ninth Five Year Plan 1997-2002. Volume 1, Development Goals, Strategy and Policies. New Delhi : Planning Commission.

Gallagher, R., (1992), The Rickshaws of Bangladesh, The University Press Limited, Dhaka.

Habitat (1987), Global Report on Human Settlements, UN Centre for Human Settlements, New York.

Habitat, International Coalition, Building the City with the people, Mexico, 1997.

Hart, J. Kelth, (1970), "Small-scale Entrepreneurs in Ghana and Development Planning"

The Journal of Development Studies, Vol. 6, pp. 104-120.

Haggblade, S. et. al. (1990), "The effect of policy and policy reforms on non-agricultural enterprises and employment in developing countries : A review of past experiences" in Stewert, F. et al.: The Other Policy, Washington, D.C.

Harriss, J., Kannan, K.P., and Rogers. G (1990) Urban Labour Market Structure and Job Access in India : A study of Coimbatore ILO/IHS.

International Labour Office (1970), *Towards Full Employment : A Programme for Colombia,* Geneva.

ILO, (1972), *Employment, Incomes and Equality : A Strategy for Increasing Productive Employment in Kenya,* Geneva.

ILO/PREALC (1993). News Letter, No. 32 September, Santiago.

ILO/PREALC (1992). News Letter, No. 29, April, Santiago.

GNCTD, "Informal Sector in Delhi (Non Agriculture)" National Sample Survey 55th Round (July 1999- 2000) State Sample, Directorate of Economics and Statistics, Government. of NCT of Delhi, June 2002.

India : Report on Urban Indicators, Government of India, Ministry of Urban Development & Poverty Alleviation.

IAMR (1992). Employment in the informal Sector : A study of selected towns, Institute of Applied Manpower Research New Delhi.

ILO (1992). The Urban Informal Sector in Asia : An annotated bibliography, Geneva.

International Development Department School of Public Policy. (1999), Slum Improvement Projects, Impact Assessment Study, Final Report. Birmingham.

Jain, A.K., 1996, The Indian Megacity and Economic Reforms, Management Publishing Co., New Delhi.

Jain, A.K., (2008), Building Systems for Low Income Housing. JM Jaina Pub; New Delhi.

Jain, A.K. (2003), The Growth and Regularization of Unauthorised Colonies in Delhi, ITPI Journal.

Jain, A.K., (2008) Low Carbon City – Policies, Planning and Practice, Discovery Publishers, Delhi

Jain A.K. (2001), Urban Ecology and Natural Resource Management, Management Publishing, Dehradun.

Jain A.K.(2007), Water – A Manual for Engineers, Architects, Planners and Managers, Daya Publications, Delhi.

Jain A.K. (2008), Handbook on Disaster Management, Pragun, New Delhi

Jain A.K. (2008), Urban Transport Planning and Management, APH Publishers, Delhi, 2008

Jain A.K., 1998 The Making of a Metropolis : The Planning and Growth of Delhi, National Books Organisation, New Delhi.

Jain A.K., (1994), The Cities of Delhi, Management Publishing Company, Dehradun

Jain A.K. (2008) School Buildings – Planning, Design and Management JBA Publications, New Delhi.

Jackelen, H.R. and Rhyne, E., 1991, "Towards a more market-oriented approach to credit and savings for the poor" in Small Enterprise Development, Vol. 2, No. 4, December.

Khandker, S., et al. (1994). "Is Grameen Bank Sustainable?" HRO Working Papers HROWP 23, The World Bank, Washington, D.C.

Kundu Amitabh and Sharma, Alakh, N. ed. *"Informal Sector in India : Perspectives and Policies"*. Institute of Human Development, New Delhi, 2001.

Kundu Amitabh, Schenk Hans, Dash B., *"Changing Role of State in Urban Governance, Provision of Basic Amenities to Poor in the Context of Unplanned Growth in Metropolitan Peripheries of Delhi and Hanoi"* Institute of Human Development, 2002, New Delhi.

Kundu, Amitabh, Soumen Bagchi and Deblina Kundu (1999), "Regional Distribution of Infrastructure and Basic Amenities in Urban India" *Economic and Political Weekly,* July 10.

Kundu, Amitabh (1993). In the Name of the Urban poor. Access to Basic Amenities. New Delhi, Sage Publications.

Kundu, Amitabh (2000a) How to Conduct Poverty Assessment for a Greater Understanding of the Urban Poverty Problem and Prioritising Related Action. Paper presented the Urban and City Management Course, Goa 9-21 January, 2000.

Kundu, Amitabh (2000b). Changing Structure of Poverty and Employment in Urban India, Issues in Formulating a Development Strategy. Paper prepared for DFID India Urban Poverty Workshop, March 2000.

Kirtee Shah & William J. Cousins, 1980, *Housing and Development,* ASAG/EZE Seminar paper, Ahmedabad.

Kannapan, S. (1993). *Employment Problem and the Urban Labour Market in Developing Nations,* University of Michigan.

Lipton M. (1980). "Migration form rural areas of poor countries: The Impact on rural productivity and Income Distribution" *World Development,* Vol. 8, No. 1.

Loughhead. S. Mittal. O. and Woods. G. (2000). Urban Poverty and Vulnerability in India: DFID's Experiences from a social policy perspective. DFID India Publication.

Linden, Jan van der; On popular participation in a culture of patronage -sites and services projects in Hyderabad, Pakistan, Environment and Urbanisation, Vol. 9, No.1, April, 1997.

Lagos, R.A. (1992). "Barriers to legality and their costs for the informal sector", in Tokman, V.E. (ed.): Beyond Regulation: The informal economy in Latin America, ILO, Colorado.

Ministry of Urban Housing and Poverty Alleviation, 2007. Report of the 11th Five Year Plan (2007-12) Working Group on Urban Housing with Focus on Slums, New Delhi.

Ministry of Urban Development, Govt. of India, (2006). Report of the Working Group on Urban Development (excluding Urban Transport), Urban Water Supply and Sanitation (including Low Cost Sanitation, Sewerage & Solid Waste Management) and Urban Environment for Eleventh Five Year Plan (2007-2012), New Delhi.

Mesa-Lago, C. (1992), "Protection for the informal sector in Latin America and the Caribbean by social security or alternative means", in Tokman, V.E. (ed): Beyond Regulation : The informal economy in Latin America, ILO, Colorado.

Mathur O.P., and Rangamannar T.s. *"Delhi Fiscal Study"* National Institute of Public Finance and Policy 2000, New Delhi.

Ministry of Urban Affairs and Employment. Department of Urban Employment & Poverty Alleviation (ed.), Second United Nations Conference on Human Settlements. HABITAT II, Istanbul 1996 - India National Report, Government of India New Delhi, April 1996.

Mongia, J.N., Role of Government, Private Sector, NGOs/CBOs and other Stakeholders in the Housing Sector, Base-cum-issue Paper. National Housing Seminar "Adequate Shelter for All' New Delhi, 7-9, 1996.

Mongia J.N. Role of Cooperaties, CBOs and NGOs in the Housing Delivery Process, in : NCHF Bulletin, New Delhi, August 1997 pp. 3-5.

Mills, E.S. and Arup Mitra, (1996) *Urban Development and Urban Ills,* Commonwealth Publishers, New Delhi.

Mitra, Arup (1992). "Urban Poverty : A Rural Spill Over? *Indian Economic Review,* Special No. in memory of S. Chakravarty.

Mohan R., (1979), "Workers of Bogota : Who They Are, What They Do and Where They Live" World Bank Staff Working Paper, Washington, D.C.

Martinez, E., Support Based Housing Process, Open House No. 2, 1978.

Misra, H. N. (1990), 'Housing and Health in Three Squatter Settlements in Allahabad, India' in Jorge E. Hardoy. Sandy Cairncross and David Satterthwaite (ed). *The Poor Die Young.* London, Earthscan Publications.

Mitlin, Diana, David Satterthwaite and Carolyn Stephens (1996). *'City Inequality' Environment and Urbanization,* Vol.8, No. 2, October.

Mukhopadhya, Alok (ed.) (1997). *Report of The Independent Commission on Health in India,* Voluntary Health Association of India New Delhi.

National Institute of Urban Affairs (NIUA) (1998), *India's Urban Sector Profile.* New Delhi, India, January 1998, Research Study series number 61.

National Institute of Urban Affairs (NIUA), (1998), *India's Urban Sector profile.* New Delhi.

Netherlands Ministry of Foreign Affairs (1991). A World of Difference, A new framework for development cooperation in the 1990s, Government of Netherlands, The Hague.

Netherlands Ministry of Foreign Affairs (1992). "Urban Poverty Alleviation in Latin America", Poverty and Development Series No. 3, Government of Netherlands, The Hague.

National Capital Region Planning Board (2005) NCR Plan, 2021, NCRPB, New Delhi.

NIUA, 1986, Dimension of Urban Poverty. A situational Analysis National Institute of Urban Affairs, Research Study Series No. 25, New Delhi.

NIUA, 1989, Profile of the Urban Poor : An Investigation into their Demographic, Economic and Shelter Characteristics, National Institute of Urban Affairs, Research Study Series, No. 40, New Delhi.

Oberoi, A.S., Sivananthiran, A., Venkataratnam, C.S., ed. *"Perspectives on Unorganised Labour"* International Labour Organisation, New Delhi, 2000.

Oberoi, A.S. and Chadha, G.K., *"Job Creation in Urban Informal Sector in India : Issues and Policy Options"* International Labour organisation, New Delhi, June 2001.

Planing Department, *"Sectoral Highlights of Annual Plan 2007-08"* Government of N.C.T. of Delhi.

Papola, T.S. (1992), "The question of unemployment" in Bimal Jalan (ed): The Indian Economy: Problems and Prospects, New Delhi.

Policy Brief (1993), published by the Midwest Universities Consortium for International Activities Inc. USA, No. 4, November.

Pollock, M. (1989). "Poverty and the labour market in Costa Rica" in Rodgers, G. (ed.): Urban poverty and the labour market: Access to jobs and incomes in Asian and Latin American Cities, ILO, Geneva.

Powell, J. (1991), "Kumasi University's involvement in grassroots industrial development" in Small Enterprise Development, Vol. 2, No. 2.

Progressive Architecture, 1968, PA 15th Annual Design Awards. USA.

Papola, T.S., (1981), *Urban Informal Sector in a Developing Economy,* Vikas Publishing House.

Report of the Sub Group on Population Projections and Demographic Profile for preparation of Master Plan for Delhi 2021, Delhi Development Authority, 2001, New Delhi (Unpublished)

Rakowski, Cathy A (1994), *"Convergence and Divergence in the Informal Sector Debate: A Focus on Latin America"*, World Development, Vol. 22, pp. 501-516.

Replogle, M., (1992), Non-motorized vehicles in Asian Cities, Technical Paper No. 162, The World Bank, Washington, D.C.

Richards, P.J., and Thomson, A.M., (1984). Basic Needs and the Urban Poor, London.

Stern, N. (1977), "On Labour Markets in Less Developed Countries", paper prepared for the Development Research Centre. The World Bank.

Todaro, M.P. (1969). "A Model of Labour Migration and urban unemployment in Less Developed countries" *The American Economic Review, Vol. LIX, No. 1.*

Slater, R. (1998). Urban Sector Review, in A. Shephered et al. Evaluation of DFID's Support to poverty Reduction, India Country Study, DFID, India.

Singh, S.P. (1198). *Sulabh Sanitation Movement,* Delhi: Sulabh International.

Swaminathan, Padmini (1997), 'Work and Reproductive Health. A Hobson's Choice for Indian Women?'.*Economic and Political Weekly,* October 25.

Seelig, MY, (1978), The Architecture of Self Help Communities, McGraw, New York.

Turner, J.F.C., Mass Housing and User Participation in Built Environment, Vol. 5, No. 2, London 1979.

Sharma, A.N. (1997), *People on the Move: Nature and Implication of Migration in a Backward Economy,* Vikas Publishing House, New Delhi.

Sparc, 1985. "We the invisible" Report on Pavement Dwellers in Bombay, SPAARC, Mumbai.

Suri, P, 1994, Urban Poor, Their Housing Needs and Government Response. Har Anand Publications, New Delhi.

Sethuraman, S.V., (1985), "Basic needs and the informal sector: The case of low-income developing countries", in Habitat International, Vol. 9, 3/4, pp. 299-316.

Stren, R., and McCarney, P. (1992). Urban research in the developing world: Towards on agenda for the 1990s, Centre for Urban and Community Studies, University of Toronto, Toronto.

Taylor, K., (2000), The Impact of Urban Services on Vulnerability. paper prepared for DFID India Urban Poverty Workshop, March 2000.

Thapan, Meenakshi (1997), 'Linkages between Culture, Education and Women's Health in Urban Slums', *Economic and Political Weekly,* October 25.

The Global Urban Observatory. Database: Analysis of Urban Indicators, (April 2001),

Uma, Adusmilli. Partnership Approaches in India, in Geoffery Panee (Editor), 1999, Making Common Ground, IT Publications, London.

UNDP, Human Development Report, 2003, Table 5, Demographic Trends, pp. 164-165.

UMP, (1991), Urban Management Progaram, Revised Prospectus, Capacity Buliding for Urban Management in the 1990s, The World Bank, UNDP and UNCHS, Washington, D.C.

UNDP, et al. (1998), Development of rural small industrial enterprise: Lessons from exprience, UNDP, Government of Nethrelands, ILO and UNIDO, Vienna.

UNDP, (1989), Urban Transition in Developing Countries, A Programme Advisory Note, New York.

INDEX

G

H

I

R

U

V